ORGANIZATIONAL LEARNING, PERFORMANCE, AND CHANGE

ORGANIZATIONAL LEARNING, PERFORMANCE, AND CHANGE

An Introduction to Strategic Human Resource Development

JERRY W. GILLEY AND
ANN MAYCUNICH

PERSEUS PUBLISHING
Cambridge, Massachusetts

Library of Congress Catalog Number: 00-102435
ISBN 0-7382-0248-7

Perseus Publishing is a member of the Perseus Books Group.

Find us on the World Wide Web at http://www.perseuspublishing.com

Perseus Publishing books are available at special discounts for bulk purchases in the U.S. by corporations, institutions, and other organizations. For more information, please contact the Special Markets Department at HarperCollins Publishers, 10 East 53rd Street, New York, NY 10022, or call 1-212-207-7528.

Text design by Jeff Williams
Set in 10-point Minion by Perseus Publishing Services

First printing, August 2000
5 6 7 8 9 10—03

CONTENTS

ILLUSTRATIONS

Figures

Tables

ACKNOWLEDGMENTS

This book would have been impossible to write had it not been for the outstanding contributions of several leaders in the field of human resource development. We would like to pay tribute to these individuals for their insight, influence, and perspective for which this book is based.

Chris Argyris for *Organizational learning II: A theory of action perspective* (1996); Peter Block, for *Flawless consulting: A guide to getting your expertise used,* (1981) and *The empowered manager: Positive political skills at work.* San Francisco, (1987); Nathaniel W. Boughton for *Stop managing, start coaching: How performance coaching can enhance commitment and improve performance.* (1996) and the *Performance challenge: Developing management systems to make employees your organization's greatest asset.* (1999); Robert O. Brinkerhoff for *The learning alliance:* (1994) and *Achieving result from training* (1987); Mary Broad and John Newstrom for *Transfer of training. Action-packed strategies to ensure high payoff from training investment.* (1992); Steven D. Brookfield for *Developing critical thinkers: Challenging adults to explore ways of thinking and acting,* (1987), and *Becoming a critically reflective teacher.* (1995); Warren W. Burke for *Organizational development: A process of learning and changing.* (1992); Neal Chalofsky for *A unifying definition for the human resource development profession.* In the *Human Resource Development Quarterly,* (1992), *A new paradigm for learning in organizations.* In the *Human Resource Development Quarterly,* (1996), and *Up the HRD ladder: A guide for professional growth* (1983); Donald Clifton for *Soar with your strengths.* (1992); Rob Foshay, Ken Silber, and Odin Westgaard for *Instructional design competencies. The standards.* (1986); Steven A. Eggland for *Principles of HRD.* (1989) and *Marketing HRD within organizations: Improving visibility, credibility and image of programs.* (1992); W. L. French, and C. H. Bell for *Organizational development: Behavioral science interventions for organizational improvement.* (1995); James L. Gibson, John M. Ivancevich, and James H. Donnelly for *Organizations: Behavior, structure, process* (1997, 9th ed.). Tom Gilbert for *Human competence: Engineering worthy performance.* (1978); E. G. Guba and Y. S. Lincoln for *Effective evaluation: Improving the usefulness of evaluation results through responsive and naturalistic approaches.* (1988); Judy Hale for *The performance consultant's fieldbook: Tools and techniques for improving organizations and people;* (1998); Joe H. Harless for *An Ounce of Analysis Is Worth a Pound of Objectives.* (1974); Edward E.

Holton, III, for *In Action: Needs Assessment* (1995) and *The adult learner* (5th Ed.) (1998); Ronald Jacobs for *Human performance technology: A systems-based field for the training and development profession* (1987) and *Structured on-the-job training* (1995); D. Katz and R. Kahn for *The Social Psychology of Organizations* (2nd ed.) (1978); Roger Kaufman for *Needs assessment: A user's guide* (1992); Donald Kirkpatrick for *Evaluating Training Programs* (1995); Gary D. Kissler for *The change riders: Managing the power of change* (1991); Malcolm S. Knowles for *Self-directed learning* (1975), *The modern practice of adult education: From pedagogy to andragogy* (1980), and *The adult learner* (5th Ed.) (1998); D. Kolb for *Experiential learning: Experience as the source of learning and development* (1984); John R. Kotter for *Leading change* (1996); Dugan Laird for *Approaches to training and development* (2nd ed.) (1985). Edward E. Lawler, III for *From the ground up* (1996); M. LeBoeuf for *Getting results: The secret to motivating yourself and others* (1985); Gordon Lippitt and Ron Lippitt for *The consulting process in action,* 2nd ed. (1986); R. Mager and P. Pipe for *Analyzing performance problems* (2nd ed.). (1984); Michael J. Marquardt for *The global learning organization* (1994), *Building the learning organization*(1996), and *Action learning in action: Transforming problems and people for world-class organizational learning* (1999); Victoria J. Marsick for *Informal and incidental learning in the workplace* (1990) and *Sculpting the learning organization: Lessons in the art and science of systematic change* (1993); Patrica McLagan, for the *Models for HRD practice* (1989) and *The age of participation* (1995); Jack Mezirow for *Transformative dimensions of adult learning* (1991) and *Transformative learning in action: Insights for practice* (1997); Oscar G. Mink for *Change at work: A Comprehensive management process for transforming organizations* (1993); Leonard Nadler for *Developing human resources: Concepts and models* (1st ed.). (1970), *Managing human resource development: A practical guide* (1986) and *Designing training programs: The critical events model* (1994); Jack Phillips for *In Action: Needs Assessment* (1995). Hallie Preskill for *The use of critical incidents to foster reflection and leaning in HRD* in the *Human Resource Development Quarterly* and *Evaluative inquiry for learning in organizations* (1999); John Redding for *Strategic readiness: The making of the learning organization* (1994); Dana Gaines Robinson and Jim C. Robinson for *Training for impact: How to link training to business needs and measure the results* (1989), *Performance consulting: Moving beyond training* (1996), and *Moving from training to performance: A practical guide* (1999); Marc J.Rosenberg for *Performance technology: Working the system. In Training* (1990) and *Human performance technology: Foundation for human performance improvement.* In W Rothwell (Ed.) *The ASTD Models for Human Performance Improvement. Roles, Competencies, and Outputs* (1996); Allison Rossett for *Analysis of human performance problems.* In H. D. Stolovitch and E. J. Keeps (Eds.), *Handbook of Human performance technology: A Comprehensive guide for analyzing and solving performance problems in organizations* (1992 & 1999) and *First things fast: A handbook for performance analysis* (1999); William Rothwell for *Beyond training and development: State-of-the-art strategies for enhancing human performance* (1996), *The ASTD models for human performance improvement: Roles, competencies, and outputs* (1996), *Beyond instruction: Comprehensive program planning for business and education* (1997), *Mastering the instructional design process: A systematic approach* (1998), and *Strategic HRD leaders: How to prepare your organization for the six trends shaping the future* (1998); Gerry A. Rummler and Alan P. Brache for *Improving performance: How to manager the white spaces on the organizational chart* (1995); Edgar H. Schein for *Organizational culture and leadership* (1992) and *The cultures of management: The key to organizational learning. Sloan Management Review* (1996); Donald A. Schon, *The reflective practitioner* (1983), *Educating the reflective practitioner* (1987), and *Organizational learning II: A theory of action perspective* (1996); Peter M. Senge for *The fifth discipline: The art and practice of the learning organization* (1990); H. Stolovitch, and E. J. Keeps for the *Handbook of Human Performance Technology* (1992 & 1999); Richard A. Swanson for *Performance at work: A systematic program for analyzing work behavior* (1986), *Forecasting financial benefits of human resource development*(1988), and *Analysis for improving performance. Tools for diagnosing organization and documenting workplace expertise.* (1994); David Ulrich for *Organizational Capability: Competing from the inside out* (1990), *Human resource champions* (1997), and *Tomorrow's HR management: 48 thought leaders call for change*(1997); Peter Vaile for *Learning as a way of being* (1996); Karen Watkins for *Informal and incidental learning in the workplace* (1990) and *Sculpting the learning organization: Lessons in the art and science of systematic change* (1993); and Ron Zemke for *Adult learning: What do we know for sure. In Training* (1995).

PREFACE

No longer can HRD professionals simply buy training programs from vendors, schedule a training session, deliver a fun-filled day of instruction, conduct simple smile sheet evaluations asking participants to react to the training event, and hope some how the employees will go forth and suddenly improve their performance. Yes, this is a grim overview of a worst-case scenario depicting HRD as a superficial, activity-based field of practice. Unfortunately, we have witnessed this example several times over the years However, the field of HRD and its professionals have changed dramatically during the past twenty-five years. Gone are the days of providing training activity hoping that employees will miraculously improve their knowledge and skills, which will some how enhance organizational performance. In their place are dedicated, determined, and professional individuals who spend their energy and effort helping their organization design learning cultures, create performance management systems, and implement change initiatives. Each of these activities is directed at altering the organization's structure, mission, strategy, leadership, managerial practices, and work climates. As a result, the field of HRD and its professionals have enhanced their credibility within organizations.

One observation that we have made during the past decade is that HRD professionals tend to align themselves with one of three philosophical orientations. This is much like joining a political party, by which HRD professionals embrace their assumptions, beliefs, policies, principles, and practices. Ultimately, these alignments affect their decisions and actions and the assumptions that they make when addressing performance issues and change initiatives. The three orientations within HRD include *organizational learning, organizational performance,* and *organizational change.* We refer to these as the professional practice domains of HRD.

Those professionals who embrace organizational learning believe that learning is the primary purpose of HRD. From their perspective, HRD professionals are primarily responsible for creating learning cultures that foster continuous employee learning. They contend that learning is the key to organizational development and change. Furthermore., they embrace the principles and practices of the learning organization, action learning, and critical reflection and their application within organizations.

When a performance problem exists within an organization, learning-oriented HRD professionals will typically rely on training solution as a way of dealing with the issue. They perceive that learning is a prerequisite to performance improvement and change. Therefore, they believe that learning is essential when dealing with most organizational problems and embrace the formal design, development, and implementation of training programs as their primary purpose within an organization. More experienced and insightful HRD professionals encourage formal learning transfer activities and believe that they are responsible for integrating action learning and self-directed learning activities in daily practice. Finally, they believe that the delivery of successful training programs will enhance their credibility within an organization.

Those professionals who embrace organizational performance believe that performance improvement and management are the essential components of HRD. They maintain that HRD professionals need to be responsible for analyzing performance problems, isolating the cause of performance breakdowns, and recommending or designing interventions used to address them. Furthermore, they believe that training is *not* the intervention of choice in most performance improvement situations. Rather, they believe that management action is most appropriate when improving organizational performance. Moreover, HRD professionals should use a system theory when examining performance shortfall. Performance-oriented HRD professionals believe that their primary responsibility is to utilize the human performance system as a way of improving organizational effectiveness. They contend that compensation and reward systems, organizational structure and culture, job design, and motivational factor should be designed to reinforce performance change and improvement. Typically, these professionals have a behaviorist approach to solving performance problems and use reinforcement schedules to bring about changes in performance and behavior. These professionals advocate the principles and practices of human performance technology and performance consulting and even create separate performance improvement departments dedicated to performance analysis, consulting, and evaluation. They believe that their credibility is improved when the organization improves its overall performance.

Those professionals who embrace organizational change believe that the alterations in the organization's culture, structure, work climate, mission, and strategy are the more important activities performed by HRD professionals. They adopt a systemic and strategic approach to organizational effectiveness. The principles and practice of organizational development are their primary orientation and they adopt the role of change agent within the organization. They contend that organizational change is the pentacle of their efforts and that organizational learning and performance often improves as a result of such alterations.

Organizational change professionals believe that they are responsible for discovering efficiencies within an organization through analysis activities. They contend that organizational development is a full-time activity and requires an independent group of professionals responsible for its implementation. Operationally, they work closely with senior executives, division and department managers, as well as with line managers as a way of implementing change. They believe that they can improve their credibility by bringing about change within the organization and managing its implementation

Each of these three professional practice domains is very complex and complicated and is a field unto itself. As with political parties, their assumptions and beliefs differ greatly. As a result, many disagreements exist regarding how to enhance organizational effectiveness, which negatively impacts the field of HRD and prevents a unified approach of organizational improvement from being adopted. Additionally, each orientation has its limitations in enhancing organizational effectiveness. However, combining the professional practice domains into one approach, HRD professionals can address any issue facing an organization. This provides HRD professionals with multiple approaches to improving organizational competitive readiness and renewal capacity. Blending these three professional practice domains allows HRD professionals to see the overlaps and linkages between learning, performance improvement, and change. It provides a fresh perspective when addressing organizational issues, problems, and breakdowns. Finally, a three-in-one approach provides HRD professionals with a several different approaches when examining performance improvement and management, organizational development, and learning.

We believe that to be successful in the 21st century, the field of HRD and its professionals need to continue to grow, develop, and change to adjust to the ever-changing conditions within organizations. This requires constant monitoring, reflection, and growth on the part of HRD professionals. To address this need, we provide a comprehensive examination for the issues, topics, principles, philosophies, and concepts facing tomorrow's HRD professionals. In keeping, the purpose of this book is to provide a framework that will help HRD professionals continue their momentum toward professionalized status, improved credibility, and influence within organizations. It is dedicated to examining the transformation of strategic HRD (Chapter 2), the role of strategic HRD leaders in ever-changing organizations (Chapter 3), and the principles of strategic HRD (Chapter 4). Moreover, we will be examining the professional practice domains of strategic HRD, organizational learning (Chapters 5–7), organizational performance (Chapters 8–11), and organizational change (Chapters 12–14), and demonstrating their relationship. Additionally, we will overview state-of-the-art analysis (Chapter 15), design (Chapter 16), and evaluation (Chapter 17) activities and how they interact with each of the professional practice domains of the field.

PART I

An Introduction to Strategic HRD

CHAPTER 1

Strategic Human Resource Development

What is *strategic human resource development?* Given the complex nature of the practice of human resource development (HRD) and the rapidity with which the field is changing, a clear definition may be elusive. Defining HRD frames practitioners' roles and competencies as well as the activities incorporated in HRD programs.

The term strategic human resource development offers clues to its meaning. Obviously, it is related to the critical development of people, but labeling people "human resources" reveals an organization's orientation, just as the terms financial resources and capital resources do. Thus, strategic HRD involves long-term development of people *within* organizations. Properly defining HRD requires a closer examination of the terms strategic, human resources, and development.

An Examination of Terms

Strategic

The term strategic is synonymous with other terms such as vital, crucial, essential, critical, important, integral, and necessary. The term also implies a long-term, organized, and planned effort to achieve an outcome or end. In an organizational context, the term strategic emphasizes the importance and critical nature of people in achieving the organization's business goals.

To achieve this outcome, HRD practice needs to be well organized and planned as well as integrated into every aspect of the organization. Furthermore, HRD practice needs to be focused on long-term goals and anchored to business strategy. Consequently, every intervention or initiative should be designed to help the organization achieve its targeted business results.

Human Resources

According to Gilley and Eggland (1989, 3), organizations utilize three types of resources: physical, financial, and human. *Physical resources* are tangible business assets such as facilities, equipment, supplies, and component parts of products, which are often referred to *as fixed corporate assets*. *Financial resources* refer to an organization's *liquid assets,* such as cash, stock, bonds, or investment capital. Financial resources impact an organization's ability to capitalize on opportunities for growth or expansion and reflect its overall financial strength. *Human resources* are the people an organization employs to produce products and provide services. Valuation of human resources proves a difficult task. Traditional measurement techniques, such as those used for physical or financial assets, are ineffective with human resources. Employees cannot be depreciated like physical resources, nor are they reflected in the net worth of an organization as financial resources are. However, human resources are just as important as physical and financial resources—in fact, more so. Unfortunately, many executives and managers overlook this fact because human resources and their intellectual capital are not given credit for the organization's prosperity.

One measure that organizational executives and managers occasionally consider is the cost of replacing valuable employees (recruiting, hiring, relocating, lost productivity, social and psychological costs, and training). However, rarely do they consider the knowledge, competencies, skills, and attitudes of their constituents—a grave oversight on their part. After all, the value of a well-trained, highly skilled, knowledgeable workforce is ultimately reflected in efficiency, productivity, and growth. Organizations must be aware of the value of human resources and include employees in their asset portfolios. When this occurs, firms will recognize the importance of HRD programs and realize that improved knowledge, skills, and attitudes are necessary to improve organizational performance and growth.

Development

The concept of development raises two questions: (1) What is meant by development? (2) What type of development occurs within organizations?

Development of employees refers to increasing the knowledge, skills, and competencies of employees, which enhances their performance capacity and capability. This reflects a philosophical commitment to the professional advancement of those within the organization (career development). But development also refers to increasing an organization's efficiency, improving its effectiveness, enhancing its renewal capacity, and improving its competitive practices (organizational development).

Individual and organizational development occurs when

1. employees participate in interventions and initiatives that expand their knowledge and skills, which improves their performance;
2. organizations remove barriers to performance;
3. organizations provide motivational factors that enhance performance;
4. organizations create work environments, systems, and processes that increase employee productivity;
5. managers provide feedback and reinforcement useful in encouraging continuous employee growth and development.

These elements are the essence of strategic human resource development.

Definitions of HRD

During the past few decades, several authors, researchers, and scholars have proposed definitions of HRD. Although many of these definitions reflect the status of the field at the time, several interesting similarities can be found. Let us briefly examine several definitions of HRD offered during the past few decades (italics added for emphasis):

- Nadler (1970, 3): "a series of *organized activities* conducted within a specified time and designed to produce *behavioral change.*"
- Craig (1976, xi): "a focus on the central goal of developing human potential in every aspect of *lifelong learning.*"
- Nadler (1983, 1): "organized *learning experiences* in a given period of time to bring about the possibility of *performance change or general growth* for the individual and the organization."
- Chalofsky and Lincoln (1983, 20): "interdisciplinary field defined as the study of how *individuals and groups in organizations change through learning.*"
- Nadler and Wiggs (1986, 5): "a comprehensive *learning system* that releases the organization's human potential; a system that that is both experience and experiential, on-the-job experiences that are keyed to the organization's reason for survival."
- Swanson (1987, 1): "a process of improving an *organization's performance,* the capabilities of its personnel."
- Smith (1988, 1): "programs and activities, direct and indirect, instructional and/or individual, that positively affect the *development of the individual* and the *productivity and profit of the organization.*"

- Gilley and Eggland (1989, 5): "organized *learning activities* within the organization in order to *improve performance and/or personal growth* for the purpose of *improving the job, the individual, and/or the organization.*
- McLagan (1989, 20): "is the integration of *training and development,* career development, and *organizational development* to improve individual, group, and organizational effectiveness."
- Watkins (1989, 427): "the field of study and practice responsible for fostering of long-term, work-related *learning capacity* at the individual, group, and organizational levels. As such, it includes but is not limited to *training, career development, and organizational development.*"
- Nadler (1990, 1): "organizational learning experiences in a given period of time to bring about the possibility of *performance change.*"
- Chalofsky (1992, 179): "the study and practice of increasing *learning capacity* of individuals and groups, collectives, and organizations through the development and application of learning-based interventions for the purpose of *optimizing human and organizational growth and effectiveness.*"
- Rothwell and Sredl (1992, 449): "*organizational learning* experience sponsored by an employer . . . for the purpose of *improving work performance* while emphasizing the betterment of the *human conditions* through the integration of organizational goals and individual needs."
- Swanson (1995, 207): "a process of developing and/or unleashing human expertise through *organizational development* and personal *training and development* for the purpose of *improving performance.*"

In each of the above definitions three areas of professional practice are identified: *learning, performance,* and *change.* In each case the purpose of HRD is focused either on the individual (personal growth, lifelong learning, expertise, etc.) or on the organization (productivity, profits, survival, effectiveness, etc.). Hence, we may conclude that HRD consists of three professional practice domains: *organizational learning, performance,* and *change.* Additionally, organizational efforts must result in *performance improvement* and *organizational change* that enhance the firm's competitiveness and efficiency. Performance improvement and organizational change, therefore, are the ultimate goals of HRD. In summary, then, strategic HRD can be defined as *the process of facilitating organizational learning, performance, and change through organized interventions and initiatives and management actions for the purpose of enhancing an organization's performance capacity, capability, competitive readiness, and renewal.* We will focus on these three practice domains and the respective roles of HRD professionals throughout this book.

Forces Causing Change in HRD

Competition, globalization, and continuous change in markets and technology are challenging today's organizations and are the principal reasons for the transformation of human resource development. Businesses large and small are in the midst of a revolution in managing people that will continue well into the twenty-first century. A flatter, less bureaucratic, more responsive organization is emerging as the model for the future. Organizations will be forced to enhance key capabilities and make these the source of their competitive advantage (Beer and Eisenstat 1996; Ulrich and Lake 1990). Moreover, Beer (1997) asserts that high levels of (1) *coordination* across functions, business units, and borders; (2) employee *commitment* to continuous improvement; (3) general management and leadership *competence;* (4) *creativity* and entrepreneurship; and (5) *open communication* will be necessary. To acquire these capabilities, organizations are struggling to realign themselves and their human resource policies and practices with new competitive realities. He suggests that a cultural revolution is underway.

Cost Effectiveness

Beer (1997) points out that the first wave of change has focused on cost effectiveness, as evidenced by the thousands of jobs lost due to downsizing, rightsizing, and reorganization of the corporate landscape. He suggests that this wave has spread to the rest of the world, which has reacted similarly in the face of economic downturn. Pressures for cost reduction not only demand a different organization; they also force the human resource development function to be cost effective. Human resource reengineering is occurring in many firms and with it, a search for new roles and responsibilities.

Many companies are discovering that downsizing is not enough. Implementation of new strategies requires fundamental changes in organizational behavior. Beer (1997) contends that streamlined organizations are not necessarily more effective. He points out that focusing on cost reduction as the principal thrust of change does not enhance long-term company performance.

People as a Source of Competitive Advantage

In recent years, several studies and works have explored the relationship among firm culture, organization effectiveness, and financial performance (Collins and Porras 1994; Denison 1990; Kotter and Heskett 1992; Pfeffer 1994). These studies show that effectiveness is much more than the aggregate talent of the firm's employees. Effectiveness is a function of the coordination around business processes the organization is able to develop (Beer 1997; Beer, Eisenstat, and Biggadike

1996; Ulrich and Lake 1990). This coordination is in turn a function of the organization's cultural context (Beer and Eisenstat 1996).

These studies have helped to establish human resources as a key to competitive advantage. The assertion that organizational behavior is linked to business success has also gained credibility. These works also point to a redefinition of human resources apart from the traditional focus on recruiting, selecting, and training employees; the new emphasis is on developing an organizational context that will attract and develop talented individuals and leaders.

Eichinger and Ulrich (1995) identify seven competitive challenges facing organizations. They are as follows:

1. Building and operating an effective customer-responsive organization
2. Gearing up for becoming an effective global competitor
3. Competing profitably with low-cost (product and service) providers
4. Transitioning from a profit-through-cost-cutting environment to a revenue-growth environment
5. Effectively taking advantage of new information technology
6. Attracting, developing, and retaining top talent
7. Operating internationally without a competitive, pro-business industrial policy matching those of foreign competitors

Each challenge greatly impacts the transformation of human resources from training department to strategic HRD.

Misconceptions Surrounding HRD as a Profession

Several misconceptions surround HRD as a profession. Overcoming these misconceptions requires HRD professionals to embrace several new actions. According to Ulrich (1997a), a common misconception of HRD is that people pursue HRD because they like people. Although it is important that HRD professionals champion the contributions and capabilities of people, HRD functions should not be designed to provide corporate therapy or provide social or health-and-happiness retreats. Moreover, HRD professionals must engage in practices that make employees more competitive, not more comfortable.

Another misconception is that the primary responsibility of HRD is to accomplish learning objectives (Brinkerhoff and Gill 1994). This belief contributes to the "training for training's sake" philosophy of HRD. Consequently, it affects HRD professionals' behavior and actions as well as the decisions they make. Learning objectives do provide structure and direction for a learning or performance improvement intervention, and they help define the purpose of training. Though important, learning objectives are not the ultimate goal. Some HRD practitioners rely too much on them and fail to focus on performance improvement interventions that add value to an organization. Gilley and Maycunich (1998a) suggest that only HRD interventions that help an organization achieve strategic business goals can add value.

Some believe that HRD deals with the soft side of a business and is therefore not accountable. Ulrich (1997a) maintains that to overcome this misconception, HRD programs need to measure their impact on business results. Additionally, HRD professionals must learn how to translate their work into financial performance. HRD activities need to be based on theory and research, and HRD professionals must master both theory and practice.

Brinkerhoff and Gill (1994) suggest that some HRD practitioners are "true believers." They honestly think that training, by itself, can change an organization and improve its performance capacity and effectiveness. When this belief is held, HRD practitioners think there is a direct cause-and-effect relationship between training and improving performance. However, employees are often so bombarded with problems, circumstances, and decisions that little of the training they receive can penetrate their mental shields (Gilley and Maycunich 1998a). Without careful and deliberate reinforcement on the job, most of what employees learn is forgotten and never applied. Ulrich (1998) contends that instead of focusing on training activity, an HRD practice needs to create value by increasing intellectual capital within the firm. Furthermore, HRD professionals must identify opportunities that enable the organization to achieve its strategic goals and objectives.

Because they believe that HRD's job is to be the learning and development police and the health-and-happiness patrol (Ulrich 1997a), many HRD practitioners spend a great deal of their time managing training events. They schedule courses, select training materials, manage enrollments, arrange conferences and workshop logistics, and collect and analyze evaluation forms (Brinkerhoff and Gill 1994). In fact, so much of their time is spent doing these types of activities that they have little time to spend on the critical issues facing their organizations, such as business process improvement, strategic planning, performance management, and change initiatives. These HRD practitioners operate as if business issues had little effect on their efforts. In fact, they are happy managing training and behave as if their department were tangential to other operational units.

HRD professionals need to realize that they do not own the learning and development processes—managers do. In addition, HRD practice does not exist to make employees happy but to help them grow and develop. Moreover, HRD professionals must help managers improve employee growth and development.

Unfortunately, some believe that HRD is driven by fads. Consequently, they feel that HRD practitioners are reactionary and do not maintain a consistent approach to practice. Swanson (1999) points out that HRD practices have evolved over time and are anchored in the fields of psychology, economics, management, change theory, systems theory, and learning theory (see Chapter 4). Additionally, he asserts that HRD professionals must see their current work as part of an evolutionary chain and must explain their work with less jargon and more authority.

Brinkerhoff and Gill (1994) report that many HRD practitioners have the attitude that training is their responsibility. Managers reinforce this belief by allowing their training responsibilities to be delegated to professional trainers (Gilley and Boughton 1996). In other words, managers wash their hands of the responsibility of developing their employees. In fact, the primary responsibility for training lies with managers because they are the only organizational players truly held accountable for employee performance and productivity (see Chapter 7). Organizations need those with real-world experience—that is, managers—to deliver training. Then managers can become the champions of training, rather than its gatekeepers, and HRD professionals can be performance consultants, analysts, evaluators, and agents for organizational development.

Ulrich (1997a) believes that HRD professionals should force vigorous debates regarding organizational effectiveness and performance. They should also be confrontive and challenging regarding state-of-the-art HRD practice. At the same time, HRD professionals should be supportive during change efforts and initiatives. It is important to remember that HRD is as important to line managers as finance, strategy, and other business domains. Thus, HRD professionals should encourage and support managers in human resource issues.

Brinkerhoff and Gill (1994) find that many HRD practitioners believe employees should enjoy training and, in fact, rely on reaction evaluations to determine whether employees find their training experiences to be enjoyable (Kirkpatrick 1995). Consequently, learning or performance improvement interventions that produce stress or cause employees to feel uncomfortable may not be viewed as positively as those designed for enjoyment. Is it any wonder that most training programs are designed to satisfy employees?

Interventions should be free from negative feedback that diminishes employee's self-esteem. However, they should be designed foremost to improve organizational performance and effectiveness. Sometimes this requires painful experiences, the type that develops employees as well as the organization.

One of the biggest misconceptions in HRD is that some practitioners believe they are in the business of "fixing" employees (Clifton and Nelson 1992). As a result, training is remedial in nature, giving employees the impression that something is wrong with them. Therefore, learning and performance improvement interventions are designed to correct employees' weaknesses rather than build on their strengths and manage their weaknesses (Buckingham and Coffman, 1999; Clifton and Nelson 1992). Such a philosophy undermines the efforts of HRD professionals and conditions employees to enter training with a negative and defensive attitude. Consequently, organizational performance and effectiveness do not improve, nor do the image and reputation of HRD professionals.

Mission and Purpose of HRD

HRD's mission is to provide (1) *individual development* focused on performance improvement related to a current job; (2) *performance management systems* aimed at improving organizational performance; and (3) *organizational development activities* that optimize human potential and organizational performance, which together improve the efficiency of the firm. Efficiency is measured by increased organizational effectiveness.

HRD's purpose, on the other hand, is to facilitate changes that lead to performance improvements, which ultimately enhance organizational competitive readiness and renewal capacity. That is, learning and performance improvement interventions and change initiatives promote on-the-job performance improvement and organizational development, thereby reducing costs, improving quality, enhancing human capital, and increasing the competitiveness of the firm.

Priorities HRD Professionals Should Address

Eichinger and Ulrich (1995) maintain that there are seven priorities of HRD, each of which must be addressed to make the transition to strategic HRD. First, HRD professionals should help the organization reinvent/redesign itself to compete more effectively. Second, they need to reinvent the HRD function to be aligned with a more customer-focused organization. Third, they need to attract and develop the next generation leaders and executives within the organization. Fourth, HRD professionals need to contribute to the continuing cost containment/management effort. Fifth, they need to continue to work on becoming a more effective business partner with internal stakeholders. Sixth, HRD professionals need to reject fads and quick fixes, sticking to the basics that work. Finally, they need to address diversity within their organizations and identify strategies to enhance it.

Creating Value Through HRD

Ehrlich (1997, 167–170) identified seven principles of creating value through HRD. The first principle is that HRD strategy must be anchored to business strategy, not programs. HRD must understand the strategy and economic realities of the business it supports and must be regarded as an essential contributor to the business mission. HRD professionals must speak the language of the business, and their activities must reflect business priorities. Nothing contributes to the credibility of HRD more than its focus on matters of genuine concern to the organization.

The second principle is that HRD is not about programs; it's about relationships. Thus, HRD's primary role is to create an environment in which individuals are committed to the success of the enterprise that employs them. Doing so requires developing attachments so that people want to work there and contribute willingly. It also includes using work teams and establishing peer review systems that provide employees with a meaningful voice in decisions that affect them. Finally, it includes engaging employees in the change process and giving them a voice in shaping their future.

Ehrlich suggests that "creating effective relationships includes providing employees with opportunities to acquire new skills to increase their capacity to contribute." This requires providing rewards and recognition that convey the importance of their contributions and an appreciation of their efforts. Effective relationships emulate a sense of community that flourishes when people work with others they admire and respect.

Third, Ehrlich contends that HRD must be known as professionals who anticipate change and understand what is necessary to implement it. In keeping with this idea, Burke (1992) suggests that HRD professionals must understand and champion the process of change by working closely with managers who are leading change and assisting those who are struggling to implement change. Ehrlich suggests that HRD professionals can help "managers appreciate that people do not resist change as much as they resist *being* changed and the top-down approach often used to introduce change. HRD can assist managers by helping them understand that employee involvement in the change process energizes them, draws on their knowledge and abilities, and helps produce desired results. HRD professionals should be viewed as thoughtful, enthusiastic advocates of change and the new ideas that contribute to business success" (168).

Gilley and Maycunich (1998a) warn HRD professionals not to be self-appointed change agents, because such attempts to impose their ideas on the organization will undermine their effectiveness within the organization. Ehrlich (1997) suggests that HRD professionals work with executives to determine what changes are needed and their effective implementation. Leaders need unbiased collaboration among peers as they focus on the change priorities of their business. HRD professionals are well suited to make that contribution.

Fourth, Ehrlich believes that HRD professionals should be outspoken advocates of employee interests, yet they must understand that business decisions must balance a range of factors that often conflict with one another. He suggests that HRD provide "thoughtful, objective, and realistic assessments of the human resource considerations surrounding pending decisions to promote reaching effective conclusions." Hence, HRD aims to ensure that performance improvement and change issues are given the attention they deserve.

Unless HRD professionals bring attention to inappropriate decisions affecting employees, they will be overlooked. This is an uncomfortable but necessary role but HRD professionals can help the organization avoid making serious mistakes that disenchant decisionmakers and negatively impact employees.

Fifth, Ehrlich believes that the effectiveness of HRD depends on its focus on issues rather than personalities. Keeping issues, rather than individuals, the topic of discussion grounds communications and helps manage conflict. Moreover, acknowledgment of others' perspectives validates their worth as persons and maintains esteem. In addition, ideas presented during a discussion that are not labeled as to their source can be discussed more objectively and evaluated more easily to reach the best solution. During this process, open-minded consideration often reveals more than one viable solution to an issue.

Sixth, HRD leaders must accept that constant learning and skill enhancement are essential to their contributions to the business. The speed of change necessitates constant learning and skill enhancement to survive. The competencies required of effective HRD professionals include functional expertise (compensation, management development, etc.), business acumen, consulting aptitude, and interpersonal skills (Gilley and Maycunich 1998a). Those in HRD must continuously expand their knowledge to avoid perpetuating old skills, notions, and styles. Thus, HRD must lead discovery of new ways for mobilizing the talent and energy of all organizational members, including themselves.

Outcomes of HRD

There are several outcomes of HRD. Brinkerhoff (1997, 146–147) identified eight outcomes of HRD, which serve as targets for interventions and initiatives.

- Type A. Current Job Performance: To provide employees the skills and knowledge they need to perform more effectively in their current jobs (includes management development, supervisory training).
- Type B. Emergency Capability: To provide employees with capability to perform effectively in emergency situations; to certify employee capability to handle emergency situations, thus reducing liability and risk.
- Type C. Advancement and Promotion: To provide employees the skills and knowledge they need to achieve promotions and other career advancement goals (career development, staff development, and staff education).
- Type D. Organizational Capacity: To build the organization's capacity to perform in an uncertain future by providing employees with the knowledge and skills they may need in future roles (development).

- Type E. Orientation and Acculturation: To provide employees with the knowledge and understanding they need to become oriented to, identified with, and to "join" their organization, knowing its business, culture, rules and policies, and so forth (employee orientation, organizational culture, diversity, business orientation).
- Type F. Employee Personal Capacity: To increase employee capacity to handle stress, work healthily, cope with change, and master the other personal resiliency skills needed to continue to grow, learn, stay healthy, and perform effectively in their continuously changing environment (development, staff development, wellness).
- Type G. Leadership Capacity: To develop leaders in the organization and give them the skills and knowledge they need to effectively formulate strategy and goals and guide the organization and its people (leadership development).
- Type H. Personal Benefits: To provide employees with learning opportunities that gratify their interests and develop skills and knowledge they personally wish to acquire but may not need for current or future performance (educational benefits, tuition reimbursement).

Challenges Facing HRD

Effective organizations possess a supply of employees willing and able to make contributions to organizational success. Thus, HRD functions must reshape themselves and revise their mental and organizational boundaries. Lawler (1996) contends that HRD must become a true business partner that helps develop new approaches to selection, training, career development, rewards, and performance improvement systems so that organizations can create strategically critical competencies and capabilities. Mohrman and Lawler (1997) believe that the HRD function faces five interrelated challenges in its attempt to make this contribution. Meeting each challenge requires blending business and HRD concerns.

Organizing for High Performance

Organization restructuring should emphasize the most effective application of human resources to accomplish the organization's mission. Mohrman and Lawler believe that "creating small, flexible, cross-functional units, aligning people around value-added tasks rather than overhead tasks, outsourcing, partnering, configuring work around core processes, and enhancing customer focus will only be successful if they transition the firm's human resources and create high levels of motivation" (243). Legitimate concerns about the condition of the workforce remaining after downsizing, reengineering, and cutbacks must be addressed.

Sustained high performance results only when new organizational forms develop due to a design process that incorporates both the nature of the task and that of people. This approach demands that HRD professionals develop a comprehensive understanding of strategy, principles of motivation, and varied approaches to goal-setting and rewards that give people a meaningful stake in organizational performance.

Deploying Employees

Because employees are more likely to move through a series of projects than through an orderly progression of jobs, managers are not likely to possess an understanding of their employees' knowledge bases. Savage (1990) contends that virtual organizations are on the rise, assembled from across the organization, often informally, and possibly connected only electronically to complete a task.

In virtual organizations, the challenge of matching employee talents to different work opportunities is intensified when combined with the need to develop people. Hall and Mirvis (1995) and Jacobs and Jones (1995) suggest that much of the employee development that takes place occurs through work or task assignments. These employees are competing for work assignments rather than for promotions up a hierarchy (Mohrman and Lawler 1997). Lawler (1996) maintains that a new information infrastructure is required to track and deploy the human resources available to the organization and the efficient, effective movement of employees between assignments. Additionally, "new compensation and reward systems are necessary to attract, develop, motivate, and retain this diverse, ever-changing workforce" (Mohrman and Lawler 1997, 224).

Managing Organizational Competencies and Capabilities

Ulrich and Lake (1990) point out that management of human resource competencies and organizational capabilities are urgent tasks that have survival implications. Because knowledge and information are increasing exponentially, organizations are required to nurture knowledge bases and enhance analytic capabilities to exploit knowledge at a faster rate than competitors.

Dynamic environments, strategies, designs, and technologies change needed competencies and capabilities—some become obsolete, noncritical, or irrelevant. Today's organizations require different, more advanced skills in group processes and organizational understanding. Although learning interventions and other approaches to development are more important than ever, Mohrman and Lawler (1997, 244) contend that "they represent only a piece of this puzzle: strategic *make-buy-partner* decisions will be as instrumental regarding human resource talent as in product and service decisions."

Managing Organizational Learning

Organizational knowledge and learning are closely related to the management of competencies. In traditional organizations, company and discipline-specific knowledge are retained by employees and shared via interaction of people in discipline-based departments and work groups.

Organizations will no longer remain competitive with informal approaches to knowledge and learning. Knowledge is an important asset to be actively managed. Increasingly, knowledge is dispersed cross-functionally and must be exploited across geographic boundaries. Embedding knowledge in organizational processes and documents, distributing information and expertise in readily accessible forms, and disseminating knowledge and accelerating learning are critical challenges facing organizations.

Defining the New Psychological Contract

Rousseau and Wade-Benzoni (1995) suggest that there is a psychological employment contract, which reflects an employee's understanding of the terms and beliefs concerning organizational members' responsibilities to and expectations of the firm. Recent changes in organizational strategies and structure have disrupted the prevailing psychological contract, which continues to evolve.

Mohrman and Lawler (1997) point out that organizations appear to be entering an era of highly differentiated psychological contracts. They contend that contracts with differing groups of employees—technical workers, salaried personnel, and temporary and part-time staff—have to address each group's particular needs and motivators, along with organizational performance expectations. Additionally, new norms and expectations must be purposefully set, and new ways of contracting for work must be devised; then employee behavior will change accordingly. Further, if the new contract does not give employees a stake in organizational performance, it is unlikely that the firm will achieve the levels of commitment found in the old era of two-way loyalty.

Ulrich (1997a, 237–254) also identifies some additional challenges that HRD faces regarding theories that HRD is based upon, tools and techniques used in HRD, HRD capabilities, governance, careers and competencies, and HRD guiding principles and values.

The HRD Function for the Twenty-First Century

The HRD function must undergo a metamorphosis in order execute the business partnership role of the future. According to Ulrich (1998), to perform effectively, the HRD function must be staffed by individuals who understand the business as well as change strategy. The HRD function must also be a valued component of management by contributing to business strategy and operational decisionmaking. In addition, the HRD function must increase outsourcing activities as a way to reduce the cost of the HRD function and to draw on expertise that is not easily built into the organization and must retain control over setting strategic direction for the organization's human resource systems, using outsourcers when appropriate.

Ulrich asserts that the HRD function needs to have high levels of competency in designing human performance systems and in managing their implementation (see Chapter 8). It needs to utilize information technology to support the development of organizational capabilities and competencies and of individuals' careers.

In the future, organizations will increasingly establish alliances and partnerships with each other, with universities, and with governments to provide services such as training and development, career and financial counseling, and development of portable benefits and other systems necessary to nourish the new workforce. Further, new resources will continue to become available to a workforce struggling to adapt to the changing employment environment.

Strategic redesign of organizations is slowly driving change in HRD practices, services, and in the way the HRD function is organized. HRD will be challenged to reinvent its structure and processes so that it can deliver the kinds of systems and business partnerships that will make its organization more effective.

The HRD Professional for the Twenty-First Century

Successful fulfillment of their roles requires HRD practitioners to develop several additional skills and to participate in varied organizational activities. Hale (1987) contends that HRD professionals need to increase their understanding of adult learning theories as well as participate in strategic planning activities. They also need to become proficient in business principles and practices. She contends that HRD professionals need to develop forecasting skills and needs assessment and performance analysis skills.

For far too long HRD professionals have entered the field from traditional learning/classrooms with little or no experience in organizational politics or theory, operations experience, or business knowledge. Recent emphasis on organizational learning and the consequences of failing to enhance organizational performance have placed pressure on HRD professionals to improve their business competence.

On the other hand, professionally identified HRD practitioners understand organizational culture, business practices, and operations. They participate in strategic planning activities and other strategic initiatives once reserved for middle or upper management. As a result, they must develop organizational development skills, change management skills, client relationship skills, and business knowledge (Gilley and Maycunich 2000). Additionally, professionally identified HRD practitioners develop forecasting skills that enable them to project future business trends and human resource requirements. These skills will be critical to HRD professionals in the next century.

The trend in today's organizations is toward performance management, human performance technology, and organizational development and change. To improve organizational learning, performance, and change, HRD professionals must expand their knowledge of job design and analysis; performance appraisal systems; performance, cause, and organizational analysis; organizational learning; performance consulting; and organizational development consulting. HRD professionals should also perfect their analysis, evaluation, project management, and partnering skills. In addition to these skills, Hale (1987, 33) reported several years ago, and it is still relevant today, that the role requires HRD professionals to be

1. *futurists,* so management is not caught off guard by changes in environment that will/could affect business viability;
2. *participants* in strategic initiatives, to better link performance improvement and organizational change to strategic business goals and objectives;
3. *performance consultants* to line management, to be in the best position to advise managers on the implications of training, coaching, and counseling;
4. *resources,* with new, more sophisticated skills in organizational learning theory, to more effectively service an assertive and aging workforce, and with business competency, to better understand and respond to business goals, performance analysis, and learning technology.

Hale (1987) points out that HRD professionals of the future must support organizational strategic goals, recompetency and/or performance formula, address higher-level problem-solving skills, and account for societal implications. She recommends that HRD professionals establish systems to better link their efforts to organizational goals. Further, evaluation of their efforts should be tied to accomplishment of those goals. They should also examine their learning and performance interventions as well as their change initiatives for legal exposure and effects on long-term social needs. She contends that future development efforts should be performance based and should follow a valid instructional development process and be based on job, task, and content analyses. HRD professionals should evaluate and select delivery systems that support affective and higher-level cognitive objectives such as socialization, problem solving, and team building. Furthermore she suggests continuing to explore using delivery systems and "smart systems" on-line to provide just-in-time training for all employees. HRD professionals should emphasize performance and/or competency-based learning supported by valid and reliable tests, the results of which can be used in promotional decisions.

Organizational Learning, Performance, and Change

To understand the complexity of strategic HRD, we need to examine the approaches of HRD (Chapter 2), identify the characteristics and components of strategic HRD leadership (Chapter 3), and analyze the principles of strategic HRD (Chapter 4). Additionally, we need to examine the three professional practice domains that constitute the field of strategic HRD: organizational learning (Chapters 5–7), organizational performance (Chapters 8–11), and organizational

FIGURE 1.1   Organizational Learning, Performance, and Change

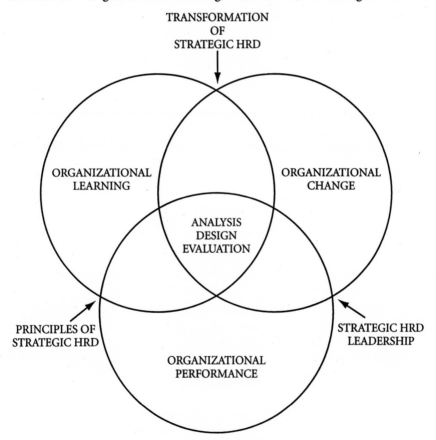

change (Chapters 12–14). Each of these domains shares three HRD practices useful in the execution of its respective goals: analysis (Chapter 15), design of interventions and initiatives (Chapter 16), and evaluation (Chapter 17). The relationship of these elements is depicted in Figure 1.1.

Conclusion

Determining an appropriate definition for strategic HRD helps to focus our attention on the critical professional practice domains of HRD: organizational learning, performance, and change. It is also important to examine the forces causing change in HRD as well as the misconceptions surrounding HRD as a profession. Identifying the mission and purpose of HRD programs and the priorities of HRD professionals shapes the focus of HRD. Identifying the outcomes and examining the challenges facing HRD are also essential, and determining what the HRD function and its professionals will look like in the twenty-first century is of vital importance to understanding strategic HRD. Finally, strategic HRD consists of several interdependent elements, domains, and practices.

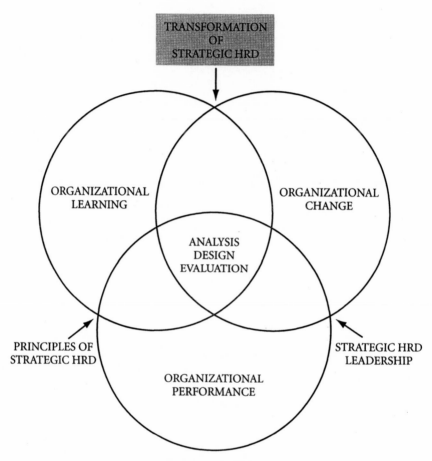

ORGANIZATIONAL LEARNING, PERFORMANCE, AND CHANGE

CHAPTER 2

Transformation of HRD

According to a number of researchers, most HRD programs are not linked to the strategic business goals of the organization (Gilley and Maycunich 1998a; Ulrich 1997a; Tarraco and Swanson 1995; Brinkerhoff and Gill 1994). Consequently, interventions and initiatives are implemented in a vacuum, as little attention is paid to the problems facing the organization and how HRD programs could be used to address them. As a result, employees fail to receive the type of learning and reinforcement needed to improve performance. Organizational performance cannot improve because interventions and initiatives are not focused on the business needs of the organization. Gilley and Boughton (1996) call this a "hit or miss" approach. Some training is on target, but most is not.

It is no longer enough for HRD programs to improve skills and knowledge; they must also improve the overall effectiveness of the organization. In other words, HRD needs to help the organization achieve its strategic business goals. HRD professionals, therefore, should create initiatives and interventions that help the organization change. This shift requires HRD professionals to change their philosophy to one of dedication to improving organizational effectiveness, rather than remaining the deliverers of training events. In short, they must become results-driven.

First-Level HRD

When the professional practice domains of HRD (learning, performance, and change) are arranged in a three-dimensional model, nine approaches can be identified (Figure 2.1). In this model, the first number represents an organization's emphasis on learning, the second represents its emphasis on performance, and the third represents change. Possible scores range from 1–1–1 to 10–10–10.

No HRD (1–1–1)

In many organizations there is no HRD program. Consequently, little or no formal learning activity is provided to employees. In addition, performance improvement interventions and change initiatives are rare, and if they exist at all, they are facilitated and led by senior management. Therefore, it is an accident when employee growth and development or organizational performance improves. Moreover, there are no performance partnerships, organizational effectiveness strategy, or HRD practice to examine.

Vendor-Driven HRD (10–1–1)

As HRD programs begin to emerge, they start to penetrate the organization. Over time they are accepted by the firm, but many are still perceived as outside the organizational mainstream. Consequently, management can easily eliminate HRD by cutting its budget. If HRD survives this period, it often completely penetrates the organization and becomes a full-fledged department. At this point, traditional training departments experience two separate and distinct approaches: vendor-driven (10–1–1) and middle-of-the-road HRD (5–5–5) (Gilley and Coffern 1994; Gilley and Maycunich 1998a).

During the vendor-driven period, HRD programs have a healthy budget and their practitioners are busy selecting and delivering training programs (Figure 2.1). This approach is characterized by the selection of training programs from a variety of vendors. It is one of management's favorite forms of HRD because programs are easy to administer and manage. They are also easy to build, downsize, and replace and are easily comprehended and justified. Unfortunately, vendor-driven HRD programs are still not viewed by management as critical to organizational success. As a consequence, HRD programs can easily be eliminated, because they have yet to become essential tools in improving organizational performance and effectiveness.

During this approach, many HRD professionals believe their job is to provide employees a comprehensive and complete list of training courses. All too often, they pay little attention to why employees participate in training as long as they attend some training class each year. Additionally, training is sometimes viewed as a reward for a job well done. Robinson and Robinson (1989) referred to this approach as the *activity strategy* of HRD.

A tremendous amount of training activity is common in vendor-driven HRD programs, although organizational performance seldom improves. During this period, the primary responsibility of HRD practitioners is to identify, evaluate, and select training programs from a myriad of outside "training houses." Gilley and Coffern (1994) refer to HRD practitioners who operate in such a manner as "brokers of training programs."

FIGURE 2.1   Approaches of HRD

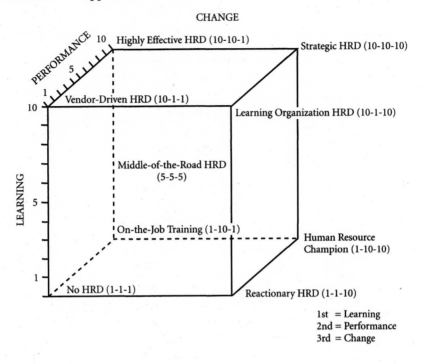

CHANGE

1st = Learning
2nd = Performance
3rd = Change

During this evolutionary approach, *training for training's sake* is an HRD practitioner's philosophy. Brinkerhoff and Gill (1994) identified five deeply held beliefs attributable to the "training for training's sake" philosophy of HRD: training
makes a difference, training is an HRD practitioner's job, the trainer's purpose is
to manage training programs, training's purpose is to achieve learning objectives,
and employees should enjoy the training they receive. Clifton and Nelson (1992)
identified a sixth belief held by HRD professionals during this period: training is
designed to "fix" employees' weaknesses. These beliefs appear to anchor HRD professionals into this philosophy, which consequently affects their decisionmaking
and behaviors.

Several traits characterize vendor-driven HRD. HRD practitioners ask more sophisticated and critical questions during the vendor-driven HRD period, such as,
"What skills or knowledge are needed for optimal performance?" Gilley and Maycunich (1998a) contend that HRD practitioners have not yet addressed the most
important question, which is, "How can HRD help the organization accomplish
its strategic business goals and objectives?"

HRD activities often provide isolated value to the organization, thus enabling
HRD to become more important. Consequently, the HRD program picks up

important sponsors and advocates that help improve its image within the firm. Unfortunately, the clearinghouse approach illustrates what is wrong with the HRD profession because it allows training activity to become the focus of HRD, which causes long-term damage to the image and credibility of HRD.

The organizational effectiveness strategy during this period is simply to improve individual employee performance. HRD practitioners pay little attention to how training enhances organizational performance, competitiveness, or efficiency. In other words, vendor-driven HRD is focused on improving employees' skills and knowledge in hopes that such development can and will help maximize organizational effectiveness and performance (Gilley and Maycunich 1998a).

As an indirect result of providing training, HRD practitioners develop performance partnerships. HRD practitioners are very customer oriented as they focus on improving organizational awareness of HRD, its interventions, and services.

HRD practice becomes more formalized during this approach. HRD practitioners conduct needs assessments to uncover skill and knowledge deficits and identify areas of training interest. They also identify the next series of training activities that organizational leaders perceive to be of value.

The primary objective of vendor-driven HRD programs is to provide formal training activities, which become the principal focus of HRD practice. In fact, to keep up with ever-increasing training demand, HRD departments hire more and more trainers. Unfortunately, little or no effort is made to ensure that training is being transferred to the job by employees (Broad and Newstrom 1992). Furthermore, managers and executives often refer to training as "something that those trainers do" and do not see employee development as a managerial responsibility. This attitude has become the Achilles heel of vendor-driven HRD programs. During this period, identifying employees' reactions to training is the only type of formal evaluation being conducted. Finally, it is common for HRD programs to separate themselves from the HR department and to establish their own structure. Although some HRD programs remain in the HR department, most operate as separate units.

On-the-Job Training (1–10–1)

Some organizations do not have a formal training department but rather conduct training on the job (OJT). Furthermore, these organizations do not have a formal change management practice nor do they employ structured performance management systems used to enhance performance (Figure 2.1). They do *"just enough"* training so that employees can do their jobs. Their emphasis is on improving short-term performance, productivity, and quality. They seldom focus on long-term organizational development strategies or foster cultures that promote learning and development.

One of the perplexing questions facing the field of HRD is, "Who should be responsible for training." Gilley (1998) believes that the person held accountable for employee performance and productivity ultimately should be responsible for training. He argues that this individual should also be responsible for conducting employee performance reviews, providing feedback, and confronting poor performance. Thus, the person responsible for training should be held accountable when productivity declines or when the organization fails to meet its goals and objectives. He concludes that the person the organization holds accountable for each of these activities is the "manager." Training is the responsibility of managers because they are held accountable for employee performance and productivity. He adds that any manager lacking the skills needed to adequately train employees should be relieved of his or her managerial responsibilities (see Chapter 6).

Having managers conduct training is helpful in improving employee knowledge and skill acquisition, but it is a futile effort when conducted in isolation. Jacobs and Jones (1995) contend that *structured on-the-job training,* planned, organized, and systematic learning at the workplace, has a greater impact on organizational effectiveness and competitiveness than traditional OJT. However, unless OJT is linked to other learning, performance improvement, management, and change initiatives, it is not very effective in improving organizational effectiveness. Therefore, incorporating OJT into an overall organizational learning, performance management, and organizational change strategy can maximize the manager-as-trainer approach. In this way, organizations embrace the strategic HRD approach to organizational effectiveness.

Reactionary HRD (1–1–10)

Some organizations react to every organization development fad that comes along. When this condition exists, an organization is experiencing reactionary HRD (Figure 2.1). Although this approach emphasizes change (organizational), the organization does not have any of the infrastructures necessary to support or manage change. The organization does not emphasize learning or maintain formal performance improvement and management systems (1–1–10). Typically, a reactionary HRD department consists of one or two persons responsible for identifying and analyzing organizational needs, designing or adopting change initiatives, implementing change activities, and evaluating their effectiveness.

Commonly, the people responsible for organizational change are not practicing professionals but rather are former line managers, salespersons, or customer service representatives who have demonstrated that they can work effectively with people. Although this competency is helpful, it fails to prepare them for the complex world of strategic HRD. Furthermore, this "practice can harm the credibility of HRD, prevent its acceptance within the organization, or prevent the evolution to result-driven HRD" (Gilley and Maycunich 1998a, 29). Moreover, such a small HRD function seldom has the time to focus on more than one activity or initiative at a time. Therefore, the emphasis is typically on the "organizational change of the day," which is done in a futile attempt to put together a successful formula that will improve an organization's effectiveness, competitiveness, and renewal capacity.

Middle-of-the-Road HRD (5–5–5)

The middle-of-the-road HRD is similar to the vendor-driven approach except that its practitioners use customized training programs to align with the organization's environment and culture as well as informal performance improvement strategies and process-level (departmental) change initiatives to enhance organizational effectiveness (Figure 2.1). During this period, formal instructional design and internal consulting activities surface (5–5–5). Consequently, HRD practitioners are responsible for designing and developing training programs to fit the organization as well as provide consulting activities used to facilitate performance improvement. On occasion, HRD professionals engage in organizational change initiatives, but always at the request of senior management.

During the middle-of-the-road HRD approach, HRD practitioners ask more sophisticated questions in their effort to address critical issues facing the organization, the most essential of which is, "How can learning, performance, and change become more organizationally focused?" The answer to this question motivates HRD practitioners to customize vendors' programs so that they complement organizational culture and meet specific business needs.

Unfortunately, the HRD philosophy during the middle-of-the-road approach is similar to what it is in the vendor-driven approach, except that the "training house" approach is brought inside the organization and combined with some modest performance management and improvement and change activity. This slight philosophical shift allows the instructional design and internal consulting roles of HRD to emerge. Although this is a positive development, HRD professionals should be more aggressive in their efforts to help executives discover ways of improving the organization's strategies, processes, or systems and improving its performance.

During the middle-of-the-road approach, HRD programs develop to full departmental status within the organization. Programs have a comprehensive and complete budget, a mission statement describing its purpose, a manager responsible for overseeing its internal affairs and providing direction, a complete staff, including trainers and institutional designers, and a formal reporting relationship and position on the organizational chart (Gilley and Maycunich 1998a). In other words, the HRD program has finally "arrived" and is considered a viable, productive department within the firm.

Roles of HRD Professionals. According to Robinson and Robinson (1996), middle-of-the-road HRD practitioners typically serve in several roles. As instructor-facilitators they are responsible for presenting information, directing structured learning experiences, and managing group discussions and processes. Program designers prepare objectives, define content, and select and sequence activities for specific interventions. Training materials developers are responsible for producing written or electronically mediated instructional materials. Internal consultants are accountable for coordinating and delivering consulting activities. Evaluators are responsible for administering forms and report results from reaction (end-of-course) project management activities (consulting), and learning evaluations.

Strategy and Partnerships. As HRD practitioners provide more and more middle-of-the-road training programs, their *organizational effectiveness strategy* begins to mature. This strategy becomes more performance oriented and incorporates organizational issues such as performance management, culture and structure, mission and strategy, leadership and managerial practices, and policies and procedures. Consequently, HRD practitioners develop an awareness of the relationship between the organizational system and the performance management process. Such knowledge is very important for the program to evolve to the more advanced phases of HRD.

Because HRD practitioners are required to customize training programs to fit the organization and provide informal internal consulting activities, they must further develop relationships with their internal clients. Since clients are expected to help HRD practitioners customize training programs, relationships are more formalized than in the previous approach. The most important element of middle-of-the-road HRD is its practitioners' work outside of their isolated departments as they interact directly with the people they serve. As a result, HRD practitioners develop an understanding of the organization and its business. Over time, such interaction will help HRD practitioners understand that their real purpose is to help the organization achieve its business goals and objectives through *management and organizational development partnerships.*

HRD Practice. One of the biggest changes in HRD practice occurs during this approach, as practitioners become instructional designers responsible for customizing training programs. Such a shift is critical to the future evolution of HRD because designing performance improvement interventions and change initiatives will be essential to maximizing organizational performance and will continue to be a useful service during the next evolutionary approach. Robinson and Robinson (1996) believe that middle-of-the-road HRD programs typically consist of identifying training needs, designing and developing training programs and other structured learning experiences, and delivering structured learning activities. They also train trainers and assure the quality of the training delivered by others. Furthermore, they provide some internal consulting activities in order to improve performance or foster change. Finally, they collect data concerning participants' reaction to training and determine whether learning occurred.

Structure.   During the middle-of-the-road HRD approach, programs are separate operating departments with a complete staff and budget. Departmental employees include an HRD manager, trainers, instructional designers, and one or two quasi-internal consultants—generally senior trainers responsible for client relationships or needs analysis activities. Typically, HRD departments are centralized in the organization's head office or headquarters as a way of improving training coordination and design and development activities. In many organizations, middle-of-the-road HRD programs are separate from HR departments, but they generally report to the same person within the organization (i.e., vice president or director of human resources).

Robinson and Robinson (1996) believe that middle-of-the-road HRD programs are commonly organized by roles or positions. When this approach is used, one or more designers, developers, instructors, and administrators report to the training manager. As a need arises in any subject area for which the function is responsible, the designer works on it and then transfers the project to the developer, who eventually hands it off to the instructor.

A second structural option is to organize by subject matter (Robinson and Robinson 1996). Some HRD professionals are dedicated to management development, interpersonal communication, project management, sales and marketing, and so forth. Therefore, the HRD program is organized to support this approach. In either case, the structure focuses on addressing training needs; therefore, positions such as designers, developers, and instructors are required.

Outcomes.   Often, middle-of-the-road HRD programs hold themselves accountable for the following measures: number of instructor days/hours, number of participant days/hours, number of different courses or new courses in a year, results from reaction evaluations, results from learning evaluations, and number of training days/hours per employee.

Higher-Order HRD

An HRD program that does not emphasize more than one of the professional practice domains of HRD (learning, performance, and change) or that emphasizes them at a moderate level will fail to improve organizational effectiveness significantly. In fact, the most effective first-level approaches, vendor-driven and middle-of-the-road HRD, focus primarily on activity. Additionally, HRD professionals that embrace first-level approaches give little thought to combining organizational learning, performance, and change efforts in order to impact their organization or help it achieve its strategic business goals. As a result, they miss opportunities to help the organization achieve its business results, improve its competitiveness, and enhance its renewal capacity.

Crossing the evolutionary line from first-level to higher-order HRD requires professionals to adopt a new philosophy that represents their new roles, responsibilities, and focus. Gilley and Maycunich (2000) suggest that HRD professionals adopt a philosophy "utilizing organizational learning, performance, and change to enhance an organization's capability, performance capacity, effectiveness, and competitiveness to achieve desired results" (10–10–10). This strategy communicates the intention of an HRD program—what it is really trying to accomplish. In essence, HRD is about achieving organizational results rather than training. A total shift in emphasis is required to accomplish this strategy.

Moving from a single dimension or the middle-of-the-road HRD approach to a higher-order HRD approach is a very difficult evolution. According to Gilley and Maycunich (1998a) and Tarraco and Swanson (1995), evolving to the higher-order level requires HRD professionals to think strategically about how HRD can have a positive impact on the organization. They assert that HRD professionals must determine which initiatives and interventions add value to the organization and which do not, always striving to improve organizational effectiveness in everything they do. They argue that HRD professionals need to understand that organizational decisionmakers are not interested in learning, performance, or change but in what these professional practice domains can do for them. Such an understanding should encourage HRD professionals to change their practice. Although it is easy to generate a lot of training activity and claim that it makes a difference, it is much harder to identify the organizational results needed and to determine a path for achieving them. When HRD professionals provide initiatives and interventions that help the organization accomplish its strategic business goals, HRD has crossed the line of demarcation that separates the activity zone from the results-driven zone.

Higher-order HRD consists of four results-driven approaches. Three of these approaches emphasize two of the professional practice domains of HRD at the highest possible level (10): highly effective training (10–10–1); learning organization HRD (10–1–10); and human resource champion (1–10–10). These approaches utilize a combination of professional practice domains to enhance organizational effectiveness, but they fail to emphasize all three. Only the strategic HRD approach emphasizes all three simultaneously and at the highest possible levels (10–10–10). It should be noted that any of the higher-order approaches is a significant improvement over the first-level approaches, in that HRD professionals are better able to improve organizational effectiveness through organizational learning, performance management, and organizational development and change.

Highly Effective Training (10–10–1)

Brinkerhoff and Gill (1994) call for a new approach in HRD. Their model focuses on using learning to improve individual and organizational performance (10–10–1), which they refer to as highly effective training (HET). This approach does not, however, emphasize organizational change nor does it provide strategies for how HET can be used to bring about long-term organizational change (Figure 2.1). Brinkerhoff and Gill contend that HET is simply a convenient name for a set of principles, strategies, tools, and methods HRD professionals have applied or observed. They explain that HET does not employ a series of cookbook-type steps because a recipe would be neither appropriate nor effective given the diverse circumstances of training in organizations. Thus, HET is composed of guidelines and suggestions for application within a simple conceptual framework that HRD professionals can use to develop and implement their own performance improvement systems. Finally, this approach is founded on the belief that enhanced learning and performance will directly bring about improved organizational effectiveness. Therefore, formal organizational change efforts and organizational development and strategic planning initiatives are not necessary or emphasized.

Purpose. According to Brinkerhoff and Gill (1994), the purpose of HET is to conceptualize, design, and implement training as an integrated system that helps organizations use learning to consistently add value to services and products. They assert that the key to HET is systems thinking, which is based on the assumption that training has an interdependent, dynamic relationship with other business processes and the total organization. This view is in contrast to the traditional view of training as a separate, secondary function that produces programs and learning that may or may not transfer to the workplace.

Roles and Responsibilities of HRD Professionals. Brinkerhoff and Gill (1994) believe that roles and responsibilities for the HET process are quite different from those in the vendor-driven or middle-of-the-road approaches. HRD activities such as needs analysis, design, delivery, and management of postlearning transfer to the workplace all require special attention. Their approach suggests that HRD professionals are responsible for four training subprocesses: (1) formulating training goals that are linked to business needs, (2) planning training strategies that will consistently and efficiently achieve those goals, (3) producing learning outcomes necessary for effective performance, and (4) supporting performance improvement that will add value to products and services.

Principles of Highly Effective Training. Brinkerhoff and Gill (1994) developed a four-part approach to performance improvement, which directly correlates to the responsibilities of HRD professionals. They maintain that this approach forces organizations to take a wide-angle view of training. This helps HRD professionals identify and assess the key factors in their organizations that enable high-leverage change.

A basic assumption, according to Brinkerhoff and Gill, is that the vision for highly effective training is always the same: to add value to organizational products. They add,

> according to this view, the end goals of training are not to produce learning, as in new knowledge, skills, and attitudes, for these alone do not benefit the organization. Only when new learning endures and is applied on the job to achieve an objective that is vital to organizational success does training pay back its costs. New learning represents only the capacity for value to be added. If that learning is not nurtured through the post-learning period into improved performance, the training fails. (Brinkerhoff and Gill 1994, 11)

The new approach to training has four principles:

1. Link training events and outcomes clearly and explicitly to business needs and strategic goals.
2. Maintain a strong customer focus in the design, development, and implementation of all training activities.
3. Manage training with a systems view of performance in the organization.
4. Measure the training process for the purpose of continuous improvement. (Brinkerhoff and Gill 1994, 77)

Linking Training to Business Goals

To derive the maximum value from training, HRD professionals need to forge clear and explicit links with vital business goals and strategic objectives (Brinkerhoff and Gill 1994). Throughout the training subprocesses (formulating training goals, planning training strategies, producing learning outcomes, and supporting performance improvement) Brinkerhoff and Gill assert that HRD professionals need to make certain that their efforts add value to the business of the organization, whether that business is producing or selling a product or providing a service. They maintain that "value is determined by the extent to which there is a need for the potential contribution of training" (91).

Maintaining Customer Focus

Since customer needs and expectations are the key to quality, products or services that meet or exceed these needs and expectations are said to have quality. Using this as a standard, Brinkerhoff and Gill (1994) argue that HRD programs need to build and maintain a strong customer focus. To do so, HRD professionals must make certain that training continuously meets customer needs and exceeds customer expectations. Brinkerhoff and Gill (1994, 115–123) identify several strategies useful to HRD professionals in maintaining customer focus: identify training customers, determine customer needs and expectations, segment training markets, tailor services, incorporate measurement throughout the training process, build an infrastructure for customer communications and involvement, create and implement a comprehensive customer service strategy, and engineer quality service into each step of the training process.

Using Systems Thinking to Integrate Work and Learning

Brinkerhoff and Gill (1994) believe that compartmentalization is a primary reason that the training-for-training's-sake philosophy has been adopted by so many training departments. Consequently, training has been shaped by an old paradigm that separates the training function operationally from other business activities. This paradigm approaches human performance as an independent aspect of organization life—which is illogical.

Brinkerhoff and Gill (1994, 125) suggest that HRD professionals manage organizational training with a systems view of learning that has its foundation in systems thinking. They believe that it is essential for HRD professionals to adopt a systems thinking approach to achieve highly effective training

Using Measurement and Feedback for Continuous Improvement

Finally, Brinkerhoff and Gill (1994, 51) contend that organizations should "measure the training process for the purpose of continuous improvement." They assert that highly effective training depends on continuous measurement to keep the process on track toward achieving business goals. They also maintain that performance improvement systems will not succeed without a continuous process of data collection and feedback.

To be effective, Brinkerhoff and Gill contend that measurement should focus on the linkage of training to business goals, needs of different customers, and the interaction of components of the organization's system. They believe that measurement can be used to identify opportunities for training, determine customer deficits in needed knowledge, skills, and attitudes, and enhance the learning process (pp. 155–156). Measurement can also be used to manage critical value-adding events, identify training problems and their potential solutions, and assess the business impact of training. Finally, measurement can be used to provide accountability for the use of resources and monitor changes in attitudes and perceptions related to training. When these four principles are fully operational within an organization, the following surface:

Formulating Training Goals.
- Line manager conducts needs analyses
- Line manager is customer of training
- Customer and training leader agree on goals
- Goals are defined as business results
- Training leader consults regarding needs analysis and goal setting
- Goals are based on measurement of performance
- Goals are based on performance systems analysis
- Training goals specify linkage to strategic goals

Planning Training Strategy.
- Includes before-during-after learning process
- Agreed on and created by line/training team
- Based on process analysis of business procedures
- Specifies accountabilities for nontraining personnel
- Provides for "just-in-time" delivery
- Specifies prelearning intervention tasks
- Specifies postlearning intervention tasks
- Specifies measurement milestones
- Based on iterative improvement cycles
- Incorporates performance support tools and tasks

Producing Learning Outcomes.
- Incorporates "just-enough" content
- Provided on or close to job
- Includes practice with performance support tools
- Includes action planning
- Specifies individual performance objectives
- Clarifies linkage to strategic goals as part of content

Supporting Performance Improvement.
- Transfer is responsibility of line management
- Frequent measurement of progress and impact
- Managed by performance support team

- Tracks performance system variables
- Training leader consults and facilitates (Brinkerhoff and Gill 1994, 19)

Learning Organization HRD (10–1–10)

Since Senge (1990) introduced the learning organization concept, many organizations have adopted its five disciplines: personal mastery, mental models, shared vision, team learning, and systems thinking. Many other authors have advocated the values and benefits of learning organizations (Marquardt 1996; Kline and Saunders 1998; Redding 1994; Watkins and Marsick 1993) and application of its principles (Preskill and Torres 1999). Consequently, we believe that it is a viable higher-order HRD strategy, which can be used to enhance organizational effectiveness.

The learning organization HRD approach views learning as a critical component in enhancing organizational effectiveness. It embraces a philosophy of continual organizational learning and transformation and advocates the management of knowledge (Marquardt 1996). It emphasizes the importance of developing a culture that enhances and encourages organizational learning and change (10–1–10). Learning organization HRD encourages the development of structures and systems to ensure that knowledge is captured, shared, supported, facilitated, and rewarded (Watkins and Marsick 1996). When the learning organization HRD approach is adopted, employee involvement is greatly encouraged and built into work structures, politics, and practices throughout the organization (Figure 2.1).

The learning organization HRD approach has been significant in that organizations emphasize learning and change as a strategic strategy for long-term success. However, this approach does not directly emphasize organizational performance as a primary outcome. Furthermore, advocates of this approach do not provide frameworks for improving organizational performance through the adoption and development of positive learning cultures (Gilley and Maycunich 2000). They do, however, emphasize an indirect enhancement of organizational performance through organizational learning and change. Although this may seem like a criticism of learning organizations HRD, it is more an observation of its focus rather than an indictment of its limitations. We examine the learning organization philosophy, strategy, and practice in greater detail in Chapters 5 and 6, as well as provide an approach that integrates organizational performance with organization learning and change (see Chapter 7).

Human Resource Champion (1–10–10)

According to Ulrich (1997a, 19), the human resource champion (HRC) model is about building competitive organizations by helping managers create more competitive organizational processes (Figure 2.1). It is also designed to help HRD (although Ulrich does not discuss HR and HRD as separate fields, the ideas expressed are applicable to both; for simplicity, we shall simply refer to HRD henceforth) professionals articulate new agendas for their roles in the organization of the future. The human resource champion approach emphasizes organizational effectiveness through organization change (both the organization and HRD function) and performance improvement and management but does advocate the use of organizational learning as an important organizational effectiveness strategy (1–10–10).

The human resource champion model is organized around the outcomes or deliverables of HRD and the activities required to accomplish these outcomes. First, Ulrich (1997a, 23–52) lays out a framework that defines four generic deliverables of effective use of HRD: strategy execution, administrative efficiency, employee contribution, and capacity for change. He believes that these deliverables represent capabilities of competitive companies and must be championed by both line managers and HRD professionals. He adds that these four deliverables also identify the roles that HRD professionals play when creating value.

Second, Ulrich (1997a, 53–82) describes how HRD can facilitate business strategy. He reviews the role of HRD as a strategic partner joined with line management in turning business strategy into action. The model provides a process for making an organizational diagnosis through which line managers and HRD professionals leverage HRD practices to deliver results. Third, Ulrich (1997a, 83–122) describes how HRD can help build administrative efficiency. He reviews the role of HRD as an administrative expert and highlights the ways in which work can be organized so that costs are reduced while quality of service is maintained. He recommends and describes the potential for reengineering HRD and links that process to organizational design choices that include outsourcing, shared services, and the learning organization. Fourth, he describes how HRD can ensure employee contribution. He reviews the role of HRD as employee champion and highlights the management of intellectual capital to create value (123–150). The model discusses specific ways that managers and HRD professionals can increase employee commitment and competence, despite post-reengineering trauma and burned-out employees, and keep employees committed in an era of increasing competitiveness.

Fifth, Ulrich (1997a, 151–188) describes how HRD can help make organizational change happen. He reviews the role of HRD as a change agent and describes how to build capacity for change. Among the topics covered are processes for improving the capacity for change and for creating fundamental transformation or culture change. Sixth, Ulrich (1997a, 189–230) believes that by applying organizational diagnostic tools to the HRD function, the model shows its professionals how to build a strategic HRD program, create HRD strategies, and establish a solid HRD function.

Principles of the Human Resource Champion.   Mohrman and Lawler (1997, 149) believe that human resource development practices are an integral part of all organization systems and are central to organization capability development. For employees to contribute to performance improvement, HRD practices must complement each other and link with the organization's strategy and design. They assert that HRD professionals must be knowledgeable about, have influence on, and be closely connected to other organization systems, while possessing a solid base of knowledge about HRD practices in order to impact performance.

Rummler and Brache (1995) maintain that the HRD function must be able to operate at multiple levels of analysis: the individual/work group, business process, organization, and cross-organizational levels. Mohrman and Lawler (1997) hold that HRD professionals cannot work exclusively at the level of the individual performer. They contend that HRD programs must contribute to the development and performance management of teams, product lines, divisions, joint ventures, consortia, and wherever else performance is strategically important. Finally, HRD professionals must also operate with a good understanding of industry trends and other competitive issues so that they can be contributors to the business.

Mohrman, Lawler, and McMahan (1996) provide evidence that the evolution of the HRD function to a business partner is under way. In some organizations, HRD is an integral part of the management team, helping to formulate strategy, improve organization performance, and develop organization capabilities that focus on speed and quality (Lawler 1995; Evans 1994).

Mohrman and Lawler (1997, 154) argue that the HRD function must have a full partnership role in each of the following key business processes: developing strategy, designing the organization, change implementation, and integrating performance management practices. First, HRD should contribute to business strategy based on its knowledge of the competencies and capabilities of the organization, its understanding of the organization changes that will be required to support different strategic directions, and its knowledge of the network of human resources available to the company including the opportunities or constraints inherent in that network. Second, HRD should be a repository of organization design expertise, and its members should play the role of internal consultants to the ongoing design and redesign that will characterize organizations and their subunits as they continually modify themselves to achieve shifting strategies, new capabilities, and higher levels of performance. Third, HRD should help the organization develop change management capabilities to weather the constant changes that will continue to be part of the environment and help with the ongoing evaluation processes required to assess the impact of change and its necessary corrections. Fourth, the HRD function should work with line managers to guarantee that the organization's performance management practices are integrated with each other, with business management practices, and that they fit with the nature of the firm's work.

Roles of HRD Professionals. Ulrich (1997a, 24) believes that to create value and deliver results, HRD professionals must begin by defining the deliverables of their work, not by identifying simple activities. He argues that deliverables guarantee outcomes of HRD work. With deliverables defined, the roles and activities of business partners can be identified.

Ulrich (1997a) identifies four key roles that HRD professionals must fulfill to make their business partnership a reality. He constructs a framework using two axes that represent HRD professionals' *focus* and *activities.* By *focus,* Ulrich means time ranges from long-term strategic to short-term operational; thus, HRD professionals must learn to be both strategic and operational, focusing on the long and short term. *Activities* range from managing processes (HRD tools and systems) to managing people. These two axes delineate four principal HRD roles: (1) management of strategic human resources; (2) management of firm infrastructure; (3) management of the employee contribution; and (4) management of transformation and change (p. 24). To understand each of these roles more fully, one must consider the deliverables that constitute the outcome of the role, characteristic metaphors or visual images that accompany the role, and activities that the HRD professional must perform to fulfill the role. (See Appendix A.)

By management of strategic human resources, Ulrich (1997a, 25–27) means that the strategic HRD role focuses on aligning HRD strategies and practices with business strategy. Executing this role requires HRD professionals to be strategic partners, working to ensure the success of business strategies. This helps an organization in three ways. First, the firm more readily adapts to change, as the time from conception to execution of a strategy is shortened. Second, the organization can better meet customer demands, because its customer service strategies have been translated into specific policies and practices. Third, the organization can achieve improved performance through its more effective execution of strategy.

Management of firm infrastructure involves designing and delivering efficient HRD processes for staffing, training, appraising, rewarding, promoting, and otherwise managing the flow of employees through the organization (Ulrich 1997a, 27–28). This is beneficial in two ways. First, HRD processes are executed efficiently. Second, HRD professionals can improve overall business efficiency by hiring, training, and rewarding managers who increase productivity and reduce waste. To be effective as administrative experts, HRD professionals need to undertake activities leading to continual reengineering of work processes.

Management of employee contribution regards involvement in the day-to-day problems, concerns, and needs of employees (Ulrich 1997a, 29–30). HRD professionals thus become employees' champions by linking employee contributions to organizational success. Management of employee contributions result in increased employee commitment and competence. Ulrich believes that active employee champions—who understand employees' needs and ensure that those needs are met—positively impact overall employee contribution. When managing employee contribution, the primary activities are listening, responding, and finding ways to provide employees with resources that meet their changing demands.

Management of transformation and change, according to Ulrich (1997a, 30–31) means helping the organization transform its culture and change by serving as both cultural guardians and catalysts. He defines *change* as the ability of an organization to improve the design and implementation of initiatives and to reduce cycle time in all organizational activities. Within this context, HRD professionals identify and implement processes for change. The basic outcome of management of transformation and change is capacity for change. As change agents, HRD professionals need to facilitate a dialogue about values as they identify new behaviors that will help to keep an organization competitive over time. Activities of change agents include identifying and framing problems, building relationships of trust, solving problems, and creating and fulfilling action plans.

HRD Practice.   The four roles or deliverables for HRD just described require new ways of thinking about and executing HRD (Ulrich 1997a, 189). If HRD professionals are to become partners and assume the four roles previously discussed, they must champion HRD practices within their firms. This means building a strategy and creating an HRD organization to deliver it. Doing so requires that three separate but related aspects of the job be understood:

- Strategic human resource development refers to the process of linking HRD practices to business strategy.
- HRD strategy refers to building an agenda for the HRD function.
- HRD organization refers to the process of diagnosing and improving an HRD function to deliver HRD services.

These three issues are related because all focus on helping an organization become more successful.

Building an HRD Infrastructure.   Ulrich (1997a, 212) contends that an effective HRD strategy sets the destination toward which the HRD function is headed, whereas the HRD organization provides the road map for getting there. An appropriate HRD organization can be developed by applying the following organizational diagnostic process.

- Shared mind-set: The extent to which the HRD function possesses a shared mind-set, or common identity.

- Competence: The extent to which individuals who have knowledge, skills, and abilities to perform their current and future work staff the HRD function.
- Consequence: The extent to which the performance management system used by HRD professionals focuses on the right behaviors and outcomes.
- Governance: The extent to which the HRD function has effective reporting relationships, communications, decisionmaking, and policies.
- Work processes/capacity for change: The extent to which the HRD function learns and adapts, and thus understands and improves processes.
- Leadership: The extent to which effective leadership permeates the HRD function (Ulrich 1997a, 212–213)

Ulrich (1997a) believes that these six factors represent the essential building blocks of an HRD organization.

Outcomes. Ulrich (1997a) identifies four outcomes that can be realized from transforming training departments to human resource champion HRD functions. They include executing business strategy, building an effective organizational infrastructure, increasing employee commitment and capability, and creating a renewed organization.

Strategic HRD (10–10–10)

HRD professionals know they have evolved to the strategic HRD level when they can positively answer the following two questions:

1. Can the HRD program help maximize organizational performance, develop an organizational culture that embraces continuous learning, implement and manage organization-wide change initiatives for the purposes of improving organizational effectiveness, enhancing competitiveness readiness, and improving renewal capacity?
2. Can evidence be gathered to support this claim?

The answers to these questions demonstrate an HRD program's commitment to making a difference in the organization and become an HRD professional's overriding passion.

To evolve to the strategic HRD level, HRD professionals must have the courage to make some fundamental changes, to question their organizational mission and its impact on the organization, and to abandon all they have achieved up to this point. HRD professionals need to be willing to forgo the enhancement of their centralized departmental structure and focus on helping operational divisions improve their learning, performance, and change capabilities, thus allowing HRD to become strategically aligned throughout the firm rather than centrally located.

Much like Cortez, the Spanish explorer, HRD professionals must "burn the mothership" and venture into uncharted lands in search of better ways of helping their organizations improve their effectiveness and performance capacity. This requires that HRD professionals be permanently assigned to business units and that they become responsible for improving the firm's productivity and performance. In other words, they become members of an operational group rather than part of a centralized HRD department. This kind of change is often quite difficult for HRD professionals, because they must become "accountable" for results and can no longer hide behind an avalanche of training activity.

The movement from a centralized department to a strategic HRD unit requires a shift in thinking on the part of HRD professionals—who must think like their clients instead of like HRD practitioners. As businesspersons, HRD professionals must understand the revenue and cost implications of their recommendations and filter their suggestions through the prism of practical reality and operational priorities. They must think strategically about the long-term implications of change prior to implementing interventions. In short, HRD professionals must become strategic business partners. For some, the transition is easy because they have always operated from this perspective or were part of an operational group prior to joining HRD. For others, the journey is a road less traveled, full of uncertainty and insecurity. As always, HRD professionals must establish credibility by demonstrating their professional competence, integrity, and sincerity.

Additionally, HRD professionals must be willing to embrace rapid change by becoming part of their organization's operational units, rather than retreating to the safety of their own centralized department (the mothership). Finally, a strategic HRD program cannot survive alongside the old centralized HRD department because their philosophies differ so dramatically. Consequently, HRD professionals must choose. Either return to the mothership and sail back across the line of demarcation to produce training activity, or go forward and help the organization achieve its strategic business goals by applying an organizational effectiveness strategy, creating and implementing performance partnerships, and unleashing HRD practice (Gilley and Maycunich 1998a).

During this approach, the centralized HRD budget shifts to the operational unit where HRD professionals are now assigned. This helps the organization and HRD in two ways. First, strategic HRD programs can demonstrate how they help their units accomplish business objectives. Thus, HRD professionals are forced to become strategic business partners within their units and, therefore, produce results. Second, organizations are compelled to view HRD as an investment rather than as a cost. For example, operational budgets are established to produce results that managers are held accountable for achieving. Staff budgets—those used to support non-revenue-producing units such as public relations, human resources, and HRD—are established to provide services for the organization. Managers of these departments are held accountable for producing service activity, not producing organizational results. Therefore, the funds made available to a centralized HRD department by definition cannot produce organizational results. Thus, HRD is viewed as a cost to the organization (to provide activity) rather than as an investment (to produce results). By creating a strategic HRD program and shifting its budget to the operational level, HRD programs become accountable for producing results and are viewed in the same way as their operational unit.

Organizational Effectiveness Strategy and Performance Partnerships. During this approach, HRD professionals' organizational effectiveness strategy is to maximize organizational performance through performance improvement and management, organizational learning, and change, rather than improving individual employee skills and knowledge. Consequently, HRD professionals concentrate on improving organizational effectiveness and achieving business results using a strategic HRD approach.

During this approach, performance partnerships become a priority because strategic HRD programs require working relationships with business units. Strategic HRD cannot succeed unless performance partnerships are formed and are functioning effectively. Performance partnerships must be formed at three levels. First, HRD professionals must be willing to become strategic business partners with clients from different business units, divisions, and departments so that they can provide them with better service. These partnerships require HRD professionals to become responsible for providing customer service, helping their clients make performance improvement and organizational development decisions, and identifying demands facing their clients and how they should respond accordingly.

Second, HRD professionals must create management development partnerships with managers and supervisors to improve organizational performance. This type of partnership can be best accomplished by helping managers and supervisors make the transition to performance coaching. With this support, managers and supervisors become responsible for the majority of training for their employees. This frees HRD professionals to help facilitate organizational change and development. This type of partnership is referred to as a *micro approach,* where performance improvement is achieved one manager and one employee at a time.

The third performance partnership is known as the *macro approach,* which occurs as a result of HRD professionals focusing their attention on improving organizational effectiveness by altering the organizational and performance management systems. Such a partnership can be formed only when HRD professionals have access to organizational leaders and decisionmakers. Its focus is on improving the organization through change and organizational development interventions that directly maximize organizational performance.

Roles of HRD Professionals.   When strategic HRD programs are in place, HRD professionals operate as internal consultants (performance consultants and organizational development change agents), which requires HRD professionals to operate on a project-by-project basis (see Chapters 11 and 14). Consequently, every strategic HRD professional is a project manager responsible for designing, managing, implementing, and evaluating performance improvement, change, and organization development interventions (Fuller and Farrington 1999). Such responsibilities include planning, organizing, directing, and controlling project outcomes that are delivered on time, within budget, and to quality specifications (Robinson and Robinson 1996).

Mohrman and Lawler (1997) conclude that today's restructured organizations demand a sophisticated business partner capability on the part of HRD professionals. As business partners, these professionals need to be able to think strategically and systematically. They also need to be part of cross-functional organization leadership teams that plan and manage the complex issues of rapid change. Such a role is a microcosm of the new organization, where more and more individuals will have to work cross-functionally. Additionally, they are expected to address business issues as well as their particular discipline's issues (Mohrman and Lawler 1997).

During this approach, HRD practice makes a serious shift that allows for the birth of the performance consulting and organizational change agent roles (see Chapters 10 and 13). As we discussed previously, strategic HRD professionals should relinquish their training responsibility to managers and supervisors, because they are ultimately responsible for improving employee performance and organizational productivity. By doing so, organizations are allowing the only organizational players accountable for performance appraisal and employee development to become the champions of HRD, rather than its gatekeepers.

As performance consultants and organizational change agents, HRD professionals are responsible for implementing performance management systems, facilitating and managing change, and championing performance improvement and change initiatives. Such activities are designed to maximize organizational performance and enhance organizational renewal capacity. Additionally, HRD professionals are responsible for helping managers make the transition to performance coaching and for implementing performance appraisals that bring about lasting change.

Change initiatives and performance improvement interventions are also being designed and implemented during this approach. Instead of simply designing training programs as a way of improving employees' skills and knowledge, strategic HRD professionals are responsible for designing and implementing efforts used to help the organization achieve operational results.

HRD Practice. Rothwell (1996a) believes that HRD professionals need to adopt a new approach to maximizing organizational performance, one that addresses the real problems of an organization and enables it to achieve needed results. Brinkerhoff and Gill (1994) maintain that HRD professionals need to develop an approach that helps them connect performance improvement interventions and change initiatives to the strategic business goals of organizations. Such an approach must focus on learning transfer strategies rather than on training activity (organizational learning). In short, HRD professionals must redesign the performance improvement and organizational change process in order to develop a strategic HRD program. This includes identifying organizational and performance needs, designing and developing performance improvement interventions and change initiatives, facilitating learning acquisition and transfer, and measuring performance improvement and organizational results.

Identifying Organizational and Performance Needs

HRD professionals need to clearly identify opportunities for learning and performance improvement and organizational development. This requires HRD professionals to examine, analyze, and evaluate possible sources of opportunity. Sources may include managers' expectations of employee performance, the strategic direction of the organization, customers' perspectives of the organization's products, and employee assessment of jobs, processes, procedures, work flow, and the like (see Chapter 15).

Designing and Developing Learning and Performance Improvement Interventions and Change Initiatives

A small group of centralized HRD professionals is needed to design and develop learning and performance improvement interventions and change initiatives. They are responsible for instructional design and coordinating organization-wide projects. As managers shoulder more and more training responsibility and HRD professionals make the transition from trainers to performance consultants and organizational change agents, this practice is essential (see Chapter 16).

Facilitating Learning Acquisition and Transfer

Before learning can be translated into value for an organization, it must be applied to the job. Therefore, no step in the performance improvement and change process is more important. Unfortunately, too many employees are on their own immediately after a training event, struggling to integrate new skills or knowledge on the job. Confused and frustrated, employees often fail to confidently and accurately transfer learned principles to their work. Consequently, much of what is learned during training is lost and never applied.

Managers and HRD professionals can help foster learning acquisition and transfer by providing practice opportunities both during and after learning or performance improvement interventions. They can also enhance learning transfer by managing learning activities, providing feedback to participants during learning activities, monitoring knowledge acquisition, and providing a supportive and positive learning environment. In addition, HRD professionals can design peer-coaching materials to reinforce on-the-job application and integration. Each of these is essential in producing learning that brings about skill development, increased knowledge, and changed attitudes (see Chapter 6).

Measuring Performance Improvement and Organizational Change

During the strategic HRD approach, performance measurement becomes a strategic weapon to determine whether performance improvement interventions or change initiatives improve organizational performance or positively impact organizational effectiveness. Interventions and initiatives that produce desired results are continued; ineffective efforts are terminated (see Chapter 17).

Structure.   The structure of a strategic HRD program is very different from the centralized approach commonly found during the vendor-driven and middle-of-the-road HRD approaches. Strategic HRD requires a much different effort. Gone are the days of delivering training as an activity, relying on employees' reactions to training in order to validate the value and importance of HRD to the organization. In their place is an HRD program with qualified professionals focused on improving organizational performance and effectiveness through learning, performance and change.

During this approach the walls of the HRD program begin to come down. HRD professionals realize that to be effective they must be integrated into the organization. As a result, centralized HRD practitioners are often assigned to operational units within the organization (Figure 2.1). HRD professionals are now held accountable for improving the results of operational units rather than generating organization-wide activity.

When strategic HRD programs are blended into the fabric of the organization, some believe there is no structural framework. They maintain that strategic HRD programs should be organized much like management consulting and professional service firms that are project based. During such projects, management consultants reside within an organization working alongside executives and managers, analyzing organizational and performance needs, providing recommendations, selecting and implementing change interventions, and evaluating the impact of change. This structure is most appropriate for strategic HRD programs.

Outcomes of Strategic HRD.   Robinson and Robinson (1996, 294) believe that strategic HRD programs are held accountable for the degree to which skills transfer to the workplace and individual or group performance improves. They are also accountable for the degree to which learning contributes to desired operational change, the quantity and quality of client relationships, and the number of performance contracts agreed to in a year. Furthermore, Gilley and Maycunich (1998a, 21) believe that by applying the principles, techniques, and strategies of the strategic HRD approach, its professionals should be able to achieve the following outcomes:

1. develop a philosophy of HRD that will help organizations achieve their business results;
2. adopt a strategic approach to improving organizational performance and development;
3. think responsively but responsibly about client requests;
4. develop an understanding of the organization and its business;
5. design, develop, and implement organizational transformation tools and techniques;
6. develop a systems approach to organizational change and development;
7. develop performance management systems;
8. develop strategic business partnerships;
9. link HRD interventions and initiatives to an organization's strategic business goals and objectives;
10. adopt a customer service approach with internal clients;
11. help managers develop their employees;
12. cultivate management development partnerships;
13. help managers link performance appraisals to performance improvement;
14. help managers develop performance coaching skills;
15. implement organizational development partnerships;
16. make the transition from trainer to organizational development consultant;
17. identify organizational and performance needs;
18. utilize organizational and performance needs as the foundation of all HRD interventions and initiatives;
19. design and develop performance improvement and change interventions;

20. create a learning acquisition strategy;
21. eliminate barriers to learning transfer;
22. implement learning transfer strategies;
23. measure the impact of HRD interventions;
24. improve the image and credibility of HRD within organizations;
25. develop a promotional strategy for an organization's HRD program.

Barriers to Strategic HRD. Beer (1997, 93) believes that one of the most formidable barriers to strategic HRD is the incapability of most HRD professionals. He contends that to play a strategic role, HRD professionals must possess analytic and interpersonal skills equal to the best external consultants used by organizations to assist with effectiveness and change issues. He argues that many HRD practitioners lack these professional skills.

To obtain individuals with these professional skills, Beer (1997) suggests transferring into HRD those executives or senior managers who have shown success in leading organizational change. This is because they already possess business knowledge and have demonstrated skills in managing organizational change. Another alternative is to train HRD professionals in the skills for organizational analysis, design, and change.

Gilley and Maycunich (1998a) identify several reasons why HRD professionals resist the transformation to strategic HRD. First, some are convinced that training is the answer to all performance problems. Therefore, they do not believe that other approaches to solving performance problems are appropriate. Second, some HRD practitioners do not have the courage to say "no" to management when a training solution is requested, because they find it hard to question management's authority and wisdom. Those individuals will have a difficult time embracing a concept as radical as strategic HRD. Third, some HRD practitioners feel overwhelmed by the complexities of solving performance problems or recommending organizational change initiatives. Consequently, they avoid making the transition to strategic HRD. Fourth, some HRD practitioners lack the skills required to apply the consulting process to identify the causes of poor performance, which is required in strategic HRD. Fifth, some simply cannot let go of their "safe and secure" training positions. They are afraid of venturing into the unknown regardless of the positive impact it can have on the organization. Sixth, some HRD practitioners have spent a lifetime building a "kingdom" within their firms, complete with a large budget, many employees, and perceived organizational respect. Changing to a strategic HRD approach requires practitioners (vendor-driven) to give up their kingdoms—a proposition many simply refuse to consider.

Beer (1997) cites an another major obstacle to the transformation of HRD, which is top management itself. Although senior management claims it wants a more strategic HRD function, they often do not understand what this entails.

Many executives still judge HRD by its effectiveness in delivering training programs. They are, therefore, unreceptive to radical ideas such as splitting off centralized HRD functions and placing them within other divisions within the organization.

Conclusion

It can be difficult to determine exactly which HRD approach an organization is using at any one period in time. Vendor-driven, middle-of-the-road HRD, and other first-order approaches are easier to document because of the tangible products they produce: training programs, on-the-job activities, and change applications. However, higher-order approaches (HET, HRC, learning organization HRD, and strategic HRD) are more difficult to assess because organizational learning, performance, and change are more integrated and less concrete.

However, most HRD professionals are making an effort to evolve from activity-oriented to results-driven HRD. There are many benefits to be derived from higher-order HRD approaches, both to individuals and to organizations.

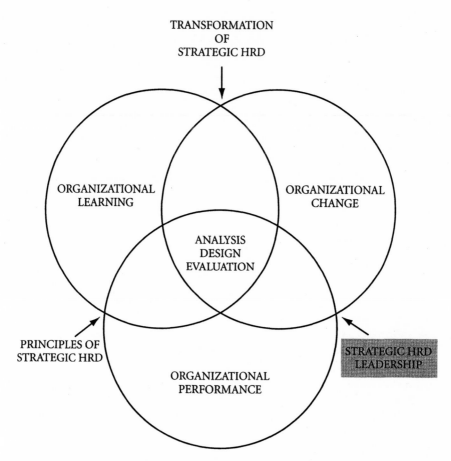

ORGANIZATIONAL LEARNING, PERFORMANCE, AND CHANGE

CHAPTER 3

Strategic HRD Leadership

Because change is a constant, organizations must continually renew themselves in order to survive. Rolls (1995, 102) believes this includes adapting, learning, and becoming change-responsive and maintains that "organizations that excel in the future will be those that understand how to gain the commitment of people at all levels and continually expand their capacity to learn." In short, organizations must transform to survive.

Today's organization must be market-driven and customer-focused because customers are demanding that product and service providers respond rapidly to their wants and needs. As a result, the relationship between providers and their customers has become critical. Employees must be more flexible, learning and adapting quickly to ever-changing conditions. In today's organization, employees are more accountable and maintain greater authority. Ulrich (1997a, 241–242) holds that these conditions further underscore the need for a transformed, developmental leader, whose organization understands employee needs and is customer-focused.

A new emphasis on partnering is required to allow leaders and followers to alternate roles, experience shared leadership, and function as teams. Interpersonal and group unity, cooperation, and organizational cohesiveness are valued. Additionally, managers are required to move from a "command and control" function to become counselors, mentors, coaches, and facilitators with the ability to establish new levels of honesty, sensitivity, trust, communication, and innovation (Gilley and Boughton 1996).

Gilley and Maycunich (2000) believe that the cornerstone of the successful organization is its ability to continuously renew itself. Rolls (1995, 103) contends that leaders of such organizations have the responsibility of creating an environment in which employees have the appropriate psychodynamics, support, and infrastructure that allows them to move from *change fragile* to *change agile*. In such an environment, the manager's principal responsibility is to encourage and facilitate learning and its application on the job.

The HRD Leaders of Tomorrow

According to Hesselbein, Goldsmith, and Beckhard (1995), today's leader is not the leader of the future. They contend that a number of shifts will occur requiring leaders (including those in HRD) to adjust their behavior and efforts. First, leadership will reside less at the top because it will be shared throughout an organization. Second, charismatic leaders will be less important than the process leaders create. Third, team leadership will replace individual leadership. Fourth, new leaders will be more likely to ask questions than to give answers. Fifth, new leaders will be less likely to look for and accept simple solutions and more likely to identify and live with paradoxes. Sixth, focus will shift from reliance on purely analytical tools in favor of integration of the analytical and the affective. Seventh, global thinking and demeanor will replace an exclusively domestic focus. Eighth, interest in questions and learning will replace focus on solutions and answers. Consequently, strategic HRD leaders must discover ways of incorporating these changes into their respective practices.

Highly aware of their employees, strategic HRD leaders are relationship oriented and create a work intimacy that unleashes the human capability. Moreover, strategic HRD leaders may come to be judged by the extent to which they develop future leaders (Ulrich 1997a). If this becomes reality, strategic HRD leaders will need to develop systems and techniques that create or develop such skills. Furthermore, strategic HRD leaders will need to demonstrate that such systems and techniques really work, requiring them to model "best practices" to improve their credibility and position within the organization. Ulrich (1997a, 242) suggests "designing and using competence models, tracking the quality of present leadership, finding creative methods for leadership development, and involving senior managers in serious leadership development."

Strategic HRD leaders must understand this organizational model and break dramatically from the old management paradigm. Rolls (1995, 107) asserts that strategic HRD leaders must become "facilitators, moral architects, coaches, stewards, relationship builders, trainers, and models of the values required of all stakeholders: trust, authenticity, courage, commitment, and partnership."

Today's leaders will benefit by adopting a *whole-self integration* leadership approach where there are no separate selves for work and personal lives (Rolls 1995, 107). Thus, strategic HRD leaders are asked to champion efforts to create a work environment where employees are nurtured, supported, accepted, and developed.

As a result, employees free up energy used to protect themselves, which they in turn use to enhance their learning and development.

Transformational Leadership

According to Rolls (1995, 108), "transformational leadership occurs when managers broaden and elevate the interests of their workers, when they generate awareness and acceptance of the purposes and mission of the group, and when they motivate their people to look beyond their own self-interests for the good of the whole group." Transformational leaders have an extraordinary effect on their employees because they create meaning for them. They provide essential conditions under which employees can develop, transform, grow, and flourish. Gibson, Ivancevich, and Donnelly (1997) note that transformational leaders model and teach the skills needed to build a learning organization.

Consequently, organizations need strategic HRD leaders who have been through their own personal transformation to facilitate the transformation of others. In other words, strategic HRD leaders need to adopt transformational leadership practices and principles to be effective in the twenty-first century. Rolls (1995, 105–106) maintains that organizations need strategic HRD leaders who "value people, growth, and learning, and who can help employees tap into inner reserves, reinvent themselves, become more attuned to interrelationships, connect to and value their own wisdom, and work with colleagues in cocreation. Without these leaders, it will be difficult to build a high performance organization."

Strategic HRD leaders manifest the characteristics of those who have mastered the "five disciplines" as identified by Senge (1990): personal mastery, mental models, shared vision, team learning, and systems thinking. They have deeply examined their core values and beliefs and have identified several leadership qualities that are most in demand: integrity, vulnerability, awareness of the human spirit, courage in relationships, curiosity, predictability, breadth, and comfort with ambiguity and presence (Schwandt 1995). Through self-reflection and change, transformational leaders establish a stronger platform from which to conduct their lives and their interactions with others.

Rolls (1995, 103) contends that strategic HRD leaders should delegate responsibility; they should invite employees to interpret the ideal future in terms of their roles and to determine how to close the gaps between current and future states. He continues by suggesting that strategic HRD leaders create conditions in which employees can experience "self-esteem, connection, dignity and security, where they can create and feel alive, be listened to and cared for, become, live their values, self-discover, risk in an environment of safety—where they can live with meaning and meaningfully contribute to the art and practice of the learning organization" (108).

Developmental Leadership

Although transformational leadership is a considerable improvement over autocratic and charismatic forms, Gilley and Maycunich (2000) believe that today's organization requires a new type of leader—one who realizes that organizational renewal and competitive readiness are totally dependent on employees prepared for future challenges, new work assignments, ever increasing competition, lifelong learning and change, and continuous growth and development. They add that each of these conditions requires innovative approaches to problem solving, creative solutions to complex issues, and new knowledge, skills, and competencies to meet competitive challenges. They refer to this type of a person as a developmental leader.

Developmental leaders constantly embrace change as a positive opportunity, spending a majority of their time creating conditions favorable to managing and implementing change. Maxwell (1998, 17) concludes that developmental leadership is about influence—nothing more, nothing less. He writes that "anyone can steer the ship, but it takes a leader to chart the course" (33). He contends that navigators can see the path ahead and make midcourse corrections to avoid dangerous water, relying on past experience as a source of information and wisdom. Navigators examine conditions before making commitments, solicit the advice of others, and have faith in others while dynamically balancing optimism and realism, intuition and planning. The navigator analogy demonstrates that developmental leadership is a twenty-four-hour, seven-day-a-week job where leaders are responsible for encouraging employees' continuous growth and development, daily nurturing and growth, trust, respect, intuition, sacrifice, shared power, mutual success, and accomplishment.

Principles of Developmental Leadership.   Gilley and Maycunich (2000) believe that strategic HRD leaders should apply ten principles of developmental leadership critical to the transformation to the developmental organization (see Chapter 7). The ten principles are clustered into four categories: (1) intrinsically oriented principles, (2) employee-oriented principles, (3) performance-oriented principles, and (4) organizationally oriented principles.

Intrinsically Oriented Principles

Intrinsically oriented principles surface when strategic HRD leaders work closely and harmoniously with managers and employees. These principles forge interpersonal relationships, demonstrate trustworthiness and respect, foster collaboration, and build teamwork. They are the principles of *personal accountability* and *trustworthiness*.

Employee-Oriented Principles

These principles demonstrate that employees are the organization's most important asset. These principles reaffirm that without employees and their contributions, organizations would not be able to achieve their strategic business goals and objectives. Thus, it makes sense that strategic HRD leaders serve as employee advocates and as conduits of employee self-esteem. These are the principles of *employee advocacy* and *self-esteeming.*

Performance-Oriented Principles

Developmental leaders rely on performance-oriented principles to help their organizations achieve desired business results and to improve employee performance and productivity through continuous growth and development. These principles provide a foundation for excellence by allowing strategic HRD leaders to communicate their expectations in a clear, motivating, and inspirational manner. They include the principles of *performance partnership, organizational performance improvement,* and *effective communications.*

Organizationally Oriented Principles

Organizationally oriented principles support the creation of work climates, environments, and organizational cultures that foster employee growth and development. They include the principles of *organizational consistency, holistic thinking,* and *organizational subordination.*

Servantship: The Key to Strategic HRD Leadership.   A developmental leader (strategic HRD leader) has the heart of a servant—willing to put the needs, expectations, interests, and success of their employees above his or her own. Gilley and Maycunich (2000, 63) believe that

> Developmental (servant) leaders advocate, support, and promote their employees, accept their overall and career development responsibilities by working tirelessly to help employees grow and develop, assist workers as they struggle to become the best they can be, share organizational success with subordinates and make certain that other decisionmakers in the organization are aware of employee contributions to achieving desired business results, accept responsibility for their employees' failures, and celebrate their successes. Above all, developmental (servant) leaders operate without regard for their own well-being or career advancement because they believe their employees are the organization's most important asset. Most importantly, developmental leaders are servants because it is the right thing to do.

When organizations ask their employees to produce business results and outcomes that require tremendous dedication and personal sacrifice, a servantship approach is critical. Boyett and Boyett (1995, 186) describe servant leaders as those who

- are servants first, driven by the need to learn and serve;
- lead by listening to their followers;
- help people articulate their own goals and those of the group by reaching consensus on a common will;
- inspire trust through their actions, beliefs, and value placed on followers; and
- take people and their work seriously, exhibiting commitment to employee growth and development.

A servantship approach implies a personal philosophy of humility and a willingness to work for the betterment of others but does not mean that leaders are weak or unable to make difficult decisions. Furthermore, servant leaders help their organization by advocating, assisting, growing, and developing its most important asset: its people. Simply stated, servantship means being a caretaker without regard for one's own personal needs or the rewards that are typically afforded leaders responsible for the professional lives of others—a tremendous responsibility, and one that should not be taken lightly.

Maxwell (1998, 215) believes that to embrace servantship, strategic HRD leaders must be willing to let their employees grow and develop above and beyond themselves, which is perhaps the most difficult aspect of becoming an effective developmental leader. He calls this the "law of legacy," whereby a leader's lasting value is measured by succession. He further asserts that "a legacy is created only when a leader puts his/her organization into position to do great things without him/her" (221).

Servant leaders delegate tasks and responsibilities to others because they are secure with themselves and realize that such opportunities for growth and development stimulate employees. Additionally, servant leaders become personally involved with employees' careers and professional lives. Over time, employees are more willing to honestly discuss important issues, without fear of negative repercussions or reprisals, and are willing to become vulnerable and exposed rather than guarded and controlled.

Decentralization of HRD

Robinson and Robinson (1996) write that there continues to be a debate over whether the HRD function should be centralized or decentralized. They believe that the human performance improvement process must be centralized, with strategic HRD leaders who complete the actual work dispersed both functionally and geographically. Strategic HRD leaders, who are responsible for the strategic side of the business, performance consulting, and organizational development consulting, are located at the site of their client groups. Thus, all requests to shape human performance in support of business goals flow through these consultants and analysts.

To move forward, however, strategic HRD leaders must have the courage to make some fundamental changes to help operational divisions improve their performance. They must be willing to decentralize their department and focus, allowing HRD to become strategically placed throughout the organization rather than centrally based. To accomplish this, several smaller operationally focused HRD units are established rather one large unit.

Decentralized performance improvement requires a much different HRD effort. Instead of delivering training as an activity, with reliance on employees' reactions to training in order to validate the value and importance of HRD to the organization, HRD programs must focus on improving organizational performance and effectiveness through learning, performance, and change initiatives and interventions.

Decentralized HRD programs rely on performance measurement to determine whether HRD initiatives and interventions improve employee performance and have a positive impact on organizational effectiveness. Interventions that produce desired results are continued; those that are ineffective are not. To help improve learning transfer and on-the-job performance, strategic HRD leaders build collaborative relationships with management. They utilize these relationships to share critical information about the organization, including changes in management, new product developments, modifications in the compensation and incentive system, and strategic decisions affecting the organization direction. This information exchange is essential for improving organizational performance and effectiveness. Robinson and Robinson (1996) and Gilley and Maycunich (1998a) agree, however, that tactical specialists, instructional designers, and compensation specialists should be organized into a shared services group, located in a centralized location.

Characteristics of Effective Strategic HRD Leaders

Nadler and Wiggs (1986) identified several characteristics of effective strategic HRD leaders. Each is viewed as essential to the development of a comprehensive and competent HRD program. First, strategic HRD leaders need to plan HRD activities that foster learning and development. These activities should be targeted at employees, managers, and organizational leaders for the purpose of improving organizational performance and effectiveness. Second, strategic HRD leaders need to establish goal priorities for the HRD activities over a one-to-five-year time span. This plan should be linked with the organization's overall strategic plan and initiatives. Third, they need to identify the most appropriate organizational structure and location for HRD, including decentralizing the HRD function within other operating units and divisions. Fourth, they need to effectively communicate their ideas and vision of the organization. Fifth, strategic HRD leaders should identify and develop effective HRD management information systems as a means of establishing good internal and external data sources (Gilley and Eggland 1989, 102). Sixth, strategic HRD leaders need to develop a mission-oriented position description for the professional HRD staff, which includes specific performance outputs, activities, and standards. Seventh, they must be role models of transformational, developmental, and servant-oriented leadership. Eighth, they need to develop technical competence and practical expertise. Ninth, strategic HRD leaders need to build confidence in their HRD staff by allowing them to become a part of the decisionmaking process and by providing opportunities for greater involvement and responsibility.

Knowledge of Strategic HRD Leaders

Burke (1997, 106) identified a brief list of "need-to-knows" for the human resource development practitioner of the next century. They are presented in an approximate order, moving from the more obvious to the less so. He starts with performance improvement, an obvious need-to-know, and concludes with power shifts, a more subtle and complex need-to-know that is not so obvious.

Burke (1997, 104) believes that there are at least three primary and overlapping benefits of these nine need-to-know categories. First, strategic HRD leaders can develop a broadened repertoire and therefore avoidance of overspecialization within the field. Second, executives need strategic HRD leaders who can tell them what to expect in the future and help plan and take action. By expanding their need-to-know areas, HRD leaders can develop an anticipatory approach to organizational issues. Third, this expanded competency helps strategic HRD leaders understand and diagnose organizational issues and problems more accurately and comprehensively.

Ulrich (1997b) identified three additional knowledge components required of strategic HRD leaders: knowledge of business, knowledge of HRD practice, and management of change processes. He contends that "knowing the business lets an HRD professional join the management team; knowing HRD practices helps the professional contribute; and managing change helps the strategic HRD leader make things happen" (251).

TABLE 3.1 The Nine "Need-to-Knows" That Strategic HRD Leaders Need to Know

Performance Improvement	Broadened measurement; determine key performance enhancers
Restructuring	What are the long-term consequences?
Organization Change	How to manage change; HR practitioner's role
Globalization	Understanding the impact cross-culturally and on small- and medium-size business
Groups and Team	Differentiation; self-directed groups/teams; large group interventions
Action Learning	"Third Wave" of training and development
Interpersonal, Intergroup, Interorganizational Relationships	Relationships at multiple levels
Timeshift	Blurring of work and personal time; "stress is prestigious"
Powershifts	More dispersion individually and organizationally, yet more toward the global corporation

Knowledge of Business

Strategic HRD leaders are able to adapt initiatives and interventions to changing business conditions when they understand how the business operates. Although it is critical for these professionals to be knowledgeable about their discipline, they must also be knowledgeable about financial, strategic, technological, and organizational capabilities of an organization in order to enter into any strategic discussion. Additionally, some strategic HRD leaders possess knowledge of human resources technology but are unable to apply it within their organizations (see Chapter 8). Ulrich (1997b) suggests that business acumen requires knowledge, and sometimes direct operational experience, in functional areas such as marketing, finance, strategy, technology, and sales, in addition to human resource development. With this understanding, strategic HRD leaders can add value to their organizations by linking performance and change initiatives to business applications.

Knowledge of HRD Practice

To enhance the credibility of and respect for strategic HRD, leaders must have the ability to deliver state-of-the-art, innovative, and effective HRD practice. HRD practices fall into several categories: analysis, intervention design, performance management, learning and development, organizational and job design, performance and organizational development consulting, and evaluation. Strategic HRD leaders who are perceived as being competent in these categories will be seen as credible designers and implementers of HRD systems. Competence in the delivery of HRD practice goes beyond knowledge; it requires that strategic HRD leaders deliver HRD practices to organization members.

Knowledge of Change Management

As the pace of change increases, organizations must change internally to be competitive. Over time, those organizations with a greater capacity for change and the ability to deal with resistance to change will be more competitive.

It is essential that strategic HRD leaders develop competencies to manage change because such knowledge is critical in helping other organization members manage change. Accordingly, this helps create an overall organizational capacity for change. When strategic HRD leaders have the capability to manage change processes, they are demonstrating the attributes of expert change agents. Therefore, they can build relationships with clients, diagnose problems, identify root causes to problems, conduct causal analyses, articulate visions, solve problems, and implement goals. Ulrich (1997b, 253) contends that the contributing competencies exhibited in change management are knowledge of change processes, skill as change agents, and ability to deliver change.

Skills of Strategic HRD Leaders

Simonsen (1997) identified several skills that strategic HRD leaders need to master in order to become transformational and developmental leaders. They include interpersonal/communication, leadership, business, and problem-solving skills.

Interpersonal/Communication Skills

Strategic HRD leaders need interpersonal skills to build and maintain relationships with individuals who may have backgrounds quite different from their own. They must be able establish rapport with employees, managers, and executives; develop a collaborative style by accepting and supporting others' ideas; and enhance conflict resolution skills so they can manage differences of opinion effectively to facilitate win-win solutions.

Much of the strategic HRD leader–employee relationship is based on clarity of understanding and straight communication. This involves active listening, which is the ability to provide full attention to the meaning and feelings behind another's words. He/she must communicate his/her perceptions in a way that maintains self-esteem and must speak clearly and effectively by articulating thoughts and ideas during oral communication.

Leadership Skills

Simonsen (1997) maintains that strategic HRD leaders are role models, and as such, they demonstrate the leadership that is desired as a result of development or opportunity to contribute. Leadership skills include providing direction by making appropriate recommendations for decisions or actions. This also includes motivating others by providing encouragement and reinforcement consistent with an employee's own motivators.

Strategic HRD leaders demonstrate leadership skills by championing change. This occurs through seeking out, initiating, supporting, and managing change or new organizational strategies. Additionally, leadership skills are demonstrated by valuing diversity, avoiding prejudging those who are different in some way, actively involving them in organizational activities, and capitalizing on their new insights and ideas.

Business Skills

Employees often expect strategic HRD leaders to help them learn about the organization, understand the culture, and gain organizational knowledge not easily acquired except through experience. Therefore, the business skills needed include extensive business knowledge (keeping up to date on work requirements and new developments and how they affect the organization) and organizational savvy (keeping up to date on organizational goals, trends, culture, and needs).

Problem-Solving Skills

Strategic HRD leaders are asked to help organizational members solve difficult and complex problems. When they successfully achieve this end, positive results occur. Appropriate problem-solving skills include diagnosing problems, identifying and analyzing alternatives, identifying root causes, conducting causal analysis, making sound decisions, and taking action. In addition to these characteristics, Shea (1994) identifies behaviors to avoid: giving advice, criticizing, and rescuing.

Abilities of Strategic HRD Leaders

Knicely (1997, 111–118) suggests critical abilities that successfully profile strategic HRD leaders. In general, these abilities tend to fall into categories such as leading and managing change, business skills, HRD technical skills, and leadership of the HRD function. He maintains that the best way for strategic HRD leaders to be successful in the future is to first focus on the three C's—credibility, competence, and courage (118).

- *Credibility* involves doing what we say we will do—in everything, maintaining a level of integrity beyond reproach and keeping confidences.
- *Competence* includes constantly upgrading business and HRD skills, broadening the professional tool kit to address changing organizational needs, being aware of shortcomings, and using good judgment to search out best practices and help from others.
- *Courage* is characterized by challenging the process of how things are done, pushing for continuous improvement, and demonstrating the willingness to take risks.

Knicely contends that strategic HRD leaders who successfully model the three C's will be not only tremendous assets to their organizations but also superhuman resource leaders in the twenty-first century.

Rothwell, Prescott, and Taylor (1998, 124–126) believe that to become an effective strategic HRD leader, one must have the ability to "envision what should be happening." This includes being able to predict customers' and employees' future needs and expectations; identify organizational strengths, weaknesses, opportunities, and threats; and forecast future competencies and workforce needs. They refer to this ability as "visionary" and have identified the following abilities:

- ability to identify customer needs and expectations;
- ability to detect threats and opportunities in the organizational environment;
- ability to locate world-class benchmarks of organizational performance;
- ability to modify the criteria of high-performance organizations to one corporate culture;
- ability to identify employee needs and expectations;
- ability to clarify ways to improve workflow to achieve breakthrough productivity increases;
- ability to forecast future competency needs;
- ability to assess future workforce needs.

Roles of Strategic HRD Leaders

The role of strategic HRD leader consists of eleven separate but overlapping components referred to as subroles. Each is vital to the development of an efficient and properly managed HRD department.

Strategic Business Partner

To increase strategic HRD leaders' credibility within the organization, they need to forge partnerships within the organization. Assuming the role of strategic partner allows leaders to improve customer-service-oriented relationships and break down walls between them and their clients. As a result, lasting commitments are created, and discoveries are made in everything pertaining to their clients' departments, activities, and goals. In this subrole, strategic HRD leaders become immersed in their clients' problems, needs, concerns, and expectations. Consequently, their organizational influence increases, which enhances their organizational impact.

Creating strategic business partnerships is one of the most important activities HRD leaders engage in, as it promotes mutually beneficial, empathic relationships between HRD professionals and their clients, resulting in client satisfaction and achievement of objectives. Strategic business partnerships are long-term oriented and interdependent, allowing HRD leaders to better understand and anticipate their clients' needs. These partnerships help HRD leaders and their function develop a responsive attitude, which is necessary for them to improve their customer-service orientation. Further HRD leaders develop trust and honesty with clients, allowing for the sharing of ideas, perspectives, and vision for the organization's future.

According to Gilley and Maycunich (1998b), HRD professionals engage in five interdependent activities to develop the strategic partner subrole, each of which enhances their credibility and acceptance within the organization while helping meet clients' business and performance needs. Thus, the organization benefits via achievement of its strategic business goals and objectives. First, they embrace a customer-service strategy committed to helping clients achieve their business goals and objectives. Second, strategic HRD leaders create a positive customer-service environment that enables them to quickly respond to client business and professional needs through development of interventions and services that improve performance and enhance organizational effectiveness. Third, they closely examine interventions and initiatives to determine their respective values and benefits, enabling them to make critical decisions about the interventions and services that most positively impact the organization. Fourth, they help clients make positive performance improvement and organizational development decisions to shape the firm's direction and ensure future viability. Fifth, strategic HRD leaders identify why clients participate in HR interventions and services, enabling human resource professionals to understand clients' motives and to adjust interventions and services accordingly.

Becoming a strategic partner positions HRD leaders to understand and deal with resistance within the organization. Block (1981, 113) believes that resistance is predictable, natural, and a normal part of the learning process. Thus, client resistance to change interventions or innovative ways of achieving business results is common. However, handling resistance involves comprehending its underlying reasons and addressing them accordingly.

Creating strategic business partnerships demonstrates HRD leaders' willingness to intimately know those they serve, as well as their ability to learn from clients. Furthermore, partnerships are based upon the business and performance needs of clients, not of the HRD program. Consequently, strategic HRD leaders "direct all efforts at satisfying their clients, including designing and developing performance improvement and change interventions in accordance with the clients' expressed interests, as well as providing consulting activities that improve the organization and performance management systems" (Gilley and Maycunich 1998a, 115).

Strategic business partnerships help HRD leaders establish credibility within the organization, which is achieved through strategic HRD leaders' ability to demonstrate professional expertise as well as understanding of organizational operations and culture. In this way, HRD provides real value to the organization.

Gilley and Maycunich (1998a, 118) contend that "better management of limited financial and human resources is another reason for creating strategic alliances. In other words, partnerships help strategic HRD leaders decide which interventions and consulting services provide the highest value and have the greatest impact on the organization." Such information helps strategic HRD leaders allocate resources that will maximize organizational performance and results.

In most circumstances, client resistance may be traced to their difficulties in dealing with unpleasant or difficult situations, which is exacerbated when decisions are forced upon clients without their input or approval. Gilley (1998, 145) identified ten reasons for resistance: (1) the purpose for change is not made clear, (2) employees affected by change are not involved in planning, (3) poor communications regarding change, (4) fear of failure, (5) cost is too high or rewards inadequate, (6) perceived loss of control, (7) anxiety over job security, (8) lack of respect or trust in the change agent, (9) past experience with change is negative, and (10) lack of management support for change.

Generally speaking, the root cause of resistance is fear (of loss of control, power, status, authority, or position). Fortunately, strategic partnerships enable synergistic relationships to be established. Such relationships foster trust and honesty, consequently diminishing, if not eliminating, client resistance to organizational change or innovation.

Finally, Gilley and Maycunich (1998a, 116) assert that "creating strategic business partnerships produces economic utility, which is measured in terms of increased organizational performance, profitability, revenue, quality, or efficiency." This strategic alliance allows HRD leaders and their clients the opportunity to work in harmony to improve the organization's economic viability.

Mohrman and Lawler (1997, 245–246) believe that HRD practices are an integral part of all organization systems and are essential to organization capability development. For an organization's human resources to contribute to performance, HRD practices must fit with each other and with the strategy and design of the organization. In order for members of the HRD function to impact performance, they must be knowledgeable about, have influence on, and be closely connected to other organization systems, as well as have a solid base of knowledge about HRD practices.

Rummler and Brache (1995) suggest that the HRD function must be able to operate at multiple levels of analysis: at the individual, work group, business process, organization, and cross-organizational levels. It cannot work exclusively at the level of the individual performer but instead must contribute to the development and performance management of teams, product lines, divisions, joint ventures, consortia, and wherever else performance is strategically important (Mohrman and Lawler 1997, 246). Additionally, the HRD function must operate with good understanding of industry trends and other competitive issues so that it can help the organization achieve its desired business results.

Mohrman, Lawler, and McMahan (1996) report that there is evidence that the evolution of the HRD function toward being a business partner is under way. In some organizations, HRD is an integral part of the management team, helping formulate strategy, improve organization performance, and develop organization capabilities that focus on speed and quality (Lawler 1995; Evans 1995).

Mohrman and Lawler (1997, 246–247) believe the expanded role of the HRD function requires a full partnership role in each of the following key business processes:

1. Developing Strategy: HRD should "contribute to business strategy based on its knowledge of the competencies and capabilities of the organization, and its understanding of the organization changes that will be required to support different strategic directions" (246).

2. Designing the Organization: HRD should be a "repository of organization design expertise, and its members should play the role of internal consultants to the ongoing designing and redesigning that will characterize organizations and their subunits as they continually modify themselves to achieve shifting strategies, new capabilities, and higher levels of performance" (246).

3. Change Implementation: HRD should help "the organization develop change management capabilities to weather the ongoing changes that will continue to be part of the environment, . . . with the ongoing learning processes required to assess the impact of change, and to enable the organization to make corrections and enhancements to the changes. . . . The organization must develop a new psychological contract, new career tracks, and ways to give employees a stake both in the changes that are occurring and in the performance of the organization" (247).

4. Integrating Performance Management Practices: The HRD function should work with "line managers to make sure that the performance management practices of the organization (goal-setting, performance appraisal, development practices, and rewards) are integrated with each other and with the business management practices of the organization and that they fit with the nature of the work" (247).

Finally, Mohrman and Lawler (1997) assert that today's organizational challenges demand a sophisticated business partner capable of thinking systematically and addressing business issues as well as their particular discipline's issues. They must be able to work cross-functionally within a number of leadership teams responsible for planning and managing the complex issues of rapid change.

Entrepreneur

Fuller and Farrington (1999, 185) suggest that establishing a performance improvement and change-management-oriented HRD program is rather like starting up a small business. Like the owner of a small business, HRD programs are offering a new service to the organization that it can either accept or reject. Therefore, strategic HRD leaders need to establish awareness among potential clients, identify and communicate the value of their service, and encourage clients to participate in initiatives and interventions that meet client needs (Meyer and Allen 1994).

According to Gerber (1995), most small businesses do not fail because of a lack of technical knowledge of the business they have chosen to enter. Rather, they fail because of a lack of entrepreneurial expertise. Consequently, strategic HRD leaders must develop entrepreneurial skills to successfully transform their training departments into strategic HRD functions (Fuller and Farrington 1999).

Evaluator

Strategic HRD leaders are the principal evaluators of the impact of HRD initiatives and interventions on overall organizational efficiency (Preskill and Torres 1999). Within this subrole, the leader is responsible for designing, developing, and implementing an evaluation strategy as well as measuring the impact evaluation efforts are having on the organization. Each evaluation activity is used to measure the effects of learning, performance, and change on the employees and the organization. Evaluating the effectiveness of performance consultants and analysts, organizational development change agents, instructional designers, performance technologists, and strategic HRD leaders is another important part of this subrole. In summary, strategic HRD leaders are accountable for the evaluation of all aspects of the HRD function, its results, effectiveness, impacts, and practitioners (Brinkerhoff 1998).

Project Manager

Every performance improvement intervention and organizational development and change initiative is a project that must be managed, implemented, and evaluated (Fuller 1997). Hence, HRD leaders are project managers and must become competent at managing projects in order to evolve to the strategic HRD level. Unfortunately, many fail to recognize this responsibility. Some even lack a practical approach and techniques for planning and managing projects.

Strategic HRD leaders should begin with a clear project definition. Fuller and Farrington (1999) suggest that the definition indicate what the project will and will not do, what the desired outcomes are, and how the organization will know when the project is successful.

Once the project definition is complete, Brinkerhoff (1998) believes HRD leaders can create the project plan, which identifies the major tasks that are necessary to accomplish the goals of an HRD intervention or initiative. It should also include a project schedule and assignments. The project plan helps to scope the project and establish the priorities. Additionally, the plan assigns resources to ensure that implementation is moving forward as rapidly as possible.

To remain viable, the plan must be managed appropriately to ensure that tasks are on schedule. Project members responsible for milestones should be held accountable for accomplishing their tasks on time, as defined in the plan. Otherwise the project is at risk in terms of quality, timeliness, and cost.

Learning Champion

A major focus of HRD is improving performance and productivity through increased knowledge, competencies, skills, and attitudes. In other words, one of the major thrusts of HRD is learning and how it affects employees and the organization. The leader of HRD is the person responsible for championing learning within the organization and developing interventions and transfer strategies used in the application of learning on the job.

A strategic HRD leader should possess knowledge of intervention design and how to evaluate learners, interventions, outcomes, instructors/facilitators (managers), and impacts. Strategic HRD leaders should also be able to supervise the facilitation of a learning intervention and provide suggestions for improvement. Additionally, they need to know how to assess the impacts that HRD is having on the organization and be able to effectively communicate such results to organizational decisionmakers.

Knowledge of adult learning theory and on-the-job, off-the-job, and through-the-job teaming activities is also needed. Finally, a strategic HRD leader must understand the importance of career development, performance management, and organizational development, and how they contribute to learning, performance improvement, and change.

Operational Manager

The operational manager subrole is often viewed as the primary role of a strategic HRD leader. It is the managerial component of the leadership role and consists of the basic elements of management: planning, organizing, influencing, and controlling. Related areas include strategic planning, staff recruitment, selection, hiring, evaluation, supervision and development, budgeting, establishing policies, procedures and standards, financial management, equipment and facilities management, material development, and scheduling.

Marketer

To develop a positive image, strategic HRD leaders must become a part of the organizational management team by participating in strategic initiatives, establishing linkage between HRD and the organization's business results, conducting strategic planning activities, and facilitating organizational and performance analysis efforts. All of these are done to demonstrate the capabilities of HRD, as well as to enhance the image of HRD within the organization. Strategic HRD leaders must also build and develop networks that communicate the importance of HRD and support its continued development. These activities are all a part of the marketer subrole.

Influencer

The influencer subrole requires strategic HRD leaders to be very directive in their attempts to influence client thinking, initiate change, and provide specific recommendations that address difficult organizational problems. To avoid conflict, HRD leaders should guard against their own personal biases and overpowering opinions, remaining receptive to others' views, ideas, and recommendations while encouraging organizational members to take risks to achieve their goals and objectives.

Strategist

As strategists, strategic HRD leaders are responsible for assessing organizational needs using quantifiable and qualifiable methodologies. They are also responsible for developing and executing business initiatives and evaluating the effectiveness of learning interventions, performance improvement efforts, and change initiatives. They help executives and senior management develop a vision for the organization and communicate this to employees at all levels. Strategists incorporate the ideas of others into directive action and strategic plans.

Problem Solver

Strategic HRD leaders as problem solvers take an active role in the decision-making and change management process. They spend a majority of their time helping clients make decisions that are beneficial to achieving desired results. Problem solvers strive to guarantee that the perceived problem is indeed the one critical to the organization by identifying the root cause and demonstrating a causal relationship before offering or implementing solutions.

Change Agent

The strategic HRD leader must develop long-range plans included in the broad human resource strategy of the client system, which includes the development of an organization-wide HRD program that is a part of the everyday operations of the firm. It is not enough to be a separate operational department of the organization; strategic HRD must be integrated into its fabric as well.

As a change agent, a strategic HRD leader must identify the HRD function's strengths and weaknesses and develop plans for its continuous development. Change agents also identify external threats, as well as opportunities, that confront the HRD function and must identify forces or trends impacting HRD. Change agents develop guidelines for implementing long-range plans and determine alternative directions for HRD. Finally, they must be able to identify and implement analyses that measure the impact of HRD on the organization (see Chapter 13).

Regardless of the subrole strategic HRD leaders embrace, they must function first as a member of the management team and second as an advocate of performance and productivity improvement and organizational development through learning, performance, and change. Strategic HRD leaders must be able to demonstrate that the HRD function is a worthwhile part of the organization. Its importance should be equal to other organizational departments and viewed as such.

Responsibilities of Strategic HRD Leaders

Strategic HRD leaders need to adopt several responsibilities to achieve the mission and purpose of HRD. We have identified twelve of the most important ones here.

Creating Cultural Change

One of the fundamental responsibilities of strategic HRD leaders is to create cultural change. Ulrich (1997a, 243–245) believes that to accomplish culture change, strategic HRD leaders must learn to engage the organization in a series of actions and help the firm commit to cultural change. In addition, they help organizations define the current and desired culture as well as expose culture gaps. Strategic HRD leaders must prepare and implement culture action plans and coordinate culture change efforts. Finally, they must measure results. Although these may not be necessary steps for every culture change, they represent some of the basic lessons that need to be applied by the strategic HRD leader of the future.

Executing Project Leadership

Strategic HRD leaders must adopt a leadership style that both motivates and empowers project team members (learning and performance improvement interventions design teams, change initiatives projects teams, strategic initiatives project teams) and that monitors and guides their progress in order to manage a project effectively. According to Weiss and Wysocki (1992), project managers must treat team members with respect and listen to their opinions and ideas until managers fully understand their team members' respective points of view.

When conflict arises, strategic HRD leaders' views, needs, and feelings must be expressed assertively, not submissively or aggressively. They believe that communicating assertively exhibits self-respect and demonstrates understanding and acceptance of their project team members. Assertive project managers stand up for their own rights, yet express their personal needs, values, concerns, and ideas in a direct and appropriate way. True assertiveness is a way of behaving that affirms the project leader's own individual worth and dignity, while simultaneously confirming and maintaining the worth and dignity of project team members.

To improve project outcomes, HRD leaders should make certain that their assertions, opinions, and requests are clear and understandable. Raudsepp (1987) identified twelve guidelines for effective project management leadership:

1. Do not over-direct, over-observe, or over-report.
2. Recognize differences in individuals. Hold a keen appreciation for each person's unique characteristics.
3. Help subordinates see problems as change opportunities.
4. Encourage employees to think more creatively and consider the types of creative contributions they would most like to make during the project.
5. Encourage self-directed work teams and behaviors during the project.

6. Respond positively to ideas rather than negatively.
7. Accept mistakes and errors as learning opportunities.
8. Create positive work environments where failure is not punished but viewed as a way of improving future performance.
9. Be a resource person rather than a controller—a helper rather than a boss.
10. Insulate employees from outside problems or internal organizational politics.
11. Participate in professional development activities that enhance creative abilities.
12. Make certain that innovative ideas are forwarded to superiors within the organization with your full support and backing.

Establishing a Strategic Focus

Strategic HRD leaders have the responsibility of shifting the focus from training needs to performance improvement and change. As a result, leaders need to help their HRD colleagues understand their roles and responsibilities in performance improvement and change. To achieve this end, Fuller and Farrington (1999, 186) identified questions that HRD professionals should ask prior to implementing any performance improvement or change initiative:

- What business needs are we attempting to achieve, and how will they be measured?
- What process was used to analyze the problem and derive the solution(s)?
- What data exist to support the solutions that were selected?
- How do we know that these interventions will solve the performance problem?

Next, strategic HRD leaders encourage managers and executives to examine the role and impact of performance improvement and change within the organization. HRD leaders should be asking the following strategic questions regarding human capital within the firm:

- What are you doing to improve the performance/worth of our human capital?
- What measurable impact have you had on the business?
- What is the return on investment of your performance improvement efforts?
- How are your efforts driven by business strategy? (Fuller and Farrington 1999)

Advocating the Benefits of HRD

According to Gilley and Eggland (1992, 209), some HRD professionals are "afflicted with what they have termed 'brochure lust,' where they believe that promotion begins and ends with the development of a brochure to describe a program. Nothing could be further from the truth." Gilley and Eggland believe that advocating HRD within the organization should begin with determining the objective associated with promoting a given intervention or initiative and followed eventually with a decision regarding how these efforts are to be advocated throughout the organization.

The primary purposes of promotion are to *inform, persuade,* or *remind* clients of the advantages, benefits, and values of performance improvement interventions and change initiatives. This should be foremost in the minds of strategic HRD leaders as they develop promotional strategies to advocate the values of their programs. Promotion can be used to improve the credibility of the HRD function, its leaders, and practitioners. It can also encourage greater participation in performance improvement interventions or rally support for a change initiative.

Facilitating Knowledge Transfer

According to Ulrich (1997a), creating systems that transfer knowledge throughout an organization will surely become a critical responsibility of strategic HRD leaders. He contends that

> knowledge transfer will help firms reduce cycle time by allowing shared insights to move easily among locations, increasing innovation by building on experience, and making better decisions derived from information from multiple sources. . . . Knowledge transfer . . . confers the ability to learn faster than competitors do, to respond more quickly to market conditions, to learn more quickly from failures and successes, and to build intellectual and human capital (242).

Creating the infrastructure for knowledge transfer requires that strategic HRD leaders work with information-systems professionals to create computer networks that share information. Basic questions that must be answered to achieve effective systems include the following:

- What do we need to know that we don't know?
- How do we find out?
- How do we share that knowledge with others? (Ulrich 1997a, 243)

Ulrich (1997a) believes that effective knowledge transfer processes have implications for who is hired, how development is done, how incentives are created, how communications are established, and how organizations are organized. He reports that strategic HRD leaders in some firms are even now being called and considered chief learning officers, an indication of the growing importance of knowledge transfer.

Implementing Strategic Visioning

Developing a strategic vision for the organization requires HRD leaders to direct their attention to the organization's future. Leaders must have the ability to anticipate business trends and processes and to break them down into manageable units for others to understand and implement. By dismantling business trends and processes into manageable components, strategic HRD leaders generate a variety of solutions that narrow the gap between what is needed and what is delivered, making the necessary adjustments to ensure organizational success.

Strategic HRD leaders have clear visions for their organizations in both human and financial terms, which allows employees to focus on a common set of goals and outcomes that give their daily activities serious meaning and determine an organization's success or failure. Moreover, strategic HRD leaders clearly know what they want to achieve and how employees can better serve their internal and external stakeholders.

Strategic HRD leaders are successful in communicating their organization's purpose and creating an environment built on employee support and involvement. Because strategic HRD leaders use an inclusive approach when designing and developing organizational vision, employees participate in the creation of this vision, share their opinions and ideas, and accept responsibility for activities that help the organization realize its goals. Strategic HRD leaders generate the support necessary for the collaborative vision to resonate throughout the firm, thereby creating an environment of employee and organizational success.

Developing an Understanding of Other Business Functions

Since the purpose of strategic HRD is to help the organization obtain business results, it is the HRD leader's responsibility to nurture and build relationships between various departments, divisions, and unit managers, as well as senior managers and executives within the firm (Fuller and Farrington 1999). Achieving this goal requires developing an understanding of other business functions.

Fuller and Farrington (1999, 191) suggest that several activities enhance strategic HRD leadership knowledge of the organization and business. First, describe the business of the organization. Second, identify the three top-selling products or services and the three most profitable products or services. Third, identify the three newest products or services. Fourth, determine the financial condition of the organization and compare it with last year's results. Fifth, identify the organization's top three competitors. Sixth, read the annual reports for the last three years and identify major messages and trends.

Strategic HRD leaders should examine their answers to determine how well they know their organization. Additionally, Fuller and Farrington (1999) suggest that if HRD leaders cannot answer most of these questions, they should create a development plan that gets them up to speed on the business. They suggest that strategic HRD leaders must first learn the language of the organization. This can be accomplished by reading the organization's annual report; attending some trade shows associated with the organization's business or products; scheduling short informational interviews with leading business managers to get their take on where the company is headed; visiting the marketing department and obtaining copies of product brochures and sales collateral; and reading the organization's press releases.

Next, strategic HRD leaders develop a working knowledge of the departments, divisions, and units within the organization. Each group has its own mission, processes, and perspectives. Therefore, HRD leaders must develop an understanding of these elements as well as discover their performance issues, major initiatives, and performance problems. In other words, strategic HRD must forge links with all the different parts of the organization. By doing so, they should understand the services that HRD can provide and what HRD might need to ask them to do in the future (Fuller and Farrington 1999).

Achieving Business Results

Strategic HRD leaders are responsible for achieving business results through people. Some believe that failing to achieve desired business results means that leaders have failed to lead (Le Boeuf 1985). Although we believe that strategic HRD leadership consists of other important characteristics, achieving desired results is a pinnacle of effective leadership and should be considered one of the critical measures of leadership aptitude and ability. To this end, Gilley and Maycunich (2000) believe that strategic HRD leaders should help their organization create work climates and environments where employees are challenged to perform at maximum levels and encouraged to demonstrate creative solutions to complex problems. They should be engaged in quality initiatives, asked to participate in continuous organizational improvement activities, and required to participate in growth and development interventions.

Achieving these high standards requires strategic HRD leaders to "understand how organizations operate, the needs and expectations of shareholders, and how to construct well-designed, long-term solutions to difficult problems" (Gilley, Boughton, and Maycunich 1999, 166–167). In other words, HRD leaders must possess business acumen, which provides them with a keen awareness and a potent operational understanding of the business. This knowledge can be used to improve the organization's performance as well as its strength and viability.

Executing Image Management

Many HRD programs are viewed as outside the organizational mainstream and are not considered an integral part of the organization. In situations such as these, HRD programs are sometimes viewed by management and employees as mere "overhead." To complicate matters, some HRD practitioners fail to demonstrate their understanding of the organization's purpose and culture. As a result, these biases produce low credibility, which ultimately results in a negative image of HRD. Strategic HRD leaders should, therefore, be interested in image management as a way of improving the credibility of HRD within the organization.

Image-oriented HRD leaders have a heightened interest in how their clients perceive them and their services. These leaders display their professional expertise as a way of demonstrating their skills and abilities. They also communicate the value-added service that they can provide the organization. Finally, leaders demonstrate their understanding of organizational operations and culture. Each of these efforts allows leaders and their programs to gain and maintain credibility.

To improve the image of an HRD program, strategic HRD leaders must first define the term image. Gilley and Eggland (1992, 12) state that "image can be defined as the sum of beliefs, attitudes, impressions, and feelings that a person has toward an object or thing." Next, they must determine the intensity of feeling that their clients have for their services. Measuring clients' awareness and favorability of HRD efforts can achieve this (Barich and Kotler 1991). Awareness refers to how conscious clients are of the interventions and initiatives provided by HRD, whereas favorability refers to the intensity of good feeling clients have toward HRD and its interventions and initiatives. To obtain an accurate image of an HRD program and its leaders and practitioners, these two elements must be used in combination. According to Gilley and Eggland (1992, 13–15), the following combinations are possible:

- High Awareness and High Favorability = Integrative HRD (Strategic HRD)
- High Awareness and Low Favorability = Activity-driven HRD (Vendor-driven HRD)
- Low Awareness and High Favorability = Selective HRD (Performance Technology)
- Low Awareness and Low Favorability = Bankrupt HRD

Strategic HRD leaders know that simply running a public relations program cannot create positive image for HRD. Rather, its image is a function of the competence of its professionals and the value-added services they provide the organization. In other words, a positive image results when HRD professionals create real satisfaction for their clients, which they communicate to other decision-makers (Gilley and Eggland 1992).

Building Consensus and Commitment for Change

To develop consensus and commitment, strategic HRD leaders build a working relationship with each client and client group. Trust can be developed during interviews used in gathering information as well as during the implementation phase. Turner (1983) suggests that an effective relationship begins with a collaborative search for acceptable answers to the client's real needs and concerns; this relationship then becomes mutually beneficial.

Strategic HRD leaders monitor client readiness and commitment to change by considering the following questions:

1. How willing are members of the organization to implement change?
2. Is upper-level management willing to learn and utilize new management methods and practices?
3. What type of information do members of the organization readily accept or resist?
4. What are their attitudes toward change?
5. What are the executives' attitudes toward change?
6. To what extent will individual members of the organization regard their contribution to overall organizational effectiveness as a legitimate and desirable objective?

Gilley and Eggland (1989, 190) suggest that "another way to gauge readiness for change is to evaluate the enthusiasm for a particular recommendation, which provides an instantaneous measure of resistance or resentment." Thus, a strategic HRD leader is able to withdraw or encourage a recommendation prior to its complete implementation.

Planning and Managing Change

Burke (1992, 140) refers to the planning and management of change as the intervention phase of an organizational development project. According to Argyris (1970), an effective intervention provides valid information for the client organization, allows for *choice* by the client regarding specific steps to be taken, and leads to commitment on the client's part to those action steps for change.

Burke (1992, 147–157) believes that two things must happen when planning change. First, the need for change must be determined. Second, the power and political dynamics of the organization must be addressed. He contends that managing the change effort is essentially transition management and concerns disengaging from the past, communicating with people about change, and involving people in implementation planning. Moreover, he contends that managing the change effort requires organizing a transition management team, using multiple leverages, and providing feedback. Finally, Burke believes that creating symbols and language to help focus the effort and stabilizing change are essential.

Evaluating the Impact of HRD

The outcomes of performance improvement interventions and change initiatives are ultimately assessed through evaluation. The most common forms of performance evaluation are formative and summative. *Formative evaluation* provides feedback for process improvement and facilitates choosing among possible modifications. Therefore, it should be used as the basis for constructively modifying HRD efforts in the future, not simply as a basis for keeping them alive or, alternatively, completing the process. On the other hand, *summative evaluation* assesses overall outcomes of the performance improvement process and leads to a decision to continue or terminate the process.

Regardless of the type of evaluation selected, strategic HRD leaders are responsible for conducting evaluations that determine the impact of their program's interventions and initiatives. Such efforts are known as impact evaluations and are discussed in greater detail in Chapter 17.

Conclusion

At the center of strategic HRD are its leaders, who provide direction, inspiration, and insight for the function. To be effective, HRD leaders need to adopt the skills and principles of transformational and developmental leaders as well as the philosophy of servant leadership. HRD leaders need to develop specialized knowledge, skills, and abilities appropriate to enhance the effectiveness of HRD within their organization. Finally, HRD professionals need to execute several roles and adopt a number of responsibilities to become effective strategic HRD leaders.

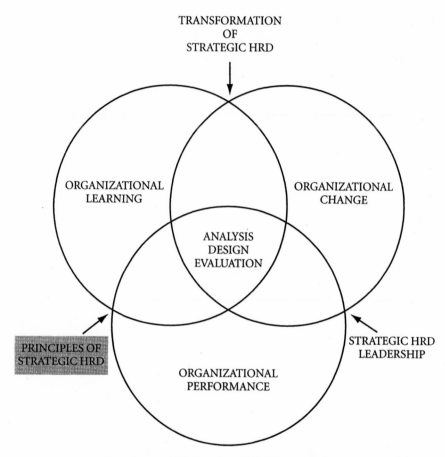

TRANSFORMATION
OF
STRATEGIC HRD

ORGANIZATIONAL
LEARNING

ORGANIZATIONAL
CHANGE

ANALYSIS
DESIGN
EVALUATION

PRINCIPLES OF
STRATEGIC HRD

STRATEGIC HRD
LEADERSHIP

ORGANIZATIONAL
PERFORMANCE

ORGANIZATIONAL LEARNING, PERFORMANCE, AND CHANGE

CHAPTER 4

Principles of Strategic HRD Practice

Several important principles guide the field of HRD in achieving critical outcomes. These principles serve as a road map for professional practice and provide HRD professionals a clear path to establishing credibility within their organizations. We have identified fourteen such principles and recognize that others may exist or will emerge as the field of HRD continues to evolve.

Principle 1: Effective HRD Practice Integrates Eclectic Theoretical Disciplines

Swanson (1999) believes that performance improvement is based on economic, psychological, and systems theories. He refers to these theories as a three-legged stool whose legs provide stability for the field of performance improvement. He (1999, 11) reports that "economic theory is recognized as a primary to survive along with its financial metrics at the organizational level; systems theory recognizes purpose, pieces, and relationships that can enhance or strangle systems and sub-systems; and psychological theory acknowledges human beings as brokers of productivity along with their cultural and behavioral nuances."

Performance improvement represents a major professional practice area of the field of HRD; hence, it stands to reason that these three theories support HRD as well. Additionally, the professional practice area of organizational learning and change requires three other theories to be added to the comprehensive foundation for HRD. They are learning, change, and organizational theory.

Economic Theory

Swanson (1999, 11) believes that unless performance improvement is founded on economic theory, "*organization development* is reduced to individual development, team development, or the pursuit of change in the hopes of achieving improved organizational performance." He questions how a responsible performance improvement function could not include direct analysis, action, and measurement of economic outcomes. In short, learning and performance improvement interventions and change initiatives contribute to the viability and profitability of an organization HRD.

Swanson identified three economic theory perspectives that are most appropriate for performance improvement: *scarce resource theory, sustainable resource theory,* and *human capital theory.*

- *Scarce resource theory* contends that there are limitations to everything (money, raw materials, time, and human resources).
- *Sustainable resource theory* is much like scarce resource theory, except that it is focused on the long term instead of the short term.
- *Human capital theory* suggests that investment in human resources is essential to organizational success.

Systems Theory

An organization's internal and external behavior can be better understood through systems theory. Internally, HRD professionals observe how and why employees inside organizations perform their individual and group tasks. Externally, they can assess organizations' transactions with other organizations and institutions.

According to systems theory, organizations are totally dependent on the larger environment in which they operate (Rothwell 1996b). All organizations acquire resources from the larger environment of which they are part and, in turn, provide the goods and services demanded by the larger environment. This essentially complex process can be simplified by employing the basic concepts of systems theory.

Basic systems theory contends that an organization is one element of a number of elements interacting interdependently. The flow of inputs and outputs is the basic starting point in describing how an organization functions. In simplest terms, the "organization takes resources (inputs) from the larger system (environment), processes these resources, and returns them in changed form (output)" (Gibson, Ivancevich, and Donnelly 1997, 19).

Katz and Kahn (1978) point out that systems theory stresses the organization's connection to the larger system of which it is a part. Every organization is part of larger systems. For example, all organizations are part of an industry, a society, and a global economy. Each of these systems places demands on the others. Demands for acceptable quality and quantity of products and services are most common; however, organizations must also satisfy demands for sustainable environments by promoting appropriate policies and actions or for global political stability by investing resources accordingly. Consequently, an organization cannot simply produce a product or service to satisfy its customers but must produce actions and behaviors to satisfy other important elements of the larger systems.

Systems theory can also describe the behavior of individuals and groups. For example, a manager asks an employee to perform a certain task (input), the employee mentally and psychologically processes the request (input), accordingly performs an appropriate group of tasks (process) and at the completion of these tasks generates a product (output). Although this is a simple linear example, it demonstrates the impact of systems theory of employee behavior. Under more realistic conditions, the work environment, motivational factors, employees' knowledge and skills, managerial feedback, communication between manager and employee, performance standards, and job interference could impact the process and negatively affect output.

Psychological Theory

Psychological theory focuses on how people make decisions and behave in organizations. Again, Swanson (1999, 15) questions how a responsible performance improvement function could not integrate and use the vast body of knowledge from psychological theory. He suggests that three psychological theory perspectives are appropriate to performance improvement: *gestalt psychology, behavioral psychology,* and *cognitive psychology.*

- *Gestalt psychology* is based on the belief that people do not see isolated stimuli but rather stimuli gathered together in meaningful configurations.
- *Behavioral psychology* is concerned with what can be seen, and therefore *actual* human behavior is studied.
- *Cognitive psychology* is used to explain goal-directed behavior and the idea that human beings organize their lives around purposes.

Learning Theory

Learning is a prerequisite to change; therefore, it is an essential pillar in the foundation of HRD. Gilley and Eggland (1989, 120–121) believe that within organizations, learning can be defined as "knowledge obtained by study and/or experience; the art of acquiring knowledge, skills, competencies, attitudes, and ideals that are retained and used, and a change of behavior through experience." This definition reminds us that learning includes change. Unfortunately, researchers and scholars do not agree on how learning occurs—or how change takes place. According to Gilley and Eggland (1989, 121), several theories of learning, each with a different view of or orientation to the *nature of the human being,* are applicable to HRD.

Behaviorist theory equates the human being with the machine; that is, an input is introduced (stimulus), which is controlled (how the input is processed is known as operant conditioning), and a predetermined output (response) results. Accordingly, the purpose of learning is to produce prescribed behaviors.

Cognitive theory focuses on the brain, in that the one thing that separates human beings from other living things is their capacity to think critically and solve problems. This theory maintains that the purpose of learning is for the brain to engage in critical thinking and problem solving.

Gestalt theory contends that individuals tend to always move in one direction: always toward a good gestalt, an organization of the whole that is regular, simple, and stable (This and Lippitt 1983). When tensions develop in a learning situation, disequilibrium results. As a result, the individual strives to move back to equilibrium. Under these conditions, HRD professionals should structure learning environments that reduce stress in order to return to a stable state.

Humanistic theory maintains that all people are unique and possess individual potential. Moreover, this theory holds that all people have the natural capacity to learn. This theoretical perspective calls for HRD professionals to encourage each individual to develop his or her full, unique potential. Another learning theory, which is based on the humanistic orientation, is known as andragogy. Andragogy, derived from the Greek word *anere* for "adult" and *agogus* meaning "leader of," refers to the art and science of helping adults learn (Knowles 1975).

Gilley and Eggland (1989, 121–122) point out that each of these theories offers its own approach to learning.

- Behaviorist theory prescribes programmatic instruction and behavior modification, computer-assisted instruction, and repetition.
- Cognitive theory fosters didactic instruction, rote memorization, and standardized testing of correct solutions to identified problems.
- Gestalt theory prescribes organized and systematic instruction beginning with a simple concept and moving toward the more complicated.
- Humanistic approach advocates the discovery model, underlining learning projects and self-directed inquiry and learning.

Argyris and Schon (1996) believe that the concepts of double-loop and single-loop learning incorporate both assimilation and accommodation as they relate to evaluating, learning, and adapting when executing a task or program. Mink, Esterhuysen, Mink, and Owen (1993, 208) believe that "single-loop learning occurs when people make errors and then correct them by examining and altering their actions or strategies by mere trial and error." Such learning is routine, repetitive, and often efficient. However, they contend that "double-loop learning occurs when people reexamine their strategies and the underlying or governing values that influence those strategies" (208). Ones guiding values, goals, and variables help them frame problems as the difference between the current and future states, which is often perceived as a gap between where they are now and where they want to be. As a result, people are motivated to close the gap through action.

Double-loop learning is learning how to learn methodology, which is sometimes referred to as meta-learning (Mink, Esterhuysen, Mink, and Owen 1993). It focuses on the way learning and perceiving are influenced by an individual's personal context, values, goals, and experiences. Furthermore, double-loop learning explores the impact of context on defining or framing problems accurately.

Organizational Theory

Another important foundational element of HRD is organizational theory, because all HRD efforts occur either for or within organizations. Therefore, it is logical to examine organizations and their operations in order to maximize the effectiveness of HRD.

According to Gibson, Ivancevich, and Donnelly (1997, 4), an "organization is a coordinated unit consisting of at least two people who function to achieve a common goal or set of goals." Organizations, obviously, consist of people, structures, and processes. Therefore, organizational theory is the study of various configurations of people, structures, and processes and how these variations impact the achievement of goals and the delivery of results.

The study of human behavior, attitudes, and performance within organizational settings is commonly known as organizational behavior. To understand organizational behavior, HRD professionals need to apply theories, methods, and principles from such disciplines as psychology, sociology, and cultural anthropology, which is necessary to learn about individual perceptions, values, learning capacities, and actions. An understanding of group behavior is also needed. Finally, HRD professionals must be able to analyze the external environment's effect on the organization and its human resources, missions, objectives, and strategies.

HRD professionals need to develop an understanding of organizational structure and processes to impact their effectiveness. Gibson, Ivancevich, and Donnelly (1997, 6) define *organization structure* as the "formal pattern of how its people and jobs are grouped" and *processes* as "the activities that give life to the organization chart." These include communication, decisionmaking, and organization development. They also believe that the culture of an organization defines appropriate behavior and actions, motivates individuals, and governs the way it processes information, internal relations, and values.

Change Theory

An understanding of change theory is critical to the success of HRD and its professionals. Lewin (1951) provided a classic description of change that serves as a prism by which change theory is reflected. He believed that change consists of three phases: unfreezing, movement, and refreezing.

The first step in the change process is *unfreezing* the present level of behavior. Unfreezing occurs when organizations create environments that are conducive for employees to examine their own work performance. During this period, employees look at the attitudes, beliefs, and values that combine to produce their behaviors. If behavior is to change, the attitudes, beliefs, and values of employees must also change. Lewin (1951) believed that if employees were encouraged to examine their present performance, determine strengths and weaknesses, and take part in learning, they would be willing to incorporate new behaviors.

HRD professionals and managers work with employees during this unfreezing phase to guarantee a slow and deliberate approach to changing behavior. A radical approach will often be perceived by employees as a threat and will severely hamper the acquisition of new behaviors.

According to Lewin (1951), every individual is in a constant search for equilibrium. "Equilibrium is a steady state, balanced between the opposing forces that drive behavior toward change and those that restrain it" (Gilley and Coffern 1994, 74). Change is often resisted because it disrupts an individual's equilibrium. Therefore, HRD professionals and managers must introduce change in ways that reduce resistance. They can reduce barriers to change by introducing change in a context employees understand. First, individual barriers to change are often difficult, if not impossible, to identify. Therefore, it's important that HRD professionals talk to participants of learning interventions to isolate individual barriers. Then they can help managers remove the barriers that prevent transfer.

Second, to reduce resistance change must be introduced to employees in small, manageable units. Introducing change in this way demonstrates an understanding of their world and the complexity of changing behavior. Providing reinforcement and supportive activities increases the incorporation of change. When change in incorporated, the second phase of change has transpired, which Lewin calls *movement*.

Lewin (1951) believes that once change has been introduced and incorporated by participants, the organization is responsible for *refreezing* the new set of behaviors. This helps guarantee that the new level of behavior is "relatively secure against change" (Burke 1992, 56). This can be accomplished by providing reinforcement and follow-up activities after a performance improvement intervention or change initiative, and by developing reward systems that recognize new behaviors. Although it is the organization's responsibility to refreeze behavior, it is an HRD professional's responsibility to create an environment that will help them do so (see Chapter 12).

According to Mink, Esterhuysen, Mink, and Owen (1993), first-order change, sometimes referred to as morphostasis, deals with routines, activities, problems, issues, and circumstances. First-order changes occur naturally as the organization grows and develops and are "minor improvements and adjustments that do not change the system's core" (Levy 1986, 10). Smith (1982, 318–319) further expands this concept by distinguishing two different types of first-order change: "those that enable things to look different while remaining basically the same . . . and those that occur as a natural expression of the developmental sequence [and are] embedded in the natural maturation process." Mink, Esterhuysen, Mink, and Owen (1993, 209) conclude that under these circumstances, "first-order changes would not necessarily require organized intervention."

Second-order change represents a fundamental shift in the organization. Ulrich (1998) and Mink, Esterhuysen, Mink, and Owen (1993) refer to this type of change as transformational change, in which leaders question their organization's basic assumptions and deal with new and unknown elements in their environment. Second-order change involves a comprehensive examination of an organization's culture, core processes (i.e., structure, management, decisionmaking, performance management system), vision, mission, values, goals, and strategies. Sometimes referred to as morphogenesis, second-order changes are alterations that are thoroughly integrated into the organization and that transform its basic nature.

Principle 2: Effective HRD Practice Is Based on Satisfying Stakeholders' Needs and Expectations

Brinkerhoff and Gill (1994) believe that stakeholders ultimately determine the level of satisfaction for products and services. Therefore, their perception of value is critically important. Allowing stakeholders to define the quality of HRD can be problematic, however, because stakeholders occasionally poorly articulate their needs, and sometimes their needs are contradictory.

A stakeholder is defined as anyone who has something to gain or lose as a result of an interaction with HRD. These gains and losses collectively frame needs and become the target for performance improvement interventions and change initiatives. The typical stakeholders of HRD include the following:

- managers—the primary customer because they endure the cost of interventions and reap the benefits;
- employees—who participate in interventions and initiatives;
- senior managers—who expect interventions and initiatives to return value and help the organization achieve its goals;
- organizations—who need the skills, abilities, and capabilities of employees to produce and deliver high-quality products and services at a profit and rely on employees' capabilities to remain competitive.

HRD professionals can direct all their efforts at satisfying client needs and expectations by developing a customer service strategy. Consequently, effective HRD interventions and initiatives are designed in accordance with the client's expressed interests, which helps assure that the HRD program is designed to maximize organizational performance. HRD programs will be supported as well as defended by clients during difficult economic periods when interventions and initiatives address their needs and when HRD is viewed as essential to the organization's long-term success.

According to Gilley and Maycunich (1998a), a customer service strategy that can be used to satisfy stakeholders' needs and expectations consists of six steps:

1. Establishing a customer service philosophy requires HRD professionals to be willing to place the business and professional needs of their clients above their own.
2. Creating a customer service environment demonstrates a willingness to listen to clients and to respond to their demands, while illustrating an interest in working with their clients in a collaborative manner.
3. Customer service opportunities are created via face-to-face interaction, the result of unwavering dedication to client satisfaction.
4. Implementing customer service requires HRD professionals to become active participants with clients rather than passive observers and embodies ample questioning, listening, and facilitating skills that lead to viable recommendations and solutions.
5. Evaluating the utility and shortcomings of customer service requires feedback from clients regarding their satisfaction with interventions and initiatives.
6. Implementing areas for improvement in customer service is always based upon the feedback received from clients.

Ultimately, an effective customer service strategy becomes a guiding principle for HRD, directing its decisions and actions.

Principle 3: Effective HRD Practice Is Responsive but Responsible

HRD professionals, like any others, need to be responsive to their stakeholders yet responsible for providing solutions that reach the heart of the issue at hand—which may not necessarily require an intervention. Strategic thinking encourages them to examine documents, interview internal confidants, prepare lists of questions to be asked during meetings, solicit input from other colleagues before reacting, and so forth to avoid serious mistakes. The purpose of gathering this type of information is to make informed decisions and recommendations.

According to Rossett (1999b), strategic thinking can include thinking before reacting, listening carefully and selectively to clients' requests, and filtering suggestions and recommendations through a strategic HRD philosophy. She also believes strategic thinking involves understanding one's role within the organization, possessing the courage to say no, and analyzing all requests as requests rather than as commands. Finally, Rossett believes that strategic thinking enables HRD professionals to maintain consistent guiding principles used to ensure credibility.

When HRD professionals fail to ask difficult questions, they create situations that may ultimately produce poor results for their programs. Gilley and Coffern (1994) suggest that HRD professionals can be in a position to think strategically when they know the organization's financial and competitive position, strengths and weaknesses, management structure and capacity, technological state, relationship to competitors, reward and compensation systems, performance appraisal and review systems, performance management system, and management's attitude toward human resources. Such knowledge helps HRD professionals maintain an understanding of the organization and the nature of its business and demonstrate understanding of business fundamentals.

One of an HRD professional's primary responsibilities is to consider the causes of performance problems or organizational inefficiencies by determining the circumstances and conditions that are impacting organizational performance. Effective HRD professionals do not focus on the status quo but continuously look for new and improved ways of enhancing the organization's effectiveness.

Strategic thinking is as much a state of mind as it is a series of techniques and processes. Rossett (1999b) believes that HRD professionals who are continually examining the state of the organization and comparing it with an ideal vision are constantly in touch with problems and issues facing the firm. That is, HRD professionals have an obligation to determine why an intervention or consulting service is needed. Obviously, interventions are sometimes appropriate; however, occasionally they are not.

Principle 4: Effective HRD Practice Uses Evaluation as a Continuous Quality Improvement Process

Evaluation is a process not an event, and it is one of the most important and powerful components of HRD practice. Effective evaluation involves all key "decision-makers, stakeholders, and influencers, and is influenced by a clear understanding of the organization's performance and business needs, as well as its strategic goals and objectives" (Gilley and Eggland 1989, 267). As a process, evaluation measures every aspect of strategic HRD, from philosophy and practice to impact and utility.

Evaluation determines the effectiveness of organizational communications, the operational efficiency of the organization, the impact of critical initiatives such as strategic planning and organizational development, and whether each of the functions within the organizational and performance management system is operating at peak efficiency. Every aspect of the organization's strategy is included in effective evaluation.

Gilley and Maycunich (1998a) and Brinkerhoff (1998) maintain that evaluation should be used as a daily continuous quality improvement process. It should preside over each component of HRD practice, including organizational and needs analysis, the design and development process, the learning acquisition and transfer process, and performance and organizational development consulting. Evaluation reveals an HRD professional's credibility and effectiveness, allowing them to ascertain the viability and utility of their efforts.

As HRD programs cross the line of demarcation from activity to results, the purpose of evaluation changes dramatically. During strategic HRD, evaluation becomes a tool for measuring performance improvement, change initiatives, and their impact throughout the organization. In this phase, evaluation is a normal and commonplace activity, used to measure every aspect and activity in the lives of HRD professionals, who understand that their role in the organization is to make a difference. Consequently, evaluation determines the credibility of HRD professionals and captures the depth and breadth of the impact HRD is having within the organization.

Gilley and Maycunich (1998a) believe that everything must be evaluated. They view evaluation as a feedback and improvement process designed to enhance individual growth and development, and customer service and quality. When strategic HRD professionals are blended into the fabric of the organization, evaluation is less of a formal event than in the vendor-driven and customized HRD phases. Strategic HRD professionals perceive evaluation as a strategy for improving overall organizational performance and effectiveness.

Traditional evaluations such as return on investment and cost-benefit analysis are historically used to "prove" the value and benefit of HRD interventions and initiatives within the organization. Unfortunately, many HRD professionals have adopted similar strategies in order to document or demonstrate their credibility within the organization. Strategic HRD professionals, to the contrary, reject the notion of demonstrating their credibility through typical reaction evaluation or documentation evaluation as they realize that improvements in organizational efficiency or productivity can be realized only through the proper use of an organizational effectiveness strategy, not "smile sheets" at the conclusion of training.

Organizational decisionmakers are not interested in the evaluation process or documentation but in improved productivity, efficiency, and effectiveness.

Strategic HRD professionals realize that their true value is their ability to help the organization achieve its desired business results. Furthermore, these professionals understand that "every project in which they engage is an opportunity to bring about change designed to improve overall organizational performance capacity and effectiveness. These projects must be evaluated to determine whether or not their desired outcomes have been achieved" (Gilley and Maycunich 1998a, 269). They also understand that evaluations conducted at the conclusion of an intervention merely constitute a collection of opinions that justify the training budget. Strategic HRD professionals realize that summative evaluations used to measure cost/benefit relationships are not a viable long-term strategy for improving HRD, because they create an adversarial relationship between HRD professionals and their clients.

Principle 5: Effective HRD Practice Is Designed to Improve Organization Effectiveness

Improving performance and effectiveness is the primary goal of HRD, whether within a large system, small division or department, or throughout an organization. Defining organizational effectiveness is not easy. According to Fallon and Brinkerhoff (1996, 14), organizational effectiveness is a company's long-term ability to consistently achieve its strategic and operational goals. The goal approach is the most widely used evaluation approach for measuring organizational effectiveness, but it is by no means the only method.

Cameron (1980) offers three additional definitions of organizational effectiveness. First, organizational effectiveness can be measured by the ability of the organization to acquire needed resources to accomplish its desired results. Under this approach, organizations are perceived to be successful when they are able to obtain the quantity and quality of resources appropriate, whether financial, material, or human resources. Second, Burke (1992, 8) and Cameron (1980) believe that organizational effectiveness can be defined in terms of how efficient the organization functions, especially the degree of absence of internal strain within the firm. This is often referred to as the *process model* of organizational effectiveness.

The extent to which the organization is able to satisfy all of its internal and external clients represents the third approach to organizational effectiveness. Employee, manager, and executive (internal clients) satisfaction is measured in terms of loyalty, motivation, esprit de corps, cooperation, and teamwork. External client satisfaction can be measured in terms of their use of organizational products and services. Satisfaction can also be measured based on the perception of the correctness of their decision to have an ongoing relationship with the organization.

The importance of organizational effectiveness is reflected in each of these definitions. Although it may be difficult to arrive at an agreed-upon definition of organizational effectiveness, it is certainly an important aspect of organizational life. HRD professionals must reach an acceptable definition of organizational effectiveness in order to help identify the agreed-upon targets that all members of the organization strive to achieve.

Principle 6: Effective HRD Practice Relies on Relationship Mapping to Enhance Operational Efficiency

Organizations have subsystems that enable them to survive just as humans have digestive, circulatory, skeletal, and nervous systems. Typically, organizations are diagrammed in such a way as to describe connections between various departments, both at the vertical and horizontal levels. On the vertical plane, organizations are categorized into subparts of various departments, usually indicating individual titles and specific reporting relationships. On the horizontal plane, various departments are indicated, which represent functions such as finance, marketing, manufacturing, customer service, and so forth.

Rummler and Brache (1995, 6) likened organizations to "silos," contending that silos are tall, thick, windowless structures that prevent interdepartmental issues from being resolved between peers at low and middle levels. They believe that silo culture forces managers to resolve low-level issues, which take time away from higher-priority customers and competitive concerns. Consequently, most employees operate within their respective silos, adopting the culture, language, and customs of their department or division. This behavior prevents cross-departmental interaction, thereby inhibiting communications, decisionmaking, performance, and quality.

According to Gilley and Maycunich (1998a), organizations that operate within the silo culture are more likely to create the organizational "Tower of Babel." The Tower of Babel is a descriptive metaphor that demonstrates the confusion rampant within organizations when silo culture pervades. Such cultural constraints prevent employees in different departments from communicating or developing a common language, thus, they tend to be isolated and operate from a narrow organizational perspective. When the organizational Tower of Babel flourishes, the culture prevents employees from working across departmental lines to achieve desired goals. Furthermore, organizational decisions are pushed up to higher levels, preventing teamwork and cross-departmental cooperation.

Overcoming the Tower of Babel syndrome requires adopting a more practical, efficient, overall organizational effectiveness strategy, which helps the firm create a universal, cross-departmental language that strengthens the entire firm and implements change both at the macro and micro levels within the organization. In essence, HRD professionals must adopt an organizational effectiveness strategy that improves individual performance as well as organizational, operational efficiency and effectiveness.

The most effective means of improving organizational effectiveness is to alter the silo culture. Rummler and Brache (1995) suggest that organizations must understand their cross-departmental interactions and dependencies. They provide a methodology known as *relationship mapping* to demonstrate this approach. A relationship map reveals that organizations are indeed systems in which employees rely on inputs (resources) and processes (interdependent tasks and activities) to produce desired results (products, services, or deliverables). The most important function of relationship mapping is identifying connections between various departments. Rummler and Brache (1995, 9) believe that "performance improvement often lies in the functional interfaces—those points in which activities are being passed from one department to another." Furthermore, HRD professionals must help organizations understand their need to create more efficient and effective interdepartmental relationships—ones that improve organizational performance capacity and effectiveness.

Principle 7: Effective HRD Practice Is Linked to the Organization's Strategic Business Goals and Objectives

A common problem encountered in organizations is that employees and other stakeholders fail to comprehend how a particular performance intervention or change initiative contributes to their work in the long run. To overcome this problem, strategic HRD leaders must look beyond short-range interventions and initiatives and focus instead on influencing long-term organizational performance and business results. The HRD horizon is more than the performance objective of a single intervention; it is a vision of the organization operating at its highest level. Executives, managers, and employees must be shown how, where, and why new learning, performance, and change will be used on the job to impact critical aspects of the business (Brinkerhoff and Gill 1994). Therefore, effective HRD practice must be linked to important organization goals.

Tarraco and Swanson (1995) and Brinkerhoff and Gill (1994) agree that the relationship of intended learning, performance, and change outcomes to strategic business goals and objectives is critical to the success of HRD. Thus, to the extent that HRD goals are compatible with and responsive to strategic goals and objectives, HRD's value increases. Conversely, when HRD's goals are not aligned with strategic goals and objectives, the value of HRD diminishes.

The link between learning, performance and change and business goals must be understood by key participants in the process. Senior management, often advocates for performance improvement interventions and change initiatives, should directly or indirectly perceive their value. Brinkerhoff and Gill (1994) assert that if management does not perceive the linkage, they will not be supportive of HRD and its professionals. Without their support, the opportunity to improve organizational performance or adopt vital change will not occur.

Tarraco and Swanson (1995) believe that strategic HRD leaders should communicate the linkage between the goals of the HRD function and the organization's business goals and objectives, and the attendant benefits and value. This helps managers and executives commit to future interventions and initiatives. Additionally, confidence is confirmed when managers and executives are aware of the value received as a result of HRD participation.

The strategic HRD approach assumes a comprehensive view of linkage. Brinkerhoff and Gill (1994, 80) believe that linkage must occur throughout the performance improvement and change process. They add that employees can "identify job-specific performance factors that are linked to needed job results, job results are linked to unit performance goals, unit goals are linked to division goals, and division goals are linked to organization strategic initiatives" (80). In such organizations, strategic HRD leaders are members of strategic planning teams, serve as change agents and performance consultants, and have strong partnership relationships with senior managers.

Principle 8: Effective HRD Practice Is Based on Partnerships

All too often, organizational leaders, managers, and employees do not view HRD professionals as vital, contributing members of the organization (capable of improving the firm's performance quality, efficiency, or productivity). HRD professionals should ask, "What can we do to prevent negative perceptions of ourselves and our programs?" This question is not easily answered but must be addressed if HRD professionals are to improve their credibility and, thus, their effectiveness.

One method is to develop strategic business partnerships, which are intraorganizational alliances formed to ensure successful completion of the organization's overall strategic plan. Gilley and Maycunich (1998a, 118) define them as mutually beneficial relationships created to help the organization better achieve its goals and objectives. Strategic business partnerships are synergistic, mutually beneficial, and oriented toward the long term in their quest to help the firm succeed. These relationships enable HRD professionals to develop a responsive, customer service orientation that better understands and anticipates client needs. The principal benefit for clients is improved performance, whereas HRD professionals enjoy increased credibility within the organization.

Bellman (1998, 39) contends that partnerships are essential to the success of any organization. He points out that a partner is a person who "takes part" with others and that partnerships involve the "parts" we each play in our work. He asserts that the two primary elements of partnership are purpose and partnering. Without a purpose, no partnership exists. Purpose may be quite clear and explicit, as that imposed by a client, or implicit, as a mutual exploration of a purpose about to be defined. Purpose, in essence, brings us together.

Partnering occurs when HRD professionals and clients pursue a common purpose together. Partnering exemplifies the visible and invisible dynamics between HRD professional, client, and purpose, the result of clarifying roles and purpose. It also embraces underlying assumptions, trust and risk, shared values, and expectations. Much that is key to partnering often goes unexpressed, and some may not be rational. HRD professionals and clients who attend to purposes but neglect partnering often fail in their work altogether (Bellman 1998).

Gilley and Maycunich (1998a) believe that creating partnerships is one of the most important activities HRD professionals engage in. They contend that partnerships are interdependent and focused on the long term, allowing HRD professionals to better understand and anticipate their clients' needs. These partnerships help HRD professionals develop a responsive attitude, which is necessary for them to improve their customer service orientation.

HRD professionals as strategic business partners break down the walls between themselves and their clients. As a result, lasting commitments are forged and investments are made in learning, performance, and change efforts. Partnerships encourage HRD professionals to fully understand their clients' contributions and the values they bring to an interaction. Consequently, HRD professionals become immersed with their clients' performance problems, needs, concerns, and expectations.

Partnerships give HRD professionals the opportunity to develop personal relationships with clients. Alliances allow HRD professionals and clients to create trust and develop a shared vision of the future through a free exchange of ideas, information, and perceptions. According to Wilson (1987), strategic business partnerships also promote establishment of working relationships based on shared values, aligned purpose and vision, and mutual support.

Bellman (1998, 41) believes that the client's role may entail products and outcomes, accountability for results, clarity of vision and values, management of resources (time, energy, money, human talent, materials, equipment, environment), creation of structure and systems, strategic decisionmaking, and so forth. The HRD professional's role exudes competence combined with adaptability in its focus on client needs. This role encompasses clarity regarding one's contributions, awareness of the organization's needs, developing alternatives, revealing new perspectives, modeling risk taking, and knowledge of the consulting process—all while honoring one's personal purpose, vision, values, and core beliefs.

Principle 9: Effective HRD Practice Is Results Oriented

HRD professionals can choose between two strategies: activity or results. These strategies differ in their focus and in their contribution to the organization.

Far too many HRD programs deluge employees with an exhaustive list of training courses (vendor-driven HRD programs). Little attention is paid to why employees participate in training as long as they attend some training classes each year. In fact, training is sometimes viewed as a reward for a job well done. Robinson and Robinson (1996, 1989) refer to this as the activity strategy of HRD. They assert that HRD professionals who embrace the activity approach report the number of courses offered and the number of employees attending them to justify their value. They suggest that activity-based HRD professionals believe that the more training is conducted, the better the organization will perform.

A results strategy is an approach HRD professionals use to improve organization performance through learning and performance interventions and change initiatives. The focus is not on how many training programs can be delivered each year or on how many employees participate in training but on the results obtained through learning, performance, and change efforts. HRD professionals who use this approach report on outcomes as a means of validating their programs.

The age-old argument of quantity versus quality characterizes the activity versus results debate. Training programs offered to employees as fringe benefits have little or no impact on organizational performance. There is an erroneous belief that throwing enough training programs at employees will improve the organization's performance. This incorrect assumption negatively impacts the field of HRD and its professionals.

It could be said that without results, training isn't of much use to managers, employees, or the organization. Although it may be easy to generate a great deal of training activity and claim that it makes a difference, it is much harder to identify needed results, design an appropriate intervention or initiative, implement it, and evaluate its impact. This approach requires a total shift in emphasis. Performance improvement interventions and change initiatives must produce specific outcomes on which the organization can rely to help it accomplish its business objectives. Gilley and Maycunich (1998a) advocate that the new HRD strategy should be learning, performance, or change to achieve business results. This indicates an effort to accomplish something specific rather than training for training's sake.

Principles 10: Credibility Is Essential to the Success of HRD Practice

Some HRD programs falter because they are not based on the needs of the organization or because they are not results oriented, whereas others fail because HRD professionals do not properly communicate the value and benefits of their interventions and initiatives to decisionmakers within the organization. Although all of these are contributing factors, most HRD programs fail because clients' business and performance needs are not satisfied; thus, HRD is not perceived as important. When clients believe that HRD is unable to help improve their performance, quality, efficiency, or productivity, they view HRD as nonessential in accomplishing the strategic goals and objectives of the organization. In other words, HRD professionals lack credibility within the organization and their programs are destined to fail.

Improved credibility results from HRD professionals' ability to demonstrate professional expertise as well as their understanding of organizational operations and culture. In this way, HRD professionals provide real value to the organization.

Ulrich (1997a, 253–254) maintains that HRD professionals need to demonstrate several behaviors in order to enhance credibility. First, they need to be accurate in all HRD practices. This includes analysis activities (performance, needs, causal, organizational), design of interventions and initiatives, performance and organizational development consulting activities, and evaluation. Second, HRD professionals need to be predictable and consistent—dependable and reliable so that decisionmakers have confidence in their actions and recommendations. Third, they must meet their commitments in a timely and efficient manner. Fourth, HRD professionals need to establish collaborative client relationships built on trust and honesty. Fifth, they must express their opinions, ideas, strategies, and activities in an understandable and clear manner and at the most appropriate times. Sixth, they need to behave in an ethical manner that demonstrates integrity. Seventh, HRD professionals must demonstrate creativity and innovation. Eighth, they need to maintain confidentiality. Ninth, they need to listen to and focus on executive problems in a manner that brings about mutual respect.

According to Gilley and Maycunich (2000, 153), HRD professionals establish credibility within their organizations in four ways. They demonstrate the ability to solve complex problems that impact their ability to satisfy client needs and expectations; exhibit professional expertise combined with understanding of organizational operations and culture; demonstrate integrity by delivering results, and network with organizational decisionmakers. In essence, credibility must be earned.

Credibility can also be established through an appropriate understanding of differing roles. When appropriate roles are executed, trust and confidence emerge, which deepen relationships and bridge performance uncertainty. Over time, improved efficiency results as collaboration and cooperation replace competition and conflict.

Anderson (1997, 148–149) offered eight steps for establishing credibility:

- Demonstrate understanding of business strategies, goals, tactics, and financial performance and connect that knowledge to the skills, competencies, practices, and people that are available to execute the business strategy.
- Establish performance goals that relate directly to business strategies.
- Provide credible follow-up to management on HRD's effectiveness in supporting the business strategy.
- Know the value of the HRD skills, competencies, practices, and business knowledge available to execute business strategies.
- Market competencies to management so that they are aware of what HRD can do to support them.
- Demonstrate problem-solving skills.
- Provide management with value-added service.
- Provide efficient and effective service.

Principle 11: Effective HRD Practice Utilizes Strategic Planning to Help the Organization Integrate Its Vision, Mission, Strategy, and Practice

Gilley and Maycunich (1998b, 22) believe that "strategic planning is a forward-thinking process that helps organizational leaders shape the future via intelligent, informed, and innovative actions . . . and that gives purpose and direction to an organization by allowing it to ascertain, in advance, what it wishes to accomplish and the means by which to achieve its ends." Simerly (1987) suggests that strategic planning provides everyone in the organization the opportunity to participate in decisionmaking, thus personally impacting the organization's future. Consequently, strategic planning can be viewed as a way of enhancing the self-esteem of employees. Strategic planning activities are designed to re-create and reinvent organizations by helping them establish a new vision and purpose. Moreover, strategic planning greatly improves organizational effectiveness by charting a new course for the firm.

When HRD leaders engage in strategic planning for their organization, they generally produce a written document that enables all decisionmakers, stakeholders, and influencers to analyze and critique the mission, goals, objectives, and strategies that will be used to help the organization achieve its desired business results (Michael 1973). Thus, strategic planning is both a process and a product (i.e., a written plan) interrelated in such complex and overlapping ways that it is almost impossible to analyze one without considering the other.

Participating in strategic planning activities also helps HRD professionals (1) improve their credibility within the organization; (2) develop strategic business partnerships; (3) enhance client relationships; (4) understand the organization; (5) create an attitude of continuous improvement and change within the organization; (6) develop learning, performance, and change partnerships; (7) create a mechanism for executing the organizational effectiveness strategy; (8) formulate a long-term decisionmaking strategy within the organization; and (9) foster change.

Principle 12: Effective HRD Practice Relies on the Analysis Process to Identify Priorities

Mills, Pace, and Peterson (1988, 5) define *analysis* as "the act and process of separating any material or abstract entity into its constituent elements, which involves determining its essential features and their relation to one another." They believe that analysis is a process designed to set goals for HRD, develop direction for the HRD function and its professionals, determine the driving forces within an organization, identify performance, management, and organization gaps, and establish purpose and priorities for HRD.

Mills, Pace, and Peterson (1988) suggest that analysis is grounded in the philosophy of problem solving, which is a process of recognizing differences between what is and what should be (a deficiency), and taking corrective action to narrow the gap between the two. Additionally, Rothwell and Cookson (1997) believe that analysis involves all of the activities associated with recognizing the existence of a problem, its causes, and consequences, and classifying the problem in terms of what interventions might reasonably be used to narrow the gap. This becomes the fundamental process of HRD and is the catalyst for organizational learning, performance, and change.

Principle 13: Effective HRD Practice Is Based on Purposeful and Meaningful Measurement

Brinkerhoff and Gill (1994, 88) report that "the process of producing a product or delivering a service is improved when people are able to measure and compare their performance to some standard for that process." Rummler and Brache (1995, 137) believe measurement data help managers communicate performance expectations, identify performance gaps, provide specific feedback, and make decisions regarding resource allocation, plans, and schedules. Furthermore, measurement data help employees know specifically what is expected of them so that they can manage their own progress, identify performance gaps, and develop performance improvement plans.

Measurement data are initially needed to identify employee performance deficits, organizational deficiencies, and improvement needs. But measurement data are also needed to identify critical activities before and after a learning and performance improvement intervention, to establish performance objectives, and to improve change initiatives. Moreover, measurement data are needed to assess the acquisition of new skills, knowledge, and attitudes and to evaluate the adequacy of HRD professionals' performance and organizational development consulting skills. Finally, measurement data are needed to gauge the effectiveness of performance management systems and to provide feedback on the implementation of interventions and initiatives.

The "purpose of measurement is to inform, illuminate, and educate" (Geis and Smith 1992, 136). HRD professionals use measurement to determine what works and what does not, which in turn helps clients become better performers, as HRD professionals improve their problem-solving capabilities. Additionally, measurement fulfills quality assurance and accountability requirements while directing projects toward worthwhile results. Measurement also helps stakeholders assess the results of their efforts and investments.

There are many possible subpurposes for measurement. Geis and Smith (1992, 133–135) believe that measurement should help HRD professionals audit the current state of affairs, determine whether an activity's effects justify the costs, and confirm that a particular procedure or treatment is being carried out as prescribed. They also believe measurement helps HRD professionals determine the effectiveness of some treatment or intervention, provide feedback to the organizational system or to an individual, and identify information that will influence decisions about where remedial actions should be undertaken. Additionally, measurement helps identify the need for revisions or alterations, support decisions to hire, fire, promote, or reassign employees, and determine the marketability of a product or service.

Rossett (1999b) suggests that the specific purpose of measurement should determine what kind of data is appropriate and when it should be gathered. When measurement is used to guide planning, it must occur early in the decision and planning process. If measurement is used to improve a process, it should be conducted throughout its design, development, and implementation. If, however, measurement is used to determine the impact of an intervention or initiative, it should occur a few months after implementation.

Since the purpose of measurement is to improve decisionmaking, it should be a guiding principle for HRD practice. Globally, the purpose of measurement is to illuminate and improve the organization. As previously discussed, measurement is a process of providing the basis for thumbs-up/thumbs-down decisions. Stufflebeam (1971) summed up the two perspectives as retroactive (whereby measurement is used for accountability) and proactive (whereby measurement is used to improve a process). Schrock and Geis (1999) believe that the current emphasis is on measurement as a means of finding out what is working well, why it is working well, and what can be done to improve it.

Principle 14: Effective HRD Promotes Diversity and Equality in the Workplace

Our nation's evolving demographic makeup has dramatic implications for business—and HRD. As women and minorities constitute an increasing percentage of workers and assume greater roles and responsibilities, their contributions to organizational success become obvious. Often, HRD professionals represent the social conscience of an organization, embracing and promoting diversity and equality as components of a progressive strategic business plan.

Developmental organizations understand the value of differences and encourage diversity. Differences are normal, healthy, and commonly occur among individuals—in fact, our differences make us interesting to others. Differences fuel creativity and innovation, allowing individuals and groups to venture beyond their comfort zones in pursuit of improvements, new ideas, alternative solutions, and challenges to the status quo. Lack of diversity leads to stagnation of the workforce, devoid of the spark needed to nourish competitive thoughts and deeds.

HRD professionals champion diversity and equality throughout an organization—from recruiting and selection to motivation and continuous development to compensation and rewards. Organizations remain competitive and capable of continually reinventing themselves in a culture epitomizing diversity and equality.

Conclusion

Principles define and guide practice within a professional field. In this chapter we have identified the major principles for the field of HRD. Each of these principles provides HRD practitioners guidance toward critical outcomes. Collectively, they serve as a foundation for practice and a prism to filter future opportunities and engagements.

PART II

Organizational Learning

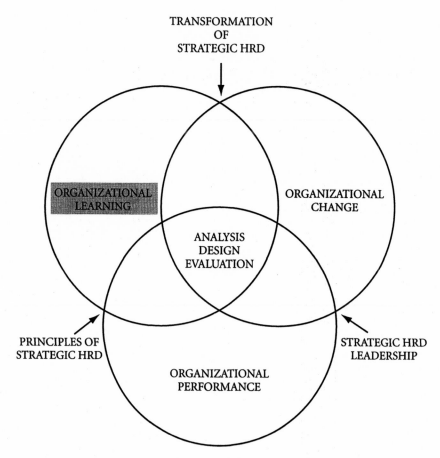

TRANSFORMATION
OF
STRATEGIC HRD

ORGANIZATIONAL
LEARNING

ORGANIZATIONAL
CHANGE

ANALYSIS
DESIGN
EVALUATION

PRINCIPLES OF
STRATEGIC HRD

STRATEGIC HRD
LEADERSHIP

ORGANIZATIONAL
PERFORMANCE

ORGANIZATIONAL LEARNING, PERFORMANCE, AND CHANGE

Learning Organizations and Action Learning

One of the critical professional practice domains is organizational learning. To properly understand this domain, we must examine four essential elements: learning organizations and action learning (Chapter 5), learning in organizations (Chapter 6), and developmental organizations (Chapter 7). Let us begin by examining the concept of organizational learning.

Organizational Learning

Organizational learning is "changed organizational capacity for doing something new" (Watkins and Marsick 1993, 152). Systemic capacity refers to an organization's ability to change fundamental ways of working, whereas transformational capacity involves a firm's ability to reinvent itself and redefine successful practices in the face of global competition or rapidly changing technology. Organizational capacity is often enhanced when a crisis requires that a company test its assumptions about what works best, when a firm alters fundamental relationships (by implementing self-managed teams), by product innovations, or new technology. When a business implements a strategy that does not work, it learns how *not* to solve a problem. Unfortunately, negative learning can diminish capacity when the results fail to inspire positive change, de-motivate, or lead to lessons in hypocrisy. Additionally, companies that subscribe to the latest fad or quick-fix strategy typically fail to invest in learning required for change at a deeper level.

Marquardt (1996, 230) defines organizational learning as "how learning occurs on an organization-wide basis" as opposed to a *learning organization,* which describes the systems, principles, and characteristics of organizations that learn as a collective entity. He identifies three levels of organizational learning.

Organization learning represents the enhanced intellectual and productive capability gained through corporate-wide commitment and opportunity for continuous improvement. It differs from individual and group/team learning in two basic respects. First, organizational learning occurs through the shared insights, knowledge, and mental models of members of the organization. Second, it builds on past knowledge and experience—that is, on organizational memory, which depends on institutional mechanisms (e.g., policies, strategies, and explicit models) used to retain knowledge. Third, organizational learning represents the enhanced intellectual and productive capability gained through corporate-wide commitment to continuous improvement. (Marquardt 1999, 21–22)

According to March (1995), learning can occur through exploration or exploitation. Learning as exploration charts new territory and is characterized by search, variation, risk taking, and play—as in research and development of new products or by learning new processes and procedures. The results of learning as exploration may be uncertain and possibly difficult to measure. Often, learning organization initiatives are exploratory in nature—attempts to revise, create, or build something new. Learners and learning teams engage in long-term learning requiring dedication, creativity, and openness to feedback and change.

Preskill and Torres (1999) contend that the majority of organizational learning models focus on learning as a change process, one that seeks to involve all of its employees in an effort to harness their intellectual capacity and knowledge capital for the purpose of individual, team, and organizational growth. In addition, Torres, Preskill, and Piontek (1996, 2) believe that organizational learning is a "continuous process of organizational growth and improvement that (a) is integrated with work activities, (b) invokes the alignment of values, attitudes, and perceptions among organizational members, and (c) uses information or feedback about both processes and outcomes to make changes." Schwandt (1995) further contends that learning in organizations is nonlinear, open, and constantly evolving to higher levels of complexity.

Preskill and Torres (1999, 49) maintain that organizational learning is grounded in a social constructivist theory of learning, which suggests that learning takes place through (a) the collective creation of meaning, (b) action, (c) the development of new knowledge, (d) an improvement in systemic processes, and (e) overcoming of tacit assumptions. Additionally, team learning occurs when individuals share their experiences, values, beliefs, assumptions, and knowledge through dialogue and engage in collaborative learning effort. It can, therefore, be said that the organization learns when individuals and teams disseminate their learning from inquiry throughout an organization.

What does organizational learning look like? Kline and Saunders (1998, 16–18) have identified a set of sixteen principles that they feel underlies organizational learning. These principles, when embraced and modeled by an organization's upper levels, influence employees' inner belief systems, becoming implicit in the organizational culture and structure. They believe that organizational learning encourages individuals at every level to be self-directed (learned helplessness has too often been the result of formal education). They view mistakes as stepping-stones to continuous learning and essential to further business growth. However, there must be willingness to rework organizational systems and structures to account for and encourage organizational learning. These include creating an organization that is supportive of continuous growth and development and that embraces the belief that ideas can be developed best through dialogue and discussion.

Kline and Saunders also believe that organizations need to celebrate the learning process for its own sake, not just its end product, as well as celebrate all learners equally. Organizations need to transfer as much knowledge and power from person to person as possible as well as encourage and teach employees to structure their own learning, rather than structuring it for them. Organizations need to facilitate the process of self-evaluation and recognize and accept as a goal the complete liberation of all human intelligence everywhere. They need to encourage employees to discover their own learning and thinking styles and make them accessible to others.

Furthermore, organizations need to recognize that different learning preferences are alternate tools for approaching and accomplishing learning. They need to cultivate each employee's abilities in all fields of knowledge and spread the idea that nothing is forever inaccessible to people. Organizations need to recognize that in order to facilitate learning, it must be logical, moral, and fun. Everything is subject to reexamination and investigation.

Learning Partnerships

Learning partnerships result from the collaborative efforts of managers (coaches) and employees to maximize learning and its outcomes. Marquardt (1996, 54) maintains that managers are obligated to develop learning partnership characterized by planning, application, and reflection. Planning involves a mutual effort by learning coaches and employees to determine the gap between the learner's existing knowledge and skills and those demanded by the learning opportunity. Partners develop learning objectives, an actionable plan to accomplish those objectives, and complete any necessary prerequisite learning.

Application requires long-term commitment on the part of both parties. A manager's primary responsibilities include coaching the learner based on learning needs (job-specific, functional, adaptive), providing the learner with needed opportunities, making certain the learner has access to references and tools, and providing guidance and feedback when needed. Learners are responsible for applying the knowledge and skills gained, utilizing available resources, reflecting on the current task being learned, and asking for assistance and feedback when needed (Marquardt 1999, 88).

Reflection involves serious consideration of past events or future implications. Employees and coaches should reflect on lessons learned and their application to the job. Will efficiency, productivity, or satisfaction improve? Employees and coaches provide feedback regarding the coaching process, learning, successes, and areas requiring improvement. Coaches encourage continuous improvement and recognize and reward accomplishments, while employees share lessons learned with others who might find the insight useful (Marquardt 1996, 54).

Learning Organizations

Marquardt (1996, 229) believes that a learning organization can be defined as a "company that learns powerfully and collectively, continually transforming itself to more effectively manage knowledge. Learning organizations empower their people to learn as they work, utilizing technology to maximize learning and production."

Marquardt (1996, 180–191) believes that the evolution from the traditional to the learning organization requires a firm to alter its environment to support learning, align learning with business operations, communicate learning's importance, and demonstrate commitment to learning. Additionally, it requires organizations to encourage continuous learning and improvement and establish organization-wide learning strategies. Furthermore, firms need to eliminate organizational bureaucracy, encourage employee involvement, and embrace continuous, adaptive, improvement-oriented learning approaches throughout the organization. Learning organizations understand that learning is the foundation upon which success is built. Employees who continually improve learning capacity are the building blocks that support improved organizational productivity, market share, and profitability. Thus, learning organizations abide by a simple assumption: When the learning reservoir of individuals improves, organizational performance capacity also improves.

In recent years, numerous models illustrating the relationship among individual, team, and organizational learning have been developed. Watkins and Marsick (1993, 10) conclude that most learning organizations share the following attributes. They develop structures and systems to ensure that knowledge is captured and shared for use in the organization memory as well as supported, facilitated, and rewarded. Learning organizations have leaders and employees at all levels think systematically about the impact of their decisions and work within the total system. Furthermore, learning organizations build learning into work structures, politics, and practice, which involves a greater percentage of the employee population. They use measurement systems to benchmark current knowledge and culture, and monitor progress toward becoming a learning organization. Finally, learning is viewed as transformative, although it is likely that some new learning will also be adaptive.

Senge (1990, 191) states, "Learning has very little to do with taking in information. Learning, instead, is a process that is about enhancing capacity. Learning is about building the capabilities to create that which you previously could not create. It ultimately relates to action, which information is not." Marquardt (1996, 32) believes that true learning exhibits several specific characteristics. First, learning is performance based and tied to business objectives. Second, the learning process (learning how to learn) is as important as the content. Third, the ability to define learning needs is essential. Fourth, the opportunities to develop knowledge, skills, and attitudes are organization-wide. Fifth, learning is, in part, a product of the activity, context, and culture in which it is developed and used. Sixth, people are more willing and able to learn when they have the opportunity to create learning engagements. Seventh, people must be developing the ability to know what they must know and to learn on their own. Eighth, continuous learning is critical for survival and success in today's world. Ninth, managers (facilitators) can accelerate learning by helping people think critically. Tenth, learning should accommodate different learning styles. Eleventh, learning is part of everyone's job description. Twelfth, learning involves a cyclical, cognitive process of planning, implementing, and reflecting on action.

Focusing on the individual's role in learning organizations, Boyett and Boyett (1995, 125) maintain that real, effective learning isn't individual, but social. They contend that true learning is anything but a passive activity and that the most important stuff for people to learn in organizations isn't the explicit stuff of rules, procedures, and so forth, but tacit knowledge (intuition, expertise, common sense, core competencies, and the like). Further, they assert that genuine learning occurs as part of the work itself, not in sterile training environments or in solitary situations.

Chalofsky (1996, 292) believes that in order to become learning organizations, institutions need to shift from

- learning based on minimal competence to learning based on continual improvement;
- learning based on fear of failure to learning based on risk taking;
- learning based on individual performance to learning based on team and collective performance;
- learning based on competition to learning based on cooperation and collaboration;
- learning based on appraisal and criticism to learning based on coaching, support, and feedback;

- learning that is formal to learning that is informal.
- learning based on one right answer to learning based on discovery of possibilities;
- learning based on abstract, logical reasoning to learning based on intuition, relationships, and context;
- learning based on outcome (the destination) to learning based on process (the journey).

Thus, Chalofsky implies that learning is intentional and contextual, the result of organizational systems and structures that encourage members to learn and grow together. Marquardt (1996, 2) believes that learning organizations possess the capability to anticipate and adapt more readily to environmental impacts and to accelerate the development of new products, processes, and services. He believes learning organizations also become more proficient at learning from competitors and collaborators and expedite the transfer of knowledge from one part of the organization to another. Additionally, learning organizations learn more effectively from their mistakes, make greater organizational use of employees at all levels of the organization, shorten the time required to implement strategic changes, and stimulate continuous improvement in all areas of the organization. Organizations that learn faster are able to adapt more quickly and thereby achieve significant strategic advantages in the global world of business.

Disciplines of Learning Organizations

Obviously, learning organizations differ from traditional organizations in critical areas. Senge (1990) identified five disciplines that represent defining characteristics of learning organizations and, thus, separate them from traditional firms: personal mastery, mental models, shared vision, team learning, and systems thinking.

Personal mastery results from the acquisition of individual expertise and proficiency through education, formal learning activities, and work experience. Exceeding expectations and extraordinary performance have been referred to as *total performance excellence* (Clifton and Nelson 1992). St. Louis Cardinal Mark McGwire's record-breaking 1998 baseball season is an excellent example of personal mastery.

Mental models encompass values, beliefs, attitudes, and assumptions, forming one's fundamental worldview. Structures, experiences, cultures, and belief systems support mental models, which guide individuals and act as filters during decision-making. Boyett and Boyett (1995) state that shared mental models, such as those relayed by storytelling and cooperative exchanges, support organizational learning by helping employees make sense out of seemingly random events.

Shared vision, a cornerstone of learning organizations, represents the collective perspectives of employees and evolves from their understanding of the firm's mission and goals. Leaders, managers, and employees hold a common perception of learning and its importance to individuals as well as the organization. In traditional organizations, unfortunately, shared vision rarely surfaces due to lack of genuine effort on management's part to internalize or engender worker commitment to the firm's mission.

Team learning encourages communication and cooperation, leading to synergy and respect among members. Participants of teams are able to expand their horizons, deepen their understandings, amplify their perspectives, develop a better sense of self, and appreciation for others as resources within the firm. Schon (1983) referred to these components as the interaction of action and reflection.

Systems thinking involves examination of and reflection upon all aspects of organizational life, such as mission and strategy, structure, culture, and managerial practices. Strategic thinking on the part of leaders, managers, and employees improves understanding and focuses actions among integrated divisions of the firm to maximize strengths, minimize weaknesses, and enhance overall operations.

According to Marquardt (1999), learning organizations consist of four subsystems: *learning, organization, people,* and *knowledge.*

Learning Subsystem

The heart and soul of the learning organization is learning, a dimension that permeates and drives the other three subsystems. True learning requires systems thinking, application of mental models, striving for personal mastery, and maintaining continuous dialogue. Learning organizations manifest three types of learning:

- Individual—the increase of skills, insights, knowledge, attitudes, and values acquired by a person through training, self-study, technology-based instruction, insight, observation, and reflection
- Team/Group—the increase in knowledge, skills, and competencies of, by, and within groups
- Organizational—the increase in learning capacity of the organization (i.e., speed of learning, depth of learning, and breadth of learning [Redding 1994]).

Individual Learning. Adult learning theories abound. Following is an exploration of some of these theories.

Behaviorism views learning as a desired permanent change in behavior. Skinner, Pavlov, Thorndike, Watson, and other behaviorists asserted that, responding to environmental stimuli, learner behavior alters along an anticipatory plane. Teachers, trainers, and managers, then, simply create the environment and provide opportunities to elicit desired learner responses. Many of today's organizations engage in one-on-one coaching, competency or skill-based instruction, and group training programs, clear examples of behaviorism.

Cognitive learning theories focus on how learning occurs, suggesting that cognitive processes control learning and behavior. As a result, learning is perceived as involuntary, with learners simply reacting automatically to situations or feedback. Although cognitive learning theories explain how, they fail to address why people learn.

Constructivist learning theories assert that learning involves "making meaning" of new knowledge or experiences, which subsequently impacts perception, thinking, and actions (Kolb 1984). Constructivism maintains that individuals constantly process new information, creating and re-creating meaning—which ultimately affects their relationships with others. As a result, adults are constantly changing and learning and are thus active participants in the learning process (Jackson and Maelssac 1994).

Social constructivist theory views learners as active agents in the learning process, constructing outcomes based upon their social settings. When members of a social setting (e.g., an organization) share their social constructs, the cycle of learning renews. Social constructivist managers function as models and guides throughout the learning process. Similarly, Dewey (1938) believed that learning is a continuous process of the reconstruction of experience. Jarvis (1992) and Kolb (1984) suggest that learning occurs when individuals have a "shared concrete experience"; they share their reactions and observations from the experience, generalize the experience to other aspects of life, and apply the learning to new situations. Further, action and reflection are critical to the learning process to ensure that individuals learn from experience rather than just have experience (Watkins and Marsick 1993).

Humanist learning theories, such as those suggested by Maslow, assert that learning is the result of the learner's self-identified needs and past experiences, with an emphasis on problem solving (Rogers 1969). Further, learners responsible for identifying, designing, and evaluating their own learning objectives experience greater success in learning (Knowles 1980; Merriam and Caffarella 1991; Tough 1979).

Group/Team Learning.   Organizations offer individuals never-ending and varied opportunities to learn. And since organizations are made up of divisions, departments, committees, and teams working closely and/or constantly toward common goals, it follows that groups share similar opportunities to learn. Stewart (1997,

163–164) believes that "interdisciplinary teams capture, formalize, and capitalize talent, because it becomes shared, less dependent on any individual."

Watkins and Marsick (1993, 99) believe that the building blocks of team learning involve an initial perception of an issue, a situation, a person, or an object based on past understanding and present input (framing). It also involves a process of transforming that perception into a new understanding or frame (reframing). Team learning involves resolving conflicts by integrating divergent views into an acceptable understanding without compromise or majority rule (integrating perspectives). It also involves action undertaken to test a hypothesis or discover something new (experimenting), and two or more individuals or teams communicate to achieve a positive end (crossing boundaries).

Watkins and Marsick (1993, 109) examined how teams learn and why they learn more or less effectively. They suggest that various group and organizational conditions influence team learning and determine whether team learning becomes organizational learning. Team factors impacting learning included appreciation of teamwork, opportunity for individual expression, and operating principles. Similarly, organizational factors included support for the operation of teams and for collaboration across lines as a way of working. (See Appendix B)

Team Factors Most Influencing Team Learning

Team learning conditions resemble group dynamics in their focus on group processes and tasks. Learning is fostered or hindered based on the way these conditions facilitate dialogue among peers, which leads to new ways of thinking. Watkins and Marsick (1993, 109–110) suggest that there are three factors that influence team learning.

- *Appreciation of teamwork*—involves the receptivity of the team to differing views and ideas, the degree to which the team is valued over the individual, and ways the team builds on the synergy of members.
- *Opportunity for individual expression*—includes the opportunity for input into mission, goals, and operating procedures; climate for expressing objections; and ease of opportunity for members to express themselves during team activities.
- *Operating principles*—include how beliefs, values, purpose, and structure are created, and how effectively the team balances tasks with relationships and learning.

Organizational Conditions Most Influencing Team Learning

Clearly, teams work within the organization system, subject to its culture, values, mission, strategies, norms, managerial practices, processes, and so on. Watkins and

Marsick (1993, 111) maintain that "organizational conditions influence whether team outcomes are shared and whether team learning leads to organizational learning." Two factors determine whether this occurs. First, is there *support for the operation of teams?* This depends to a large extent on whether managerial support is positive, which can be measured by managers' attitudes, behaviors, and openness to team recommendations that challenge existing norms or practices, along with reward and recognition programs for the team. Second, is there *support for working across functional, divisional, and hierarchical lines?* This reflects organizational and managerial support for and understanding of the value of cross-boundary collaboration and the corresponding values and rewards for participants.

Assessing Team Learning

Watkins and Marsick (1993, 113) believe that assessment is the first step in enhancing team learning, and they provide the following questions to gain understanding of the conditions and processes by which the team functions.

Organizational and team conditions

- To what extent do team members have an opportunity to define and develop the team's objective?
- To what extent is team effort valued over individual achievement?
- To what extent do senior managers support the outcomes of work teams?

Learning processes

- To what extent can team members drop their departmental perspectives and think from an organization-wide perspective?
- To what extent do team members seek out, listen to, and incorporate the perspectives of all team members in analyzing problems?
- To what extent does the team invite people from outside the team to present information and have discussions?

Capturing and transforming learning

- To what extent do members pass on what is learned to people outside the team through informal channels?
- Are there mechanisms to convey the findings from work teams to the right people?
- To what extent are electronic bulletin boards used to ask for help?

Changing Learning Conditions

Changing learning conditions can either originate "from the top," as a means of improving the environment, or from within the teams themselves, by establishing codes of cooperation, engaging in group training or team-building activities, and utilizing group dynamics tools and constant feedback (Watkins and Marsick 1993).

Adversity and challenge present opportunities for major breakthroughs and often require new ways of thinking or approaching situations. Group members are stretched beyond their normal capacity. According to Shipka (1995, 147–148), together they delve into deep inquiry of complex questions and dilemmas and experience the discomfort of not having ready-made answers; members develop unified, resolute, ardent vision and engage in creative problem solving. Thus, group members change, grow, and draw from the deeper, less physical senses—trusting more of what is learned from each other.

Organization Subsystem

According to Marquardt (1996), the second subsystem of a learning organization is the organization itself, which consists of four key dimensions: culture, vision, strategy, and structure.

An organization's *culture* includes its values, beliefs, attitudes, practices, procedures, and customs. A learning organization's culture emphasizes the critical importance of continuous learning—at all levels, functions, and divisions—throughout the firm. Learning is everyone's responsibility and serves as a key component of each and every job, an integral part of all organizational operations. A culture of learning encourages individual and team growth and development by valuing creativity, teamwork, continuous improvement, and self-management.

Vision reveals an organization's goals, objectives, and direction for the future. A learning organization's vision reveals the importance of learning in achieving future goals, building the desired firm, and continuously recreating the company in order to sustain constant growth and development.

Strategy refers to the actions, tactics, and methods used to achieve an organization's vision and goals. In learning organizations, these strategies encourage and maximize the learning acquired, transferred, and utilized in all departments, actions, and initiatives of the firm.

A firm's *structure* entails its configuration of units, departments, and divisions. Learning organizations exhibit seamless, streamlined structures that minimize separation of people and processes while maximizing contact, information flow, and collaboration among individuals and teams.

People Subsystem

The third subsystem of the learning organization includes employees, managers/ leaders, customers, business partners (suppliers, vendors, and subcontractors), and the local community. Each group, valuable to the learning organization, must understand its importance and how it can influence a firm's direction and success. First, employees as learners are empowered and expected to expand their knowledge base, to plan for their future competencies, to take action and risks, and to solve problems. Second, managers/leaders as learners carry out coaching, mentoring, and modeling roles with the primary responsibility of generating and enhancing learning opportunities for the people around them. Third, customers as learners participate in identifying needs, receiving training, and being linked to the learning of the organization. Suppliers and vendors as learners can receive from and contribute to instructional programs. Fourth, alliance partners as learners can benefit by sharing competencies and knowledge. Fifth, community groups as learners include social, educational, and economic agencies that share in the providing and receiving of learning (Marquardt 1996, 26).

Knowledge Subsystem

A learning organization's knowledge subsystem includes its management of acquired, created, stored, transferred, and utilized knowledge within the firm. The knowledge subsystem of organizational learning is ongoing and interactive instead of sequential and independent. The collection and distribution of information occurs through multiple channels, each having different time frames (Marquardt 1996, 90). These include the collection of existing data and information from within and outside the organization (acquisition). It also includes new knowledge that is created within the organization through problem solving and insights (creation) and the coding and preserving of the organization's valued knowledge for easy access by any staff member, at any time, and from anywhere (storage). Finally, it includes the mechanical, electronic, and interpersonal movement of information and knowledge, both intentionally and unintentionally, throughout the organization as well as its application and use by members of the organization (transfer and utilization).

Characteristics of Learning Organizations

Marquardt (1996, 19–20) identifies a number of important dimensions and characteristics of the learning organization:

- Learning is accomplished by organizational systems as a whole, almost as if the organization were a single brain.

- Members of the organization recognize the critical importance of ongoing organization-wide learning for the organization's current and future success.
- Learning is a continuous, strategically used process—integrated with and running parallel to work.
- There is a focus on creativity and generative learning.
- Systems thinking is fundamental.
- People have continuous access to information and data resources that are important to the company's success.
- The corporate climate encourages, rewards, and accelerates individual and group learning.
- Workers network in an innovative, community-like manner inside and outside the organization.
- Change is embraced, while unexpected surprises and even failure are viewed as opportunities to learn.
- The learning organization is agile and flexible.
- Everyone is driven by a desire for quality and continuous improvement.
- Activities are characterized by aspiration, reflection, and conceptualization.
- There are well-developed core competencies that serve as taking-off points for new products and services.
- The learning organization possesses the ability to continuously adapt, renew, and revitalize itself in response to the changing environment.

Conditions Necessary for Building Learning Organizations

According to Thompson (1995, 96), a number of conditions, considered critical success factors, must be present or created within organizations in order to foster an environment in which people feel supported and encouraged to enter a new relationship with learning. He believes that critical success factors include having senior management committed to making learning capability a key part of the organization's ongoing competitive strategy. Another success factor is having a clear blueprint for change and a compelling vision of the desired learning organization that employees feel a part of and excited by. Another factor is having committed leadership willing to model desired changes and to drive fear out of the organization. Organizations also need to institute immediate corrective action with leaders who resist change. Additionally, they need senior management committed to significant investment of time and resources.

Another critical success factor includes having a performance management system that links compensation to achievement of the desired vision. An organizational culture that encourages and acknowledges experimentation, collaboration, innovation, and new paradigm thinking is also essential. At the same time, organizations must have a sense of urgency but resist the temptation to adopt quick fixes. Finally, organizations need to establish multiple feedback structures and learning channels to maximize reinforcement and learning opportunities.

Admittedly, these conditions are very difficult to create in today's complex, fast-paced business world. As a result, organizational leaders must be deeply committed to creating a learning environment and willing to model the approach to learning that they desire for the firm and its members. "All organizational employees must have a clear model for the kind of change that will be required of them as they reorient themselves to learning" (Thompson 1995, 99).

Action Learning

According to Marquardt (1996, 39), "one of the most valuable tools for organizational learning is *action learning*." He describes action learning as "both a process and a powerful program that involves a small group of people solving real problems while at the same time focusing on what they are learning and how their learning can benefit each group member and the organization as a whole" (1999, 4). In his work, Marquardt has built upon the concepts of Reginald Revans, a pioneer of action learning and learning organizations. Revans believed that "there is no learning without action and no action without learning." Thus, the learning equation is: Learning = Programmed Instruction (i.e., knowledge in current use) + Questioning (fresh insights into what is not yet known) or, L = P + Q. "Action learning builds upon the experience and knowledge of an individual or group and the skilled, fresh questioning that results in creative, new knowledge" (Marquardt 1996, 40).

According to Senge (1990), action learning transforms organizations into learning environments. Watkins and Marsick (1993) argue that action learning enables program planners to become learning and change facilitators. Additionally, Rothwell and Cookson (1997) believes action learning captures the power of incidental learning and helps promotes application on the job.

Action learning enables people to effectively learn and to simultaneously handle difficult, real-life situations. By questioning existing knowledge and reflecting on actions engaged in during and after problem solving, individuals, teams, and organizations begin to learn and think critically and, thus, are better able to respond to change.

Action learning helps organizations in a number of ways. It can help improve communications and teamwork and can enhance shared learning throughout various levels of the organization. It can increase participants' self-awareness and self-confidence due to new insights and feedback. Action learning helps employees develop skills and knowledge through the process of reflecting on actions taken when solving real problems. It can facilitate organizational change by encouraging participants to address organizational problems from new perspectives (Marquardt 1996, 1999).

Action learning teams learn from the problems they are solving, which may involve unfamiliar issues. To solve these new problems, past assumptions and actions are challenged. Addressing unusual or unfamiliar situations leads to fresh perspectives and provides individuals and teams with opportunities to learn and apply new approaches.

Characteristics of Action Learning

Marquardt (1999) asserts that action learning teams help create learning organizations because (1) team members develop solutions to problems that serve as valuable information in future problem-solving episodes, and (2) the body of knowledge and the pace of learning increase in organizations that encourage action learning. Marquardt and Reynolds (1994, 23) identify characteristics of action learning that contribute to forming learning organizations:

- Is outcome-oriented
- Is designed to systematically transfer knowledge throughout the organization
- Enables people to learn by doing
- Helps develop learning-how-to-learn skills
- Encourages continual learning
- Creates a culture in which learning becomes a way of life
- Is an active rather than a passive approach
- Is done mainly on the job rather than off the job
- Allows for mistakes and experimentation
- Develops skills of critical reflection and reframing
- Is a mechanism for developing learning skills and behavior
- Demonstrates the benefits of organizational learning
- Models working and learning simultaneously
- Is problem-focused rather than hierarchically bound
- Provides a network for sharing, supporting, giving feedback, and challenging assumptions
- Develops the ability to generate information
- Breaks down barriers between people and across traditional organizational boundaries
- Helps an organization move from a culture of training (in which someone else determines and provides the tools for others' development) to a culture of learning (in which everyone is responsible for his or her own continuous learning)

- Is systems-based
- Applies learning to other parts of the organization as appropriate.

Principles and Skills of Action Learning

The following proven principles of adult learning are demonstrated and practiced as people participate in action learning. First, learning is increased when people reflect on what they experience. Second, people become empowered to seek their own solutions when they are not relying solely on experts. Third, when people are able to question the assumptions on which actions are based, they learn critical thinking skills. Fourth, people learn best when they receive accurate feedback from others. Fifth, the results of one's problem-solving actions provide constructive insight. Sixth, the greatest learning occurs when people work on unfamiliar problems in unfamiliar settings. Seventh, when nonhierarchical groups from across organizational departments and functions are assembled, people are better able to gain new perspectives and, therefore, new learning. Eighth, action learning is most effective when the learners are examining the organizational system as a whole. (Marquardt 1996, 40)

Participants gain several key organizational learning skills via the action learning process. Action learning provides employees new ways of thinking about the organization by addressing unfamiliar problems. It enables employees to develop self-understanding from the feedback of others in the group. Furthermore, action learning helps employees develop critical reflection and reframing skills. These skills can help employees test assumptions that may be preventing them from acting in new and more effective ways. Finally, action learning helps employees acquire teamwork skills as a result of their participation in problem-solving teams (Marquardt 1996, 41)

Action learning proves a valuable tool in addressing a wide variety of problems, from complex issues that impact varied elements of the organization to scenarios that are organizational rather than technical in nature. Examples of problems solvable by action learning include reducing turnover in the workforce, improving information systems and reduction in paperwork, increasing sales by a predetermined amount, and resolving a problem between research and development and production. Additionally, action learning can be helpful in increasing the use of computers in a company, reorganizing a department, closing a production or line, and improving productivity in retailing or manufacturing companies (Marquardt 1996, 41).

Learning Capacity

Action learning teaches individuals how to learn effectively as well as how to learn about and for oneself. In action learning groups, learning occurs at the individual, team, and organizational levels. Whether individually or as a team, learners think and create, generating valuable knowledge and taking action as a result of analysis of complex issues.

According to Redding (1994), action learning also involves learning in three dimensions. Action learning accounts for how fast the group is able to move through the learning cycle (i.e., planning, implementing, and reflecting) and complete each iteration (speed of learning). It also accounts for how well the group is able to learn at the end of each iteration of the cycle by questioning underlying assumptions and improving the capacity to learn in the future (depth of learning). Finally, action learning accounts for how extensively the group is able to transfer the new insights and knowledge derived from each iteration of the learning cycle to other issues and other parts of organizational, team, or individual life (breadth of learning).

Components of an Action Learning

Marquardt (1999, 5) asserts that action learning programs derive their power and benefits from six interactive and interdependent components: (1) the problem, (2) the group, (3) the questioning and reflection process, (4) the resolution to take action, (5) the commitment to learning, and (6) the facilitator. He asserts that the success of action learning relies on the effective interaction of these six elements.

The Problem. The problem (concern, issue, task, or project) serves as the catalyst for action learning and may emerge at the individual, team, or organization level (Pedler 1991). The problem should represent a significant, relevant concern to the action learner(s), be within his/her/their responsibility, and provide opportunities for testing current or new knowledge that will lead to reflection and learning.

The Group. The ideal action learning group/team is composed of four to eight individuals whose challenge involves examining a pertinent organizational problem for which there is no easily identifiable solution. To guarantee fresh perspectives and unbiased input, groups should be comprised of a variety of people—from those in cross-functional departments to individuals outside the organization (stakeholders, such as customers or vendors).

The Questioning and Reflection Process. Questioning is one of the most difficult skills to master and is a critical task of action learning teams. Open questions (How? Why?) encourage the free flow of information, whereas closed questions (Does? How many? Which?) solicit one-word answers that clarify thoughts and direct focus. Used in combination, open and closed questions reveal what individuals and the team do or do not know and help clarify the nature of the problem. Reflection follows, which allows the team to identifying possible solutions before taking action.

The Resolution to Take Action.   Reflection is powerless without action, for implementation reveals whether or not reflection is accurate and learning has taken place. Action learners must have the authority to initiate action themselves or be assured that their recommendations will be implemented, absent any significant change within the firm or in the group's critical information. Action aids learning by providing a basis for reflection.

The Commitment to Learning.   Learning is equally important as action in action learning, which emphasizes task accomplishment concurrently with individual, team, and organizational learning and development. Failure to commit to learning relegates action learning teams to simple task groups.

The Facilitator.   Facilitators help action learning teams reflect on their learning by directing discussion regarding participant listening skills, ability to reframe problems, the feedback process, planning and organization, how assumptions and values may shape their beliefs and actions, individual and group achievements or difficulties, processes being employed, and implications of each. The facilitator may be a member of the group who is familiar with the issue or may be an external advisor who possesses facilitation skills for action learning.

Steps in Action Learning

In contrast, Pedler (1991) believes the basis of action learning is a spiral consisting of nine dependent steps:

1. Transitioning from earlier action to learning—taking into account previous life experiences
2. Identifying the problem—learning happens in response to a problem or crisis
3. Taking ownership of a learning experience—accepting responsibility for planned learning
4. Creating a learning system—developing a support system for learning (i.e., individual and small groups) used to facilitate learning acquisition and transfer
5. Establishing contact over time—working cohesively with others to overcome a problem or crisis
6. Addressing conflict and tension—adjusting to various phases of groups (i.e., forming, storming, norming, performing) to maximize learning

7. Developing identity—creating a learning identity through group cohesiveness and togetherness
8. Making a transition—consolidating learning through debriefings at the end of a learning project
9. Preparing for later action and learning—planning for future learning to meet needs identified during the action learning experience

Applications of Action Learning

Action learning, according to Marquardt (1999, 5), may be applied simultaneously to the five most important needs facing organizations today: problem solving, organizational learning, team building, leadership development, and professional growth and career development. Action learning programs find solutions to complex organizational problems—the more difficult the problem, the better suited action learning is to meeting the challenge (problem solving). Action learning is the DNA of organizational learning; the action learning team serves as a model and an impetus for individual, group, and company-wide learning (organizational learning). Action learning helps develop strong teams and builds skills for individuals to work effectively in future teams (team building). It has become the premier way for training future and current managers in organizations throughout the world because it prepares and develops leaders to deal with real problems (leadership development). Action learning helps employees develop high levels of self-awareness; self-development and continuous learning are gained via action learning (professional growth and career development).

Principles of Learning Enhanced by Action Learning

"Solving a problem provides important, immediate, short-term benefits to an organization or individual. The greater, longer-term benefit of action learning, however, is the learning gained by the group members and the application of their learning on a system-wide basis throughout the organization and/or in other parts of their lives" (Marquardt 1999, 35). In essence, lessons learned via action learning are more valuable than problem solution. Through the process of action learning, individuals become responsible and accountable for their own learning and development and, ultimately, that of the team and the organization.

Unique, unfamiliar situations present individuals, teams, and organizations with optimal learning opportunities. When confronted by the unfamiliar, learners rely on past experiences to shed light on possible approaches, formulate concepts in different ways, and seek new information relevant to the current problem. Thus, action learning exemplifies numerous learning principles:

- Learning is increased when we are asked questions (or ask ourselves questions).
- Learning intensifies when we reflect on what we did in the experience.
- Greater learning occurs when we are given time and space to deal with problems and reflect on our decisions, when a sense of urgency exists, when we can see results, when we are allowed to take risks, and when we are encouraged and supported in our deliberations.
- We can learn critically when we are able to question the assumptions on which our actions are based.
- We learn when we receive accurate feedback from others and from the results of our problem-solving actions.
- When we do not rely solely on experts, we become empowered to seek our own solutions.
- Nonhierarchical groups from across organizational departments and functions are often better able to gain new perspectives and therefore augment learning.
- Action learning is most effective when learners are examining the organizational system as a whole.
- Group responsibility for the task empowers the members and enhances learning.
- We are most challenged when we work on unfamiliar problems in unfamiliar settings, where we can unfreeze some of our previous ways of doing things and develop new ways of thinking.
- By working cooperatively with others on real issues, the group can move to a higher level of learning relative to application, synthesis, and evaluation.
- People learn when they do something, and they learn more as they feel more responsible for their task.

Action learning is built upon the entire learning cycle: learning and creating knowledge through concrete experience, observing and identifying the problem, reflecting on this experience, experimenting, analyzing and forming generalizations from experiments, planning solutions, testing the implications of the generalizations in new experiences, and beginning the process again (Marquardt 1999, 35–36).

Conclusion

Organizational learning has become a critical professional practice domain within HRD. However, it is often confused with the learning organization. The following explanation provided by Marquardt (1996, 19) furnishes some critical insight:

A learning organization, systematically defined, is an organization that learns powerfully and collectively and is continually transforming itself to better collect, manage, and use knowledge for corporate success. It empowers people within and outside the company to learn as they work. . . . [When we refer to] learning organizations, we are focusing on the *what*, and are describing the systems, principles, and characteristics of organizations that learn and produce as a collective entity. Organizational learning, on the other hand, refers to *how* organizational learning occurs, i.e., the skills and processes of building and utilizing knowledge.

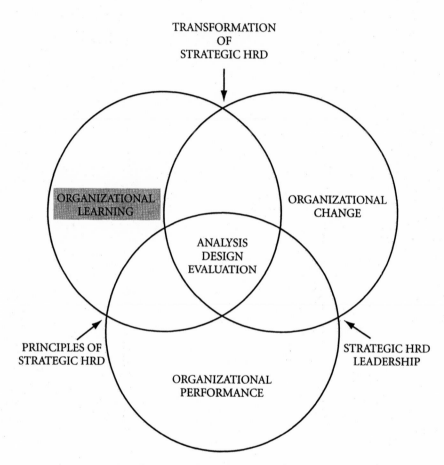

TRANSFORMATION
OF
STRATEGIC HRD

ORGANIZATIONAL
LEARNING

ORGANIZATIONAL
CHANGE

ANALYSIS
DESIGN
EVALUATION

PRINCIPLES OF
STRATEGIC HRD

STRATEGIC HRD
LEADERSHIP

ORGANIZATIONAL
PERFORMANCE

ORGANIZATIONAL LEARNING, PERFORMANCE, AND CHANGE

CHAPTER 6

Learning in Organizations

Learning is the crucial component in the transformation from the traditional organization to the developmental organization. The learning process itself promotes continuous organizational renewal and improved performance capacity. Without learning, individual, team, and organizational growth and development cannot occur.

Learning has been defined as "knowledge obtained by self-directed study and/or experience; the art of acquiring knowledge, skills, competencies, attitudes, and ideas retained and used; a change of behavior through experience" (Gilley and Eggland 1989, 120–121). Most agree that true learning occurs when an overt action results—and is demonstrated when behavior changes. Individuals reflect upon experiences and consequences, consider results of actions, and learn lessons accordingly. According to Marsick, Volpe, and Watkins (1999, 92), the first step toward enhancing learning in organizations is to become more "intentional about (1) what one wants to learn (learning goals); (2) how this learning will help further one's own life or career goals and those of the organization (without assuming that these goals are always congruent); and (3) how one can best accomplish this kind of learning, given differences in learning styles, personality and motivation variables, and constraints within the organization."

Learning focuses on building developmental capacity at the individual, team, and organizational levels. As a result, each level produces new outcomes while continuously growing and developing.

To better understand the learning process in organizations, four critical questions must be answered. First, who is responsible for learning in the firm? Second, what type of learning occurs in organizations? Third, what phases of the learning process must be addressed to enhance individual employee capability and performance capacity? Fourth, how do learning process phases explain the types of learning engagements occurring within organizations? Four approaches address these questions: (1) determine who is responsible for learning in organizations, (2) identify the type of learning in organizations, (3) identify the five phases of the learning process, and (4) apply the learning process model.

Who Is Responsible for Learning in Organizations?

In many organizations the responsibility for learning belongs to a specialized group known as training and development practitioners, who are regarded as experts in the design, development, and presentation of training programs. Most training and development practitioners possess excellent communications skills, enthusiastic and energetic personalities, and a solid foundation in adult learning theory and practice. Unfortunately, this highly talented group of professionals has limited impact on improving organizational performance because they are not held accountable for employee learning, growth, development, or performance. Utilization of new knowledge, skills, or competencies—in essence, learning—is beyond the scope of their responsibility and accountability.

Who should be responsible for the growth and development of the organization's most important asset—its employees? *Managers.* According to Gilley and Boughton (1996) organizations should hold managers accountable for employee performance and productivity. It follows, then, that managers should also be charged with learning, since the learning process underlies improvements in employee performance and productivity. Effective managers employ interpersonal and communications expertise to secure results through people, which are the same critical skills necessary to be influential in the learning process. Managers who fail to possess these skills or are unable to acquire them shouldn't be managers at all.

If managers are responsible for learning, what role do training and development practitioners hold in the learning organization? Given their expertise, training and development practitioners are excellent employee champions, performance consultants, and change agents. Training and development professionals in these roles are able to forge learning partnerships that improve employee performance and organizational productivity through developmental engagements. Partnerships such as these require training and development professionals to team with managers as facilitators of the learning process, teach managers the intricacies of facilitating the learning process, and help managers perfect their training and development skills. Doing so allows training and development professionals to concentrate on designing and implementing developmental activities if managers are not qualified to function as instructional designers.

Since the learning process consists of both the dissemination of information and the facilitation of learning, managers will occasionally be responsible for providing employees with new information or encouraging them to initiate self-directed learning activities to deepen their experiences and understandings. The Latin root words for education refer to the infilling *(educere)* and drawing out *(educare)* of information and content. Chadwick (1982) refers to the process of disseminating information as infilling, while drawing out involves activities and experiences.

The purpose of infilling, whereby managers present ideas, facts, concepts, theories, and data, typically with little interaction between themselves and employees, is to increase employees' reservoir of knowledge. Drawing out, which emphasizes interaction between managers and employees via use of activities or discussion, refers to the application of ideas, facts, concepts, theories, and data, based upon employees' experiences and background. Effective learning partnerships are founded on these two critical approaches.

Types of Learning in Organizations

Adaptive Learning

According to Marquardt (1996, 38), adaptive learning occurs when an individual or organization learns from experience and reflection. He believes the process in adaptive learning is as follows: (1) the organization takes an action intended to further an identified organizational goal; (2) the action results in some internal or external outcome; (3) the resultant change is analyzed for congruence with the goal; and (4) a new action or a modification of the previous action is initiated based on the outcome.

Adaptive learning can be either single-loop or double-loop learning. Marquardt (1996, 38) writes that:

> single-loop learning is focused on gaining information to stabilize and maintain existing systems where the emphasis is error detection and correction. Single-loop learning is concerned with obtaining direct solutions to the immediate problems or roadblocks encountered by the individual or organization. Single-loop learning is by far the one and only loop learning used in most organizations today. Double-loop learning is more in-depth and involves questioning the system itself and why the errors or successes occurred in the first place. Double-loop learning looks at deeper organizational norms and structures. It raises questions about their validity in terms of organization, action, and results.

Most organizations are unwilling to engage in double-loop learning because it involves disclosure of errors and mistakes as well as the questioning of existing assumptions, norms, structures, and processes (Argyris and Schon 1996; Schein 1992).

Self-Directed Learning

Knowles (1975, 18) suggests that the term self-directed learning refers to a process in which individuals take the lead "in diagnosing their learning needs, formulating learning goals, identifying human and material resources for learning, choosing and implementing appropriate teaming strategies, and evaluating learning outcomes." The following steps can be used in designing a learning plan: (1) What is the question I want to answer? (2) What are the data I need to answer this question? (3) What are the most appropriate and feasible sources of these data? (4) What are the most efficient and effective means I can use to collect these data from these sources? (5) How shall I organize and analyze these data to get an answer to my question? (6) How will I report my answer and test its validity (Knowles 1975, 25)?

Knowles (1975, 62) suggests a somewhat more elaborate and rigorous format known as a learning contract, which is a binding agreement between two or more individuals consisting of four parts: learning objectives, learning resources and strategies, evidence of accomplishment, and criteria and means of validating evidence. However, self-directed learning is not as easy as it looks. As Marsick, Volpe, and Watkins (1999, 92) contend, "for reasons internal to the learner or extrinsic in the environment (or both), . . . many people are not in the habit of continuously learning and may need help developing the skills needed to plan and carry out learning initiatives."

Experiential Learning

Another instructional approach is to use structural exercises or experiential learning designed to utilize the experiences of the learners. Some HRD professionals, however, prefer simply to expose learners to knowledge, using such traditional content-oriented techniques as the lecture. According to Dean and Gilley (1986), these individuals do not use experiential exercises for three reasons: (1) they do not know when it is appropriate to use the exercise, (2) they do not know how to plan and design such an exercise, and (3) they are unsure about how to achieve closure following the exercise. Some HRD professionals do not recognize experiential learning as a valid method of formal instruction because their training was only in traditional, content-oriented approaches. Others recognize the value of the experiential approach, but they lack the energy needed to design and present experiential exercises. Experiential learning is appropriate (1) to develop highly complex cognitive skills such as decisionmaking, evaluating, and synthesizing; (2) to positively impact the learners' values, beliefs, or attitudes; (3) to induce empathy (understanding); (4) to sharpen interpersonal communication skills; and (5) to unlearn negative attitudes or behaviors (Kolb 1984; Thiagarajan 1980, 38).

According to Gilley and Eggland (1989, 140–141), implementing an experiential exercise consist of five distinct stages: (1) experiencing (doing the activity); (2) publishing (sharing reactions, observations, and emotions from the activity); (3) processing (discussing the group dynamics that occurred during the activity); (4) generalizing (inferring principles from the activity that relate to the real world); and (5) applying (planning more effective behavior for actual use in the real world). During the learning activity, HRD professionals or managers (change agent or trainer) act as facilitators, guiding the individual learner or the group through each element of the learning cycle.

Transformative Learning

Transformative learning is directed at personal change (Mezirow 1991). Unfortunately, it is often undervalued and unrecognized in favor of demonstrated performance. Transformative learning is central to one's ability or motivation to learn about the organization or the job. Gilley and Eggland (1989, 33) suggest that "this type of learning takes on additional salience in managerial development, since many of the abilities needed by middle and senior level managers are moderated by a manager's view of the world and his or her place in it."

Learning takes place through a process Mezirow (1981) originally identified as "perspective transformation." Mezirow (1991) maintains that adults reconstitute the meaning perspective by which they order their understanding of themselves and their world, which enables them to obtain further insight into their own values and belief systems, as well as achieve greater self-assurance and self-esteem. He (1997) has referred to this as "frames of reference that define a person's world." Marsick, Volpe, and Watkins (1999, 93) contend that

> frames of reference are broad, comprehensive habits of mind that show up in different situations as a point of view that shapes interpretation of a specific event. Frames of reference and points of view can be psychological, political, social, cultural, economic, or epistemological. . . . Frames of mind are reflected in pedagogical choices, such as choice of reading material or learning activities, selection of people to answer questions—or to work on particular projects, and even in seating arrangements.

Therefore, learners need to cultivate their ability to identify and critique the assumptions behind their actions in order to transform their thinking and future behavior and action (i.e., improving their performance). Schwinn (1997) refers to this process as "assumption testing."

The introspection process just described is often referred to as critical reflective learning (Schon 1987; Brookfield 1987). It is essential to adaptive learning, self-directive learning, and experiential learning. The notion of critical reflective learning can impact the way an HRD professional designs learning and performance improvement interventions as well as encourage the continuous assumptions, values, and beliefs testing so essential to organization development (Preskill and Torres 1999).

Five Phases of the Learning Process in Organizations

According to Gilley and Maycunich (2000), the learning process consists of five phases. In the following, we examine each phase and demonstrate how each is critical to enhancing organizational renewal through learning.

Phase 1: Preparation for learning
Phase 2: Information exchange process
Phase 3: Knowledge acquisition and practice process
Phase 4: Transfer and integration process
Phase 5: Accountability and recognition process (Figure 6.1)

Preparing for Learning

For learning to be effective, organizations must adequately prepare for the acquisition of new knowledge in order to ensure significance, reflection, and application (Figure 6.1). The following four elements must be addressed adequately in preparation for learning: learning readiness, self-direction, linkage, designing knowledge acquisition plans.

Learning Readiness.   Individuals must be ready, willing, and able prior to successful engagement in any activity, especially learning. Individuals, teams, and organizations receptive to and excited about learning acquire knowledge, engage in actions, and reflect on outcomes by allowing their natural curiosity and analytical skills to surface (Caffarella 1993). Individuals seek learning experiences to cope with specific life-changing events; hence, practical learning processes encourage employee participation (Zemke and Zemke 1995). Learning organizations understand learner receptivity and create conditions by which individual and team learning flourishes, which ultimately influences organizational learning and prosperity. Conversely, if organizations fail to acknowledge employee readiness or accept their innate motivation for learning, subsequent facilitation and developmental activities will fall short of achieving desired ends.

Understanding learning readiness requires examination of how individuals focus on learning, beginning with attention, which has been defined as directing one's mind on an internal or external object. Internal attention involves reflecting on the meaning of an idea or recalling a past experience. External attention regards observing formal procedures or the execution of a specific skill. Gilley and

FIGURE 6.1 Five Phases of the Learning and Change Process and Its Impact

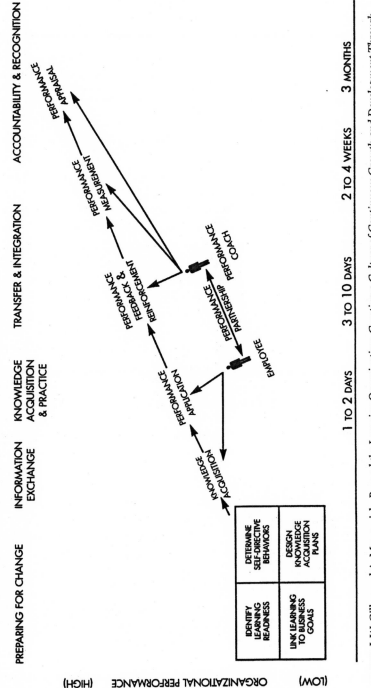

SOURCE: J. W. Gilley and A. Maycunich, *Beyond the Learning Organization: Creating a Culture of Continuous Growth and Development Through State-of-the-Art Human Resource Practices* (Cambridge, Mass.: Perseus Publishing, 2000).

Eggland (1989) maintain that learning captures three types of attention—passive, active, and secondary passive, each of which reveals understanding of learning readiness.

Passive attention occurs when individuals exert little or no effort, and often react instinctively, by simply following the strongest present stimulus. Passively attentive individuals rarely concentrate effectively and hold little or no interest in learning or remembering information being shared.

Active attention refers to choosing between two stimuli by consciously selecting the appropriate one and concentrating accordingly (Gregory [1884] 1978). In learning situations, managers may employ a variety of methods such as role-plays, group discussions, simulations, or demonstrations to focus participants' attention. Active attention promotes easier mastery of skills and retention of information but requires, however, tremendous dedication and exertion of energy. Learning organizations and their managers utilize active attention strategically and in relatively short, manageable periods of time so as not to exhaust learners.

Secondary passive attention, like passive attention, involves little or no effort on the part of learners as knowledge or skills are interesting in and of themselves. In secondary passive attention, learners focus on the subject matter, which they perceive to be fascinating, challenging, and somewhat enjoyable—in essence, a pleasant learning experience. Effective learning managers appeal to workers' personal interests whenever possible, adapt the length of developmental activities so as not to completely exhaust learner attention, employ diverse presentation methods to arouse and maintain participant attention, minimize distractions, and encourage learner participation in the design, development, and implementation of learning activities. Learning facilitators may enhance secondary passive attention by posing thought-provoking questions prior to each interaction with learners and by pausing until focus returns whenever concentration wanes or has been interrupted.

Two primary detractors of attention are apathy and distraction. Apathy refers to the learner's lack of interest in a topic or activity, whereas distraction occurs when outside stimuli distract one's attention. Learning organizations assess individual interests and goals to ensure alignment between participant and learning objectives, while concurrently guaranteeing undisturbed focus for employees on the learning event.

Self-Direction.   Learning and change flourish when individuals are autonomous, self-directed learners. Self-direction means taking control of learning situations and teaching oneself about a particular subject. Knowles, Holton, and Swanson (1998, 135) define autonomy as "taking control of the goals and purposes of learning, and assuring ownership of learning—leading to an internal change of consciousness in which the learner views knowledge as contextual, and fully questions what is learned."

Autonomous, self-directed learning and change activities allow employees to take responsibility for their own destinies (Brockett and Hiemstra 1991). Self-directed learners seek assistance via networks and resources to maximize personal growth and development. Further, Knowles (1975) believes that self-directed learners must be able to differentiate assumptions about learners and the skills required in teacher-directed learning versus those of self-directed learning. They need to view themselves as independent, self-determining, autonomous, and self-directing and must possess the ability to relate to peers collaboratively, seeing them as resources for diagnosing needs, planning learning and change activities, and providing feedback or constructive criticism when necessary. They should also be able to diagnose their own learning needs realistically with the assistance of peers and other resources, translate learning needs into performance objectives via formats that ensure their accomplishment, and relate to managers as facilitators, helpers, and change agents, taking initiative to utilize them as resources. Finally, learners should be able to identify human and material resources appropriate for different types of performance objectives, identify and select effective strategies for making use of learning resources, implement these tactics skillfully and with initiative, and collect and validate evidence that demonstrates accomplishment of their performance objectives.

Linkage.   Organizational leaders, managers, human resource professionals, and employees must link all learning and change activities to the firm's strategic business goals and objectives to become developmental. From this perspective, linking learning and change to strategic goals and objectives ensures that all employees focus on developmental results critical to the firm's success (Brinkerhoff and Gill 1994). Learning and change that fails to support achievement of organizational goals and objectives ceases to be of value.

Each business unit, department, and division must link its goals to the organization's strategic business goals and objectives. Doing so enables each manager and employee to understand how achieving his or her personal performance goals and objectives ultimately drives the organization's success. Focusing on business results permits employees to feel more like owners and to participate accordingly.

Designing Knowledge Acquisition and Transfer Plans.   Organizations can prepare their employees for learning and change by collaboratively creating knowledge acquisition and transfer plans. These plans are used to help employees attain performance results that enable them to accomplish their personal goals and objectives (see Chapter 16).

Information Exchange

During information exchange, content is taught to or acquired by learners. Content includes any information designed to enhance an employee's performance capacity (Figure 6.1). The information exchange process allows employees to obtain content necessary to improve their knowledge, skills, or behaviors. This process incorporates five interrelated elements: the learning environment, the learning agent, the adult learner, the communications process, and the instruction process.

The Learning Environment.   The learning environment must support the free exchange of ideas and feelings and allow learners to feel secure and to participate in open two-way communications (Hiemstra 1991). A nonthreatening, comfortable environment nurtures individual growth and development, demonstrates deep concern for employee well-being, and improves interpersonal relationships.

Developmental managers exhibit empathy, acceptance, and understanding by creating learning environments that are participative and respectful, yet dynamic. Managers are able to build lasting relationships with their subordinates, deepen their understanding of employees' developmental needs and the risks associated with acquiring new knowledge and skills, carefully protect employees' self-esteem, and create trust that brings about honesty and candor.

The Learning Agent.   The individual responsible for presenting information to employees in a meaningful, manageable way is the learning agent (Brookfield 1994). Learning agents combine knowledge of the subject with job experience to help employees apply new information on the job.

A manager's knowledge and experience are his or her tools. Competent, well-prepared, passionate managers inspire others, awakening in their employees the desire to learn, grow, and develop. Enthusiasm, combined with knowledge, subconsciously fuels employees' interest and curiosity and can be quite contagious. Inexperienced managers, on the other hand, lack the knowledge and experience necessary to garner employee respect, trust, or confidence and, thus, are ineffective.

Effective learning agents relate information to their employees' lives, illustrating new ideas in terms of common experiences that provide individuals with familiar references (Marquardt 1999). They present information in a logical order, from simple to complex, so that learners are better able to grasp difficult concepts. Learning agents devote time to study for each learning session, which helps them gather fresh perspectives and insight prior to engagement with employees. Finally, they recruit allies to assist in motivating employees to acquire developmental perspectives throughout their careers.

Unfortunately, many managers lack or fail to adequately develop learning agent competencies. One reason is their mistaken belief that employees are solely responsible for their own growth and development and that management has no role in their subordinates' success. Managers such as these are often indifferent and ill prepared to teach employees new and innovative ways to approach their work—potentially harming current job performance and future developmental potential. Poor organization skills and lack of planning (for learning) by managers further hinders employee learning and development.

Role of Learning Facilitator

The facilitator's role in learning is essential for maximizing learning opportunities. The facilitator's main purposes are to assist individuals or groups in learning events and to help participants maintain their commitment to the learning process (Marquardt 1999). They act as a catalyst for learners, "position" the importance of learning and, specifically, the current engagement, and orient participants to the fundamentals of learning (e.g., all individuals have valuable experiences and insight to share, listening to the views of others is essential, etc.). Facilitators then take on the responsibility of mentor to learners, allowing individuals to explore and uncover their own learning. They do this by questioning, confronting, encouraging, and supporting learners, thereby acting as mirrors that reflect learning opportunities back to participants. As a result, facilitators greatly influence the ultimate success of individual and group learners by providing perspectives regarding the learning that has occurred.

Facilitators focus primarily on processes, ensuring that all learners are permitted adequate time to voice their experiences, opinions, concerns, and reflections (Marquardt 1999). Facilitators encourage support among participants, guiding their reflection on problem solving, personal learning, and application of this new insight to their individual work or organizational challenges. In group situations, facilitators help members examine their group behavior, including how they listen, provide each other with feedback, develop solutions, plan activities, and challenge one another.

Modes of Facilitation

At the start of learning engagements, facilitators play a key role in guiding and directing how individuals and groups function. As time progresses, facilitators help individuals assume increasing responsibility for their learning, thus encouraging their autonomy. Heron (1989) identified three modes of facilitation, which reveal how facilitators can move from a directive to a less authoritarian role:

Hierarchical: The facilitator directs the learning process by clarifying procedural questions, learner goals, and appropriate participant behaviors. In this mode, already, the facilitator encourages learners to support, question, and challenge one another.

Cooperative: As individual confidence with the learning process increases, the facilitator shares power and dynamics with participants or the group. Individuals and groups no longer require the facilitator to help them implement learning processes and procedures. The facilitator will, however, address issues that harm or help learning not yet noticed by members.

Autonomous: In this mode individuals are on their own, enlisting others for encouragement, clarification, or as sounding boards of reflection. The facilitator subtly creates and supports the conditions that allow participants to direct and determine their own learning. A group may or may not, at this point, be ready to self-facilitate learning.

How Facilitation Accelerates the Learning and Development Process

Effective facilitators help individuals learn how to learn on their own and create new meaning. They focus their attention on increasing ability and the speed with which individuals learn by engaging in the following four key activities: asking questions, breaking up complex ideas and tasks into smaller parts, "testing" to see how much or what one has learned, and focusing learning on a specific goal or action (Heiman and Slomianko 1990).

Facilitators help individuals and groups implement each of these activities, which increases the quality and rapidity of their learning. They also assist participant learning by making the process explicit, thereby allowing learners to become more conscious of the process, outcomes, and possible applications (McGill and Beaty 1995). Finally, facilitators are instrumental in reflection. As Boud, Keogh, and Walker (1985) note, the reflection process is one that learners can only learn for themselves; it is an intentional event. Reflection is a complex activity in which feelings and cognition are closely interrelated and interactive, and it is part of a cyclical process.

Facilitators enhance the reflection process by reviewing and replaying experiences, addressing feelings associated with experiences, and reevaluating experiences in light of participants' descriptions and feelings. Attention to all aspects of an experience reveals its potential for learners.

Internal, External, and Self-Facilitation

Learning facilitation may occur in a variety of ways. The role of facilitator may be assigned to someone within the organization (internal facilitation), outside the organization (external facilitation), or rotated among participants (self-facilitation).

External facilitators tend to lack the biases harbored by learning participants or internal facilitators. Thus, they are able to remain objective and focus on critical processes and issues surrounding the learning experience. Caution should be exercised during internally or self-facilitated sessions as the facilitator may lose necessary objectivity. For this reason, the facilitator should not be involved in questioning, reflecting, and decisionmaking.

Facilitators are particularly effective if they are able to help individuals and groups focus on learning, question their current assumptions, or overcome negative past experiences (Marquardt 1999). Again, it is often the external facilitator who is able to offer unbiased advice and direction regarding patterns of thinking, behavior, options, and possible insight. Many learning groups may not need an external facilitator once they understand the principles of learning and have changed their ways of functioning as a group. Effective facilitators allow and encourage group members to assume this function, after which the facilitator can exit from the group. Some organizations believe that a facilitator is necessary for individual or team learning and growth; others provide facilitators "by invitation only"—at the request of the learners.

Self-facilitated groups encourage each member to take and share responsibility for facilitation. Some organizations utilize staff as facilitators or rotate the role of facilitator to develop as many employees as possible with these competencies.

Questions for Improving Facilitation

Certainly, facilitation is a challenging endeavor. Facilitators can better prepare for this exciting role by addressing the following questions:

1. What is the need for the learning intervention?
2. Who is the client or sponsor?
3. What are the expectations and commitment of the client or sponsor?
4. What other key decisionmakers in the organization have an interest in this intervention?
5. What are their expectations?
6. What is the scope of the learning intervention?
7. What is the time frame of the learning intervention?
8. What other individuals or groups may be affected by the learning intervention?
9. What are their expectations?
10. What related learning interventions have been implemented in the organization?
11. What were the results?
12. What sources of support exist for the learning intervention?
13. What are the possible constraints to the intervention?
14. What other economic, political, or cultural factors may affect the success of the intervention? (Spitzer 1992)

The Adult Learner.   The topic of adult learning continues to generate much research and debate. In the early 1960s and 1970s, Malcolm Knowles identified several assumptions necessary to the art and science of helping adults learn, which he termed "andragogy." First, adults need to know *why* learning a new skill, acquiring new knowledge, or changing their behavior is important. Adults want purpose, combined with thorough, thoughtful explanations as to why the proposed learning is necessary and how it will benefit them.

Second, adults desire control over their actions and the ability to influence outcomes (Merriam and Caffarella 1991). Thus, learning and change must support adult learners' self-concepts. Third, adults possess a wealth of personal and professional experiences that are invaluable to the learning process. Adult learners benefit by sharing these experiences and interacting with each other.

Knowles (1975) maintains that adults are pragmatic, desiring learning intended to help them cope with real-life situations. In fact, Knowles contrasted adult learners with children and adolescents via their orientation to learning: adults are life centered (task or problem centered), whereas children and adolescents are subject centered. Adults are motivated to learn to the extent the learning will help them perform tasks or deal with problems confronted in their lives (Knowles, Holton, and Swanson 1998).

Adults are very responsive to external motivation such as promotions, advancements, increased compensation, recognition, and other rewards. Knowles, Holton, and Swanson (1998) contend that the most potent motivators are intrinsic, enabling adult learners to increase their job satisfaction, self-esteem, and quality of life while acting on and demonstrating their values and beliefs. Organizations must consider these motivators when determining appropriate recognition and rewards for employees who engage in learning activities. Further, adult learners respond favorably to positive reinforcement, embracing honest, factual, constructive feedback designed to improve their skills, abilities, and competencies (Merriam and Brockett 1997).

Most adults respond positively to authority and demonstrate respect, yet some learners will test change agents until credibility is established or fear (of learning, of change) is eliminated (Galbraith 1991). Adult learners abide by a set of guiding principles, values, attitudes, and beliefs that affects their behaviors; thus, contrary learning or change activities may be challenged if perceived negatively.

Finally, adult learner personal and professional experiences, relationships, assumptions, beliefs, and values can either accelerate or impede the learning and change process. When past experiences pose negative predisposition to development, problem isolation and correction are necessary to alter these assumptions and maximize learning opportunities.

Zemke and Zemke (1995) identified twelve principles of adult learning to be considered when providing individuals with organizational learning opportunities.

Adults tend to be problem centered in their outlook. Adults want programs that address their immediate personal and professional problems. Effective program planning may query participants about the problems they are currently facing in their lives or on the job. Rothwell and Cookson (1997, 119) assert that HRD professionals may wish to consider questions such as the following: What problems are participants presently facing that relate to their lives and work? How can these problems focus program design and delivery? HRD professionals can then plan instruction around how to deal with the practical problems facing learners.

Adult learners can be motivated by personal growth or gain. Adults are also motivated by a desire to improve their lives or future job prospects. How will learners benefit from instruction? What do they *want* in terms of benefits? Appeals to self-interest will often work; hence, participants should be questioned about their interests and desires for personal gain. Rothwell and Cookson (1997, 119–120) encourage HRD professionals to ask the following: What do learners want to know about a program? Why do they want to know it? How can the information they want be obtained? Addressing these questions enables HRD professionals to develop keen insights about participants and design learning experiences to meet their wants and needs.

Motivation to learn can be increased. HRD professionals can enhance participants' motivation to learn by helping learners understand how a program will benefit them. Important questions to consider include the following: What are the participants' present levels of motivation to learn? How obvious are program benefits to participants? What can be done to increase participant motivation? (Rothwell and Cookson 1997, 120).

Preprogram assessment is important. Effective program planning begins by assessing HRD professionals' knowledge of the program's subject matter and by determining their competencies. In addition, what is the current knowledge and experience level of participants? Program failures are sometimes linked to planners making incorrect assumptions about the participants' level of knowledge or experience.

Exercises and cases in programs should be realistic and should stem from the experiences and work settings to which program participants can relate. Activity success is closely tied to the relevancy to learners' lives or work. Thus, HRD professionals should examine the environment in which program participants will apply what they learn.

Feedback and recognition should be planned. Learners should be provided with ample opportunity to receive feedback on their learning progress. As a result, HRD professionals will need to know their participants well. In particular, they should encourage the kind and frequency of feedback and recognition likely to be successful with learners.

Planned learning experiences should, when possible, account for learning-style differences. Individuals learn in different ways. HRD professionals should identify participants' learning styles, account for differences, and incorporate them into program design. Learning style assessment may include surveys, questionnaires, or one-on-one discussions.

Program designs should accommodate adults' continued growth and changing values. Adult interests and needs change throughout their lives. Effective program design adapts to these changes. Discovering participants' values, including what they want and why (values clarification), allows HRD professionals to isolate issues associated with those values that will correspond with participants' needs.

Program plans should include transfer strategies. Participants should be encouraged to apply learning on the job. Broad and Newstrom (1992) identified numerous transfer strategies, including having participants bring a work project to be completed on the job, having participants write a letter to a supervisor to pledge on-the-job behavior change resulting from what was learned, and having participants write a performance contract with the trainer, pledging to change specific on-the-job behaviors.

Adults need a safe and comfortable environment in which to learn. What is considered safe and comfortable by participants in one program may be quite different from what participants in another program consider safe or comfortable (Zemke and Zemke 1995). For example, "safe" may mean that participants do not feel threatened with physical or mental harm during the program or in the environment surrounding it. Or "safe" may mean that they are able to practice their new knowledge or skills on the job, without fear of the consequences. One of the authors worked for a firm that reprimanded a supervisor for speaking out about low company morale during a weekly staff meeting. Obviously, this action sent a powerful message throughout the division—don't discuss poor morale (which was caused by working conditions), bury it. "Comfortable" can also have a range of meanings—from the types of chairs used to the psychological climate of the setting. Those who are comfortable with their peers will be more likely to express ideas, opinions, and concerns more freely.

For adults, facilitation tends to be more effective than lectures. Various research indicates that the adult attention span averages eight to twenty minutes and that adults prefer to be involved. Facilitation focuses on group interaction, encouraging collaboration among learners and self-directed learning climates. Hence, facilitators who work to achieve effective group interaction eventually foster a climate in which participants can learn on their own.

Activity promotes understanding and retention. It is most effective to introduce learners to a topic and provide them with opportunities to work in small groups on an action-oriented problem situation. Group members should then share their approaches to the problem situation. The facilitator's role is to encourage discussion and information sharing.

Davis (1984) identified several characteristics of adults useful when designing or delivering learning. Adults are people who have a good deal of firsthand experience; have established habits and strong tastes; possess some amount of pride; hold very tangible things to lose in a learning setting; have developed a reflex toward authority (such as a resistance); have a great many preoccupations outside a practical learning situation; have developed group behavior consistent with their needs; have established a rational framework composed of values, attitudes, and tendencies; have developed selective stimuli filters; will respond positively to reinforcement; need a purpose for existence; possess the ability to change; have a past that can positively influence learning; and bring ideas to contribute. Each of these should be incorporated into learning situations to enhance learning (cited in Gilley and Eggland 1989, 125).

The Communications Process.   The medium of communication used by learning agents to facilitate learning plays an important role in the information exchange process. Thoughts and feelings are defined through words, symbols, and signs.

Language, the instrument of thought, consists of words and symbols whose meanings are based on common experiences and understandings. Words are tools that managers utilize to convey information and bring about comprehension. Because ideas become inculcated in words, they take the form of language and stand ready to be studied and known, marshaled into the mechanism of intelligible thought (Gregory [1884] 1978). Hence, learning will be incomplete without language that is plain, understood, and common to the learner.

Since symbolism often represents highly technical information that is a language unto itself, learning agents must frequently test learners' understanding of signs and symbols to guarantee their correct usage. Study of organization, manager, and employee language reveals the words and symbols they use and their meanings. If learners fail to comprehend, ideas and information should be rephrased or an analogy used to illustrate meaning. In addition, using the simplest and fewest words possible to express meaning decreases confusion and possible misunderstanding.

Language also functions as the storehouse of knowledge, allowing us to convey all that we know about subjects, theories, or cultures via the written or spoken word. Thus, words are not only the expression of our ideas but the tools we use to construct themes and explain what we believe to be true—we master knowledge by expressing it. In learning situations, employees express their understanding by using specific language, words, or symbols.

Many individuals do not appreciate the character and complexity of language, take language for granted, or misuse it in haphazard attempts to convey their knowledge. The use of slang or highly technical words, for example, may confuse or intimidate learners who have no context for such language. Misunderstandings also occur when employees fail to ask for explanation when confused or exhibit facial expressions and other body language that managers mistake for understanding. Occasionally, the information being shared with learners simply falls outside their realm of experience. In this instance, effective learning agents should identify and incorporate more familiar terms and symbols into the learning engagement.

The Instruction Process.   What is the role of instruction in learning? Should instruction be the cornerstone of learning or an instrument to convey information? Should managers disseminate information or facilitate learning? Although many believe that learning cannot take place without an instructor, research has shown the opposite—individuals can and do learn without facilitators. The most effective learning occurs when individuals actively participate in the process by directing their own learning actions.

When managers are required to act as learning agents who deliver information, they begin with an awareness of their employees' knowledge and skill levels, which becomes the starting point of instruction. Effective managers present information in a way that intrigues employees, who then become absorbed by it (secondary passive attention). As previously mentioned, information should be presented logically, in a practical, problem-centered approach, and one concept at a time, so that each step leads naturally to the next. The use of illustrations, examples, and stories, while encouraging employees to share experiences, provides a common framework on which to base the learning event. Finally, learning agents encourage employees to utilize their knowledge during formal learning activities and on the job. Learning agent (manager) support is critical if learning is to be transferred to the job.

Commonly occurring mistakes in the learning process include information overload, failure to relate information to previous data, failure to heighten employee interest and enthusiasm for learning, and managers holding inappropriate attitudes toward employees regarding their abilities, skills, or level of comprehension. Furthermore, criticizing workers' lack of learning acceleration or memory and failing to familiarize employees with elementary facts or definitions prior to presenting new information can negatively impact learning.

Information overload is a commonly occurring phenomenon in the learning process; this occurs when too much material is presented in too little time (Hiemstra and Sisco 1990). As a result of information overload employees may become confused, overwhelmed, or de-motivated. Consequently, learning falls short of desired goals, and employee performance on the job fails to improve.

An effective method in overcoming information overload is the concept-unit approach, which allows learners to absorb and apply new information by presenting concepts in small units of a single idea group. Each learning session lasts only two to three hours, with the entire program spread over several weeks. Although the same amount of information is covered, the length of time allotted to do so is expanded.

To ensure successful learning, learning agents (managers) should adhere to the following practical rules for instruction:

1. Ask thought-provoking questions to excite learner interest in the topic or information.
2. Place themselves in the learners' position and join their search for additional knowledge.
3. Allow learners time to sort out material and gain insight and understanding.
4. Repress the desire to tell all one knows about a subject or lesson.
5. Encourage learners to ask questions when they are confused or do not understand.
6. Allow learners ample time to answer questions or complete exercises on their own.
7. Accept responsibility to awaken learners' minds; do not rest until each individual demonstrates his or her mental activity and involvement.
8. Adapt learning activities to the experience, preparation, and skill of participants.
9. Be dedicated to begin each learning session in a manner that stirs learners' interest and enthusiasm.
10. Teach individuals to ask who, what, how, where, and when questions to encourage better understanding of information.
11. Avoid answering your own questions and allow learners to struggle with thought-provoking questions (which will enhance their learning).
12. Avoid information overload.
13. Repress impatience with learners' inability to grasp concepts or master skills.
14. Carefully consider the information to be presented, identify points of contact with the lives, interests, and experiences of learners (Gilley and Eggland 1989).

Knowledge Acquisition and Practice

Learning occurs when certain activities cause an individual to transpose information into new awareness that ultimately alters behavior (Figure 6.1). Four types of learning are most common: *natural, formal, personal,* and *developmental*. Natural learning is the result of spontaneous individual interaction with the environment. Formal learning occurs when others choose information and present it to the learner. Personal learning means an individual self-directs intentional learning activities to improve knowledge, skills, or behaviors (Gibbons 1990). Developmental learning is a combination of formal and personal learning. In other words, learners participate in content-driven (formal) programs that utilize self-directed techniques and practical application.

Three fundamental elements support the knowledge acquisition and practice process: *enlightenment, repetition,* and *review.*

Enlightenment.   In his 1884 classic *Seven Laws of Teaching,* John Milton Gregory stated,

> Learning is not memorization and repetition of words and ideas of the instructor. . . . Contrary to common understanding this is much more the work of the learner than the instructor. . . . Learning comes by progressions of interpretation, which may be easy and rapid. . . . No real learning is wholly a repetition of the thoughts of another. The discoverer borrows largely on facts known to others, and the learner must add to what he or she studies from his or her own experience. His or her aim should be to become an independent searcher in the fields of knowledge, not merely a passive learner at the hands of others. . . . The practical relationship of truth and the forces that lie behind all facts are never really understood until we apply our knowledge to some of the practical purposes of life and of thought. . . . Thus, what was idle knowledge becomes practical wisdom. (Gregory [1884] 1978, 106–107, 109)

In essence, the process of learning involves internalizing knowledge and applying it in some form or fashion—which we call enlightenment. The learning process is not complete until the last stage, enlightenment, has been reached.

According to Gilley and Maycunich (2000), learning agents help learners reach enlightenment when they help individuals form a clear idea of the work to be done and ask learners to express in their own words or in writing the meaning of the information or content as they understand it. They help by asking questions of learners in a nonthreatening manner, encouraging them to embellish and share their point of view, and helping individuals become self-directed, independent investigators responsible for their own learning, growth, and development. They also help by challenging learners' perceptions regarding reproduction of information in a correct, acceptable form and by providing assistance whenever they are unable to grasp concepts and ideas quickly. As Gregory ([1884] 1978) stated, "instructors (managers) should constantly seek to develop in employees a profound regard for truth as something noble and enduring" (112).

Learning agents (managers) make common mistakes during the enlightenment period, such as failing to insist on original thinking by learners and consistently neglecting practical application of information and content. Another common error is providing inadequate instruction or assistance in the application of information or content, as well as assuming that individuals' failure to ask questions implies understanding of material.

Knowles, Holton, and Swanson (1998) maintain that *whole-part-whole learning* avoids these common mistakes (see Chapter 16 for additional sequence approaches). Learning agents first share the "big picture" or end result with individuals, disseminate information little by little, correlate this with desired results, and then wrap up with discussion and review of the topic. For example, a manager provides a comprehensive picture of an employee's job. In this job overview, tasks are broken down into component parts and it is shown how each piece fits in the scheme of things. Individual job segments are explained in detail only after the employee comprehends the overall picture. After each part is understood, the manager summarizes and briefly explains the job once again to reinforce or review. This approach enables a manager to illustrate where an employee's responsibilities lie in the organizational framework, allowing for greater appreciation of the worker's value to the organization.

Repetition.   A skilled athlete's performance may lead us to conclude that it is easy. The performances of Michael Jordan, Peggy Fleming, and Mark McGwire appear natural and relaxed. But were these individuals always experts? Certainly not. Each of them experienced the pain of poor performance early in their careers and occasionally thereafter. Over time and through a process known as practice, they were able to grasp the skills and techniques needed to excel. Baseball is a prime example. With proper instruction and practice, most individuals are able to strike a ball with a wooden stick. This achievement is important because it marks the point where learning moves from theory to practicality—the point at which new awareness and insights prevail. Practice also allows individuals to "unlearn" incorrect information or an improper method.

Practice can be conducted on one's own or during formal learning events in safe environments (Broad and Newstrom 1992). Opportunities for practice should be as realistic as possible, encourage failure that results in learning, protect individual self-esteem, and not harm productivity. Practice should occur throughout the learning process as new activities or tasks are introduced. Practice may also occur on the job. According to Gilley (1998, 83), "one of the best ways of improving learning transfer is by allowing employees to fail in safe environments such as work simulations and case studies. Employees allowed to fail in comfortable, supportive settings will learn a great deal about what skill levels will or will not work on the job."

Review.   Any exercise or activity using previously presented information is considered a review, which is an important step in the learning process. Effective reviews enhance learning when individuals rethink, reproduce, or apply recently acquired information, which deepens learners' understanding and allows them to make new associations and derive new meaning from the activity (Gregory [1884] 1978). Effective reviews also pose realistic problems and offer employees opportunities to apply new skills or knowledge accordingly. Controlled scenarios such as these are safer than actual job situations and permit mistakes that otherwise might harm the individual or financially burden the organization. Often, in our haste to complete the learning process this step is overlooked.

Effective learning agents (managers) always include review (and feedback) and are aware of its crucial role in the learning process and its ability to integrate new material with old. They establish appropriate and sufficient time for reviews, usually at the end of each learning session. Learning agents understand that a final review may be their last opportunity to challenge employees to incorporate information into personal understandings and orientations prior to returning to work.

Transfer and Integration

Whether personal or professional, learning that does not transfer and integrate into real-life or job experiences is meaningless. Gilley, Boughton, and Maycunich (1999, 252–253) state that "before learning can be translated into value for the organization it must be applied to the job. Unfortunately, many employees are on their own immediately after participating in a learning intervention. Management fails to assist in integrating change, skills, or knowledge on the job, causing confusion and frustration on both sides. Consequently, much of the change is lost."

Individuals who are abandoned after a learning event rarely transfer their new knowledge to their lives or to their jobs (Brinkerhoff and Gill 1994). Without support, learners take the path of least resistance and revert back to their old habits instead struggling with application of new knowledge and skills. Many reasons prevent employees from transferring learning to the job, such as fear of change, lack of confidence, no reward for trying new skills or knowledge, on-the-job failure when applying new skills, peer pressure, and lack of manager encouragement and support.

Learning agents (managers) take care before, during, and after learning activities to ensure knowledge transfer. Prior to learning, they develop performance standards and share these with learners, show their support for learning and its importance, identify rewards, and sharpen their performance coaching skills. During learning events, managers promote a positive learning environment, ensure individual learning readiness, encourage participation, use practical learning exercises, give positive feedback, and reward and recognize learners. Afterward they provide additional training, refresher courses, or follow-up activities to boost learner confidence, encourage discussion of how new knowledge and skills have been applied, mentor learners, and track improvement via daily journals (Gilley and Coffern 1994).

Lack of support or involvement on management's part accounts for the majority of employee failure to transfer learning to the job (Broad and Newstrom 1992). Many managers fail to coach their employees, reinforce learner behavior, establish performance standards, communicate expectations (which set the stage for poor performance), confront poor performance, be positive role models, or create work environments conducive to learning.

Organizations hinder learning transfer by creating counterproductive policies, procedures, work environments, and managerial practices. Additionally, many business leaders believe that employees are easily replaced and thus that learning is a waste of time. Human resource professionals further compound the problem when they ignore the fact that learning is everyone's responsibility, fail to involve stakeholders in the learning process, relinquish learning activities to managers and supervisors, or do not link learning to strategic business goals and objectives (Brinkerhoff and Gill 1994).

The following questions will help organizations, human resource professionals, managers, and employees improve learning transfer:

- How are knowledge, skills, and attitudes being used on the job?
- What barriers prevent learning from being transferred?
- What role do managers and supervisors play in transferring and reinforcing learning on the job?
- What should be done before, during, and after implementing the learning acquisition plan to enhance learning transfer?
- What role do employees play in learning transfer?
- What role does the organization play in learning transfer?
- What activities should be used to improve learning transfer?
- What can be done to increase learning effectiveness and efficiency?
  (Gilley, Boughton, and Maycunich 1999, 260)

Application. People learn by doing. Participating in an activity involves learners to the fullest, allowing them to immediately apply new knowledge, practice skills, or alter behaviors. Research indicates that the most effective learning occurs when application immediately follows training.

Applying new knowledge or skills may temporarily harm an individual's performance; hence, managers should employ *failure analysis* to ascertain the impact on overall productivity (Gilley and Boughton 1996). Through failure analysis, managers and employees identify possible barriers to integration of learning so that they may be proactively planned for.

Learning agents (managers) who understand the process do not demand perfection the first time an individual applies new knowledge or skills. Allowing application and learning failure emphasizes long-term over short-term performance improvement. Learning failure helps employees enhance their long-term productivity and improve their overall performance (Gilley 1998, 83). Thus, the principle of application is simple: Permit learners the opportunity to utilize their new knowledge or skill, allow failure, and preserve self-esteem.

Reinforcement and Feedback.   Individuals are more likely to repeat activities for which they receive positive reinforcement and feedback; thus, learning is enhanced (Rothwell and Cookson 1997). Reinforcement and feedback may take the form of a simple approving nod, congratulations for a job well done, recognition during department meetings, or encouragement to continue. Regular performance reviews are prime opportunities for managers to provide employee-learners with reinforcement and feedback regarding their application of new knowledge or skill on the job.

Performance reviews or appraisals that contain specific learning components communicate the importance of knowledge transfer and learning. If new skills and knowledge are being evaluated, they must be worth obtaining (Gilley 1998). Additionally, most individuals desire reinforcement that their performance is satisfactory. Gilley and Coffern (1994) believe that learning agents/managers should follow several guidelines when providing reinforcement and feedback to employees, including being specific so employees know what they did correctly, being sincere so employees accept feedback without manipulation, and delivering feedback immediately after employees perform tasks correctly. They add that managers can help by giving specific, individualized feedback, giving feedback frequently but randomly to strengthen performance behavior, and conveying feedback clearly and concisely so employees understand it.

Reflection.   Reflection is a critical step in the learning process and one of the most powerful activities employed by individuals to enhance transfer and integration of new knowledge, skills, or behaviors. As noted previously, reflection activities are numerous. Peterson and Hicks (1995) maintain that the goal of reflection is to solidify one's insight and to guarantee that mistakes and/or successes just learned are remembered, identify themes and patterns of performance, challenge one's assumptions to ensure appropriate learning, and remain open to new learning opportunities. Further, they assert that learners should reflect regularly. Daily reflection might occur after important events or crises, completion of big assignments, or major milestones in a project; monthly or quarterly reflection should follow completion of each significant job assignment or project. As a result, individuals will have ample opportunity to examine the impact of new knowledge, skills, or behaviors on their personal or professional lives.

Reflection encourages individuals to consider upcoming opportunities or different situations where their new knowledge and skills may be applied, as well as what they might do differently under current circumstances (Preskill and Torres 1999). Finally, learners assess potential improvements the next time they are able to apply the knowledge and skills being reflected upon. Reflection enables individuals to learn from their mistakes, analyze their own thoughts and feelings, cope with personal and professional barriers, and strategize future use of learning.

Accountability and Recognition

Although individuals must be held accountable for their learning, they must also be recognized for their efforts and improvements (Figure 6.1). Learning agents/managers partner with learners to assess successes as well as failures and to strategize what might be done to improve future performance.

Expectation and Inspection.   Gilley and Boughton (1996) maintain that a two-way technique known as expectation and inspection allows learning agents/managers to share with individuals how they are expected to perform as a result of new learning, including the quantity and quality of their performance outputs. These expectations are discussed with learners prior to engaging in learning activities.

Expectation and inspection allows for managerial scrutiny of learner behavior to determine whether established performance standards have been met and how learning actions facilitated improvement. Thus, expectations are linked with accountability, which ultimately enhances learning transfer. Learners/employees know what they are being asked to do and how they will be held accountable.

Recognition and Reward.   Those who pursue or engage in learning to improve their knowledge, skills, or behaviors should be rewarded and recognized for their efforts. Appropriate rewards and recognition encourage individuals to continuously grow and develop via learning. Le Beouf (1985, 9) asserts that "the things that get rewarded get done." Thus, linking recognition and rewards to individual growth and development is a vital component of learning acquisition plans.

Managers must plan for celebration of new learning prior to their employees' engagement in learning actions. Active participation by management encourages learning and reinforces its importance. Examples of celebration include departmental ceremonies honoring learners, gifts or prizes, and the like. Failure to recognize and reward learning (and its resultant performance improvement) discourages employees from transferring their new knowledge and skills to the job.

Applying the Learning Process Model

In a previous work (Gilley and Maycunich 2000), we introduced a three-dimensional learning process model, which reflects the phases and elements of learning (Figure 6.2). The first and last phases (preparing for learning, accountability and recognition) are inputs, depicting the relationship among the information exchange process (vertical component), the knowledge acquisition and practice process (diagonal component), and the transfer and integration process (horizontal component).

The learning process model indicates the operational relationships of the three components, each of which is portrayed by a series of numbers. The first represents the information exchange process and its importance to learning. The second number depicts the knowledge acquisition and transfer process and its use in learning. The third symbolizes transfer and integration, revealing the amount and degree of transfer and integration that occur as a result of learning.

Applying numerical values to each dimension describes eight different types of learning:

Content–centered learning (9-1-1) presumes instructors are primarily disseminators of information. They emphasize content with little or no focus on learning transfer, practice, or integration.

Trial and error learning (1-9-1) occurs when employees are on their own and responsible for acquiring the knowledge and skills necessary to be effective. Little or no instruction is provided regarding job duties or responsibilities, and feedback or reinforcement are virtually nonexistent. Learning occurs occasionally but not frequently. If learners are fortunate enough to acquire the necessary knowledge and skills, they will be successful; if not, they will be organizational casualties.

Accidental learning (1-1-9) results when little or no emphasis is placed upon sharing information, helping learners acquire knowledge, or practice new skills. Yet somehow, individuals integrate appropriate skills for the job—they learn by accident. These learners often demonstrate acceptable performance but typically fall short of the level of mastery needed by organizations of the next century.

Anticipatory learning (5-5-5) is a process by which information exchange, knowledge acquisition and practice, and transfer and integration are equal partners in learning. Although usually acceptable, anticipatory learning fails to maximize its full potential because it usually occurs at a mediocre level of intensity.

Incidental learning (9-1-9) occurs most often as a by-product of another activity; thus, learning is unintentional (Marsick and Watkins 1990). Learning occurs as a result of mistakes that happen on the job. Consequently, learning is deeply internalized and remembered.

151

FIGURE 6.2 Learning and Change Cube

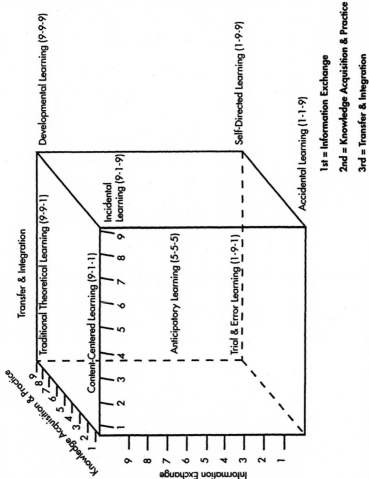
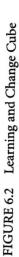

1st = Information Exchange

2nd = Knowledge Acquisition & Practice

3rd = Transfer & Integration

SOURCE: J. W. Gilley and A. M. Maycunich, *Beyond the Learning Organization: Creating a Culture of Continuous Growth and Development Through State-of-the-Art Human Resource Practices* (Cambridge, Mass.: Perseus Publishing, 2000).

Traditional theoretical learning (9-9-1) represents most training and development activities. Individuals participate in formal training activities to enhance their performance. Unfortunately most organizations do not grasp the importance of transfer and integration on the job, nor do they provide support (e.g., policies and procedures) for it to occur. Thus, learning transfer does not materialize.

Self-directed learning (1-9-9), one of the most important types of learning, occurs when individuals are responsible for knowledge acquisition and practice, and the transfer and integration thereof. The risk is that employees are alone in determining appropriate sources for acquiring the knowledge and skills necessary to be successful. Thus, learning is still left to chance. Marsick and Watkins (1990) refer to this type of learning as informal learning.

Developmental learning (9-9-9) represents the epitome of learning, with equal emphasis on information exchange, knowledge acquisition and practice, and transfer and integration at a high level. Developmental learning embraces and exhibits the importance of learning preparation, accountability, and recognition. Individual and organizational learning are maximized by combining the strengths of traditional theoretical and self-directed learning, allowing managers to forge learning partnerships with employees.

Conclusion

The learning process should be the heart of any organization. In this chapter we discussed the roles of managers and human resource professionals. We also identified the phases and elements necessary to enhance the learning process. Finally, we reviewed the application of these phases by constructing an interactive, three-dimensional model representing eight different types of organizational learning. The pinnacle of our model is developmental learning, whereby information, learning acquisition and practice, and transfer and integration work in harmony to improve individual knowledge and skill. Developmental learning perpetuates learner growth and development both personally and professionally. As a result, individual and organizational renewal capability increases, as does performance capacity.

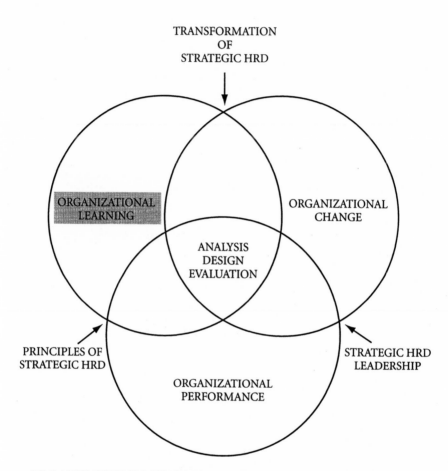

ORGANIZATIONAL LEARNING, PERFORMANCE, AND CHANGE

CHAPTER 7

The Developmental Organization

In many organizations, employees are treated as disposable resources to be used and disposed of as the organization sees fit. Because of this approach, many of an organization's best employees leave, seeking opportunities for growth, development, and appreciation in other organizations. One reason for this phenomenon is a disconnect between the perceived importance of employees and their treatment within the organization. Another reason is managers' refusal to mentor and develop their employees, which displaces responsibility for their employees' performance. Consequently, many employees fail to meet performance expectations, which reduces their morale, loyalty, and commitment.

According to Gilley (1998, 45–46), organizations need an optimal number of qualified, talented employees to produce the products and services demanded by clients. They can fulfill this need in two ways. First, organizations can recruit and hire needed resources from the open market if an adequate supply of talented individuals exists. Second, organizations can grow, develop, and promote employees within the firm. Since employees desire challenges that contribute to their continuous growth and development, organizations can better retain talented employees by providing them with growth and development opportunities. Organizations benefit via enhanced competitiveness, productivity, and profitability.

Comparing Learning and Developmental Organizations

Senge (1990) maintains that an organization that is characterized by a culture dedicated to improving employees, their productivity, and overall business performance via continuous lifelong learning is likely to achieve business results on a more consistent and higher level. Although learning is a prerequisite to development, it is not the final outcome. Simply increasing an organization's reservoir of knowledge does not necessarily produce better business results. They recommend taking learning to its highest form, development, which enables employees to reach their full potential while organizations focus on outcomes that produce better business results. They advocate the evolution to the next phase of organizational transformation—that of the developmental organization. This chapter examines a blueprint by which organizational leaders and human resources professionals can accelerate beyond the learning organization.

Every organization possesses the capability to evolve beyond the traditional sphere to that of learning or developmental. Gilley and Maycunich (2000) distinguish one type of organization from another based on the importance of human resources in achieving strategic business goals and objectives, the type of leadership guiding the firm, the type and focus of developmental activities adopted by an organization, the capacity for organizational renewal, and the desire to improve competitive readiness. (See Appendix C)

Traditional Organizations

More than 80 percent of all organizations currently reside in the traditional phase. Some produce satisfactory results and achieve sufficient business outcomes, whereas others struggle to meet revenue goals and profitability requirements (Figure 7.1). Their effectiveness could be greatly increased by making the shift to a higher, more efficient plane—one where the organization's ability to renew itself and maximize competitive readiness are greatly enhanced and employee importance is increased substantially.

Learning Organizations

Learning organizations theoretically maintain a significantly higher capacity for organizational renewal and competitive readiness than traditional firms because they emphasize the importance of human resources in achieving desired business results, utilize transactional and transformation leadership, and focus on application and reflection designed to enhance personal mastery and self-awareness respectively. These outcomes are achieved by demonstrating the value of continuous learning and change.

Marquardt (1996) believes the role of leader within the learning organization is that of synergist, responsible for creating an environment where the whole is greater than the sum of its parts. Leaders take on the responsibility for creating a type of esprit de corps and camaraderie unfamiliar to traditional organizations. Additionally, managers assume the role of learning partner, fostering and encouraging employee learning on an ongoing basis. Within learning organizations,

FIGURE 7.1   Evolution of Organizations

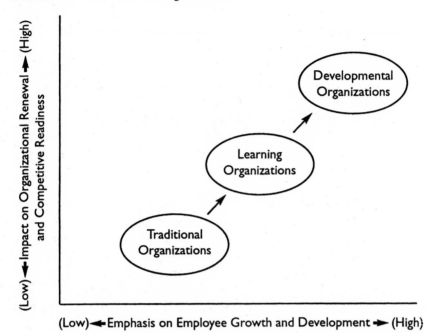

SOURCE: J. W. Gilley and A. Maycunich, *Beyond the Learning Organization: Creating a Culture of Continuous Growth and Development Through State-of-the-Art Human Resource Practices* (Cambridge, Mass.: Perseus Publishing, 2000).

managers readily accept their responsibility for learning application, mastery, reflection, and self-awareness on the part of their employees. HRD professionals assume the role of employee champion, advocating strategic learning direction within the firm to improve and maximize learning opportunities. Finally, employees accept the role of self-directed learner, accountable for their own learning acquisition, application, and reflection. They understand the importance of learning to themselves and the firm.

Transactional leadership and transformational leadership are the most common in learning organizations, and they differ dramatically from the type of leadership in the traditional organization. Both of these leadership styles emphasize the importance of learning in everyday interactions. According to Gibson, Ivancevich, and Donnelley (1997, 313–314), transactional leadership occurs when leaders help employees identify what must be done to achieve a desired result. Transactional leaders identify what employees want or prefer and help them achieve levels of performance that result in satisfying rewards. Transformational leaders motivate employees to work toward long-term strategic goals instead of short-term self-interest and toward achievement and self-actualization instead of security. Consequently, transformational leaders possess the ability to inspire and motivate employees to achieve results greater than they originally planned, with as much emphasis on internal reward as external reward.

In most learning organizations, a team or project-centered organizational structure prevails. Watkins and Marsick (1993) report that learning organizations reconfigure themselves to foster group and team performance and learning. Most learning organizations do not radically reengineer their operations, structure, or culture but instead rely on a simple shift in orientation and operations. This sometimes is a barrier to learning organizations' success in focusing on learning as a centerpiece of the firm.

Types of Developmental Activities.   Marquardt (1996) identified two types of developmental activities most commonly found in the learning organization: duetero learning and action learning. Duetero and action learning are conscious efforts on the part of individuals to review and reflect upon their actions or those of others. He suggests that duetero learning is a process of learning about learning, whereas action learning involves working on real problems, focusing on learning acquired, and actually implementing solutions.

Focus of Developmental Activities.   Morris (1995, 328) believes that "learning organizations are important because they provide meaning to work and reflect the beginnings of a fundamental restructuring of the purpose of business and of society. Constructing them with a development strategy will provide the internal focus to link individual fulfillment and organizational attainment and to galvanize both." Learning organizations focus on application and reflection. Application involves using learned information in new and concrete ways and applying its steps, methods, concepts, principles, and theories on the job. The outcome of application on the job is personal mastery—defined as a high level of proficiency in one's area of expertise, skill, or subject matter. Therefore, learning organizations encourage integration of new knowledge and skills on the job to enhance and improve an individual's proficiency.

Another critical focus of developmental activities involves reflection. Preskill and Torres (1999) believe that reflection permits individuals to constantly search for new awareness, insight, and understanding regarding actions and beliefs. Thus, the outcome of reflection is self-awareness—obtaining or gaining a greater cognizance of who one is and why one behaves as one does.

Furthermore, Preskill and Torres assert that knowledge acquisition brings about comprehension, which functions as a prerequisite to the developmental activities of the learning organization. In other words, the evolution from traditional to learning organization is a result of utilizing all components and respective outcomes from knowledge acquisition through and including self-awareness.

Developmental Organizations

Morris (1995, 326) believes that learning organizations must become developmentally focused:

> Deciding to become a learning organization holds the possibility of enabling companies to create new visions, and to initiate and implement new or "reinvented" business processes. However, to gain the high ground and the greatest long-term competitive advantage, an even greater shift is required. Organizations need to purposefully move through the stage of being a learning organization to committing to a development strategy. . . . Therefore, the type of learning organization needed is one that consciously and intentionally develops its people and constantly transforms itself. In such an organization the concept of development is central to its identity and pivotal to purpose and strategy.

According to Gilley and Maycunich (2000), the final phase of evolutionary movement is that of the developmental organization. They contend that beyond the learning organization lies the epitome of individual and organizational growth and performance. Thus, they argue that learning itself doesn't guarantee employee or business growth and development. Developmental organizations extend themselves further along the evolutionary plane, engaging in activities that promote and reward long-term individual and organizational growth. Consequently, developmental organizations enjoy a heightened capacity for organizational renewal and improved competitive readiness.

Type of Leadership. A developmental champion is needed within an organization to promote the developmental philosophy and orientation required to truly transform an organization to the highest plane. Gilley and Maycunich (2000, 23) suggest that "developmental organizations require developmental leadership embracing the following ten principles: personal accountability, trustworthiness, employee advocacy, employee self-esteeming, performance partnership, organizational performance improvement, effective communications, organizational consistency, holistic thinking, and organization subordination." Simonsen (1997, 60) believes that leadership in a developmental organization is less about position and more about skills and knowledge. She suggests that the people who do move to senior management positions are collaborators who lead an informed group of skillful and knowledgeable employees and even form alliances with competitors when it is in the best interests of both parties.

Types of Developmental Activities.   Morris (1995, 328–329) argues that a strategy that focuses on enhancing the development of and investment in people is needed in developmental organizations. She contends that a development strategy can be seen as a "natural response to the change from making economic decisions based on the distribution of scarce natural resources to making those decisions based on choices among similar services, differentiated by perceived values created by knowledge."

Within the developmental organization, "the type of developmental activity most common is . . . developmental learning, which incorporates one's ability to acquire new knowledge and skills, comprehend, transfer, and integrate them on the job" (Gilley and Maycunich 2000, 24). Additionally, employees analyze, synthesize, and evaluate the outcomes of their performance, enabling them to change and continually grow. The result is new meaning and improved organizational renewal and performance capacity.

Focus of Developmental Activities.   Gilley and Maycunich (2000, 24) maintain that the principal focus of "developmental activities is to bring about *change* within an individual. This is the result of gaining new insight, awareness, and understanding of oneself brought about by critical reflection." Change alters an individual to the point that he or she can never return to his or her original state. This type of change is a reconfiguration of oneself. New meaning heightens individuals' desire to change the way they interact on a daily basis. This permanent change propels individual employees to a higher plane.

Another focus of developmental activities is *continuous growth and development.* Continuous growth is a process of never-ending expansion, taking into account new and different things, the outcomes of which are improved renewal and performance capacity. Thus, continued growth and development enhances an employee's reservoir of performance capabilities, which he or she can use when needed. As this process continues over time, the organization's overall aggregate renewal and performance capacity increases, allowing organizations to avoid the slippery slope of decline.

Enhancing Individual Potential

Morris (1995, 328) supports the view that organizations should modify processes and practices to enhance people's abilities to be in a learning mode and to focus on continual learning and self-development. Doing so requires organizations to accept the basic assumption that work and learning are two sides of the same coin. In other words, employees work when they learn and learn when they work. Moreover, organizations must create supportive learning environments that emphasize development in order to heighten the integration between work and learning. This type of organizational culture allows organizations to build performance expertise and improve work processes.

Linking Individual and Organizational Development

According to Morris (1995) and Gilley (1989), organizational actions supportive of linking individual and organizational development include career planning and institutional career management. More specifically, these activities include identification of competencies that are aligned with organizational goals; redesign of systems and processes to support long-term development; recruiting, selection, and human resource allocation to build employee expertise; and performance appraisal and evaluation that fosters continuous growth and development.

Creating a Developmental Organization.   According to Simonsen (1997, 56–62), although employees embrace change, organizational systems are often not modified to support change. Organizations need to create systems that support new behavior to achieve the results needed to survive and thrive. To make the greatest impact, the approach to development must align with and support the organization's new or desired culture.

Simonsen (1997) believes that organizations should create a new developmental culture by defining the desired future state. She suggests that it is better to leave the present circumstances behind and focus on the future. Essential stakeholders should be asked to contribute to the future vision. Simonsen has identified several questions that can help define the future state:

- What will be the characteristics of the organization in this future state?
- What will people be doing?
- How will behaviors be different?
- Does everyone agree on the desired outcomes?

From these questions, Simonsen was able to identify several characteristics of developmental cultures. They include trust, open and direct communication, listening for understanding, making commitments, reliability, respect, honesty, and openness.

Barriers to Becoming a Developmental Organization.   Gilley and Maycunich (2000, 41–47) identified a number of circumstances preventing organizations from developing their employees. First, many organizations select managers that are unproductive, unprofessional, incompetent, or unable to secure results through people. Second, many maintain poor human resource practices that prevent adequate development of their employees. Third, many organizations boast a client-oriented philosophy rather than an employee-oriented one; thus, their efforts are directed at satisfying clients instead of meeting the needs of employees. Fourth, organizational success often creates an atmosphere of overconfidence, leading to a feeling of invincibility that causes developmental blindness. Fifth, some lack an inclusive problem-solving approach. Consequently, employees are excluded from the decisionmaking process, which wastes valuable talent and breeds mediocrity as employees focus on tasks instead of creative, collaborative, problem solving. Sixth, organizations neglect to incorporate an organization-wide diversity strategy, which mitigates the firm's ability to maximize creativity and innovation. Seventh, some fail to link developmental activities and strategies to their strategic business goals and objectives (Brinkerhoff and Gill 1994). Eighth, organizations fail to account for the laws of fast forgetting, which occurs when an organization's perceived success causes them to forget the basic management and organizational principles that were instrumental in bringing about financial and operational success. Ninth, many organizations are slow to learn from their mistakes and are, consequently, doomed to repeat them. Tenth, some are guilty of organizational stupidity, the worst sin of all, which occurs when firms repeat the same decisions, tasks, or activities over and over again expecting "different results."

According to Gilley and Maycunich (2000, 47), evolution to developmental status requires the following:

- organizational cognizance of the importance of people in the success equation,
- avoidance of self-defeating and dysfunctional behaviors by breaking the cycles of fast forgetting, slow learning, and organizational stupidity,
- realization of when fears are realistic versus unrealistic so that healthy fears can be managed.

Doing so focuses organizations on a developmental perspective that ultimately transforms the firm, causing it to rely on employees and encourage investment in their ever-increasing abilities. Thus, a developmental organization is created.

Guiding Principles of Developmental Organizations

Gilley and Maycunich (2000) identified ten guiding principles that underpin developmental organizations. These guiding principles represent the infrastructure of the developmental organization, without which the organization may fail to adapt to change. They assert that these guiding principles serve as the underlying philosophy in accordance with which all business decisions are made.

Servant Leadership

Developmental organizations require a different type of leadership. Servant leadership, the leadership most appropriate for developmental organizations, reinforces the philosophy of synergy between leaders and employees.

Servant leaders serve others by advocating, supporting, and promoting employees' contributions and efforts—in essence, their employees are number one. They assist staff in their struggle to become the best they can by working tirelessly to help employees grow and develop. They share organizational success and make certain that other decisionmakers are aware of their employees' contributions to achieving business results. Additionally, servant leaders accept responsibility for their employees' failures and celebrate their successes.

Performance Mastery

The principle of performance mastery maintains that organizations orchestrate best practices by applying an effective, efficient performance management system. Performance mastery occurs when individuals rely on their strengths and perform without conscious awareness of the steps involved. When employees are allowed to demonstrate performance mastery, they enjoy supreme satisfaction because they feel invincible and powerful. As a result, they want to repeat the performance over and over again, which enhances their self-esteem and shapes their confidence. Through repetition, employees develop performance expertise—a cycle that developmental organizations maximize to achieve goals. When employees enjoy caring, supportive environments that allow them to be their best, exemplary performance occurs. Thus, employees take responsibility for their own growth and development, and they focus on both current and future obligations.

Changeability

In developmental organizations, change is constant; thus, executives, managers, employees, and HR professionals must adopt new roles and accept new responsibilities in order to enhance organizational preparedness for growth and development. Changeability is an essential ingredient required for organizational renewal and competitive readiness.

Knowledge Construction

The principle of knowledge construction and continuous lifelong learning is the backbone of the developmental organization. It asserts that employees are responsible for the acquisition, application, transfer, and integration of knowledge. When employee performance and productivity improves, knowledge construction is generally demonstrated. Ultimately, employees are accountable for obtaining knowledge on the job and are responsible for continuous growth and development.

Coachability

Developmental organizations select employees based on their aptitude and desire for growth and development. These individuals maintain a high coachability index in that they are receptive to constructive criticism, suggestions, and honest efforts to help improve their performance. Moreover, they are willing to accept or learn new ways of performing. Furthermore, coachable employees are enthusiastic about learning, interested in new methods and innovations, receptive to performance feedback, career-focused, inclined to compare themselves with high achievers, and predisposed to developing reflective and critical thinking skills.

Continuous Renewal and Performance Capacity

When employees are allowed to apply the principle of continuous renewal and performance capacity, they are willing to acquire new and different information that expands their reservoir of performance capabilities. As a result, developmental organizations enjoy enhanced competitive readiness and ability to constantly grow and develop.

Internal Systems Working in Harmony

The critical functions of a developmental organization (leadership, structure, culture, mission and strategy, management practices, work climate, and policies and procedures) work together in harmony to guarantee success. Each of these functions is an independent component that either directly or indirectly impacts each of the others. Consequently, developmental organizations anticipate breakdowns or failures in any or all of these functions and plan accordingly.

Right Person–Right Place–Right Time Theory

Developmental organizations adhere to the principle of the right person at the right place at the right time. This is what human resource planning, recruiting, and selecting are designed to accomplish. When successful, these activities enable an organization to have the type, quantity, and quality of human resources needed to foster organizational renewal and enhance competitiveness. Additionally, developmental organizations appropriately link learning and change interventions, career development activities, performance management processes, and compensation and rewards programs to growth and development strategies. Such linkage positively impacts employee performance and provides continuous feedback to employees, thus ensuring improved business results.

Philosophy of Endless Possibilities

In developmental organizations, a partnership is forged between employees and the firm for the purpose of enhancing employee knowledge, skills, and abilities. Career development is a quintessential organizational development activity, providing linkage between individual and organizational development, allowing for improved individual proficiencies, enhancing organizational renewal, and improving performance capacity (Gilley 1989). Moreover, the principle of endless possibilities reveals that there are countless career development opportunities for employees. As a result, developmental organizations encourage employees to identify their strengths and build on them accordingly, while creating strategies for managing weaknesses.

Continuous Motivation Theory

Developmental organizations embrace continuous motivation, utilizing strategies, philosophies, and goals to inspire employees to improve their performance and productivity. Thus, compensation and reward programs must be responsive to employee needs while simultaneously helping the organization accomplish its business goals. These reward systems are linked to employee growth and development plans. In other words, the principle of continuous motivation is the foundation of all compensation and reward programs; thus, a well-designed compensation and reward program fuels employee growth and development, improves employee self-esteem, and enhances performance, resulting in a healthier organization.

Outcomes of Developmental Organizations

The process of changing from a product- and revenue-centered approach (traditional) to a people-centered one (developmental) produces an atmosphere of cooperation, respect, and dignity that yields synergy. Additionally, this process generates outcomes essential to enhancing organizational renewal and competitive readiness as well as the continuous growth and development of employees.

Enhanced Dialogue

In the developmental organization, dialogue involves active listening, sharing, high-quality two-way communication, and the free exchange of thoughts, ideas, and feelings. Such communication reveals active engagement between individuals attempting to understand another's perceptional world. Dialogue is an intense interaction in which people suspend their own views and assumptions to better understand another. Participants become linked through their solidarity, affiliation, and association.

Dialogue, an important outcome of the evolution to a developmental organization, is fostered through managers' involvement with their employees. Involvement requires a manager's active participation in his or her employees' problems and needs, whereby leaders, managers, and employees engage in activities that allow face-to-face contact.

Risk Taking

Simonsen (1997, 60) believes that a developmental organization encourages smart risk taking. Change requires exploring the unknown, which ultimately means taking risks. Employees are encouraged to be open to new ideas, challenge their own perceptions, and engage in learning and change activities that will bring about growth and development. In a developmental organization, risk taking is rewarded, not punished, and innovation as a result of risk taking is celebrated (Simonsen 1997, 60). As a result, leaders, managers, and employees understand the difference between unnecessary risks and calculated intelligent risks and know how to monitor risk factors. This understanding reduces the likelihood of failure and increases the probability of success.

Harmony Through Respect

Harmony can be defined as a pleasing arrangement of parts, an internal calm. This definition describes the work climate and organizational culture found in developmental organizations. Such peace and tranquillity is not commonly found in traditional organizations. Harmony is achieved through respect—respect for individual performance, achievement, thoughts, ideas, and efforts. In other words, developmental organizations exhibit respect for individuals as persons of worth.

Developmental leaders and managers facilitate harmony by creating environments conductive to sharing, demonstrating acceptance through a willingness to allow employees to differ from one another. This willingness is based on the belief that each employee is a complex being made up of different experiences, values, beliefs, and attitudes.

Managed Conflict

Simonsen (1997, 59) offers the following advice on managing conflict: "Conflict that is not identified, understood, and managed effectively can lead to inefficient use of organization resources, stress on the conflicting parties, and misdirection of the energies of those affected by the conflict situation. On the other hand, conflict that is effectively managed can result in increased creativity and innovation, a rethinking of goals and practices, and a better informed work group." When developmental organizations adhere to these practices, leaders, managers, and employees have more time to focus on the critical strategic issues facing the organization.

Interpersonal Reciprocity

Another critical outcome of the developmental organization is a process known as interpersonal reciprocity. This process involves the mutual exchange of actions and behaviors between two or more individuals. Interpersonal reciprocity requires empathy, attentiveness, and understanding. Interpersonal reciprocity enables leaders, managers, and employees to treat others the way they themselves are treated. Thus, it is the ability to recognize, sense, and understand the feelings that another person communicates through his or her behavior and verbal expressions and to accurately communicate this understanding to that person.

Strategic Direction and Communication

According to Simonsen (1997), developmental organizations provide clear and focused direction that eliminates internal competition and helps coordinate projects and initiatives. As a result, employees can manage their careers strategically by identifying paths that enhance their professional success. Moreover, managers will be better able to keep their people informed of and involved in the direction the corporation is taking.

Collaboration and Teamwork

In developmental organizations, there is an overt shift from authoritarian control to participation. Because participation is less threatening to employees, it allows employees to become agents of change, who support decisions made. Participation encourages open, honest relationships between and among employees that are based on a deep concern for the well-being of others.

Participation fosters collaboration and teamwork. Additionally, collaboration and teamwork require employees to have the courage to relinquish control and dominance over their organizational partners. These behavioral shifts produce organizational synergy, heightened cooperation, and tolerance. When collaboration and teamwork are present, employee motivation improves, which results in increased productivity, enhanced performance, and improved communication.

According to Simonsen (1997, 58), developmental organizations focus on external competitors and build collaboration internally. She suggests that professional development is not about beating out other employees for a promotion but about successful teamwork that allows everyone to add value and contribute to team goals and organizational success. Additionally, development is about ensuring one's own career security, not job security, which becomes a win-win situation for everyone.

Sense of Belonging

When organizations encourage dialogue, harmony through respect, interpersonal reciprocity, collaboration, and teamwork, they provide employees with a sense of belonging. This brings about an ownership attitude, which encourages continuous involvement and participation, the results of which include improved quality, increased employee engagement, better performance, and enhanced organizational efficiency and effectiveness (Gilley and Maycunich 2000).

Employees are more willing to participate in quality improvement initiatives, change activities, reengineering efforts, and organizational development interventions when they feel they are an intricate part of the organization. Moreover, employees that think and act like owners are more willing to give of themselves and make sacrifices for the good of the organization.

Shared Reality and Purpose

In developmental organizations, employees have a shared reality and purpose, knowing how their efforts contribute to the achievement of business results and their respective value. A common complaint among employees of traditional organizations is that they do not know where the firm is going or how they fit into the overall picture; thus they feel hopelessly lost amid the fog of organizational complexity. These employees never become actively involved in the improvement of the firm and resign themselves to doing their jobs without the enthusiasm necessary to bring about performance mastery. By contrast, employees in developmental organizations know their contributions and efforts are appreciated and how their performance outputs blend into the organizational tapestry. Consequently, employees are able to assess their value and contributions, which enhances their worth and self-esteem.

Active Engagement

Developmental organizations encourage active engagement by creating conditions that permit employees to become totally committed to the organization and its goals. Employees become active change agents in search of ways to improve the firm and become absorbed in daily business operations as well as the strategic direction of the firm, sharing their perspectives, ideas, thoughts, and insights with management to improve the organization's effectiveness and efficiency.

By increasing their knowledge of job-related problems and expanding employee levels of influence to solve problems, organizational leaders promote active engagement. Furthermore, the successful alignment of these two goals results in a more harmonious, efficient organization. To a greater extent, developmental leaders encourage risk taking on the part of employees by providing a supportive decisionmaking climate. Larson and LaFasto (1989, 126) suggest that developmental leaders create this climate through the following actions:

- trusting team members with meaningful levels of responsibility;
- providing team members with the necessary autonomy to achieve results;
- presenting challenging opportunities that stretch the ability of individual team members;
- recognizing and rewarding superior performance; and
- standing behind employees and supporting them.

System Alignment

According to Simonsen (1997), developmental organizations reward appropriate behavior, such as open communication and risk taking. Compensation and reward systems are structured to recognize and reward contributions rather than tenure or position. Developmental organization leaders provide intrinsic rewards by showing respect and acknowledging employees' work and value. Decisionmaking is encouraged at all levels of the organization. Finally, senior managers and leaders model the behavior they want demonstrated throughout the organization. In other words, they "walk the talk."

Inspired Growth and Development

Inspired growth and development on the part of employees is the principal outcome of every developmental organization. It separates developmental organizations from traditional and/or learning organizations. Gilley and Maycunich (2000, 343) argue that "unless organizational leaders foster inspired growth and development, the benefits of the developmental organization will not be realized. Performance, productivity, organizational quality and efficiency, organizational effectiveness, organizational renewal and competitive readiness will not be improved. In fact, inspired growth and development is the very reason developmental organizations exist."

Learning as a Standard

Simonsen (1997, 62) maintains that in a developmental organization everyone is expected to learn from experience and apply what they have learned to improve their own work and contribute to the goals of the company. Consequently, employees are encouraged to engage in career planning activities to determine appropriate learning and development needs.

A developmental organization expects employees to expand their personal self-awareness by getting to know themselves and where they want to go. This is done so they can reach out, listen, and be open and willing to share ideas (Simonsen 1997). Additionally, work groups are asked to concentrate on team goals and on those who are contributing to and committed to goals. Work groups are sensitive to members' needs and generate cooperative interaction with other teams. At the organization level, leaders share information and resources as well as encourage interaction, teamwork, and cooperation in an effort to achieve the goals of the firm.

A Blueprint for Creating the Developmental Organization

According to Gilley and Maycunich (2000), the evolution from traditional to learning to developmental organization can be a difficult journey—one that requires a blueprint to facilitate and expedite the transition. In accordance with this belief, they have created the *developmental organization blueprint,* a planning tool consisting of five separate but interrelated components: (1) developmental leadership, (2) organizational system, (3) organizational readiness, (4) reinventing human resources, and (5) state-of-the-art human resource practices (Figure 7.2).

The first four components are preconditions to the developmental organization and serve as its foundation. By foundation, they mean preconditions, alignments, changes, or considerations necessary to bring about a successful transformation to the developmental organization. In other words, an organization must be willing to (1) adopt new leadership techniques, (2) reconfigure its organizational system, (3) reexamine employees' critical roles and responsibilities, and (4) reinvent human resources in order to evolve to this higher level. These four preconditions must be addressed before an organization can begin its final evolutionary journey.

The final component is state-of-the-art human resource practices. Gilley and Maycunich (2000) believe that most organizations deploy these HR practices, but it is their utilization, unique configuration, and application that produce the synergy necessary to evolve to the developmental level. Figure 7.2 illustrates the relationships among each of these components. The ultimate outcome of the developmental organization is enhanced organizational renewal and performance capacity.

FIGURE 7.2 The Developmental Organization Blueprint

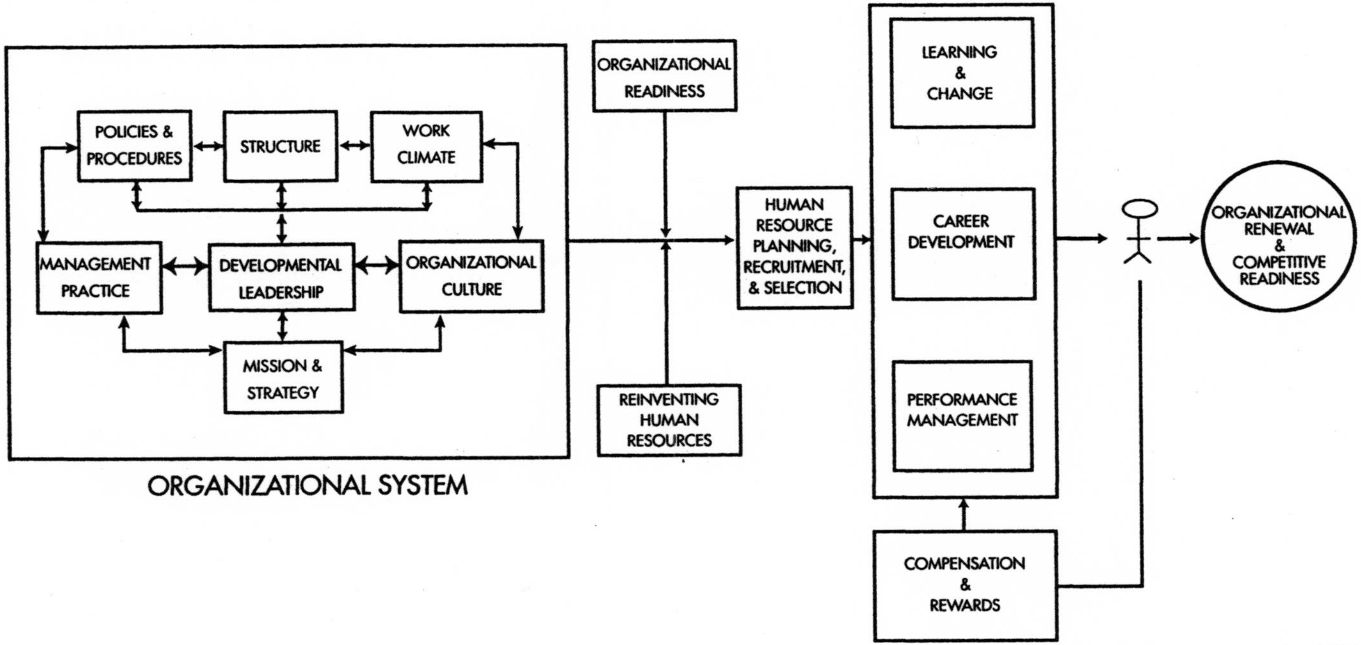

SOURCE: J. W. Gilley and A. M. Maycunich, *Beyond the Learning Organization: Creating a Culture of Continuous Growth and Development Through State-of-the-Art Human Resource Practices* (Cambridge, Mass.: Perseus Publishing, 2000).

Developmental Leadership

Identifying the organization's developmental leadership capability, its current leadership philosophy, and aptitude for change is the first step of creating a developmental organization. This enables organizations to determine their current baseline of leadership talent and their developmental readiness. Once identified, organizations can select strategies designed to continuously improve developmental leadership capability. One such strategy is to recruit, select, and train developmental leaders and managers. This approach allows organizations to concentrate on maximizing leadership strengths.

Gilley and Maycunich (2000) believe that developmental leaders are servants of their employees and the organization. Such an approach demonstrates to employees that they are, indeed, the organization's greatest asset, worthy of organizational investment in continuous growth and development opportunities. Consequently, organizations should apply the principles of developmental leadership (see Chapter 3).

Organizational System

The next part of the developmental blueprint is to examine the organizational system to determine its strengths, weaknesses, opportunities, and threats—a SWOT analysis. An organizational system consists of seven components: culture, structure, managerial practices, work climate, leadership, policies and procedures, and mission and strategy. Carefully examining each allows for identification of critical ingredients necessary for businesses to manifest developmental environments. Only through critical assessment of the entire organizational system will firms improve their processes, procedures, and management effectiveness along the journey of developmental evolution.

Transforming the organizational system into one that facilitates and supports employee growth and development is essential. Successfully building an organizational system that supports employee growth, development, reflection, and renewal requires integration of all components of organizational life and manifestation of a developmental culture within each. This effort requires commitment and dedication from all organizational members—leaders, managers, employees, and human resource professionals.

Organizational Readiness

The third step in building a developmental organization is examination of readiness for the transformation process. To do so, an organization must critically examine the attitudes and beliefs of executives, managers, and employees to determine whether they are willing to change and adopt new roles and responsibilities. Absent sufficient indicators of readiness, leaders and managers should avoid proceeding and work on building organizational preparedness. If indicators are positive, leaders and managers can motivate and prepare all organizational members for upcoming change, stressing the benefits to both individual employees and the organization itself.

Reinventing the Human Resources Function

Most organizations require a massive reinventing of the human resource function in order to meet ever-increasing demands from their employees and stakeholders. Such a redesign requires human resource professionals to undertake new and exciting roles and responsibilities that allow them to function as change agents and partners within their organizations. As fully integrated members of the organization, human resources professionals will be equal contributors to organizational success, on the same level as other functions such as marketing, finance, and research and development.

Human Resource Practices

Unquestionably, organizations must offer state-of-the-art products and services. They must also operate within a well-defined mission, vision, and strategy in order to bring about financial success. Human resource practices enabling organizations to have the right people in the right places at the right time are equally important. Accordingly, developmental organizations cannot evolve without implementing state-of-the-art human resource practices.

What organizations need are serious, workable solutions to their problems— ones that will help them improve their competitive readiness and enhance organizational renewal rather than "creative, innovative, simple, and painless" solutions that promise guaranteed success with little or no effort or commitment. Organizations need to return to proven, commonsense, even boring solutions to secure the results they need. Although these solutions may not be spectacular techniques possessing catchy names and slogans, they are at the heart of achieving results through people. These solutions are simple human resource practices common to virtually every organization: (1) human resource planning, recruitment, and selection, (2) learning and change process, (3) career development strategies, (4) performance management process, and (5) compensation and rewards.

Although these practices are not new, they work especially well when organizations are committed and determined to execute them in an effective, efficient manner. Firms must be enthusiastic about their application, dedicated to their success, and willing to passionately and forcefully implement these practices. The primary difference is that these practices must be state-of-the-art practices (meaning, best practices), executed at the highest possible level.

Each of these human resource practices has been perceived to be an organizational panacea, although no singular practice has been able to bring about lasting, permanent change. However, when these five human resource practices are performed at their highest levels of proficiency and appropriately combined, they transcend organizational barriers and internal resistance to change, enabling organizations to enhance their competitive readiness and improve their renewal capabilities.

Human Resource Planning, Recruitment, and Selection. Developmental organizations actively seek individuals with high coachability and growth and development readiness. The goal of this process is to secure employees that are predisposed to lifelong learning, who have discovered the advantages and benefits of continuous growth and development. These employees view challenges as opportunities, accept feedback as constructive, seek new ways of approaching problems or situations, and constantly search for new knowledge or meaning—in essence, employees possessing a high coachability index. Highly coachable employees desire to continuously develop, recognizing the importance of growth in their personal and professional lives.

Learning and Change Process. Developmental organizations create a learning and change process that prepares organizational members for developmental learning. Gilley and Maycunich (2000) describe this as a prerequisite to reflection and renewal necessary to enhance continuous growth and development at the individual and organizational levels.

Career Development. Organizational neglect of employee development is nothing new. Most fail to adequately plan for workers' long-term developmental needs or to incorporate them into strategic human resource planning strategies. As a result, many organizations have no strategy focused on long-term career development or performance enhancement. Obviously, these organizations are short-term oriented when it comes to developing their employees.

Developmental organizations create career development programs that build on employees' strengths while managing their weaknesses. Identifying strengths and weakness is just as critical at the organizational level as it is at the individual level. After all, organizations are merely compilations of the collective strengths, weaknesses, talents, and abilities of their members. Maximizing strengths leads to champion performance, whereas strategies designed to "fix" weaknesses merely make employees adequate.

Performance Management.   Essential to creating a developmental organization is the implementation of performance management processes at the organizational and individual levels. Performance management involves analysis and recognition of the reasons why employees fail to achieve desired results. Understanding these causes allows developmental managers to implement the principles of performance improvement and apply the performance alignment process (see Chapter 9). Successful implementation leads to performance greatness, a desired outcome for any individual and any firm.

Compensation and Reward Programs.   Developmental organizations redesign their compensation and reward programs to support growth and development. Such a program rewards the "right things" (e.g., leadership, creativity, entrepreneurship, learning new skills, growth and development).

A critical characteristic of the developmental organization is its ability to be flexible, adaptive, responsive, and willing to change in order to meet long-term goals. Because change is inevitable, no single formula exists for making the transformation to the developmental organization other than the collective desire of all organizational members to be the best that they can be. Dedication and commitment to individual growth and development leads to the same outcome at the organizational level, along with achievement of desired long-term business results.

Conclusion

Developmental organizations require specific types of leadership, activities, philosophy, guiding principles, and focus. Their purpose is to enhance the organization's competitive readiness and renewal capacity. Finally, the developmental organization blueprint, consisting of five separate but interrelated components, serves as a planning tool that HRD professionals can use to achieve the goals of the developmental organization.

PART III

Organizational Performance

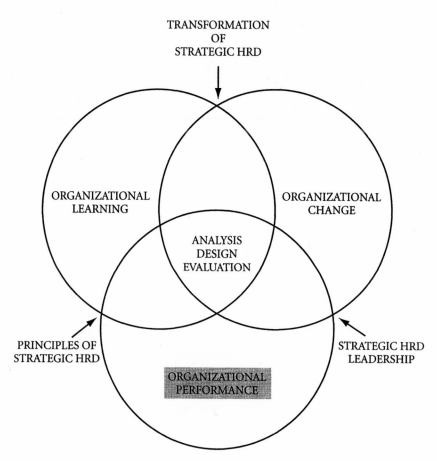

TRANSFORMATION
OF
STRATEGIC HRD

ORGANIZATIONAL
LEARNING

ORGANIZATIONAL
CHANGE

ANALYSIS
DESIGN
EVALUATION

PRINCIPLES OF
STRATEGIC HRD

STRATEGIC HRD
LEADERSHIP

ORGANIZATIONAL
PERFORMANCE

ORGANIZATIONAL LEARNING, PERFORMANCE, AND CHANGE

Human Performance Technology

Another critical professional practice domain is organizational performance. To properly understand this domain, we must examine four essential elements: human performance technology (Chapter 8), performance improvement and management (Chapter 9), performance consultants (Chapter 10), and performance consulting (Chapter 11).

A Definition of Human Performance Technology

Rothwell (1996b, 5) describes human performance technology (HPT) as a "systematic process that links business strategy and goals and workers' abilities to achieve them with a variety of interventions, including environment redesign, learning and training, and incentive system reconfiguration." The primary outcome is individual and organizational performance improvement. Through causal analysis of performance problems or business opportunities, underlying causes are identified for which effective solutions can be generated for any given performance challenge.

Spitzer (1999, 163) maintains that "human performance (HP) technologists are in the business of improving performance in organizations." Like other consultants who have no direct authority over organizational change, HP technologists rely on indirect influence in the form of interventions (Block 1981), which may be any type of organizational change, from a relatively small modification of a tool, to a training program, to a completely new organizational system or structure.

According to Stolovich and Keeps (1992, 3), "human performance technology is a field of practice that has evolved largely as a result of the experience, reflection, and conceptualization of professional practitioners striving to improve human performance in the workplace." They add that since the term human is included in the name, the focus of this field of application is on human performers in organizational and work settings. In short, they believe that HRD professionals work with the performance of people (employees) operating within results-oriented systems.

The term performance is defined as an accomplishment, execution, outcome, or achievement. It denotes a quantified result or a set of obtained results. Swanson (1999) defines performance as the outcomes of behavior. Stolovitch and Keeps (1992, 4) argue that "behavior is individual activity, whereas the outcomes of behavior are the ways in which the behaving individual's environment is somehow different as a result of his or her behavior." Within an organizational context, Gilbert (1978) asserts that performance is an "accomplishment" that is valued.

The term technology is perhaps the most confusing in that it has incongruous connotations. But when joined with the word performance and introduced into an organizational context, it implies an objective, systematic procedure for examining performance issues from both individual and organizational perspectives. Thus, "human performance technology is a field of endeavor that seeks to bring about changes to a system, in such a way that the system is improved in terms of the achievements it values" (Stolovitch and Keeps 1992, 5).

Rothwell (1996b, 3) asserts that "human performance technology requires a systematic process of discovering and analyzing important human performance gaps, planning for future improvements in human performance, designing and developing cost-effective and ethically justifiable interventions to close performance gaps, implementing interventions, and evaluating the financial and nonfinancial results." This definition can be further explained.

By "systemic," Rothwell (1996b, 15) implies that human performance improvement is approached in an organized, open systems approach, whereby the organization system absorbs environmental inputs (people, raw materials, capital, and information), uses them in such transformational processes as delivering service or manufacturing products, and discharges them as outputs such as finished goods or customer services. "Discovering and analyzing" means identifying and examining present and future barriers that prevent an organization, process, or individual from achieving desired results. "Human performance" refers to a quantified result or a set of obtained results. "Planning for future improvements in human performance" indicates performance improvement is focused on averting future problems or realizing improvement opportunities as well as examining past and present performance problems or breakdowns. "Designing and developing cost-effective and ethically justifiable interventions" refers to discovering optimal, sensitive, and efficient means of solving past or present performance problems or planning for future performance improvement opportunities. "Implementing interventions" includes installing and maintaining performance improvement solutions. Finally, "evaluating results" gathers persuasive evidence that demonstrates the solution's effectiveness.

Fuller and Farrington (1999, 94) add insight into human performance technology with their definition: "HPT is a systemic and systematic approach to defining a business need or opportunity, identifying barriers to achieving the desired business result, implementing solutions to remove the barriers to performance, and then measuring bottom-line results." This definition differs from previous ones in that it has additional considerations:

1. Using a systematic approach. HPT follows well-organized procedures, using a step-by-step approach, method, or system that is known for achieving results.
2. Defining a business problem or opportunity. Fuller and Farrington (1999) assert that HPT as a process makes certain the organization knows what the problem is that practitioners are trying to solve.
3. Identifying barriers to achieving the desired business result. HPT uses process, performance, and causal analysis to assess the root cause of the problem or the reason why an opportunity is not being realized. This is done in order to ensure that practitioners go beyond the symptoms of a performance problem to identify the performance issues within the firm.
4. Implementing solutions to remove barriers to performance. HPT eliminates barriers to performance by offering a number of solutions (i.e., work environment, motivational factors, knowledge, and skills), since most performance problems or business opportunities require a combination of interventions.

Stolovitch and Keeps (1999) maintain that HPT is concerned with measurable performance and the structuring of strategies within the organizational system to improve performance. As a result, the HP practitioner must identify and analyze factors within the organizational system that may affect performance and the consequences of employee performance (rewards and punishments) to uncover root causes of inadequacies so that a performance solution can be constructed to address them.

Basis of Human Performance Technology

HPT is grounded in general systems theory as it applies to organizations. HP practitioners adopt a holistic philosophy of performance problems: They examine problems (defined as a gap between desired and actual states) from a broader context of the organizational system in which it actually occurs. Not all performance problems require an endless examination of all systems; however, each is studied in relation to the overall goals and mission of the organization within which it is identified.

Stolovitch and Keeps (1999) warn that HPT should not be applied to all organizational systems because it is a results-driven, productivity-oriented process that may be inappropriate in social systems. They believe that it is particularly valuable for business and industry, where organizational purposes and goals are generally clearly defined.

Relevance of Human Performance Technology to Organizations

HPT is particularly relevant to organizations for several reasons. First, HPT adopts an organizational systems view in that it seeks to link the actions and interventions of all organizational elements (selection, training, feedback systems, incentives, and organizational design) that affect overall performance rather than operating piecemeal (training-only approach) (Rummler and Brache 1995). Second, it uses a systematic approach to performance improvement through the orderliness of technology, ensuring that the analysis and evaluation of performance problems are based on solid scientific, theoretical, and empirical foundations. This provides a coherent approach to the solution of performance problems, as opposed to the more eclectic procedures adopted by most vendor-driven training departments (Gilley and Maycunich 1998a). Third, HPT practitioners are more cause conscious than solution oriented because they rely on the results of performance and causal analysis prior to proposing interventions or solutions (Rothwell 1996b). Fourth, HPT is bottom-line oriented, which makes it particularly credible to money-conscious decisionmakers (Fuller and Farrington 1999). Fifth, HPT is a rational, logical, and transparent approach to performance improvement because it requires thorough performance analyses to identify all factors contributing to the current level of performance. Moreover, HPT requires a precise statement of the mission(s) of the system in which improved performance is being sought (Stolovitch and Keeps 1999). Sixth, HPT is dedicated to linking training, environmental redesign, feedback systems, or incentive systems to measurable performance in order for the organization to achieve its business goals and objectives (Brinkerhoff and Gill 1994).

Goals of Human Performance Technology

The goal of human performance technology is to guarantee that the right individuals have the knowledge, skills, motivation, and environmental supports to do their jobs effectively and efficiently (Fuller and Farrington 1999). Rummler and Brache (1995) define effectiveness as employee accomplishments that are of value to the organization as well as to the individual. They believe efficiency involves production in a manner that requires the least amount of resources (time, financial, human, and material). The result is improved organizational performance and renewal capacity (Gilley and Maycunich 2000).

Principles Underlying Human Performance Technology

Jacobs (1987, 41) identified eleven important principles of human performance technology, which serve as a foundation for other elements such as performance and causal analysis, stakeholder evaluation, design and development techniques, implementation strategies, and evaluation procedures.

1. Human performance and human behavior are different, and knowledge of their differences is important for achieving goals.
2. Any statement about human performance is about organizational performance as well.
3. Costs of improving performance should be regarded as investments in human capital, yielding returns in the form of increased performance potential.
4. Organizational and individual goals must be considered to define worthy performance.
5. The domain of human performance technology consists of management functions, development functions, and systems components.
6. Knowing how to engineer human performance and the conditions that affect it is as important as explaining why the behavior occurred.
7. Diagnosing problems requires analysis of the present system and examination of differences between it and an ideal system. Avoiding anticipated problems requires analyzing the planned system and modifying it to approximate the ideal.
8. Exemplary performance provides the most logical reference for establishing job performance standards.
9. Human performance problems have differing root causes that originate either from the person, from something in the environment, or both.
10. The performance of one subsystem affects the performance of other subsystems in somewhat predictable ways, requiring that root causes be analyzed at more than one level of the organization.
11. Many different solutions may be used to improve human performance. Selection of any one solution is dependent upon the cause and nature of the performance problem, and the criteria used to evaluate a solution must include its potential to make a measurable difference in the performance system.

Process of Human Performance Technology

Instructional Systems Design.   According to Rosenberg, Coscarelli, and Hutchison (1999), HPT relies on instructional systems design (ISD) as a generalized systematic model. They contend that instructional requirements must be identified to determine the precise instructional needs of learners. Thus, instructional program design links with analysis. Moreover, instructional materials are produced and delivered in accordance with design. In every situation, evaluation data are collected and revisions are made to align outcomes of the learning process with identified needs as closely as possible. Today, this systematic model has come to be known simply as ADDIE (analysis, design, development, implementation, and evaluation).

The ISD framework has a few limitations. First, a variety of needs cannot be met through instructional programs alone, regardless of how well learning interventions are designed. Further, learning does not always result in improved performance. As HRD practitioners have become better at identifying problems, they have realized that their repertoire of instructional solutions can solve only a small set of problems; thus, a broader paradigm is required (Rosenberg, Coscarelli, and Hutchison 1999).

Analytical Systems.   Harless (1974) realized that analysis of learner needs often occurs too late in the instructional process. He believed it was critical to complete the analysis process before design of an instructional program. Over time, front-end analysis became the first step in the instructional design process.

Rummler and Brache (1995) maintain that organizational structures are a collection of integrated systems (finance, manufacturing, human resources, and marketing). Through systemic analysis they discovered that individual performance is influenced by organizational performance, and vice versa. They suggest that all organizational systems (and their subsystems) are influenced by a complex and ever-changing variety of outside forces. Rosenberg, Coscarelli, and Hutchison (1999) argue that organizational analysis is required to examine this interrelationship and the impact of external forces. They also suggest that several other factors are a critical part of the process of HPT, including the following:

Cognitive engineering is an applied cognitive science that draws on the knowledge and techniques of cognitive psychology and related disciplines to provide the foundation for principle-driven design of person-machine systems.

Ergonomics and human factors are disciplines that developed in response to the world's increasingly complex technology.

Psychometrics is the measurement of human achievement and capabilities.

Feedback systems are directly related to motivation, incentives, and rewards. According to Tosti (1986), the critical characteristics of feedback are tied to who gives it, what the content of the feedback is, and when and where the feedback is given.

Intervention systems are responses to identify causes of human performance problems or to opportunities for improving performance, and are often referred to as *solutions, strategies, tactics,* or *human resource functions.*

Management of Human Performance Technology

HPT is more complex than managing a single intervention. However, the management of HPT has been primarily based on overlaying the human performance system within an organization, applying HPT models, or through utilization of one of three types of practitioner.

Hutchison (1990) identified two types of HPT practitioners: the *performance technologist,* concerned primarily with analysis, management, and evaluation, and the *intervention specialist,* focused on the design and implementation of specific interventions. One or more individuals, depending on the complexity of the performance problem or business opportunity, may perform these roles. Robinson and Robinson (1996) identified a third type of practitioner: the *performance consultant.*

Rosenberg, Coscarelli, and Hutchison (1999) argue that many HP practitioners assume that combinations of interventions, taken from a variety of fields, provide greater value when applied to a performance problem or opportunity than any specific intervention does when used alone. Gilley (1989) notes that career development within an organization is enhanced when the training and organizational development processes and strategies are linked together. Pucel, Cerrito, and Noe (1989) assert that the linkage between selection, training, and performance appraisal can result in a defensible human resource system that contributes to management's ability to improve organizational productivity.

Implementation of Human Performance Technology

Galpin (1996) warns HRD professionals not to take a haphazard approach to the transition from training to performance improvement, because it will invite resistance, delays, confusion, and potential rejection of the entire strategic HRD approach. Fuller and Farrington (1999, 57) advocate a planned approach to building an effective performance improvement practice within an organization. There are four phases in this planned approach: (1) prepare for performance technology by building capability and gathering resources; (2) demonstrate results by implementing small projects that have a clear, positive impact on the organization's business needs (cost, quality, quantity, and timeliness; (3) build organizational awareness by communicating and demonstrating ways to achieve results; and (4) address the barriers to implementation.

Competencies of HPT Practitioners

Few systematic efforts have been made to identify the competencies necessary for success in human performance technology. Jacobs (1987) identified fifteen competencies for training and development professionals who set their sights on becoming performance technologists. Most recently, Stolovitch, Keeps, and Rodrigue (1995) identified sixteen skills/competencies of the performance technologist:

1. Determine appropriateness of project.
2. Conduct needs assessment/front-end analysis.
3. Assess performer characteristics.
4. Analyze the structural characteristics of jobs, tasks, and content.
5. Write statement of performance improvement intervention outcomes.
6. Analyze the characteristics of a setting (learning/working environment).
7. Sequence performance intervention outcomes.
8. Specify performance improvement strategies.
9. Sequence performance improvement activities.
10. Determine the resources appropriate to the performance improvement activities and create all components.
11. Evaluate human performance technology interventions.
12. Create human performance technology intervention, implementation, monitoring, and maintenance.
13. Plan, manage, and monitor human technology projects.
14. Communicate effectively in visual, oral, and written form.
15. Demonstrate appropriate interpersonal, group process, and consumer behaviors.
16. Promote human performance technology as a major approach to achieve human performance results in organizations.

Human Performance System

According to Dean (1999), the conceptual domain of human performance technology can be defined by three key aspects: (1) functions to manage the development of human performance systems or other management operations, (2) functions to develop human performance systems, and (3) the components of human performance systems. Combining these aspects reveals the following definition of HPT. HPT is the development of human performance systems and the management of that development, using a systems approach to achieve organizational and individual goals.

The human performance system accepts that organizations are open systems that are absolutely dependent for success on their external environments (Rothwell 1996b). Katz and Kahn (1978) argued that open systems receive inputs from the environment, process them, and release outputs into the environment. Rummler and Brache (1995) describe inputs as resources used to produce products or deliver services; processes are the work methods applied to the inputs; and outputs are the results of processes, such as finished goods or services.

Rothwell (1996b) believes each part of an organization is a subsystem (part of the organizational system) interacting with a suprasystem (the environment external to the organization). Consequently, each part of an organization contributes to its mission. Furthermore, changes in one part of the organization will affect others. This reflects the interdependencies of open systems.

Many researchers have found that efforts to improve human performance must take into account the environments within which performance occurs. Rothwell (1996b, 32) identified four environments that practitioners should examine:

- The *organizational environment* is synonymous with the suprasystem. It is everything outside the organization (the external environment).
- The *work environment* is everything inside the organization (the internal environment).
- The *work* consists of processes used to transform inputs into outputs.
- The *worker* is the individual who performs work and achieves results.

According to Fuller and Farrington (1999, 14), the human performance system is a process where organizational inputs, people, and their behaviors lead to performance, consequences, and feedback, which loops back through the system to the organization and the people in it, and so on. Moreover, the components of this system exist within an environment that also affects performance. (Appendix D)

Organizational Inputs

The system begins with organizational inputs such as raw materials, people, financial capital, and information. Additionally, organizations have business goals and objectives, values, guiding principles, and an overall work climate that affect the way employees operate within them. Moreover, organizations exist within a culture, sometimes referred to as behavioral norms, that identifies how work is to be done and how members of the firm are to treat one another. In short, culture is "how things get done around here" (Gilley and Maycunich 1998). Those individuals who fail to abide by the culture are socially punished by members of the organization, or choose to leave because they don't fit in, or are fired for failing to demonstrate teamwork (Aronson 1995).

Most organizations provide employees with a written job description that indicates what their role is within the organization and what results they are expected to achieve on the job. Ideally, job descriptions present a clear picture of employees' roles, responsibilities, required outputs, and standards used to judge the quality of their performance. If a job description is poorly written or dated, the employee could easily end up performing inappropriately or pursuing incorrect performance objectives.

People

By applying their existing knowledge, skills, and attitudes to available input, employees (people) produce product and services for the organization. If their capabilities are inadequate, employees may perform their tasks incorrectly, poorly, or not at all (Fuller and Farrington 1999). In the human performance system, employee capabilities are not the only element needed to achieve desired performance. The mistake that HRD professionals typically make is focusing exclusively on the people component of the human performance system while ignoring the other components. Although this approach may yield highly talented and capable employees, they nevertheless will struggle to produce results in a suboptimized organizational work environment. This condition creates high levels of frustration that have been demonstrated to increase attrition, since high performers who desire a less frustrating working environment will secure a position with another organization (Greenberg 1994).

Behaviors

Behaviors are measured in terms of specific actions and are influenced by organizational inputs. Fuller and Farrington (1999) revealed that job-related behaviors can be observed through the actions, problem solving, and decisionmaking of individuals and groups. Ultimately, job-related behavior impacts the achievement of desired business results.

Performance

Performance is measured in terms of outcomes that are desired and valued by the organization (i.e., reduced product costs, increased quality, or increased productivity). Although appropriate job-related behavior is important, performance makes the organization successful. Gilbert (1978) contends that firms obsessed with controlling or improving behaviors will have difficulty improving both individual and organizational performance. In essence, employees can demonstrate desired behaviors yet not achieve desired outcomes.

Consequences

Consequences may include rewards, incentives, recognition, status, power and authority, responsibilities, or compensation and should be linked to job performance (Fuller and Farrington 1999). In it simplest application, consequences that reinforce desired performance are likely to continue, whereas those that punish for undesired performance are likely to extinguish it over time.

To be effective, organizations should align consequences of performance with organizational inputs. When out of alignment, people are forced to choose between what they are told to do and what actually gets rewarded within the organization (Fuller and Farrington 1999, 18). Under these circumstances, employees will appear to follow organizational mandates, while spending most of their time doing what gets rewarded, which negatively impacts the organization in the long term.

Feedback

Feedback is simply information about employee performance and the consequences of their performance. Employees will modify their job-related behavior to optimize their performance when they are able to associate their work with specific consequences. Without frequent, accurate feedback, people are far less likely to improve their performance over time.

Environment

Four environmental factors significantly impact performance: job processes, performance barriers, information, and tools. Environmental factors have the potential to seriously impede performance even if organizational inputs such as people, abilities, behaviors, consequences, and feedback are of the highest quality. As Rummler and Brache (1995) point out, if you put a good performer up against a bad system, the system wins every time.

Whole-System Solutions

Fuller and Farrington (1999, 21) assert that "if people are to achieve top-level performance, all the components of their human performance system must be optimized." When any of these components break down or are ignored, individual and organizational performance decreases. Performance consultants are then called upon to remove performance barriers by installing appropriate performance improvement solutions (Chapter 10).

Simply examining the human performance system provides evidence of the complexity of performance, its management, and improvement. For this reason, training by itself is an insufficient approach to improving performance. Although training can positively impact the people component of the human performance system, it cannot fix performance barriers in the areas of organizational inputs, consequences, feedback, or the environment (Fuller and Farrington 1999; Swanson 1999; Gilley and Maycunich 1998a). Organizations, in turn, are obligated to create performance improvement solutions that address each of the broken elements of the performance system.

Rummler and Brache (1995, 25) believe that the human performance system relies on the premise that people are motivated and talented, and if they do not perform adequately the cause is most likely in the system (i.e., organization, process, or job/performer level) in which they work. Organizations that effectively manage the human performance system should positively respond to the following questions:

- Do performers understand the outputs they are expected to produce and the standards they are expected to meet? (Performance)
- Do performers have sufficient resources, clear signals and priorities, and a logical set of job responsibilities? (Performance)
- Are performers rewarded for achieving job goals? (Consequences)
- Do performers know whether they are meeting job goals? (Feedback)
- Do performers have the necessary skills and knowledge to achieve job goals? (Behavior)
- In an environment in which the five questions listed above are answered affirmatively, do performers have the physical, mental, and emotional capacity to achieve job goals? (People)

Models of Human Performance Technology

Human Performance Enhancement

Rothwell (1996a, 42) believes in the need for a new model of human performance technology that can be applied both situationally (Mager and Pipe 1984) and comprehensively (Gilbert 1978). Such a model, called the *human performance enhancement* (HPE) model, focuses attention both outside the organization (customers, suppliers, distributors, and other stakeholders) and inside, thus giving due consideration to the four environments that affect human performance (worker, work, work environment, organizational environment). He concluded that the model could become the basis for selecting, training, developing, appraising, and rewarding HRD professionals.

The model requires that HRD professionals work in concert with stakeholders to do the following:

1. Analyze what is happening (performance).
2. Envision what should be happening (performance).
3. Clarify present and future performance gaps.
4. Determine the present and future importance of the performance gaps.
5. Identify underlying cause(s) of performance gap(s).
6. Select human performance enhancement strategies, individually or collectively, that close performance gaps by addressing their cause(s).
7. Assess the likely outcomes of implementation to minimize negative side effects and maximize positive results.
8. Establish an action plan for implementation of human performance enhancement strategies (performance improvement intervention/solutions).
9. Implement HPE strategies.
10. Evaluate results during and after implementation, feeding information back into Step 1 to prompt continuous improvement and organizational learning.

HPE is a systematic approach to identifying or anticipating performance problems and improvement opportunities (Rothwell 1996a, 44).

Human Performance Technology Approach

Strategic HRD professionals maintain a philosophy that provides insight into complex performance situations. But how does this philosophy become converted into action? Required is an approach that addresses the range of performance improvement opportunities but always begins with the premise that performance problems are indicated by a clear gap between desired and actual performance.

HPT effectively addresses this range of situations in a systemic, performance-focused, and data-driven approach (Rummler and Brache 1992). The steps in the process are summarized as follows:

Step 1: Problem/Opportunity Definition. The objective of the first step is to identify and agree on the performance problem to be examined, which is the starting point (and the ending point, since it will ultimately be the basis for evaluating the project's effectiveness) of the process (Rummler and Brache 1992, 42). During this step, HRD professionals identify performance desired by the organization and the level(s) (organizational, business process, performer/job) of the performance problem.

Step 2: Analysis. During this step, HP technologists apply the HPT framework to diagnose the problem, determine its causes, and identify or prescribe a solution.

According to Rummler and Brache (1992, 42–44), this analysis should be focused at three levels within the organization:

- Organizational level to determine cross-functional processes that prevent appropriate performance.
- Process level to determine which process steps are not being performed properly and are leading to poor performance, to determine the action required to improve performance, and to identify the jobs that are critical to the successful performance of the process.
- Job/performer level to determine what job outputs of which critical jobs need to be improved in order for the key processes to work effectively and produce the desired quality and to identify the action required to improve the job output.

Step 3: Design and Development of Performance Improvement Interventions. At this point, HRD professionals consider possible ways to close past, present, or possible future performance gaps by addressing their root cause(s). The objective of this step is to design and develop performance improvement solutions that help close the performance gap. Interventions may be used individually or in combination, depending on the cause(s) of the gap(s). Rummler and Brache (1992, 44) suggest that this may include "a broad range of actions, from modifying organizational strategy to process and job redesign to the design of a new measurement system, a performance management system, or training." They further add that a critical component of this step is development of a process to evaluate the effectiveness of the solution.

Step 4: Implementation. Key to the success of implementing a performance management solution is planning and installing an intervention. Of course, top management's support is critical to successful implementation and can be assumed, provided that a significant organizational performance problem is being addressed.

Rothwell (1996b, 15) points out that human performance improvement specialists help the organization install an intervention. They may assist performers, managers, process owners, and other stakeholders in carrying out the following:

- examine what the organization currently is doing to address the cause(s) of the human performance gap;
- determine what the organization should do in the future to address the cause(s) of the human performance gap;
- assess changes inside or outside the organization that may affect the intervention as it is implemented;

- clarify and emphasize how the intervention will help the organization meet its needs, achieve its mission, and realize its strategic planning goals and objectives;
- identify the best sources of talent and resources to implement the intervention.

At the conclusion of this step the organization should have a clear understanding of the desired outcomes to be achieved from the intervention. To be effective, however, any intervention requires a long-term commitment and constant oversight by HRD professionals, stakeholders, and decisionmakers.

Regardless of the level of the organizational system, Silber (1992, 61) recommends the use of five different types of performance improvement interventions by HRD professionals.

- *Isolated Training.* The simplest (not necessarily the most effective or cheapest) form of intervention uses training to fix an isolated performance problem.
- *Isolated Performance.* These solutions involve job aids, minor environmental redesign, and incentive/motivation system changes to fix an isolated performance problem.
- *Total Training.* The approach takes a broad view of the problems it addresses and does a more effective and efficient training job to solve them but is limited to the solution set it considers: training.
- *Total Performance.* This approach includes studying information, environment/work design, incentives/motives, skill/knowledge, and management problems and solutions by taking into account cost effectiveness and return on investment for implemented solutions.
- *Total Cultural.* The total cultural intervention incorporates examination of problems and solutions, in the context of addressing the total organization's values and corporate culture, by providing techniques that determine the influence of larger-scale affective issues that underlie performance and for effecting changes that improve related performances.

Step 5: Evaluation. Evaluation entails gathering data on performance, assessing whether chosen solutions are producing desired results and, if not, how they can be modified to achieve the desired outcome (Rothwell 1996a). Although evaluation appears last in this process, Rummler and Brache (1992) point out that evaluation starts in step one, problem or opportunity identification, where the performance to be improved is identified. They assert that evaluation procedures should be developed along with solutions and should be part of the ongoing management of the performance improvement initiative. The data gathered and analyzed will determine whether the performance improvement solution eliminated or significantly mitigated the performance problem. If the solution is deemed inadequate, treatment is discontinued or a new remedy is prescribed.

Rothwell (1996b, 15) provides several questions that help to determine the effectiveness of a performance improvement solution:

- How well did the intervention achieve desired and measurable results?
- How well realized were the forecasted and measurable improvements targeted for the intervention?
- What were the positive and negative side effects?
- What side effects of the intervention were noticeable?
- What lessons were learned from the intervention that could be applied in the future?
- How well has the intervention been adopted in the corporate culture?
- What best practices or lessons learned resulted from the intervention?

Evaluation properly targeted at the subject for change (such as employee performance) and at the intervention (the means to an end) answers these key questions:

- Did results match intentions?
- Was a human performance gap eliminated or a human performance improvement opportunity realized?
- Were organizational needs met?

Measurement determines how much change and how much improvement occurred and answers the following questions:

- What were the impacts of the intervention strategy?
- What value was added in economic and noneconomic terms?

Conclusion

Human performance technology (HPT) differs from other fields, such as training and organizational development, in its unique approach to performance problem solving. HP technologists design and develop interventions that have four fundamental characteristics: They should be *results-oriented* (measurable), *cost-effective* (designed to save more than they cost), *comprehensive* (solve the whole problem, not just part of it), and *systemic* (well integrated into the entire organization).

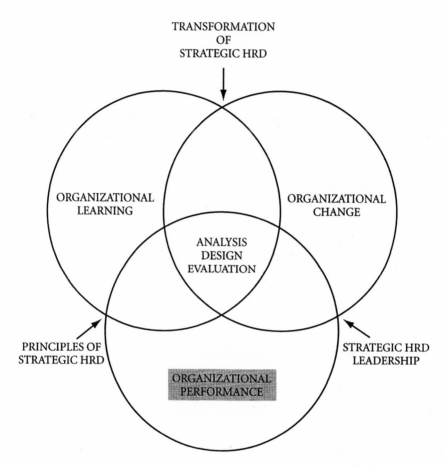

ORGANIZATIONAL LEARNING, PERFORMANCE, AND CHANGE

CHAPTER 9

Performance Improvement and Management

The first step in improving and managing performance is to define the term performance. Understanding the meaning of performance is essential to transforming traditional training departments into strategic HRD functions. It is also critical to improving an organization's performance capabilities. According to Rothwell (1996a, 26), "perform" means "to begin and carry through to completion; to take action in accordance with the requirements of; fulfill." "Performance" means "something performed; an accomplishment." He stresses that performance is synonymous with outcomes, results, or accomplishments.

Rothwell (1996a) asserts that performance should not be confused with the terms behavior, work activity, duty, responsibility, or competency. He maintains that a *behavior* is an observable action taken to achieve results, whereas a *work activity* is a task or series of tasks taken to achieve results. Thus, a work activity has a definite beginning, middle, and end. On the other hand, a *duty* is a moral obligation to perform, and a *responsibility* is an action or a result for which one is accountable; a *competency* is an area of knowledge or skill that is critical for producing key outputs. Moreover, he contends that a "competency is an internal capability that people bring to their jobs, a capability that may be expressed in a broad, even infinite array of on-the-job behaviors" (26). Robinson and Robinson (1996) assert that identifying and evaluating competencies typically means determining the underlying characteristics shared by outstanding performers.

A distinguishing characteristic between ineffective and effective organizations is that ineffective firms commonly fail to achieve the results required of them. Historically, ineffective organizations have well-written, meaningful mission statements and strategic plans but are ineffective in bringing about business results needed to remain vibrant and competitive. They boast that employees are their greatest asset and most valuable resource, while reality reveals this couldn't be further from the truth (Gilley and Maycunich 1999).

Ineffective organizations fail to possess or embrace a comprehensive performance management process instrumental in bringing about the performance improvements needed to secure desired business results. Consequently, ineffective organizations' strategic business goals and objectives are often unrealized. Ineffective organizations believe that their employees are easily replaced; thus policies and procedures demonstrate a revolving-door philosophy toward human resources.

Gilley, Boughton, and Maycunich (1999, 2) report that ineffective organizations exhibit an attitude of corporate indifference whereby they "wash their hands of any responsibility for their actions and decisions regarding employee performance, and are quickly willing to blame scapegoats for their own failings." They contend that the dilemma facing today's organizations is their ignorance regarding how to manage performance, develop people, or create systems and techniques that enhance organizational effectiveness. In short, organizations must transform employees into high performers who are their greatest asset, which requires creating a performance management process that allows firms to achieve their strategic business goals and objectives, enhance organizational renewal, improve performance capability, and increase competitive readiness.

Performance Improvement

Gilbert (1996, 7) cautions HRD professionals to avoid focusing on behavior rather than performance. He calls this common problem the "cult of behavior," which he refers to as and describes it as "the appeal to control or affect behavior in some way." In such cases, "there is little or no technology of ends and purposes. Indeed, behavior itself is viewed as an end rather than as a means to an end." HRD professionals need to be on guard to ensure that they do not fall into this pervasive trap. Gilbert maintains that the cult of behavior typically manifests itself in one of three specific areas: work behavior, knowledge, or motivation.

The cult of work behavior is common when expenditures of energy in the form of hard work are encouraged regardless of the results achieved by work efforts. Fuller and Farrington (1999) suggest that organizations caught in this trap encourage employees to work exactly like specific top performers (benchmark) and to value activity rather than results.

The cult of knowledge admires and reveres knowledge regardless of whether performance improves. Fuller and Farrington (1998) maintain that organizations locked into this behavior cult overemphasize employee development. Needless to say, placing highly developed employees in a dysfunctional work environment does not necessarily result in improved performance.

The cult of motivation is present when the organization overlooks results or achievement as long as employees demonstrate eagerness and a positive attitude and rally around company objectives. In this case, Fuller and Farrington (1999) find that organizations typically focus on building morale and teamwork. Although these are desirable outcomes, they are usually insufficient when performance is inadequate.

> Although the HRD professional's objective is to improve performance, too much emphasis on behaviors is particularly dangerous. HRD professionals need to remember that organizations value performance, not behavior. Additionally, specific behaviors do not necessarily lead to desired performance because environmental factors may interfere. Furthermore, some employees display "correct" behaviors yet never achieve the desired level of performance, while others exhibit contrary behaviors and achieve superior performance (Fuller and Farrington 1999, 31).

Principles of Performance Improvement

Why do employees behave the way they do, sometimes failing to achieve the performance results required of them? We believe that three fundamental principles explain most employee behavior and why organizations fail to secure the results they desire. These principles include performance/reward disconnect, performance whitewashing, and inspection failure.

Many employees fail to perform adequately because there is no correlation between their performance and that rewarded by the organization *(performance/reward disconnect)*. Many organizations, for example, embrace the concept of team building and invest much time and money training their people in the skills, knowledge, and practice of self-directed work teams; however, they continue to compensate their employees for individual performance. Thus, performance behaviors that an organization desires are ignored or punished in the workplace.

> Organizations send mixed messages by demanding quality work yet establishing unrealistic deadlines for completion; expecting projects to be finished on time but doing nothing when a senior manager delays until the last minute to begin; or rewarding those employees who look the busiest or work the longest hours, while emphasizing other results such as speed or efficiency. Improving organizational performance requires a direct correlation between desired performance and rewards. Individuals rewarded for the right performance will continue to produce similarly, as will those rewarded for improper behavior. (Le Boeuf 1985).

Inappropriate performance also occurs when managers fail to communicate which results are the most important and treat all performance results the same, which we refer to as *performance whitewashing*. This behavior confuses employees and causes them to prioritize results according to their own perspectives, which may or may not align with organizational expectations. The problem, however, is not with employee performance but with managers' inability to prioritize performance outcomes and communicate these to staff. Correction requires managers to determine which results are truly important and which are less so. These priorities must be communicated to employees and rewarded accordingly.

Some employees fail to produce desired performance outcomes because managers neglect to inspect their work *(inspection failure)*. Since some managers spend little time reviewing or inspecting employees' outputs, employees are on their own to produce results they perceive to be important to the organization. Effective managers link expectations with inspection, which can occur during performance coaching or developmental evaluations. Employees must know what is important to produce and that their managers will be inspecting performance outputs.

Models of Performance Improvement

Simonsen (1997) asserts that any performance improvement initiative should consist of seven essential elements. First, it should be driven by business needs. Second, models should identify their vision and philosophy of performance improvement. Third, performance improvement initiatives should have senior management support. Fourth, they should identify and allocate appropriate resources to improve performance. Fifth, performance improvement initiatives should guarantee management involvement. Sixth, initiatives should encourage employees' ownership of and responsibility for their own growth and development. Seventh, they should make necessary performance improvement resources available to employees.

The Performance Improvement Process Model

A large number of performance improvement models have surfaced over the years. Although they may differ in their construction, most contain the essential elements of problem definition, root cause analysis, and solution implementation and evaluation. Fuller and Farrington (1999, 25–28) provide a straightforward, simple performance improvement model based on these elements (see Figure 9.1).

Phase 1: Problem Definition.   The first phase of the performance improvement process is problem definition, where performance consultants (HRD professionals) determine what they are attempting to achieve (Chapters 10 and 11). An effective performance improvement initiative always begins with organizational

FIGURE 9.1   Performance Improvement Process Model

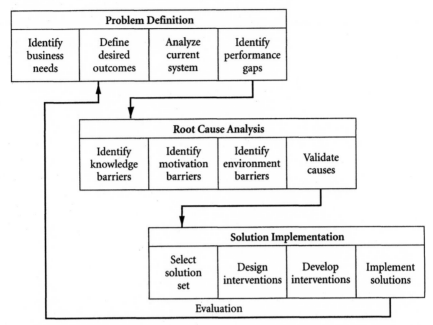

SOURCE: J. Fuller and J. Farrington, *From Training to Performance Improvement: Navigating the Transition* (San Francisco: Jossey-Bass, 1999).

needs. Essentially, the purpose of performance improvement is to increase the organization's success. By focusing on organizational needs, performance consultants keep performance improvement initiatives on course. While defining these business needs, performance consultants illuminate desired outcomes of the initiative and identify evidence indicating when the project has met its goals.

Performance consultants also determine the levels of performance necessary from employees. Comparing current performance with the desired performance to identify gaps accomplishes this and prevents performance consultants from creating performance improvement solutions when none are needed.

Phase 2: Root Cause Analysis.   Root cause analysis isolates what is actually creating the performance gap(s) (Chapters 9, 11, and 15). Once isolated, valid root causes become the target of the performance improvement solutions. In essence, eliminating root causes of poor performance allows employees to achieve desired performance, which leads to meeting the organization's business goals. Solutions should specifically eliminate identified root causes as efficiently and effectively as possible. Additionally, the cost of eliminating performance barriers should be weighed against the benefit of achieving business goals.

Phase 3: Solution Implementation. Fuller (1997) suggests that implementing solutions be undertaken with attention to implementation management and change management issues. Furthermore, the effectiveness of the performance improvement initiative should be evaluated based on achieving the original business goals identified in the performance analysis phase.

Systems Model of Performance Improvement

According to Swanson (1999, 2), a systematic process effectively addresses performance improvement efforts. The general performance improvement process consists of five phases: analysis, design, development, implementation, and evaluation within the organizational and external environments. The external environment is further delineated in terms of economic, political, and cultural forces surrounding the organization; the organization's environment reflects mission and strategy, structure, technology, and human resources. Performance improvement is displayed as only one process within the organization, which interacts with other organizational processes such as marketing, production, distribution, and research and development (Rummler and Brache 1995).

Analysis, the first and most critical phase, requires performance consultants and managers to work on establishing performance requirements, goals, or standards of the organization (Swanson 1999). They also determine whether management actions, development efforts, or a combination of both effect performance change. Performance consultants and managers determine precisely what people are required to know and what skills they must possess to perform a specific job.

Swanson (1994) divides the analysis phase into two parts, organizational performance diagnosis and work expertise documentation. Performance diagnosis is a problem-defining method that examines the systemic nature of the organization. The results include identifying actual and desired performance of the organization and its employees, and the desirable systems improvements to be made by management.

Work expertise documentation reveals the knowledge, skills, and abilities required of employees to perform on the job. Tools and techniques used in diagnosing workplace performance include job description, task inventory, performance activity, output, standard analysis, and task analysis. Performance consultants then develop a competency map for each position within the firm.

The analysis phase defines and frames the entire performance improvement effort. Therefore, the quality of analysis is critical because it impacts all remaining phases, which include design, development, implementation, and evaluation. Major errors can be made in any of the phases, but a fatal error in analysis not discovered until evaluation can prove very costly. Additionally, errors in the later phases are less costly to repair. (Swanson 1994)

White Spaces Performance Improvement Model

Rummler and Brache (1995) developed a performance management framework that reflects three levels of performance and their interdependent relationship: organization, business process, and job/performer. This framework is sometimes referred to as the White Spaces Performance Improvement Model.

Organization Level. At the organization level one examines the nature and direction of the business and the way it is set up and managed. This includes organizational goals, design, and management.

Organization Goals

At the organization level, goals are part of the business strategy. Organizations must establish clear systemwide goals that reflect decisions regarding (1) the organization's competitive advantage(s), (2) new services and new markets, (3) emphasis it will place on its various products or services and markets, and (4) resources it is prepared to invest in its operations and the return it expects to realize on these investments (Rummler and Brache 1995, 20; Rummler 1998).

Organization Design

This variable focuses on the structure of the organization. The systems view of performance suggests that structure should include more than where departmental boundaries have been drawn and who reports to whom. Structure includes the more important dimension of how work gets done and whether it makes sense.

Organization Management

Regardless of an organization's goals and design, it must be managed appropriately to operate effectively and efficiently. At the organization level, Rummler and Brache (1995, 21) maintain that management includes the following:

- Goal management: Creating functional subgoals that support achievement of overall organization goals.
- Performance management: Obtaining regular customer feedback, tracking actual performance along the measurement dimensions established in the goals, feeding back performance information to relevant subsystems, taking corrective action if performance is off target, and resetting goals so that the organization is continually adapting to external and internal reality.
- Resource management: Balancing the allocation of people, equipment, and budgets across the system.

- Interface management: Ensuring that the "white space" between functions is managed. In this capacity, managers resolve functional "turf" conflicts and establish infrastructures to support collaboration that characterizes efficient, effective internal customer-supplier relationships.

Business Process Level.   Every organization is organized into separate functions, which perform specific duties and activities. These functions offer identity for employees and provide them a connection within the organization. Rummler and Brache (1995, 22) argue that the "systems view does not enable us to understand the way work actually gets done, which is a necessary precursor to performance improvement." As a result, performance consultants should look at *processes* because most performance breakdowns or opportunities for efficiencies occur within cross-functional processes, such as order handling, billing, procurement, product development, customer service, sales, and marketing. These are known as business processes.

Accordingly, each function exists to serve the needs of one or more internal or external stakeholders. For external stakeholders, "the functions should measure the degree to which its products and services meet needs. If a function serves only internal stakeholders, it should be evaluated based on the way it meets stakeholders' needs and on the value it ultimately adds to the external stakeholder. In both cases, the key links to the customer are the processes to which the function contributes" (Rummler and Brache 1995, 22).

Process Goal

Because business processes are the means through which work gets produced, organizations need to set goals for processes. These goals should be derived from organization goals and other stakeholder requirements, as they are targets that link external stakeholders to the organization. The goals for internal processes (i.e., planning, budgeting, and recruiting) should also be based on the needs of internal stakeholders.

Process Design

Once organizations have established process goals, organizations need to make sure that their processes are structured (designed) to meet the goals efficiently (Rummler 1998). Processes should be logical, streamlined paths to the achievement of goals. Rummler and Brache (1995, 23) ask one simple question that addresses this variable: "Do the company's key processes consist of steps that enable it to meet process goals efficiently?"

Process Management

Any process will be ineffective unless it is managed appropriately. Rummler and Brache (1995, 23) maintain that process management includes the same ingredients as organization management:

- Goal management: Establishing subgoals at each critical process step.
- Performance management: Regularly obtaining customer feedback on process outputs, tracking process performance along dimensions established in goals, feeding back performance information, identifying and correcting process deficiencies, and resetting process goals to reflect current customer requirements and internal constraints.
- Resource management: Supporting each process step with the equipment, staff, and budget needed to achieve goals and make expected contributions to overall process goals.
- Interface management: Managing the "white space" between process steps, especially those that pass between functions. As at the organization level, where the greatest opportunities for improvement lie between functions, the greatest process improvement opportunities often lie between process steps.

Job/Performer Level. Regardless of how well organization and process levels are organized and managed in terms of goals, design, and management, a breakdown will occur unless employee needs are met. This is because employees are responsible for organization and process performance. If processes are the means by which an organization produces its outputs, employees (performers) are the means through which processes operate.

Rummler (1998) believes that organizations must establish goals for employees in those jobs that support processes (job goals). In addition, the job should be designed to make optimum contributions to job goals (job design). In other words, has the organization structured the boundaries and responsibilities of its jobs so that they enable job goals to be met? Finally, organizations must manage the human performance system to survive.

Rummler and Brache (1995) maintain that managers must create a supportive environment free of fear for employees, who ultimately determine whether company strategy becomes reality. They also argue that relationship mapping (Chapter 4) and the interface between performance standards, outputs, activities, and competency maps (see the Performance Alignment Model this chapter) are essential in managing and improving performance as well as managing the "white spaces" of the organization.

Performance Management

According to Kissler (1991), performance management should begin by determining why it should take place at all. He believes that performance management helps organizations sustain or improve performance, promote greater consistency in performance evaluation, and provide high-quality feedback. Performance management helps organizations link evaluations to employee development and to a merit-based compensation plan. Moreover, it forms a basis for coaching and counseling, permits individual input during the evaluation process, and allows for a blend of qualitative and quantitative evaluations. Performance management provides a process that helps manage employee expectations of job demands and factors that reveal how well the job is done.

Characteristics of Top Performers

Fuller and Farrington (1999, 22–24) identified several characteristics of top performers. First, top performers typically examine closely the processes they use to achieve their objectives or results and then eliminate unnecessary steps. Second, they determine what additional steps or actions need to be taken to achieve success or avoid failure. Third, top performers use information or documentation, such as diagrams, schematics, repair manuals, and so forth, that is not widely distributed throughout the organization. As a result, these individuals can outperform others in organizations that are not familiar with the information source. Fourth, they assemble or create their own job aids based on their work experience, which provides them a significant advantage over others, which have to discover the information for themselves. Fifth, top performers are successful in scouting out sources of information outside of their own workplace. Sixth, they rapidly realize that standard-issue tools (software, equipment, etc.) are inadequate for the job and begin to accumulate additional tools through other sources, usually at their own expense. Seventh, top performers have an intrinsic motivation that helps them take initiative in overcoming barriers in the performance system that the organization is not addressing. Eighth, they receive better guidance and feedback, which leads to constantly improving performance over time. Ninth, top performers enjoy incentives that motivate them to achieve excellence. Tenth, they do not excel because of more or better training. Although training does significantly contribute to performance improvement for poor to medium performers, it does not impact the achievement of top performers who optimize other components of the human performance system (see Chapter 8: inputs, consequences, feedback, environment).

Measurement of Performance

According to Bates (1999), measuring performance depends on having or developing good measures. He summarizes the difficulty of measuring performance:

> The availability of good measures assumes that particular attributes of interest can be identified and assessed. However, the attributes like performance can sometimes be difficult to quantify because of their complexity and magnitude. Problems of performance definition, measurement, and interpretation can also be compounded by the social context of organizations. . . . When performance attributes resist accurate and

consistent definition, measurement problems—such as low reliability, contamination, and inaccuracy—arise. Inevitably, there are then difficulties in data interpretation because the information is ambiguous. (Bates 1999, 51)

Benefits of Performance Management

According to Simonsen (1997, 66), there are several benefits to developing and implementing performance management systems. Performance management systems help organizations reduce turnover of highly skilled or experienced employees by providing environments conducive to growth and development and help eliminate outdated expectations for career opportunities after flattening or reorganizing an organization. She contends that such systems help to motivate employees, who take responsibility for their own development and continue to add value, encourage employees and managers to support continuous learning, and help managers develop their employees.

Performance management systems permit employees to understand the urgency of keeping skills and abilities current and increase retention of experienced employees by providing career advancement. They enable employees to create meaningful development plans and match realities in the organization to recruiting promises. They also help encourage equal opportunity for minorities and women. Finally, performance management systems help organizations develop competitive readiness through productive and motivated employees and cultivate flexible employees who can move out of functional "silos" or narrowly defined roles.

Outcomes of Linking Performance Management to Business Strategy

Kissler (1991) identified several outcomes of linking performance management to business strategy. They include developing clearer work goals and objectives in support of organization strategy and creating greater overall commitment from employees at all levels. Other outcomes of this linkage include improving individual performance, creating a stronger link to rewards and career management, and reducing administrative burden by encouraging involvement. Finally, this linkage results in improving managerial skills in performance management and increasing employee involvement in the overall performance improvement process.

Organizational Responsibilities in Performance Management

When developing and implementing performance management systems, organizations are responsible for identifying stakeholders' performance needs and expectations, organizational design, human resource planning, and job analysis. Successful achievement of these responsibilities results in the execution of an effective performance management system.

Identifying Stakeholders' Performance Needs and Expectations

Organizations have the responsibility of identifying their stakeholders' needs and expectations. Previously, we defined stakeholders as anyone who has something to gain or lose as a result of an interaction with the firm. Thus, organizations must focus their performance management efforts on these individuals.

Needs are the problems or issues that must be resolved for an organization to reach its business goals and objectives. They are the gaps that must be filled in order for an organization to function effectively and provide value to all stakeholders. The most common stakeholders' needs include improved business results, higher return on investment, more effective hiring and retention practices, better organizational communications, and improved developmental strategies. Effective organizations identify the needs most prevalent among their stakeholder groups and design performance improvement strategies to fulfill them.

Identifying expectations reveals employee strategies for meeting organizational goals. However, expectations differ from needs. Expectations are outcomes desired by stakeholders as a result of their performance, whereas needs are requirements that stakeholders must have met in order to perform satisfactorily. In other words, needs are the minimal or baseline conditions that must be met for the stakeholder, whereas expectations are the outcomes that stakeholders hope to achieve as a result of their performance. Achieving performance goals requires organizations to meet their stakeholders' needs and expectations.

Expectations are the outcomes that internal stakeholders (employees) anticipate from their performance within an organization. These should be motivational and fair since they establish satisfaction levels for internal stakeholders. The most common expectations include compensation, recognition, rewards, feedback, and coaching.

Organizational Design

According to Dean (1999), organizational design is the configuration used by a firm to transform resources into products or services to create competitive advantage. Competitive advantage occurs when one organization is more successful than another in influencing the decisions of three key constituencies: customers, suppliers of capital and funds, and current and potential employees (Jewell and Jewell 1992).

Competitive advantage surfaces by understanding where an organization has or can have leverage over their competitors and then devising strategies and operational procedures to maximize this leverage. An organization can also achieve competitive advantage by providing greater perceived value for its products and services than its competitors do. This allows an organization to gain market share, broaden its customer base, and force competitors to adjust their strategy. Another way is by providing higher return on investment for risk taking. When successful, organizations can influence their financial partners (suppliers of internal and external funds) to underwrite key initiatives and strategies. As a result, organizations have greater access to the funds they need to grow.

By attracting and retaining human resources with exceptional talent or potential, organizations can gain a competitive advantage over their competitors. Dean (1999) believes that organizations can further enhance their competitive advantage by developing each employee's knowledge and skills, creating structures and systems that focus and support each individual's ability to contribute, and gaining individual commitment to the vision and objectives of the organization. In fact, organizational long-term ability to compete in the marketplace depends on the competence, creativity, and commitment of its human resources. This strategy is enormously important in building a developmental culture (Morris 1995). All of these require mastery of the organization's performance management system.

Organizational design can improve performance management systems by creating structures, systems, and a culture that embraces performance and quality. This focuses human resources on continuous improvement, further developing and utilizing the diverse capabilities and potential of all employees. Organizational design can create work environments that meet the critical and changing needs of every employee.

Human Resource Planning

Cascio (1995, 142) defines human resource planning as "an effort to anticipate future business and environmental demands on an organization, and provide qualified people to fulfill business needs and satisfy demands." Gilley and Maycunich (2000) maintain that human resource planning is a process of systematically organizing the future, of putting into place a plan designed to address upcoming performance problems or productivity and quality requirements. They view human resource planning as a process, not merely a component of an HR professional's job description. As such, human resource planning focuses on identifying an organization's human resource needs under changing conditions and developing the interventions and initiatives necessary to satisfy those needs.

A performance improvement–oriented organization's long-term success depends on its employees' capabilities, which can be developed internally or acquired on the open market. Strategic human resource planning, instrumental in this success, is a complex activity that requires careful analysis, forecasting skill, and input by organizational leaders, managers, and employees.

Human resource planning should be integrated with organization-wide strategic planning and implementation, as well as performance management activities. Absent this integrative approach, human resource planning will be unable to positively impact the type and quality of employees needed to ensure effective organizational renewal and competitive readiness.

Job Analysis

Once human resource planning efforts have been identified, HRD professionals and organizational leaders engage in job analysis. Job analysis identifies job requirements within the organization, which in turn creates a solid basis on which to make job-related employment decisions (Schneider and Konz 1989). Through this process, organizations can establish interviewing criteria, develop performance appraisal systems, identify selection requirements, and provide a framework for performance coaching—all of which are important elements of a performance management system.

Cascio (1995) believes job analysis can further improve performance management by clarifying job requirements and the relationships among jobs, forecasting human resource needs, identifying training, transfer, and promotion requirements, evaluating employee performance, and conducting compensation reviews. Additionally, job analysis is helpful in recruiting future employees, enhancing career planning and counseling activities, improving job design, and developing job classifications. Finally, job analysis is useful in resolving grievances and jurisdictional disputes, improving working methods, and identifying job classifications useful in developing selection, training, and compensation systems.

Organizational Leaders' Roles and Responsibilities in Performance Management

In most organizations, leaders are considered executives and senior managers. Although this has been true for many years, Hesselbein, Goldsmith, and Beckhard (1995) believe that a number of shifts occurring within organizations regarding leadership are having a profound impact on performance management. Leadership will be shared throughout the firm rather than only at the top. They note that leaders will be more likely to ask questions than give answers or provide solutions and to focus on learning and its implications on organizational renewal. Leaders will shift from reliance on purely analytical *tools* in favor of integrating analytical *approaches* to problem solving. Simple solutions to complex problems will be abandoned as unrealistic in favor of identifying interventions and solutions that will impact the organization throughout its life. Finally, team leadership is increasing and will be the primary emphasis in tomorrow's organizations.

Ulrich (1997a, 242) believes that "systems must be created to mold future leaders. These systems might include designing and using competency models, tracking present leadership quality, finding creative models for leadership development, and involving senior managers in serious leadership development." Additionally, organizations will seek leaders who possess "the right stuff," those philosophies, qualities, and skills essential to championing the performance management needed for evolution to the developmental level.

Leaders' Roles

When performance management systems are used, leaders adopt two principal roles: *champions for change* and *advocates for performance improvement.*

Champions for Change. Improving performance within an organization requires leaders (executives) to accept their role as its champion, identifying key success factors for building performance capacity. Ulrich (1997a) identified seven critical factors of success in building capacity for performance management and improvement. Leaders must

1. lead performance management and improvement initiatives;
2. mobilize commitment for performance management and improvement;
3. change systems and structures to support performance management and improvement;
4. monitor employee progress through performance management initiatives;
5. make performance improvement last by reinforcing and rewarding employee growth and development;
6. create a shared need for performance management and improvement;
7. shape a vision for performance management and improvement initiatives.

Ulrich contends that few executives employ these factors when implementing performance management and improvement initiatives. He further argues that performance management and improvement present a paradox, one that requires the utilization of a clearly defined performance management model to resolve.

Advocates for Performance Improvement. Organizational leaders should serve as advocates during the performance management process, acting as guides, providing and interpreting information, identifying problems, facilitating solutions, and evaluating outcomes. According to Gilley and Maycunich (1998a), advocates are pro-active "scouts" pioneering ways the organization can successfully implement the process. As scouts, leaders focus on the success of performance management; hence acting as change ambassadors within the firm.

In order for leaders to become advocates for performance improvement they must possess credibility with other decisionmakers, stakeholders, influencers, and human resource professionals. Because advocates ask the organization to take risks that may seriously impact its competitiveness and financial viability, credibility is essential. As advocates for performance improvement, leaders demonstrate vision.

Leaders' Responsibilities

During performance management initiatives, leaders are primarily responsible for initiating organizational transformation. According to Gilley and Maycunich (2000, 36), "organizational transformation is the re-creation, redesign, and redefinition of a firm to meet continuous, ever-changing competitive challenges." Leaders are responsible for initiatives that cause organizations to shift their culture, structure, work climate, job and work designs, and fundamental identification of products and services necessary to enhance a firm's competitive readiness.

Performance improvement–oriented leaders demand that HRD professionals focus on outcomes instead of activities. Consequently, leaders need to shift their HRD philosophy from activity-based to outcome-based solutions. Ulrich (1998, 133–134) describes four approaches that accomplish this change. First, leaders communicate to all organizational members that performance management is critical to business success. Second, leaders explicitly define the deliverables for HRD professionals, holding them accountable for results. In this way, HRD professionals will be responsible for initiatives similar to other departments, divisions, and units. As such, they will track, measure, and evaluate results and be rewarded accordingly. Third, leaders invest in innovative HRD practices and utilize new technologies and practices to transform the organization through performance management. By promoting new HRD practices, leaders signal to the organization that its human resources are worthy of the organization's investment, attention, and time. Fourth, leaders insist on increased professionalism of their practitioners, which is perhaps the most important innovation in which leaders may engage to support performance management. Organizations need HRD professionals who know the business, understand the theory and practice of human resources, and are able to coordinate performance management activities.

Leaders are ultimately responsible for increased profitability, efficiency, and effectiveness through performance management, although they rely on managers and employees to ensure that improvement occurs. Although leaders initiate and guide performance management activities, employee participation is needed to create a shared vision of performance excellence. Managers sponsor performance improvement by mobilizing commitment, modifying systems and structures, monitoring progress, and making change last.

Ulrich (1997a, 160) maintains that effective leaders own and champion the performance management process, publicly commit to making performance management happen, obtain the resources necessary to sustain performance management, and make a personal commitment to the performance management process.

Managers' Roles and Responsibilities in Performance Management

Managers drive the process of and are responsible for performance management. Performance-oriented organizations require managers to dramatically shift their roles to accommodate and encourage employee growth and development. They are the decisionmakers, energizers, and guides for their employees, serving as conduits for performance improvement and organizational change.

Managers' Roles

Managers engage in at least five different roles in performance management. These include performance coach, facilitator of learning, mentor, performance confronter, and career counselor.

Performance Coach.   Employing performance management systems requires a dramatic shift in the role of manager. According to Peterson and Hicks (1996), managers should assume the role of performance coach—responsible for establishing rapport with employees, encouraging face-to-face communications, being active participants with workers rather than passive observers, and relying on good listening, questioning, and facilitation skills to achieve desired business results. Performance coaching is *person-centered management,* a series of one-on-one exchanges between managers and their employees that solve problems, improve performance, and achieve results through personal growth and development (Gilley and Boughton 1996).

Facilitator of Learning.   In the facilitator of learning role, managers guide and direct employees, helping them acquire new skills, knowledge, and appropriate behaviors. As learning facilitators, managers operate as partners in performance management, using feedback and summarization techniques to help employees fully grasp the concepts being taught. They serve as one-on-one tutors sharing information that will ultimately impact employee growth and development. Effective managers successfully communicate and demonstrate how additional skills, knowledge, and appropriate behaviors will produce desired outcomes. Typically, training comes in the form of on-the-job training but can involve formal developmental activities.

Several benefits are realized from the facilitator of learning role. They include increased technical competence and breadth of understanding, improved interpersonal interactions and relationships between managers and employees, enhanced problem-solving skills, improved employee performance and quality, improved managerial competence in technical and interpersonal areas through repetitive instruction, and commitment to continuous growth and development.

Mentor.   Mentors are valuable guides for employees, sharing their personal and professional experiences in an effort to help employees grow and develop. Simonsen (1997) believes that mentoring allows employees to benefit from a manager's experience—both successes and failures—and reduces fears, concerns, or frustrations, while promoting celebration of success, victories, and job accomplishments. They suggest that mentoring helps employees avoid costly mistakes and pitfalls so damaging to careers. It helps improve the relationship between managers and employees.

Gilley and Boughton (1996, 40) identified several outcomes realized by mentoring. It helps employees develop political awareness and savvy; understand and appreciate the special nature of the organization's culture; create a personal network within the firm; build commitment to organizational goals, guiding principles, and values; advance their careers; and enhance their personal growth and development.

Simonsen (1997, 160–162) maintains that managers are responsible for understanding the benefits of mentoring for all involved, including the organization. They should be responsible for knowing the purpose and goals of the mentoring program and participating in orientation and training sessions to better understand and support it, encouraging employees to adopt a developmental attitude, and offering help when appropriate. Furthermore, they are responsible for making time available to employees and establishing a climate of open interaction as well as establishing realistic expectations. Additionally, they are responsible for working with employees to set realistic goals and appropriate action plans, fostering relationships with them by listening and being open-minded about the their ideas and opinions. Managers are responsible for encouraging professional behavior and confronting negative attitudes as well as identifying obstacles and exploring ways to overcome them. Moreover, managers are responsible for offering encouragement and standing by employees in critical situations, identifying appropriate resources, and sharing critical knowledge and insight into organizational realities. Finally, they are responsible for triggering self-awareness and providing genuine confidence-building experiences and encouraging employees to explore options.

Performance Confronter. Managers have the unique responsibility of improving employee performance and thus are obligated to confront poor performance. Effective managers address inadequate performance immediately yet in a nonthreatening, participatory manner, shifting from an authoritative role to a participatory one by relinquishing control and dominance. Employees participate as equal partners in examination of their careers or performance challenges. As a result, the manager/employee relationship improves significantly.

Managers who adopt a nonthreatening, participatory approach encourage employees to share in problem solving and decisionmaking, while advocating the free exchange of ideas, opinions, and feelings. Employees benefit from the resulting positive communication climate, feel more secure, and openly express their thoughts and ideas. Such a climate is comfortable, conducive to sharing, and even nurturing to employee development.

Career Counselor. From a performance management perspective, the role of career counselor might be the most important. Managers actively engaged in this role encourage employees to make independent yet informed decisions regarding their future career paths. Effective managers *guide* employees through a reasonably in-depth review and exploration of their interests, abilities, beliefs, and desires pertaining to their present and future careers. They partner with employees to evaluate alternatives, explore careers inside or outside the organization, and examine career commitment. They present differing point of views to help them develop a more in-depth analysis of career options. One of the primary activities in which career counselors engage is applying developmental evaluations and creating employee growth and development plans.

As career counselors, managers help organizations better allocate human resources by providing a direct link between employees and the business when considering the quality and quantity of workers needed to maintain or enhance organizational competitive readiness. Simonsen (1997) identified several functions of career counselors, which include providing assistance to individuals for career planning within the organization, conducting formal and informal individual assessments and interpretation, and identifying relevant written resources and making information available to employees. She contends that career counselors are helpful in identifying and coordinating organizational resources, such as contacts, networks, or executive briefings, and making referrals to external sources as appropriate, such as counseling, testing, training, or outplacement services.

Managers' Responsibilities

To enhance organizational performance, every manager should be held accountable for several responsibilities such as building synergistic relationships, establishing appropriate goals, enhancing performance improvement, and performance overviewing. They should also be responsible for conducting developmental evaluations, creating growth and development plans, and conducting succession planning. Finally, managers are responsible for linking compensation and rewards to growth and development and sponsoring performance improvement and change.

Building Synergistic Relationships.   Ineffective organizations typically pluck managers from the ranks of day-to-day operations because they possess advanced technical knowledge. Unfortunately, little or no attention is paid to the interpersonal and leadership skills necessary to secure results through people. Promoting individuals in this manner discounts the importance of the interactive people skills necessary to achieve desired business results. As a result, employees are subjected to inexperienced, ineffective, or incompetent managers. Because organizations fail to focus on the necessary interpersonal skills needed to enhance manager-employee relationships, they miss opportunities to develop effective performance management practices.

Gilley and Boughton (1996, 34) believe that managers have an obligation to build synergistic relationships that enhance employee commitment to improving performance and quality and increasing productivity. Synergistic relationships anchor a performance management process that enhances employee self-esteem, increases productivity, improves organizational understanding and communication, and enhances commitment.

Establishing Appropriate Goals.   Every job within an organization contains one or several goals to be accomplished. A goal is a global statement of purpose and direction toward which all objectives, activities, and tasks will point. According to Weiss and Wysocki (1992), goals define outcomes in terms of end products or services, act as continual points of reference for settling disputes and misunderstandings about the project, and keep all objectives and associated work on track. Gilley and Coffern (1994) add two more functions: Work goals enable employees to stay focused on desired results and promote agreement and commitment regarding performance outcomes. Randolph and Posner (1992) maintain that goal statements help managers and employees know when a successful outcome has been achieved. In essence, performance goals reveal to everyone involved what the end will look like. Effectively written performance goals—the result of collaboration between managers and employees—are specific, measurable, attainable, realistic, and time-based (SMART). Performance goals that meet this SMART criteria are more easily measured and allow employees greater understanding of expectations.

Enhancing Performance Improvement. Continuous performance improvement is the heart of performance management. Effective managers communicate specifically what employees need to improve and why. Performance improvement focuses on problems and behaviors, not people; confronts to produce desired change without causing employees to become defensive; and maintains positive relationships with employees.

Many managers, unfortunately, have difficulty confronting employees who do not perform adequately. They may be uncomfortable with confrontation. Occasionally, some managers avoid addressing poor performance until it has reached the point where dramatic action must be taken. Overcoming these inhibitions requires managerial knowledge of the difference between confrontation and criticism. Confrontation focuses on the performance problem and its consequences, identifies specific performance shortfalls, and offers appropriate corrective actions to improve future performance. Concurrently, managers concentrate extensively on building and maintaining relationships with their employees. Conversely, criticism attacks an employee's faults, often in the form of general, nonspecific statements that place blame for performance deficiencies. Typical criticism is a self-serving, self-centered, counterproductive action that allows managers (critics) to vent anger and frustration toward their employees.

To enhance performance, effective managers communicate performance standards, identify performance shortfalls, collaboratively develop strategies for performance improvement, obtain employee commitment for continued improvement, encourage employees to perform increasingly difficult tasks, and encourage employee growth and development.

Performance Overviewing. According to Kissler (1991, 153), performance overviewing allows managers to examine performance in a variety of ways. At times the focus is on certain business processes, such as marketing, research and development, or human resources; at other times the emphasis is on current performance as compared to desired performance. In any case, managers are responsible for reviewing performance throughout the organization for the purpose of making recommendations for change.

Conducting Developmental Evaluations. Most organizations require regularly scheduled employee performance appraisals, whereby managers judge employee performance and bestow compensation increases accordingly. In theory, performance appraisals are an effective developmental activity that rewards past performance, improves future performance, and encourages career development. In reality, performance appraisals often fail to achieve any of these objectives.

According to Gilley, Boughton, and Maycunich (1999, 91),

> One reason for the disparity between performance appraisal theory and practice is in the execution of the performance appraisal process. Many organizations rely on performance appraisal or review forms that allow managers to painlessly evaluate their employees by assigning numbers for every possible performance category. Making the process as simple as possible prevents managers and employees from thinking developmentally. We believe that these forms are more damaging than beneficial—preventing managers from working collaboratively with employees in their development. Overcoming this obstacle requires managers to be given freedom to work with their employees to identify performance problems, solutions, and developmental opportunities. Eliminating useless, wasteful performance appraisal and review forms, and substituting them with an opportunity to conduct developmental evaluations, solves this problem.
>
> Developmental evaluations allow managers the opportunity to assess employee strengths and weaknesses; thus, managers analyze worker knowledge, skills, and behaviors to determine areas of excellence and those needing improvement. These evaluations present opportunities for managers and employees to discuss current and future developmental goals and objectives along with plans to achieve them, reviewing the "fit" between organizational expectations and those of the employee. Constructive discussion regarding developmental and career planning actions to be implemented will follow. Most importantly, developmental evaluations are a vehicle for discussing future growth and development actions that will enhance employees' abilities and competencies, as well as their careers.
>
> Developmental evaluations are an excellent tool for analyzing employee performance and making recommendations for improvement. They help managers isolate obstacles that prevent exemplary performance, and identify strategies to overcome them. Thus, development evaluations provide formal, summative evaluations of an employee's current performance, skills, and aptitudes designed to help employees adopt corrective actions or identify activities that will enhance their future potential.

Creating Employee Growth and Development Plans.   A critical component of the performance management process is the employee growth and development plan, which allows managers and employees to discuss ways by which to improve performance results. Growth and development plans examine employee strengths, weaknesses, and areas requiring improvement and formulate strategies for continuous improvement and success. These plans are long-term, developmental strategies (not quick fixes), mutually designed by managers and employees, and realistic, specific, attainable, and tied to a timetable.

Growth and development plans are the cornerstones of the developmental organization because they help shift emphasis from short-term performance results to long-term development strategies that enhance an organization's competitive readiness (see Chapter 7). This shift in focus prepares employees to build their personal renewal and performance capacities.

Managers and employees partner to design plans that help employees acquire new knowledge and skills and to apply them to their jobs. This mutually beneficial partnership allows employees to acquire critical skills and competencies that enhance their performance and career development opportunities, while managers enjoy better business results. Collaborative partnerships permit managers to motivate their employees, create a self-esteeming work environment, delegate tasks and responsibilities, build on employee strengths while managing their weaknesses, and design learning acquisition and transfer plans.

Kissler (1991) suggests that development plans should include career interests (both short-term and long-range), technical, managerial, and interpersonal qualifications, future development requirements, and the employee's perceptions of development activities. Additionally, managers are responsible for providing a brief review of the employee's accomplishments, an assessment of his or her qualifications in terms of strengths and areas needing improvement, development opportunities, career recommendations, potential next assignments, and assessment of the individual's stated career route and goals.

Simonsen (1997) identified several benefits of developmental plans. First, organizations have a record of employees' interests, mobility, and goals. Second, information can be available in a database for promotional consideration and human resource planning. Third, development plans serve as a needs assessment that can be used in designing and developing learning interventions. Fourth, they reveal employee involvement in career management. Fifth, development plans can help identify employee readiness to upgrade skills and keep them current. Finally, an annual development plan is a means of accountability.

Conducting Succession Planning.   Succession planning allows managers to identify, mold, and mentor replacements for key employees in the organization. Despite its obvious benefits, Kissler (1991, 150–151) contends that succession planning fails when top-level management is not involved in the process or shows little interest. Succession planning also fails when the data gathered is not valid and when replacement nominations are accepted without review. Finally, succession planning is ineffective when backup candidates are chosen only by top-level managers or when the succession process itself is not reviewed for improvement.

Linking Compensation and Rewards to Growth and Development.   Historically, compensation and reward programs have been performance based, with little consideration given to rewarding employees for enhancing their skills or competencies. Employee performance increases dramatically when organizations link compensation and rewards to employee growth and development. Thus, compensation and rewards become a vehicle forever increasing employee development as opposed to mere performance achievement.

Performance without growth and development prevents an organization from maintaining the growth phase of the organizational life cycle. Failure to perpetuate the growth phase leads to organizational stagnation and eventual decline. Shifting compensation and reward programs to rewarding employee growth and development ensures that employee skills and competencies continue to evolve, thus guaranteeing an organization's competitive readiness, renewal, and performance capability.

The shift from rewarding performance to rewarding growth and development involves a remarkable transformation. Managers must develop a compensation and reward philosophy, align compensation and rewards with guiding principles, and select appropriate compensation and reward strategies. Effective managers identify performance growth and development goals and offer rewards that enhance employee growth and development. Finally, developmental managers integrate components of effective compensation program and link compensation and rewards to performance growth and development outcomes.

When growth and development actions are rewarded and reinforced they will be repeated, which further enhances employee commitment and loyalty. In this way, organizations encourage employees to develop their performance competencies so they are better able to produce desired results.

Sponsoring Performance Improvement and Change.   Successful implementation of performance management systems mandates significant change in organizational philosophy, operations, and strategy. This monumental effort requires organizational players—*managers*—to sponsor change, since they are the frontline *doers* responsible for incremental performance improvement.

Performance management systems need managers to generate excitement and mobilize commitment for performance improvement and change, alter systems and structures to better support performance improvement and change initiatives, oversee progress, and encourage actions that make change last. Ulrich (1997a, 160) believes that being a performance improvement and change catalyst requires managers to build coalitions of support for performance improvement and change and to recognize others who must be committed to performance improvement and change. They need to also enlist support from key individuals in the organization and build a responsibility matrix to bring about performance improvement and change. He agrees that managers must also be able to modify systems and structures to keep performance improvement and change alive. This requires managerial understanding of how to link performance improvement and change to other HR systems such as training, appraisals, compensation and rewards, communication, and so forth. Furthermore, sponsoring change requires managers to measure the success of performance improvement and change, identify its results, and recognize benchmarks of progress. Effective managers identify the important first steps needed to start, and maintain employee interest in performance improvement and change in both the short and long term. Finally, successful managers have a plan for adapting performance improvement and change over time.

HRD Professionals' Roles and Responsibilities in Performance Management

HRD professionals' roles and responsibilities are discussed throughout this book. Roles include performance consultant (Chapter 10) and organizational development change agent (Chapter 13). Responsibilities include developing learning transfer strategies (Chapter 7), managing the performance management process (performance alignment model, this chapter), evaluating the performance management process (Chapter 17), and performance consulting (Chapter 11).

Additionally, HRD professionals are responsible for designing and installing an employee involvement system to encourage participation in performance management and identifying customer/client satisfaction measures to determine overall product/service satisfaction. They are responsible for identifying competencies required for each job classification within the organization and for establishing performance goals and objectives for operating units or divisions. Other responsibilities include identifying the principal outcomes or outputs produced by each job classification, creating competency maps that can be used as the foundation for training and development activities, and identifying performance standards for each job classification.

HRD professionals have the responsibility for developing performance measures, creating a performance evaluation system for each job classification using performance measures to compare actual performance with performance standards and identifying training and development strategies designed to close performance gaps discovered during performance evaluation. Finally, HRD professionals are responsible for developing performance feedback and reinforcement systems designed to foster performance improvement and identifying compensation and reward systems linked to performance improvement. Once a performance management system has been established, managers are responsible for implementation and use in improving employee performance.

Employees' Roles and Responsibilities in Performance Management

During the performance management process, employees are ultimately responsible for their development, improvement, and change. Therefore, they must understand the relationship between developing knowledge and skills, performance improvement, and change. Employees are responsible for career planning and identifying their most appropriate career paths; thus they are gatekeepers of their own success. As a result, their primary responsibility is to identify the skills, knowledge, and competencies needed for current and future job assignments.

Employee Roles

The principal employee role in performance management is that of *doer* by utilizing available personal and organizational resources to the best of one's ability. The success with which employees secure these results lies with their ability to function as a personal change agent, individual career advocate, and career planner.

Personal Change Agent.   As personal change agents, employees take advantage of opportunities to positively impact their lives within the organization. This can range from improving relationships with coworkers and supervisors to positioning themselves for promotions due to exemplary performance over time. Personal change agents recognize and cultivate significant *transformation points,* those instances that provide opportunities for personal breakthroughs that will influence their organization's success and, as a result, their own.

Career Advocate.   The performance management process requires employees to take responsibility for their own careers even though they don't receive desired recognition or rewards (more responsibility, authority, raises, and promotions). As career advocates, employees are self-promoters, taking the initiative to inform management of their talents, interests, and career desires. Career advocates clearly demonstrate their wishes and back them up with solid evidence (work samples, special projects, portfolios, and the like) indicative of their knowledge and skills. Furthermore, career advocates routinely share their career aspirations with managers, maximizing formal or informal interaction, performance evaluations, and feedback opportunities to attain success.

Career Planner.   As career planners, employees proactively strategize to maximize their full potential, plotting a course that incorporates additional training, education, and experience to gain the knowledge, skills, and attitudes necessary to achieve their personal career goals. Strategic career planners constantly assess, reflect, and renew themselves throughout their careers, understanding the importance and impact of personal growth and development on their professional lives.

Employee Responsibilities

In order for the performance management process to be successful, employees must accept the responsibility for *making it happen* within the organization. Primarily, they are advocates of change.

In the final analysis, employees are responsible for implementing change, bringing leaders' visions to life through managers' policies and procedures. All too often, employees are overlooked as an essential element in bringing about lasting change in spite of the fact that they are instrumental in helping create the conditions conducive to establishing effective organizations. Ulrich (1997a, 160) contends that because employees are contributors to and benefactors of effective organizations, it is important that they understand the reason for change implementation, why it is important, how it benefits them and their organization, and how it benefits customers and other stakeholders.

The Performance Alignment Process

Gilley, Boughton, and Maycunich (1999, 4) insist that "the performance challenge facing every organization is to develop management systems that make employees the organization's greatest asset." To do so, an organization must design, develop and implement a *performance alignment process* intended to improve its performance and competitiveness, in other words, a process that addresses the performance challenge. The performance management process must incorporate an organization-wide approach that combines the entire performance improvement process into one cohesive operating system. He further contends that an organization-wide performance alignment process links performance to compensation and rewards, to the organization's strategic business goals and objectives, and to client needs and expectations.

According to Gilley, Boughton, and Maycunich (1999), the performance alignment process consists of seven separate but interrelated steps:

Step 1: Conducting stakeholder valuation
Step 2: Improving job design
Step 3: Establishing synergistic relationships
Step 4: Applying performance coaching
Step 5: Conducting developmental evaluations
Step 6: Creating performance growth and development plans
Step 7: Linking compensation and rewards to performance growth and development

Each step builds upon the others, forming a systematic and comprehensive approach to addressing the performance challenge (Figure 9.2). This approach separates performance alignment into two distinct phases. Conducting stakeholder valuations and improving job design are the responsibility of the organization, whereas the remaining steps are the responsibility of managers and employees. At the heart of the performance alignment process is the belief that employees are the center of influence that drives business results. Their employees understand and align their performance with the organization's strategic business goals and objectives.

Step 1: Conducting Stakeholder Valuation

Identifying client needs and expectations is the first step in achieving an organization's desired business results. Organizations must actively seek to understand their stakeholders and the value they place upon the products and services they receive. Employees who have little or no direct contact with external clients may not fully appreciate client needs and expectations. Even those who interact frequently with other employees may not view their coworkers as internal clients. Consequently, they fail to solicit their coworkers' input, recommendations, and suggestions.

Developmental organizations design strategies that allow each employee to understand his or her impact on both internal and external clients. If employees clearly understand how their clients think, they are able to identify needs and provide solutions that help the organization achieve long-term success. Organizations will then have a more effective, productive workforce through the alignment of employee understanding with client needs and expectations.

Identifying client needs and expectations can be accomplished through the process of stakeholder valuation. This process requires organizations to formally identify the needs and expectations of critical stakeholders; this information is obtainable through surveys, focus groups, and interviews. Once identified, stakeholders needs and expectations drive the organization's efforts to deliver value to clients. Consequently, stakeholder valuation serves as the genesis of the performance alignment process and must be completed prior to implementing step two.

Step 2: Improving Job Design

Jobs are designed to help the organization achieve strategic business goals and objectives, which become the targets for the entire performance alignment process. Strategic business goals and objectives represent the criteria used in measuring the entire organization's success. Increasing sales revenue, market share, and profits are the most common examples of strategic business goals and objectives.

Once the organization's strategic business goals and objectives have been identified, the job design process can begin. This process consists of five interdepen-

FIGURE 9.2   Performance Alignment Process

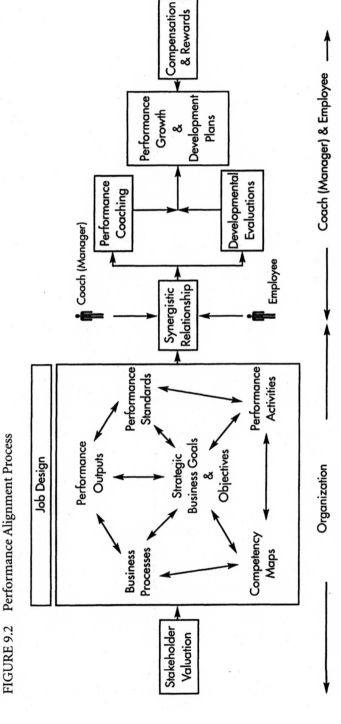

source: J. W. Gilley, N. W. Boughton, and A. Maycunich, *The Performance Challenge: Developing Management Systems to Make Employees Your Organization's Greatest Asset* (Cambridge, Mass.: Perseus Publishing, 1999).

dent functions used to produce a product or service: business processes, performance outputs, performance standards, performance activities, and competency maps.

Business Process. Every job is housed within an organizational function where various departments interact with one another. Rummler and Brache (1995) maintain that at this level important business processes (i.e., financial analysis, selling, record keeping, claims processing, customer service) can be identified. They also believe that part of the job analysis process involves identifying interfaces between business processes in order to eliminate breakdowns or isolate areas of improvement that ultimately impact organizational performance capacity. Therefore, job analysis uncovers opportunities for performance improvement and employee growth and development.

Performance Outputs. Rummler and Brache (1995) define performance outputs as the tangibles and intangibles employees are paid to produce—in essence, an employee's job. According to Gilley (1998, 91), performance outputs may represent the number of sales calls made by telemarketing representatives, sales made per month by sales personnel, service claims handled by customer service representatives, the number of packages delivered per day by postal workers, and so on. Hence, outputs represent the hourly, daily, weekly, monthly, quarterly, and/or yearly expectations of employees in a specific job classification.

Performance outputs are also the internal deliverables used as inputs by other employees in execution of their jobs, whereas external deliverables are the products and services produced for customers outside the organization. They are the tangible outcomes of employee performance that defines one's contribution within the organization.

Performance Activities. Employees engage in performance activities to create performance outputs. It is the responsibility of HRD professionals, managers, and employees to identify the activities required of employees. Each performance activity consists of small tasks, which collectively form the components of an employee's job.

In job analysis, HRD professionals need to examine performance activities to determine possible breakdowns. If a problem is identified, a growth and development intervention should be designed to help employees demonstrate acceptable performance.

Job descriptions demonstrate the relationship between performance outputs and activities and should be written to achieve three goals. First, job descriptions should be written to clearly identify performance outputs for each job. Second, they should identify the performance activities required by employees to produce these deliverables. Third, they should demonstrate the relationship between activities and outputs. Quite simply, a job description is simply a written document that describes an employee's performance activities and deliverables.

Performance Standards.   Rummler and Brache (1995) contend that performance standards are excellent criteria for measuring product and service quality and worker efficiency. They provide measures against which employees compare their actions and output to determine whether they are performing at acceptable levels. In other words, performance standards represent the targets used to measure the quality of employee outputs and the efficiency of their performance activities.

Performance standards enable employees to regulate the quality of their performance outputs and activities, avoid needless mistakes, and maintain consistency. Ultimately, this leads to better organizational results. Additionally, performance standards help managers determine acceptable performance and measure the quality of performance outputs. Without performance standards, managers and employees are not able to ascertain whether they have created performance outputs or executed performance activities acceptable to internal and external stakeholders.

According to Berke (1990), performance standards are based on performance outputs, rather than on the way employees do their jobs, and should be achievable, specific, measurable, time based, and written. Managers and employees should also easily understand them. He believes that performance standards allow employees to monitor and correct their performance because employees can determine for themselves how well they are performing and whether they are producing satisfactory performance outputs. Performance standards encourage employees to continue to produce at an acceptable level. Consequently, they will know when they are doing their jobs well.

Competency Maps.   Once performance outputs, standards, and activities are identified, HRD professionals can identify the competencies employees need to accomplish them. Gilley, Boughton, and Maycunich (1999) refer to these as *competency maps*, which represent the cumulation of the knowledge, skills, behaviors, and attitudes an employee possesses to complete job tasks that constitute performance activities. Competency maps are useful in recruiting and selecting employees for given job classifications, determining the growth and development activities in which employees must participate to master performance, and revealing employee strengths and weaknesses, thereby guiding formulation of career development activities as well as performance growth and development plans.

Examination of each of these five steps and determining their dependencies allows organizations to identify efficiencies that enable them to be more profitable and competitive. In fact, it could be said that an organization is only as efficient and effective as its job design.

Step 3: Establishing Synergistic Relationships

Organizations cannot possibly address the performance challenge without establishing positive working relationships between managers and employees—ones that enhance employee commitment to improving performance and quality and to increasing productivity and organizational results. A "positive working relationship" benefits all parties, allowing each to receive the specific outcomes desired. "Employee commitment" refers to an employee's willingness to make personal sacrifices to reach his or her team, department, and organizational goals. To enhance commitment, managers must clarify the goals of the team, department, and organization, provide the training necessary to improve the competencies required, and allow greater employee influence in decisionmaking. In exchange for their enhanced commitment, managers should reward employees appropriately. "Improving performance and quality, and increasing productivity and organizational results" refers to a manager's ability to create work environments dedicated to continuous improvement.

Step 4: Applying Performance Coaching

Understanding the manager's role in transforming employees into the organization's greatest asset is one of the most critical components of the performance challenge. Without a doubt, the most common and debilitating problem facing organizations today is the lack of qualified managers. Unfortunately, many organizations employ managers who are indifferent toward their employees, possess superior attitudes, consider employees as something to use and abuse, have poor listening, feedback, and interpersonal relationship skills, cannot produce a positive relationship with their employees, and cannot delegate, develop their employees, conduct performance appraisals, or establish priorities. It is common for such managers to criticize their employees' efforts, creating work environments characterized by fear and paranoia. When these conditions are allowed to continue, organizations are encouraging and fostering *managerial malpractice*, which is simply encouraging and supporting practices that enable unprofessional, unproductive, and incompetent managers to function within an organization.

The existence of managerial malpractice can be determined by examining whether the organization practices the following:

- keeping managers who are not good at getting results through people;
- promoting people to management roles before determining their "managerial aptitude";
- selecting new managers because they are the best performers or producers without regard for their people skills;

- spending valuable time "fixing" managerial incompetence instead of hiring qualified managers;
- keeping managers who preach the importance of teamwork, yet reward those individuals who stand out in the crowd;
- allowing managers to say one thing and do another (Gilley and Boughton 1996, 1).

Evidence of these symptoms within an organization reveals it is guilty of managerial malpractice.

The most efficient solution to this problem is to simply select managers for their people skills and hold them accountable for securing results through people. This requires managers to become involved with their employees by establishing rapport and encouraging face-to-face communications. Second, organizations must learn how to transform managers into performance coaches in order to overcome managerial malpractice. Performance coaching requires managers to shift constantly from one role to another, including training, counseling, confronting, and mentoring. Each role enhances employee self-esteem and helps the organization achieve better business results.

Step 5: Conducting Developmental Evaluations

Most organizations have some kind of annual performance appraisal process designed to provide managers with an opportunity to judge the quantity and quality of employee performance. The performance appraisal process should be transformed into a developmental opportunity, with performance appraisals evolving to developmental evaluations. Developmental evaluations should be used to determine whether employees are demonstrating acceptable performance activities and generating adequate outputs that meet or exceed performance standards. Developmental evaluations should also be used to determine whether the needs and expectations of internal and external clients have been satisfied, to assess employees' strengths and weaknesses by comparing their competencies against job requirements, and to examine how employee performance is helping the organization achieve its strategic business goals and objectives. Further, developmental evaluations are an excellent tool when confronting employee performance and making recommendations for improvement.

Step 6: Creating Performance Growth and Development Plans

The primary purpose of developmental evaluations is to identify the strengths and weaknesses of employees and discuss ways of enhancing employee performance growth and development. From this perspective, performance growth and development plans become a long-term strategy instead of a quick fix.

Clifton and Nelson (1992) believe that one of management's biggest temptations is to "fix" employees rather than discover things that they do well. As a result, most training and development activities are designed to *fix weaknesses* instead of to maximize employees' strengths. To develop areas of expertise that enable employees to maximize their personal productivity, effective managers create employee growth and development plans based upon employees' strengths, not weaknesses. If an employee's areas of expertise produce high levels of performance, it makes sense to build on these areas.

Additionally, managers should assist employees in the design, development, and implementation of a learning transfer plan because learning is a complete waste of time, energy, effort, and money if not transferred to the job. Consequently, performance growth and development plans must be designed in such a way that employees are able to apply learning to the job. Broad and Newstrom (1992) maintain that if employees fail to transfer learning to the job, the performance management process is utterly destroyed; thus, no other activity is more important to learning transfer.

Step 7: Linking Compensation and Rewards to Employee Growth and Development

Managers must establish a clear link between positive performance and recognition of employees' efforts. According to Le Boeuf (1985), research has shown that the performances that get rewarded and reinforced are repeated. Consequently, organizations are challenged to incorporate compensation and reward systems that build commitment and improve employee motivation. That is, organizations must reward the right things. Once proper compensation and reward systems are in place, performance coaches link performance enhancement with them.

Le Boeuf (1985) identified seven reward strategies that help performance coaches enhance employee commitment and secure results. They include rewarding long-term solutions, entrepreneurship, leadership, performance growth and development, teamwork and cooperation, creativity, and employee commitment and loyalty. Each of these strategies provides a better understanding of the impact of compensation and rewards on employee and organizational performance.

Conclusion

In order for performance improvement and management to be effective, the organization, leaders, managers, and employees must embrace their roles and meet their responsibilities. In addition, organizations need to identify their stakeholders' needs and expectations and design jobs appropriately. Managers need to establish positive working relationships with their employees, provide performance coaching, conduct developmental evaluation, create growth and development plans for their employees, and link compensation and rewards to employee growth and development. When these activities have been performed correctly, organizations will have appropriately addressed the performance challenge.

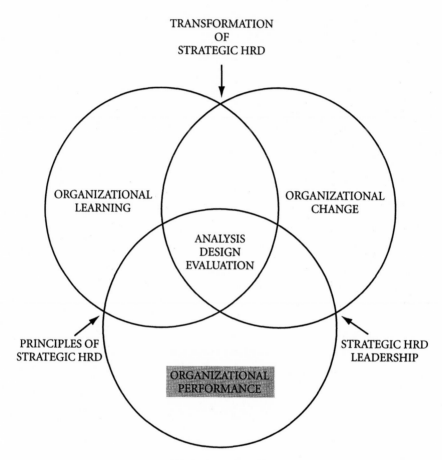

TRANSFORMATION
OF
STRATEGIC HRD

ORGANIZATIONAL
LEARNING

ORGANIZATIONAL
CHANGE

ANALYSIS
DESIGN
EVALUATION

PRINCIPLES OF
STRATEGIC HRD

STRATEGIC HRD
LEADERSHIP

ORGANIZATIONAL
PERFORMANCE

ORGANIZATIONAL LEARNING, PERFORMANCE, AND CHANGE

CHAPTER 10

Performance Consultant

Some HRD practitioners attempt to improve organizational effectiveness through classroom-oriented training. This approach relies on instructional design delivered under safe, controlled, artificial situations to improve employee skills and knowledge. HRD practitioners' credibility depends upon expert knowledge of predetermined learning activities (Bellman 1983).

Performance consultants, on the other hand, possess a very different perspective. Their focus emphasizes helping organizations achieve goals and objectives by improving overall organizational performance. This approach relies upon performance management and systems thinking skills to bring about organizational change, with emphasis on the overall human system rather than on individuals within the system. From this vantage point, performance consulting represents a "macro perspective" of overall organizational effectiveness. In essence, the performance consulting process treats the organization as the principal benefactor of any learning and change intervention, while employees are secondary benefactors.

Performance consultants partner with clients to provide services, determine what must be accomplished, and ensure that business problems are resolved to the client's satisfaction (Fuller and Farrington 1999). Robinson and Robinson (1996) believe that performance consultants are responsible for encouraging organizational leaders to take action in order to improve organizational performance.

The performance consultant's principal role is enhancing organizational efficiency and change; thus they must help the organization properly utilize its resources (inputs) by generating (through business processes) improved results (outputs). Performance consultants view the organization as a system containing inputs, such as financial, physical, and human resources, that produces outputs such as products and services through a series of business processes.

Performance Consultant Roles and Subroles

Many HRD professionals view themselves as "brokers of training," making little or no effort to customize training for the organization and paying little attention to overall organizational performance (Gilley and Coffern 1994, 26). Effective organizations, however, view learning as a strategy to help improve their overall performance so they can compete in a global economy. Consequently, HRD professionals are instrumental in producing results that improve organizational effectiveness. They do not have the luxury of simply being trainers any longer.

An increasingly important role is that of performance consultant. Due to the complexity, ambiguity, and demands commonly found in the world of performance consulting, many HRD professionals have difficulty evolving to this role (Hale 1998; Robinson and Robinson 1996). Performance consultants have little time for the preplanned solutions so common in workshops and training classes. Rather than leading clients through a carefully prepared training class, performance consultants delve into problems with creative zest. Additionally, to isolate and resolve performance problems, HRD professionals conduct performance and cause analysis and develop and provide recommendations for solutions.

Robinson and Robinson (1996, 287) maintain that performance consultants should serve as client liaisons. In this subrole they partner with management to identify and contract performance improvement initiatives that address business needs. Performance consultants are performance analysts, identifying the ideal and actual performances required to meet business needs and determining the causes of performance discrepancies. The performance analyst defines performance problems or issues to be addressed, determines gaps in performance (making sure the root cause analysis is conducted), and recommends solutions for eliminating barriers to performance (Fuller and Farrington 1999; Rossett 1999b). When performance consultants serve as impact evaluators, they identify and report the impact of an intervention on individual performance and organizational effectiveness.

Another subrole is that of performance consulting champion, who is responsible for spreading the word about the benefits of the performance improvement process. Performance consultants also serve as root cause analysts, determining root causes of identified gaps in performance. Once necessary solutions to performance problems have been determined, a solution developer builds them. Performance consultants occasionally function as instructional designers (creating learning interventions), compensation analysts (designing new compensation and reward systems), or organizational development specialists (managing change, restructuring the organization, or reengineering business processes). Once a solution is developed, solution implementers put them in motion—yet another subrole of performance consultants.

Performance consultants sometimes serve as scouts, answering questions, providing guidance, or assisting in solving problems that arise during the course of a performance improvement project. Since many projects are complex, performance consultants function as project managers to ensure that the project remains on schedule, within budget, and at an acceptable level of quality (Hale 1998). Furthermore, performance consultants facilitate focus group activities—managing difficult participants, drawing out ideas from reticent individuals, and generally ensuring that the best information is captured from the group. Finally, "whenever change is involved, people may have negative reactions to the change. Even if the change is widely perceived as positive, difficulties in making the change can occur. Someone should be managing the change process to ensure that the change as proposed will have the desired result and will transfer to common practice in the workplace" (Fuller and Farrington 1999, 153). Performance consultants serving in this subrole act as change advisors.

Fuller and Farrington (1999, 150–153) agree that performance consultants can engage in several different subroles, but every performance improvement intervention needs a sponsor. This person advocates the performance improvement process. Sponsors may change from project to project, but the sponsor is typically the performance consultant's primary client. Performance consultant sponsors need not describe or understand the performance improvement process; they only need to recognize that a business problem exists and recommend an investigation of it.

Robinson and Robinson (1996) point out that the term performance consultant can also be used as a job title. The *job* of performance consultants may involve all of the above roles. Additionally, one person may play the majority of these roles in many projects.

Performance Consultant Responsibilities

Performance consultants are responsible for traditional organizational learning activities, such as identifying training needs, designing and developing learning interventions and other structured learning experiences, helping managers deliver structured learning experiences, training managers to become trainers and assuring the quality of training delivered by others, and evaluating learning and change interventions. Robinson and Robinson (1996, 285) further contend that performance consultants are responsible for developing performance and competency models to identify performance gaps and for determining the causes of performance gaps. They also maintain that performance consultants are responsible for measuring the impact of training and nontraining actions undertaken to change performance, advising management on business and performance needs, and identifying performance implications for future business goals and needs.

Additionally, Robb (1998, 235) asserts that performance consultants need to partner with clients to identify, build, and maintain a strong business relationship, assess performance to gather data, and analyze data for patterns and connections. Additionally, they need to collaborate with clients to identify impacts on business goals and to secure agreement on actions to be taken and measures of success. He also holds that performance consultants are responsible for implementing interventions, managing and facilitating performance improvement efforts through internal and external partnerships, and measuring and reporting results.

Competencies and Skills of Performance Consultants

The roles and subroles of a performance consultant require a set of skills or competencies in order to function successfully. Robinson and Robinson (1996) report that these skills are unique and that people who are successful in traditional training roles (i.e., instructors) may not be successful in performance improvement roles, and vice versa. The following ten general capabilities are essential for a performance consultant:

1. Business knowledge
2. Systems thinking skills
3. Interpersonal skills
4. Consulting skills
5. Project management skills
6. Change management skills
7. Teamwork skills
8. Working with experts
9. Knowledge of performance technology
10. Partnering skills

Business Knowledge

Effective performance consultants think like their clients, which requires an understanding of how things are accomplished inside the organization and how decisions are made (Brinkerhoff 1998). Business understanding involves awareness of how organizations operate and why they exist, including knowledge of business fundamentals, systems theory, organizational culture, and politics. Business understanding helps performance consultants to be perceived as members of the organizational family, which enables them to generate solutions to business problems (Gilley and Maycunich 1998a).

Fuller and Farrington (1999) believe that performance consultants should be able to speak intelligently about their organization's business, which requires an understanding of its products, services, markets, and customers. Additionally, performance consultants should be able to describe primary functions within the firm and critical processes used to create products and services to meet both internal and external clients' needs (Hale 1998). Lack of such knowledge prevents the establishment of credibility so essential to organizational success.

Successful performance consultants avoid using HRD jargon when explaining performance problems, relying instead on straightforward language to describe processes and approaches to solving them. Moreover, performance consultants describe solutions in business terms rather than in technical HRD terms, which helps establish clear communication and permission to proceed. Steinburg (1991, 30) further argues that performance consultants must understand the financial and marketing language that managers utilize every day. "Talking their language" allows performance consultants to establish joint partnerships.

To establish an in-depth knowledge of the business, Robinson and Robinson (1996) suggest that performance consultants read their organization's annual report and demonstrate understanding of it. They should converse with managers regarding the critical ratios used to measure the firm's operational health in order to compare current performance with goals. From such conversations, performance consultants should be able to determine return on equity, whether operating revenue is on target, and if not, why, what business actions must be taken to close any gap, and the external forces that challenge the organization's ability to meet its business goals. Performance consultants should be able to discuss competitors' strategies and actions and their implications for the organization. Finally, they should be able to skillfully use the business terminology unique to the organization and the industry.

Because business challenges and goals change, performance consultants must take the initiative to remain current. Robinson and Robinson (1996) suggest that performance consultants read trade journals relevant to the organization, review organizational documents that provide information about the firm's vision, mission, strategic goals, and performance, and volunteer to serve on task forces or committees formed to address particular business issues. Furthermore, they believe performance consultants need to volunteer to work on special assignments in areas such as manufacturing, customer service, or maintenance and to identify key performers in a business unit or division and ask permission to "shadow" them for a few days.

Systems Thinking Skills

Identifying, analyzing, and evaluating systems within an organization is an essential part of performance consulting. Fuller and Farrington (1999, 162) believe that this requires the ability to assess which elements of a system are related to one another and determine which inputs, processes, and outputs from one element of a system interact with other elements of that system. Moreover, they contend that performance consultants need to predict which parts of a system are likely to change when another part of the system changes and use the human performance system framework to determine where change may affect other elements of a system (Rossett 1999b).

Performance consultants need to develop an understanding of the characteristics of open systems as described by Katz and Kahn (1978), who maintain that every organization bears ten key characteristics. These characteristics form a framework for appraising an organization's internal environment, isolating performance problems, and identifying relationships critical to organizational effectiveness.

1. Importation of Energy.   Organizations obtain resources such as raw materials from their external environment. Referred to as *production inputs,* these consist of materials and energies that are directly related to producing products or delivering services (i.e., transformation processes). *Maintenance inputs,* such as organizational policies and procedures, guide employees as they carry out their activities as members of the system.

Rothwell and Cookson (1997, 105) identified the following questions that can be used by performance consultants when examining the organization's importation of energy:

- What are the production and maintenance inputs of the organization as a whole? Of each part of the organization?
- How are those inputs changing to respond to external environmental change?
- How should those inputs change in the future to respond to external environmental change?
- How do present and future changes in inputs affect program planning efforts?
- How should present and future changes in inputs affect program planning efforts?

2. Throughput.   The process of transforming raw materials (inputs) into products and services is known as throughput. Rummler and Brache (1995) refer to throughputs as business processes, which describe the steps employees go through to create products and deliver services.

Rothwell and Cookson (1997, 105) again provide several questions that help performance consultants when appraising an organization's throughputs:

- What are the throughputs (transformation processes) of the organization? Of each part of the organization?
- How are throughputs changing to respond to external environmental change?
- How should throughputs change in the future to respond to external environmental change?
- How do changes in throughputs currently affect program planning efforts?
- How should changes in throughputs affect future program planning efforts?

3. *Outputs.* At the completion of the throughput process, organizations have created outputs, which are products and services critical to their survival (Katz and Kahn 1978). The quality and quantity of the outputs consumed by customers (external environment) determine the firm's profitability. Performance consultants use the following questions to appraise an organization's outputs:

- What are the outputs of the organization?
- How are outputs changing in response to external environmental change?
- How should outputs change in the future in response to external environmental change?
- How do changes in outputs currently affect program planning efforts?
- How should changes in outputs affect future program planning efforts (Rothwell and Cookson 1997, 106)?

4. *Cycle of Events.* Katz and Kahn (1978) report that the input-throughput-output cycle flows smoothly as long as the organization maintains its current processes and procedures. Change, however, can cause breakdowns or impose barriers, or performance consultants may simply wish to improve the efficiency of processes. Therefore, they need to examine the relationship among inputs, throughputs, and outputs to detect existing or desirable changes and their impact on present and future programs (Rothwell and Cookson 1997).

5. *Negative Entropy.* According to the law of entropy, organization tends to move toward disorganization, chaos, and demise. Thus, performance consultants ought to take steps to avoid such imbalance within the organization. The actions taken to address an organization's natural tendency is known as negative entropy. In practice, organizations demonstrate negative entropy by planning for the future, such as by setting aside funds, credit, or other resources to reestablish equilibrium. These excess resources are often referred to as "organizational slack." Performance

consultants examining an organization's internal environment look for evidence of entropy, negative entropy, and organizational slack. How is the organization preparing itself to handle problems in the future? How do such efforts impact performance consulting? How should they?

6. *Informational Input.*   Of fundamental importance is how an organization obtains information from its internal and external customers, partners, and employees regarding their needs and expectations. Information such as this permits the organization to predict and manage change. Mismatches in this area can lead to loss of external customers, turnover among employees, and poor partnerships. Such losses result when organizational products and services fail to match customers' needs and expectations. Therefore, when performance consultants evaluate an organization's informational input they may wish to pose the following questions:

- How is the organization obtaining information about the needs of customers, employees, and partners?
- How are decisionmakers and prospective change participants using that information?
- How should they be using that information to make adaptive or even proactive change to meet or exceed customer, employee, and partner requirements?
- How is performance improvement intervention supporting efforts to obtain and use information to meet or exceed current customer, employee, or partner requirements?
- How should performance improvement intervention support efforts to obtain and use information to meet or exceed customer, employee, or partner requirements in the future (Rothwell and Cookson 1997, 107)?

7. *Steady State and Dynamic Homeostasis.*   Katz and Kahn (1978, 26) argue that "a steady state is not a motionless or true equilibrium. There is a continuous inflow of energy from the external environment and a continuous export of the products of the system." For performance consultants who are examining the steady state and dynamic homeostasis, Rothwell and Cookson (1997, 107) offer the following questions:

- How does the organization maintain stability amid turmoil?
- What functions help to preserve order?
- How are these functions changing to respond to external environmental change?
- How are existing programs helping to preserve order?

- What programmatic changes are necessary to adapt to or anticipate changing external environmental conditions?

8. Differentiation. Katz and Kahn (1978, 29) report that differentiation occurs when "diffuse global patterns are replaced by more specialized functions." Advanced organizations become more specialized and differentiated in the products and services (outputs) they provide to the marketplace (environment). Hamil and Prahalad (1994) believe that for-profit organizations focus on their *core competencies*—that is, what they do especially well—and secure a market niche. Gilley and Eggland (1992) add that specialized organizations focus on targeted market niches in order to maximize their revenue. Again, Rothwell and Cookson (1997, 109) provide valuable questions for performance consultants who are responsible for examining an organization's differentiation:

- What does the organization do best and why?
- How is the organization beginning to focus on specialized customers or needs?
- How are programs changing, or how should programs change, in response?

9. Integration and Coordination. As differentiation and specialization increase, organizations need to establish mechanisms and controls to coordinate divergent segments. They may set priorities, establish organization-wide rules and regulations, increase organizational communications, establish performance standards, identify operating procedures, coordinate production scheduling, or establish quality improvement standards. To appraise an organization's integration and coordination efforts, performance consultants should address the following questions:

- Through what methods is the organization unified and coordinated?
- How are these methods used?
- What role is played by performance improvement interventions at present as a tool for achieving integration and coordination?
- What role should be played by performance improvement interventions in the future as a tool for achieving integration and coordination? (Rothwell and Cookson 1997, 108)

10. Equifinality. According to Katz and Kahn (1978), equifinality is the tendency of open systems to attain their objectives by various means. Unfortunately, this can cause confusion and conflict among members of a firm. Performance consultants can help an organization avoid such confusion by asking:

- How much variation exists in pursuit of common goals or results in the organization?
- How are those variations manifested?
- What are the impacts of these variations on performance improvement efforts at present?
- What should be the impacts of these variations on performance improvement efforts in the future? (Rothwell and Cookson 1997, 108)

Interpersonal Skills

In order to be effective, performance consultants need to develop the ability to interact with executives, senior managers, and managers from diverse functional backgrounds (i.e., finance, engineering, marketing, sales, manufacturing, facilities, information resources). Fuller and Farrington (1999, 164–165) identified a variety of interactions that performance consultants are responsible for, which include communicating the status of a project, presenting ideas persuasively, and selling a concept or approach. They also believe performance consultants are responsible for holding an exploratory discussion to search for information one on one or in groups, managing focus groups, and using appropriate and nonbiasing questioning techniques (for example, asking open-ended and closed questions effectively, asking nonleading questions, and so on).

Hale (1998) maintains that performance consultants are responsible for fostering inquiry and advocacy to further the goals of an interaction and for focusing a conversation to gather information efficiently while making sure that participants neither go off on tangents nor neglect to share information critical to the project's success. Finally, performance consultants are responsible for defusing potential emotional reactions to problems while gathering needed information. Each of these activities requires interpersonal skills.

Consulting Skills

Robinson and Robinson (1996) define performance consulting as a synergistic process through which the expertise of both the client and the consultant is maximized. In essence, the whole is greater than the sum of the parts—which epitomizes the synergistic consulting process. Therefore, performance consultants must develop skills that enable them to enter into discussions with potential clients, determine what services and results clients require, and formulate contracts with clients (Fuller and Farrington 1999; Nilson 1999; Gilley and Maycunich 1998a; Hale 1998).

As performance consultants work through the steps of the human performance system, performance improvement, or performance management models, they rely on consulting skills. This includes maintaining contact with the client, communicating the status of the project as appropriate, negotiating any changes in the contract, providing support and maintenance as required, and terminating the engagement.

Block (1981, 18–22) has identified three consulting styles that are used with frequency: the pair-of-hands, expert, and collaborative styles.

The Pair-of-Hands Style.   This style allows clients to retain almost all of the control during the performance improvement project. Typically, the client determines the problem and arrives at a solution, which the performance consultant then implements. Block (1981, 20) provides some clues for determining when performance consultants are acting from a pair-of-hands style. They include taking a passive role when interacting with clients, allowing clients to control conversations and decide how to proceed, and allowing clients to decide how change will be implemented. Additional behaviors that demonstrate this style include limited collaboration and two-way communication.

The Expert Style.   As an expert, the performance consultant assumes the majority of control, makes recommendations, and tells the client what would be best to do during a performance improvement project. Although the client may make suggestions, the performance consultant is clearly in charge. During this type of relationship, the client plays an inactive role, with little two-way communication or buy-in. Decisions on how to proceed, technical controls, and information gathering are made primarily by the performance consultant. Consequently, the client's role is limited to judging and evaluating "after the fact," which requires little or no collaboration. Finally, the performance consultant's goal is to solve the immediate problem (Block 1981, 19).

The Collaborative Style.   Block (1981) and Robinson and Robinson (1996) believe that the collaborative style is the most effective approach for performance consultants because it utilizes both the consultant's specialized knowledge and the client's knowledge of the organization and its processes. In the collaborative style, decisions regarding actions to take and implementation plans are all shared responsibilities. Decisions are made bilaterally, data collection and analysis are joint efforts, and collaboration is essential (Block 1981, 21). Control resides equally and is a matter of discussion and negotiation. Two-way communication is encouraged, and implementation of solutions is jointly determined through discussion and agreement. According to Robinson and Robinson (1996, 20–21), the advantages of this style include improved diagnosis, increased support of decisions made because clients participate in making those decisions, and improved results from projects because all actions are identified and accounted for. They also believe that the collaborative style improves learning for both the performance consultant and the client and that better relationships are developed because mutual trust and respect are developed.

Project Management Skills

Every performance improvement intervention is a project. Consequently, performance consultants need project management skills to lead such projects from beginning to end (Brinkerhoff 1998). Fuller and Farrington (1999, 165–166) believe that project management skills overlap with the skills required for consulting and change management in that performance consultants need to define the relationship with the project sponsor and define the performance improvement intervention. They also need to analyze risks to project completion and engage in contingency planning to help minimize those risks, write requests for proposals, and select and manage vendors (Brinkerhoff and Gill 1994). Performance consultants need to manage the entire project, making sure that its requirements are being fulfilled, that people working on the project are aware of their roles and responsibilities, that timing and scheduling of the project are going according to plan, and that the budget is within limits. They also need to manage communications.

Planning a project is a complex skill that should not be underestimated. A project's many facets include creating a work breakdown structure and a schedule estimation, determining the interdependencies in the schedule, optimizing the schedule, and researching the project (Fuller 1997).

Change Management Skills

According to Dormant (1992), every time performance improves, a change has occurred that represents a new way of working. For some employees the change may be insignificant, whereas for others it may be quite drastic. Fuller and Farrington (1999, 166–167) believe that to deal with resistance to change and to foster an environment that is conducive to change, change agents need to enlist the support and cooperation of sponsors, advocates, early adopters, team members, and others involved with the change. Performance consultants need to recognize and minimize weaknesses in an intervention and to recognize the stages of change and employ the appropriate strategies for each stage (Kissler 1991).

Teamwork Skills

Because performance improvement projects are often complex, performance consultants must possess knowledge of teamwork and team-building skills (Hale 1998). These competencies, including planning, directing, coordinating, and managing team performance, ensure that projects function smoothly. Activities include identifying roles and responsibilities clearly, implementing the necessary communication processes, managing meetings, accounting for interdependencies, sequencing complex resources, scheduling tasks, dividing the work into manageable units, and assigning work.

Knowledge of Human Performance Technology

Rothwell (1992, 1) defines human performance technology as "a systematic approach to analyzing, improving, and managing performance in the workplace through the use of appropriate and varied interventions." Human performance technology acknowledges that employee performance is a function of many influences: feedback, accountability, skills and knowledge, rewards or incentives, motivation, and so forth (Nilson 1999). Consequently, performance consultants need to examine performance problems using the human performance system model (Rossett 1999b). Another concept associated with human performance technology is the idea that these influences are interdependent; it is the combination of these factors that results in desired performance.

Robinson and Robinson (1996) believe that performance consultants must cultivate knowledge of performance technology and operate from a systems approach each time a problem or performance challenge is presented to them. Thus, they strive to understand the current system and identify what it must become if the desired performance is to be achieved. To accomplish this, performance consultants assume that performance is a function of a system and not simply one element (Hale 1998). Consequently, solutions to performance problems will be systemic in nature as opposed to one-dimensional (i.e., training).

Partnering Skills

According to Robinson and Robinson (1996), performance consultants must take the initiative to meet, work with, and gain the trust of managers and others within their organization. This requires building trust with clients, which takes a tremendous amount of time and effort. One way of forging partnerships with executives, senior managers, managers, and subject matter experts is for performance consultants to form liaisons.

Another technique used to forge partnerships is networking. Networking involves identifying people throughout the organization, in various positions and levels, with whom ongoing contact would be mutually beneficial (Simonsen 1997). Members of the network provide performance consultants with information regarding strategic plans, departmental objectives, initiatives, and employee attitudes, morale, and concerns.

Accountabilities and Abilities of Performance Consultants

According to Robinson and Robinson (1996, 254), performance consultants are held accountable for the following types of measures:

- Degree to which skills transfer to the workplace and individual or group performance improves.
- Degree to which training contributes to desired operational change.
- Quantity and quality of client relationships.
- Number of performance contracts agreed to in a year.

Abilities of Performance Consultants

According to Rothwell (1996a), performance consultants must have the ability to determine the importance of gaps between what is and what should be in the organization's interactions with the external environment. Moreover, this means using strategic thinking skills and having the ability to compare an idealized vision of the future with organizational reality (Nilson 1999). Rothwell (1996a, 149) provides two essential questions that will help performance consultants in this effort:

- How will the most important *present* challenges facing the organization eventually play out in its dealings with customers, stockholders, suppliers, distributors, and other important external groups?
- How will the most important *future* challenges facing the organization eventually unfold in its dealings with customers, stockholders, suppliers, distributors, and other important external groups?

Rothwell (1996a, 149) also believes that performance consultants must have the ability to determine the importance of gaps between what is and what should be happening within the organization. To determine what is happening within the organization requires examination of organizational structure, culture, work climate, and policies and procedures to discover real or perceived problems (Rossett 1999b). Additionally, performance consultants should be able to determine the importance of gaps between what is and what should be in work processing. Hale (1998) maintains that to uncover these gaps, performance consultants should lead, coordinate, or participate in efforts at the work level to examine workflow, work processing, and the inputs, outputs, and transformation processes involved in producing the work or delivering services. According to Rothwell (1996a, 152), this ability requires performance consultants to examine how work flows into a division, department, or work unit/team and the raw (untransformed) states in which materials, people, and information flow into a division, department, work unit, or team. They must know how materials, people, and information *should* flow into the division, department, work unit, or team. Next, they need to identify the gaps that exist between what is happening and what should be happening, identify the consequences that stem from existing gaps between what is and what should be happening in workflow as well as the importance of those consequences (Rossett 1999b).

Rothwell (1996a, 152–154) maintains that performance consultants should have the ability to determine the importance of gaps between what workers can do and what they should be able to do. In order to do this, performance consultants need to lead, coordinate, or participate in matching work requirements to worker competencies. As a result, they will need to discover answers to the following questions:

- What competencies are available among workers to function effectively in the organization's internal and external environment and to deal with work processing requirements?
- What competencies *should* be available among workers to function effectively in the organization's internal and external environment and to deal with work processing requirements?
- What gaps exist between worker competencies *required* now and those *available* now?
- What gaps exist between worker competencies required in the *future* and those available *now*?
- How important are the gaps in worker competencies?
- What consequences stem from—or are expected to stem from—these competency gaps?

Furthermore, performance consultants should serve as strategic trouble-shooters and as such must possess the ability to isolate strategic mismatches in the organization's interactions with the external environment and the ability to benchmark other organizations in the industry or "best-in-class" organizations (Rothwell 1996a, 178–180). They also must possess the ability to isolate large-scale and small-scale causes of gaps within the organization (Rossett 1999b). Finally, performance consultants need to have the ability to troubleshoot causes of gaps in the work or workflow and the ability to troubleshoot causes of performance gaps between worker and other performance environments.

Areas of Expertise

In addition to the general abilities just reviewed, the performance consultant needs specific expertise in using the human performance system and performance improvement and management models. Using these models requires skills in the following areas:

- Establishing and managing client relationships
- Conducting analyses
- Identifying root causes
- Creating performance relationship maps
- Developing models of performance
- Recommending and implementing solutions
- Evaluating results

Establishing and Managing Client Relationships

One of the most critical elements in improving organizational performance is establishing and managing client relationships, which is necessary for fostering trust and cooperation between consultants and clients. It provides an environment of open and honest communication that can improve understanding and reduce resistance. Also, a positive client relationship reduces the impact of hidden agendas so commonly found during organizational change.

The most important issue to be resolved is that of control (Hale 1998). The balance of power between clients and consultants must be established at the outset, with a clear understanding of who will make what decisions. According to Gilley (1998), Burke (1992), and Lippitt and Lippitt (1986), power can be shared in one of three ways. First, the power to make decisions can reside with the performance consultant. Second, it can reside with clients, who dominate the decisionmaking process by deciding when and how the performance consultant's knowledge and skills are to be used. Third, power can be mutually shared. Clients and performance consultants mutually diagnose needs, generate and select solutions, and implement and evaluate solutions. Except for the client's ultimate veto, neither clients nor performance consultants have greater power.

Conducting Analyses

Conducting analysis requires interacting with clients to determine the business need, performance problem, and expected outcomes (Nilson 1999; Rossett 1999b). This expertise requires performance consultants to communicate with clients about the business in business terms and about performance improvement and management in a straightforward and understandable way. Additionally, performance consultants need to examine the organizational system, define business issues with their clients, obtain permission to proceed with a performance analysis, and decide what measures will be used to determine whether the performance improvement or management initiative has been successful (Gilley and Maycunich 1998a).

Fuller and Farrington (1999) believe that performance consultants must analyze the business issue and determine what performance is necessary to solve the problem. Clark and Estes (1996) further contend that performance consultants need to determine what results must actually be accomplished to meet business goals and to avoid being distracted by irrelevant behaviors that may have been erroneously associated with desired performance in the past.

Performance consultants need to be able to define the current state, the desired state, and to identify gaps. Interviewing, focus groups, observation, and facilitation techniques may be required to identify the root causes of inadequate performance.

Identifying Root Causes

Determining the root causes of a performance gap can be achieved in a number of ways. Brassard (1996) believes that using techniques such as fishbone diagrams, affinity diagrams, or interrelationship maps are helpful in isolating the root cause. Fuller and Farrington (1999) propose asking "Why?" until the layers of confounding ideas about root causes have all fallen away. Comparing performance gaps against the three major types of causes (knowledge and skills, motivation, and environment) may prove useful in pinpointing root causes. Using proven models such as the human performance system (Fuller and Farrington 1999) and the performance alignment framework (Gilley and Maycunich 1998a) to test gaps can isolate the root cause. They can determine whether the root cause is a gap caused by the organization, its people, their behavior, consequences for performance, feedback, or other environmental factors (Fuller and Farrington 1999).

After the root cause has been identified, performance consultants must validate them in a reliable manner, such as through observations, interviews, and the like (Rossett 1999b). In order for an observation to be effective, the information uncovered must not relate to changes in the environment as a result of the performance consultant's presence.

Creating Client Relationship Maps

Robinson and Robinson (1996, 53–54) believe that performance consultants can best influence management when they can illustrate how actions being proposed will positively affect the business. To do this, performance consultants must illustrate the interrelationships among business goals, performance requirements, training, and work environment needs. They must also be able to determine the performance needed if business goals are to be realized as well as the current capability of individuals to demonstrate this required performance. They must also determine the training and work environment actions that will be needed to change performance.

According to Robinson and Robinson (1996), a performance relationship map should include (1) identified business goals, (2) desired operational results, (3) desired employee performance, (4) current employee performance, (5) current operational results, and (6) external factors and internal forces that have an impact on the desired performance. Once developed, performance consultants and their clients will have a good understanding of current performance and operational results as compared to the desired performance and results. They will have also isolated the factors and forces impacting performance and operational results.

Developing Performance Improvement Models

Developing performance improvement models begins with identifying needed performance results. Isolating the type of model to be used (performance or competency), the criteria used to measure performance, and environmental factors impacting performance follow.

Performance Results.   Robinson and Robinson (1996) define performance results as the outcomes a performer must achieve on the job if the organization's business goals are to be attained. This could be the number of parts manufactured, products or contracts sold, insurance claims processed, or sales revenue generated (Rummler and Brache 1995). According to Robinson and Robinson, most jobs require between ten and fifteen performance results. To enhance performance, these results should be shared with employees in order to raise their understanding and obtain support.

Best Practices or Competencies.   Performance consultants need to select between a best practices (performance) or competencies approach. Best practices are what the very best, or exemplary, performers actually do on the job to achieve each of the performance results for a specific position (Rossett 1999b; Robinson and Robinson 1996). Also called benchmarking, this is the most common approach to identifying best practices, which is determined by observing and interviewing exemplary performers.

If performance consultants decide to describe the skills and knowledge required to produce results, then a competency model is formed (Hale 1998; Robinson and Robinson 1996). Competency models compile a comprehensive list of skills, knowledge, and attitudes required to do a job.

Quality Criteria. Effective performance consultants establish criteria to measure the quality of performance results and the way they are achieved (Gilley and Maycunich 1998a). Criteria should be identified for each performance result and the steps and tasks of a performance activity (Rummler and Brache 1995). In this way, performance consultants can measure performance at a micro level or evaluate performance results individually.

Work Environment Factors. Finally, a performance model should include a list of the forces, within and outside the control of the organization, that will either encourage or inhibit the accomplishment of each performance result (Fuller and Farrington 1999; Hale 1998; Robinson and Robinson 1996). If the forces are outside the organization, employees must learn coping techniques and skills that enable them to optimize positive factors and overcome negative influences. If the factors are within the organization, leaders must eliminate or manage them.

It is important to remember that performance models define performance that is causally linked to accomplishment of business goals (Robinson and Robinson 1996). The business goals of the organization are the targets to which performance models are directed. Furthermore, it is critical for performance consultants to fully comprehend their organization's business goals. Without this understanding, performance consultants risk developing inaccurate or incomplete performance models.

Recommending and Implementing Solutions

Recommended solutions should be instrumental in eliminating the barriers to performance by addressing root causes. This requires a fluent knowledge of the human performance system and an ability to match interventions with types of root causes (Rossett 1999b).

Fuller and Farrington (1999, 171) assert that performance consultants must answer the question, "When something is broken in this part of the human performance system, then which interventions are required?" Doing so requires performance consultants to either develop and implement the required solutions alone, or influence others to do so, or work collaboratively with others to create and deliver these solutions. Influencing, negotiating, project management, and teamwork skills are invaluable in this phase.

Solutions can be either instructional or noninstructional (Silber 1992). Instructional interventions primarily require training and learning activities, transfer of learning efforts, and evaluation. When solutions involve noninstructional interventions, the performance consultant designs and creates those interventions or partners with someone who can (Hale 1998). Noninstructional interventions include writing job descriptions, creating feedback systems, redesigning incentive or pay systems, using process engineering, making cultural changes, and using change management and information or knowledge engineering (Nilson 1999).

Evaluating Results

Measuring the overall success of the project determines whether initial goals have been met and the business issue resolved. Effective evaluation starts in the analysis phase when the decision is made about what to accept as evidence that business goals have been met (Fuller and Farrington 1999; Swanson 1994). During the evaluation phase, performance consultants identify the evaluation criteria used to measure whether project goals have been achieved (Brinkerhoff 1998). They are expected to perform a number of evaluative actions such as conducting peer reviews, requesting client reviews, and establishing a feedback mechanism from members of the group or groups whose performance is being analyzed and modified (Fuller and Farrington 1999).

Conclusion

Performance consulting is by its very nature a spontaneous activity. Effective performance consultants adopt a planning approach that enables them to anticipate and solve potential problems. Such an approach frames a long-term process that requires various members of the organization, who possess different orientations, to develop a common view of the firm and its future. Performance consulting requires a thorough understanding of the organization and its operations, strategic planning that emphasizes the importance of identifying goals, determining organizational values, and action planning. Performance consultants' credibility relies on asking appropriate questions and finding acceptable answers.

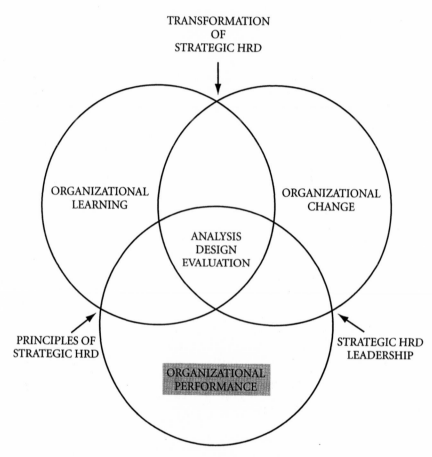

TRANSFORMATION
OF
STRATEGIC HRD

ORGANIZATIONAL
LEARNING

ORGANIZATIONAL
CHANGE

ANALYSIS
DESIGN
EVALUATION

PRINCIPLES OF
STRATEGIC HRD

STRATEGIC HRD
LEADERSHIP

ORGANIZATIONAL
PERFORMANCE

ORGANIZATIONAL LEARNING, PERFORMANCE, AND CHANGE

CHAPTER 11

Performance Consulting

When organizations fail to achieve their desired business goals and objectives, it *could* be because employees lack the skills, knowledge, or abilities to perform their jobs. It *could* also be because the employees are not performing adequately or managers are not doing an acceptable job of supervising their employees. Performance breakdowns *could* occur because the organization fails to create environments or design jobs that enable employees to perform proficiently. In any case, performance consulting is a process that can be used to uncover the reason(s) (root cause) for inadequate performance and failed business results and to provide solutions for overcoming them.

Robinson and Robinson (1996) coined the term performance consulting to illustrate the roles and responsibilities of performance consultants and the approach they use to identify performance problems, isolate root causes, identify solutions, implement performance improvement solutions, and evaluate performance results and outcomes. Hale (1998, 9) defines performance consulting as the "practice of taking a disciplined approach to assessing individual and organizational effectiveness, diagnosing causes of human performance problems, and recommending a set of interventions."

Why Employees and Organizations Fail to Achieve Desired Performance Results

The process of performance consulting begins with a simple question: "Why do employees and their organization fail to achieve desired performance results?" The search for an answer to this question is at the heart of individual and organizational performance improvement. Furthermore, it is the principal purpose for the performance consulting process.

To find an answer to this question, we need to examine four possible performance problem areas: employees' skills, knowledge, and abilities; performers' actions and behaviors; managers' actions and behaviors; and the organization's actions and behaviors.

Employees' Knowledge, Skills, and Abilities

The performance consulting process should begin by examining employees' knowledge, skills, and abilities (KSAs) to do their jobs. Performance consultants should determine whether employees fail when using KSAs on the job and whether they have an immediate application for the skills. Additionally, performance consultants need to determine whether employees know how to do their jobs and whether they understand their job responsibilities.

If adequate KSAs exist, performance consultants need to determine whether employees see a payoff for using the skills and have sufficient confidence to use the skills (Robinson and Robinson 1996). Finally, performance consultants need to determine whether employees know when they are effectively using the skills.

Performers' Actions and Behaviors

Another essential purpose of performance consulting is determining the adequacy of performers' actions and behaviors In other words, what actions or behaviors do performers exhibit that inhibit the achievement of desired performance results? When performance consultants can isolate these behaviors, they are well on their way to identifying a positive performance improvement solution.

Some of the common actions or behaviors include not feeling safe asking for help or being fearful of repercussions for doing their jobs incorrectly. Some employees don't trust their managers, whereas others have personal problems that prevent them from doing their jobs. Others think they are doing their jobs correctly but fail to realize that they are not, whereas others focus on less important activities. Still others think there is a better way of doing their jobs and thus do not adhere to proven performance standards. In any case, employees struggle to produce acceptable results.

Managers' Actions and Behaviors

The heart of every organization, large or small, manufacturing or service, is its managers. Organizations assign managers the task of securing results through people. They serve as guides, directors, decisionmakers, and energizers for their employees. "Managers are the conduits of organizational change and development; without them, organizations struggle in mediocrity" (Gilley, Boughton, and Maycunich 1999, 71).

Unfortunately, most organizations have managers who are abusive and indifferent toward employees, possessing superior attitudes and poor interpersonal skills. They have managers with poor listening and feedback skills, who fail to delegate, develop people, or conduct developmental evaluations. They have managers who create work environments full of fear and paranoia and fail to confront employees when they do not perform their jobs correctly. These managers exercise little or no patience with their employees as they struggle to improve performance and criticize employees' personalities rather than focus on their work performance. Some managers fail to provide feedback to the employees regarding the organizational impact of their use of knowledge, skills, and abilities (Robinson and Robinson 1996). As a result of these actions and behaviors, employee morale, performance, and productivity remain low, which leads to poor-quality products and services, and higher costs.

The Organization's Actions and Behaviors

Performance consulting is used to address the organization's failures as well. In fact, the organizational system is the biggest unconscious conspirator to inadequate or poor performance (Rummler and Brache 1995). For example, organizations allow task interference, including lack of time, a poor physical environment, conflicting policies and procedures, and lack of authority, to inhibit employees as they attempt to use their knowledge, skills, and abilities on the job (Robinson and Robinson 1996). Organizations fail to link organizational performance to strategic business goals and objectives and fail to identify performance breakdowns (Gilley, Boughton, and Maycunich 1999).

Some organizations fail to focus on stakeholders' needs, which leads to producing inadequate products and services. Still others fail to encourage employee involvement and support or fail to manage performance (Fournies 1988). Most organizations fail to focus on long-term results or to remove barriers and obstacles preventing adequate performance (Fuller and Farrington 1999). Others simply do not design jobs adequately or fail to measure or evaluate employee performance (Rossett 1999a). Many organizations do not reward employees for doing their jobs or reward them for doing less important activities (Flannery, Hofrichter, and Platten 1996). Some organizations ask employees to do one thing (e.g., work as a team) but reward them for another (e.g., compensation and bonuses for individual performance) (Le Boeuf 1985).

Simply stated, performance consulting is used to identify the present state of employees' knowledge, skills, and abilities and to uncover inappropriate and inadequate actions and behaviors of performers, managers, and organizations so that they can be addressed accordingly.

Identifying Different Types of Clients

The performance consulting process begins by identifying the individuals who have something to gain or lose as a result of the performance analysis or recommendations for performance improvement. Unfortunately, one of the biggest mistakes performance consultants make is treating all clients in the same way. Some clients have the power to make decisions and provide the financial and human resources needed to implement and support change. Some can derail the performance analysis or intervention before it is implemented or completed, whereas others can affect the outcome by altering the perceptions of individuals regarding organizational performance. Some clients are able to provide the technical advice needed to ensure performance improvement, and others can guide the interaction between client groups and provide insight into the implementation of the performance improvement intervention.

In any decisionmaking situation there are four different types of clients, each of whom has a distinct purpose for participating. Their organizational roles often affect their behavior, interaction, and decisionmaking. The types of clients include decisionmakers, stakeholders, influencers, and scouts (Gilley and Maycunich 1998a). To become effective analyzers of performance and business needs, performance consultants must understand and address each type of client.

Decisionmakers

Decisionmakers, most commonly senior executives and managers, have the authority to give final approval to performance consultants for improvement interventions. Decisionmakers have direct access to financial and human resources and can assign them to help implement performance improvement interventions. Moreover, decisionmakers enjoy veto power and can prevent an intervention from being implemented.

A decisionmaker's primary focus is the bottom line and the impact that a performance improvement intervention will have on the organization. Decisionmakers are most interested in the return on investment that the organization will receive by implementing change. Performance consultants address decisionmakers' concerns by answering their questions and providing evidence that supports their recommendations for change and improvement. The impact of performance improvement interventions, such as increased profitability, enhanced revenue, or improved performance, must be clearly communicated in ways easily understood by decisionmakers.

Stakeholders

Stakeholders are those individuals who have the most to gain or lose as a result of implementation of a performance improvement intervention. Stakeholders are responsible for supervising and implementing these performance improvement interventions; therefore, their impact on departments, divisions, and units within the organization must be evaluated. Stakeholders must live with the performance improvement intervention; consequently, it becomes a very personal decision for which they will be held accountable. Stakeholders understand the consequences of implementing performance improvement interventions that fail to improve organizational performance and effectiveness.

To meet stakeholders' needs and expectations, performance consultants must reassure them that performance improvement interventions will indeed help improve organizational performance and effectiveness. Effective performance consultants communicate their intent and level of involvement during these interventions. This information reassures stakeholders that performance consultants will help them implement complex interventions as well as assist in overcoming employees' resistance to change.

Influencers

Many influencers serve as gatekeepers by impacting the perceptions of decisionmakers and stakeholders regarding selected performance improvement interventions. In most performance improvement or organizational development situations, influencers do not have the authority to approve the selection of an intervention but can greatly impact the selection process.

Some performance consultants avoid, discount, or minimize the impact of influencers, which is a serious mistake. One of the best ways of dealing with influencers is to validate them by soliciting their opinions, ideas, and assistance. Additionally, performance consultants can address their concerns with quantifiable, measurable evidence or by demonstrating how influencers benefit as a result of the change being proposed. Such an approach elevates influencers in the eyes of decisionmakers and stakeholders, which is precisely what influencers desire.

Scouts

In every performance improvement situation, someone serves as a point person, acting as a guide during interactions with performance consultants, decisionmakers, stakeholders, and influencers. He or she provides and interprets information about the problem, potential causes, types of clients involved, client expectations, and ways to proceed. A point person may be found anywhere in the organization, including the performance improvement department, among stakeholders, or within other operational units and divisions.

Scouts focus on the success of an intervention because they believe the intervention will improve organizational effectiveness. Consequently, scouts are change ambassadors within the firm.

Before performance consultants solicit the help of scouts, they must make certain that scouts have credibility with other decisionmakers, stakeholders, and influencers. Scouts must firmly believe that the performance improvement interventions being proposed will improve organizational performance and effectiveness.

Performance consultants should work closely with credible scouts, soliciting their advice unless it seriously violates professional values or ethics. Credible scouts often have organizational insight and understanding that performance consultants lack. Scouts possess awareness and intuition about what will or will not work within the organization and are conscious of how each decisionmaker, stakeholder, and influencer will benefit from a successful intervention. This insight is invaluable to performance consultants in their struggle to effect organizational change.

Focusing Performance Consulting Efforts

Performance improvement occurs at three levels within an organization: organization, process, and job/performer. To be successful, performance consultants focus their efforts at each or all of these levels simultaneously (Rummler and Brache 1995).

Organization Level

Rummler and Brache (1992, 42) argue that "the objectives of this step are to determine what changes are required in the variables of the organization level to improve the desired performance and to identify the cross-functional processes that, because they are affecting desired performance in a negative manner, should be examined further." This generally requires performance consultants to develop a systems picture of the organization to depict how various functions and processes are related to and affect desired performance, analyze performance data to identify gaps in performance, and name the critical processes involved.

Process Level

The objectives at this level are to determine the changes required to improve performance and identify the jobs that, because they are key to effective performance of these processes, should be examined further. Completion of this analysis requires performance consultants to determine the performance of key processes (in terms of desired performance goals), identify which process steps are not being performed properly and are leading to poor performance, determine the actions required to improve performance of the processes, and identify critical jobs in the successful performance of the process that need to be analyzed further (Rummler and Brache 1992, 43).

Job/Performer Level

At this level, objectives are to determine which critical jobs and their outputs must be improved in order for key processes to work effectively and produce desired quality and to identify the actions required to improve job outputs (Rummler and Brache 1992, 43). This step consists primarily of identifying gaps between desired and actual job outputs and using the human performance system framework (Chapter 8) or other performance consulting models to determine the cause(s) of poor job performance and appropriate corrective action(s).

Responsibilities in Performance Consulting

Performance consultants assume several responsibilities in order to help their organizations achieve desired business goals and performance improvement.

Developing and Managing Client Relationships

One of the major responsibilities in performance consulting is developing long-lasting, positive, working relationships with clients. Doing so initiates client partnerships that are essential during the analysis process.

Performance consultants engage in four activities to accomplish this end, including meeting with the client, discussing the client's background, establishing rapport, and developing trust. Although these seem very straightforward and commonsensical, they are far more difficult to master than might be anticipated. Gilley and Boughton (1996) identified eight critical components to a healthy, functional relationship:

1. Elevator conversation—sharing pleasantries or participating in small talk about low stress topics (e.g., the weather).
2. Fear free interactions—an atmosphere in which clients are encouraged to participate, thus allowing both sides the opportunity to cultivate positive, healthy relationships.
3. Personal interaction—one-on-one exchanges that help develop rapport.
4. Acceptance—willingness to work with others as they are and to allow them to be themselves, regardless of their differences.

5. Dialogue—a deep personal exchange of ideas, philosophies, insights, and feelings.
6. Trust—an environment exemplifying truth, confidence, mutual respect, and open and straightforward communication.
7. Honesty—adherence to the truth, even if that means presenting clients with information they'd rather avoid.
8. Self-esteem—mutual, reciprocal respect and confidence; two parties work collaboratively to achieve desired results.

Robinson and Robinson (1996) attest that although it would be wonderful for clients to view the relationship between themselves and performance consultants as a partnership, it seldom happens. Consequently, performance consultants face difficult challenges in managing client relationships. In most situations, performance consultants are simply trying to help clients make decisions that are "for their own good." Unfortunately, many clients still perceive performance consultants as trainers who provide training courses. This can be especially true if the group has not made the transition from a training department to that of a performance improvement group.

Robinson and Robinson (1996, 127–128) provide several suggestions for helping clients make the best use of performance consultants' services. Performance consultants should define performance consulting for clients. Explain the roles and services they should expect and provide concrete examples. They should provide samples of what other performance consultants have done for other internal clients. Performance consultants are responsible for protecting the performance improvement team so that it can focus on critical tasks. They also help clients produce communications, activities, and accomplishments concerning performance improvement that can be taken to senior management.

The performance consultant should explain clearly the responsibility that clients retain during solution selection, design/development, and implementation. Robinson and Robinson (1996, 127–128) point out that these responsibilities generally include reviewing selected performance improvement interventions with their rationales and providing input on economics, feasibility, and organizational acceptability. They include legitimizing the change initiative through communications to the performer groups involved; approving solutions and participating in or approving selected resources; and providing information and content expertise (personally or through appropriate specialists). Responsibilities also include facilitating access to required content information/subject matter experts or targeted performers for tryouts and reviewing budgets and timelines. Further responsibilities include participating in planning, decisionmaking, and troubleshooting, where necessary, and providing feedback and reinforcement for success. Overall, managing clients means ensuring that they do all that is necessary to achieve results they themselves value.

Managing Resistance

Client resistance to change occurs for a variety of reasons. Most commonly, they resist when the purpose for change is not made clear, the persons affected by change are not involved in planning, or an appeal for change is based on personal reasons (Ulrich 1998). Additionally, clients resist when work group habit patterns are ignored, poor communication is present, or there is a fear of failure (Rummler and Brache 1995). Sometimes clients resist change when excessive work pressure is involved or costs are too high. At other times, they resist when rewards are inadequate, anxiety over job security is not relieved, or there is a clear "vested interest" on the part of an individual, department, or unit (Block 1981). Furthermore, clients resist change when there is a lack of trust in or respect for the initiator or when clients are satisfied with the status quo (Hale 1998). Finally, resistance exists when change is too rapid, when past experience with change is negative, or when there are honest differences of opinion on how to proceed (Gilley and Maycunich 2000).

Resistance Resolution Method.   Resistance hampers implementation of performance improvement initiatives. Performance consultants, therefore, adopt approaches for dealing effectively with resistance, such as the conflict resolution method developed by Gilley and Eggland (1992). They maintain that resistance is simply the result of differing perspectives and fear of losing one's current state. The resistance resolution method is an effective tool in addressing clients' differing perspectives. This approach should be thought of as a set of skills that help performance consultants govern conflict. The objective of this method is to uncover underlying fears that cause resistance so that they can be addressed. The resistance resolution method consists of four steps: (1) acknowledging resistance, (2) clarifying resistance, (3) problem solving, and (4) confirming (Gilley and Eggland 1992).

Acknowledging Resistance

The resistance resolution methods begins with acknowledging resistance, which consists of listening and sharing. First, performance consultants listen carefully to clients' messages to determine their meaning. In fact, the very process of listening converts tension into words that reduce anxiety, even if they do not actually reveal the nature of the tension or the reason for it.

Sharing feelings with clients conveys support. When performance consultants demonstrate their understanding of clients' feelings and are not surprised or upset by negative statements, it illustrates their support for their clients—which reduces tension. To be successful in this stage, performance consultants should exhibit empathy and concern for resolution.

Clarifying Resistance

The second step is to clarify client thinking to reveal the reasons for their behavior. Clients "learn to cover up the plausible reasons, explanations, and justifications, all designed to prove that they're acting in a well thought out and logical manner" (Gilley and Boughton 1996, 160–161). There's a word that explains this thinking process—rationalization.

The challenge facing performance consultants is to learn how to defuse client statements without causing clients to lose face. Asking nonthreatening, open questions allows clients to express their thoughts more freely, which clarifies their resistance. By encouraging clients to give examples and illustrations, performance consultants encourage them to grasp their own meaning more clearly.

Problem Solving

Once performance consultants have clarified client resistance, they are ready to help clients identify solutions to their problems. A five-step problem-solving process is recommended, which includes identifying the problem, offering possible solutions, analyzing alternatives, selecting and implementing a viable remedy, and evaluating results.

Confirming

When an acceptable solution has been identified, clients must make a commitment—typically some kind of immediate action—that reinforces their willingness to accept the remedy. At this time, client feedback is essential in evaluating the continuing viability of the solution and the relationship in general.

Identifying Needs.

Robinson and Robinson (1996) believe that performance consultants are responsible for identifying organizational and client needs. They argue that there are four common needs: business, performance, learning, and work environment. *Business needs* are expressed in operational terms, such as goals for a unit, department, or organization, and represent the quantifiable data measures used to monitor the organization's "health." Product and service organizations express business needs differently, yet both are quantifiable. For example, manufacturing business needs may be expressed as the number of parts processed per hour. In service firms, business needs can be expressed by the percentage of customers that are satisfied with service.

Robinson and Robinson (1996, 28) identified two types of business needs: problems and opportunities. *Business problems* define a gap between what is actually occurring at the present time and what should be occurring operationally. Examples are excessive waste, falling profitability, low sales, high production costs, poor quality, and reduced customer satisfaction ratings. Robinson and Robinson assert that business problems exist when two criteria are met. First, there is a deviation between what should be occurring operationally and what is occurring. Second, someone in management feels "pain" about the deviation and is, therefore, motivated to address the problem.

Business opportunities focus on a future operational goal; no current problem needs to be fixed, but rather an opportunity needs to be optimized. Business opportunities exist when operationally defined goals are expected to be met, and when some members of management desire to gain from the opportunity. In essence, business problems require pain, whereas business opportunities leverage perceived gain.

Performance needs describe what people should do in order to meet business needs. These are on-the-job behavioral requirements of people who are performing a specific job. Performance needs provide guidance to employees as to their productivity requirements and serve as a yardstick for managers to gauge the adequacy of performance.

Robinson and Robinson (1996, 25) maintain that *learning needs* identify what people must learn if they are to perform successfully. Learning needs represent areas where performers lack the skill or knowledge to perform satisfactorily. These needs are the foundations for training programs and knowledge acquisition plans.

Hale (1998) asserts that *work environment needs* identify what systems and processes within the employee's work environment must be modified if performance and business needs are to be achieved. Work environment needs represent the aspects of the system that must be modified to ensure that the needed performance is adequately supported.

These four types of needs should be examined together. Business needs are the most important because they are the very reason most organizations exist. Learning and work environment needs are linked to business needs through performance needs in that positive learning and environmental change bring about improved performance, which results in the attainment of business needs (Robinson and Robinson 1996).

Conducting Performance Analysis.

Rossett (1992, 157–160) argues that performance analysis is a major and vital phase of a performance improvement project. Performance consultants use this process to identify the critical performance roles and factors that must be improved in order to achieve the business goal. Formative evaluation at this phase is critically important because analysis helps to prevent the wrong performance from being improved, or the wrong performance improvement factors from being addressed. Thus, performance analysis is used to "assess individual and organizational performance" (Hale 1998, 9). Additionally, performance analysis is critical to make certain that improvement factors are not overlooked.

Performance analysis presents a clear picture of existing and desired conditions surrounding performance. As a result, analysis answers four key questions:

1. What results (performance outcomes) are being achieved?
2. What results are desired?
3. How large is the performance gap?
4. What is the impact of the performance gap (Rothwell 1996b, 13)?

Performance analysis typically identifies three levels of performance improvement needs: primary needs, secondary needs, and tertiary needs (Rossett 1999b). Primary needs are specific improvements in performer behavior or results needed to positively impact desired business objectives. Often, performance analysis reveals that employees cannot increase performance on their own and that they need some sort of performance support tool to aid their development. This is an example of a secondary need. Performance analysis also reveals additional needs in the work environment, such as the need for a new organizational structure to facilitate or support a performance initiative. These are referred to as tertiary needs.

Hale (1998) maintains that performance improvement efforts in a complex performance environment may require numerous interventions and changes across several layers and levels of the firm. Rarely does a performance improvement effort involve a simple fix, such as training alone. In most situations, poor performance, that which has fallen below established standards, occurs for a variety of reasons. The changes needed to bring performance up to an acceptable level may include training, performance coaching, additional compensation and rewards, environmental change, or any combination of these.

To identify and describe past, present, and future human performance gaps, performance consultants should assess desired versus actual performance. Rothwell (1996b, 13) provides several questions to guide performance analysis:

- What is the performance gap or difference?
- Who is affected by the performance gap? Is it one person, a group, an organization, or a work process?
- When and where did the performance gap first occur, or when and where is it expected to begin?

- When and where were its effects, side effects (symptoms), and after effects (consequences) first noticed?
- Have they been noticed consistently or inconsistently?
- How has the gap been affecting the organization?
- Have the effects been widespread or limited?
- Is the performance gap traceable to individuals, work groups, locations, departments, divisions, suppliers, distributors, customers, or others?
- What are the immediate and direct results of the gap?
- How much has the gap cost the organization?
- How can the tangible economic impact of the gap best be calculated?
- How can the intangible impact of the gap be calculated in lost customer goodwill or worker morale?

As performance complexity increases so does the opportunity for mistakes in the performance analysis process. The three-level need framework helps clients understand the needs tied to a particular performance improvement effort and tracks linkages among them. This framework also allows performance consultants to assess the relative importance of needs at each level.

Evaluating the performance analysis process ensures accurate and complete needs identification. Each need, regardless of its level, must logically and validly relate to the desired primary performance improvement objective. Since performance consultants devote a significant portion of their time, energy, and effort to designing performance improvement interventions that address client needs, and clients allocate more resources implementing these initiatives, it is critical that these interventions be on target. Dedicated performance consultants systematically revisit and reflect on the performance analysis process, double-checking for errors and oversights.

Rossett (1992, 160) identified several questions useful in evaluating a performance analysis activity:

- Have sufficient primary performance improvement needs been identified?
- Are performance objectives clearly and specifically linked to business goals?
- How valid, reliable, and complete are available performance data?
- How likely is it that identified performers can improve performance to the levels needed to positively impact business goals?
- Have all of the right performers and performance improvement objectives been identified?
- Are the projected performance improvement objectives sufficient to accomplish business goals?
- Have sufficient secondary and tertiary needs been identified?

- Is there sufficient reason to believe that external factors (acquisition of the company, changes in competition, political shifts, economic climate) will not overwhelm efforts to improve performance?
- How clear, specific, and complete are performance improvement objectives?

Conducting Cause Analysis

Cause analysis reveals the real reason(s) a performance problem or gap exists. Hale (1998, 9) contends that cause analysis is also used to identify factors impeding and contributing to performance. Determining the causes of performance gaps requires HRD professionals to consider the following:

- Do employees have the knowledge, ability, skills, time, and other resources necessary to perform?
- What are employees' expectations of performance?
- Are employees motivated to perform adequately?
- Do performers possess the ability to perform their jobs correctly?
- What is the adequacy of environmental support and feedback?
- Are employees providing sufficient data and information regarding their performance?
- What are the rewards and incentives for performing correctly, and are they adequate to motivate acceptable performance?
- What are the results and consequences for performing inadequately?
- Are performers penalized or otherwise given disincentives for achieving desired work results?
- How well are people given the data, information, or feedback they need to perform at the time they need it? Are performers given important information they need to perform on a timely basis?
- How well are performers supported in what they do by appropriate environmental support, resources, equipment, or tools?
- Do performers have the necessary job aids and working conditions to perform satisfactorily?
- How well are individuals or groups able to perform?
- Do performers want to achieve desired results? What payoffs do they expect? How realistic are their expectations (Rothwell 1996b, 13–14)?

Designing, Developing, Implementing, and Evaluating the Solution

Performance consulting involves designing solutions to individual and organizational performance problems. Hale (1998, 18) believes that this requires performance consultants to describe their audiences (direct and indirect) and specify necessary long-term support, communication and implementation requirements, costs and benefits, other relevant success measures, the pilot test and rollout plans, and how and who will measure results.

Developing solutions, according to Hale (1998, 18), includes preparing or securing materials, systems, and other required elements. Preparing collateral and management support materials, public relations pieces, and employee communiques may also be involved.

Implementing the solution requires establishing an implementation team, conducting the pilot test, analyzing findings, and launching the solution throughout the organization. Finally, measuring the solution's results includes gathering data, comparing the data with pre-established measures, assessing findings, and reporting results (Hale 1998, 18).

Performance Consulting Model

Robinson and Robinson (1996) provide an eight-step approach to the performance consulting process. Each step is designed to help uncover the root cause of performance problems and identify appropriate performance improvement solutions. The steps are as follows:

1. Mapping the components of performance (the performance relationship map)
2. Identifying business needs in operational terms
3. Developing models of performance
4. Identifying actual performance
5. Identifying factors impacting performance
6. Implementing performance improvement interventions
7. Managing performance consulting projects
8. Measuring and reporting results

Mapping the Components of Performance: The Performance Relationship Map

The performance relationship map is a tool for helping both performance consultants and clients understand the complex interrelationships of human performance (Robinson and Robinson 1996, 53). This map is illustrated in Figure 11.1.

First, a specific business need is written at the top of the map. Performance consultants then indicate desired results in the form of specific business goals. Recorded in box 2 is the type of performance employees *should* demonstrate if desired operational results are to be achieved.

FIGURE 11.1   Performance Relationship Map

Business Need:

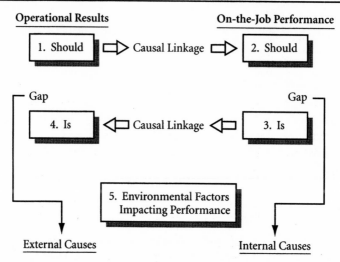

SOURCE: Reprinted, by permission from the publisher, from D. G. Robinson and J. Robinson, *Performance Consulting* (San Francisco: Berrett-Koehler, 1996).

In box 3, employees' current performance is identified and compared to desired performance. Performance consultants need to determine what kinds of gaps exist. After all, current performance determines current operational results.

In box 5 are the factors and forces that impact desired performance. According to Robinson and Robinson (1996), factors are external causes outside of a client's control that affect operational results and performance requirements (e.g., economic conditions or technological state). Forces are internal and within the client's control. Examples might include the lack of skill or knowledge to do what is required on the job, ineffective compensation and reward systems, poor job design, or an inadequate performance feedback system.

Identifying Business Needs in Operational Terms

Business needs should be identified in operational terms (Robinson and Robinson 1996, 80–81). Thus, performance assessments must begin with a clear definition of business goals, objectives, and strategies for a unit, division, department, or entire company. These serve as the foundation to which all performance requirements will be anchored. First, performance consultants need to define business needs in operational or measurable terms, including identification of any gap between actual and desired results. Next, they need to determine the driving forces and reasons behind needs. Once this is accomplished, performance consultants need to identify business strategies that will be used to meet needs. Following this activity, performance consultants need to determine the external and internal factors that affect accomplishment of business goals. Finally, they need to identify any implications for performance as envisioned by clients (Robinson and Robinson 1996, 80). This information can be obtained through interviews with the client team or senior management and by reviewing internal and external documents.

Developing Models of Performance

As discussed in Chapter 10, a model of performance consists of four components: (1) performance results, (2) best practices or competencies, (3) quality criteria, and (4) work environment factors. Performance models can be written in two ways: as best practices or as competencies. When using performance language, the model describes actual techniques and behaviors used by exemplary performers to secure results (Robinson and Robinson 1996, 104). Best practices are determined by asking employees who consistently do a superior job to communicate what they do step by step. Performance consultants then build a pattern of techniques, practices, and approaches that will achieve the desired result in an excellent manner (Rossett 1992).

According to Robinson and Robinson (1996, 107), performance language is a guide or road map for people who are new to the position. It helps provide specific activities that can be reviewed by others to determine whether they are, in fact, doing what should be done. Performance language provides a strong framework for learning interventions and curriculum design and helps performance consultants analyze a *specific job*.

A competency model describes the knowledge, skills, and attitudes required in accomplishing a task or job. Again, exemplary performers are instrumental in identifying the knowledge, skills, and attitudes necessary to achieve desired results (Robinson and Robinson 1996, 106). Competency-based performance models yield a common language across positions within an organization. It is the best approach when creating a performance management system, and it enables performance consultants to identify *core capabilities* required of any employee in any position across the entire organization.

Competency-based performance models can be easily translated into training curricula and are the best approach when a job cluster is being assessed (Robinson and Robinson 1996, 110–111). Robinson and Robinson (1996) encourage the use of a performance model when performance consultants are describing "should" performance for a specific position or job cluster. In essence, performance models describe an employee's best practices for a particular job, as well as the knowledge that all employees (ones performing identical jobs) must have to be successful.

Identifying Actual Performance

Performance consultants identify actual performance to establish a baseline for future comparisons through a process known as performance assessment. Performance assessment is a three-phase diagnostic process (Robinson and Robinson 1996). First, performance consultants obtain the client's perception of desired operational results and create operational measurement indicators. The outcome of this phase is agreement with the client on business goals, initiatives, and challenges, and how they will affect employee performance requirements. Second, detailed descriptions are developed of the performance required to achieve desired operational results to secure agreement with the client on acceptable performance models. Third, performance consultants identify current performance strengths and gaps as compared to desired performance. In addition, they isolate any external factors or internal forces that challenge both operational goals and required on-the-job performance. Ultimately, successful performance assessment leads to agreement with the client on actions to be taken. These can include learning interventions that will provide employees with needed skills and knowledge, initiatives that enhance employee motivation, or organizational actions required to remove work environment barriers and maximize effectiveness.

Silber (1992) maintains that performance consultants engage in two primary activities when identifying actual performance. First, they use front-end and needs-analysis techniques to identify problems (problem identification). Second, they break a problem down into its component parts, identify and categorize related issues, and then isolate the cause(s) of the problem(s) (problem analysis).

Identifying Factors Impacting Performance

Performance consultants are responsible for identifying factors impacting performance. Earlier in this chapter, we examined four primary contributors to performance breakdown: employees' knowledge, skills, and abilities; performers' actions and behaviors; managers' actions and behaviors; and the organization's actions and behaviors.

Implementing Performance Improvement Interventions

Implementing performance improvement interventions is an area in which performance consultants generally are the most comfortable and competent. The purpose of this phase is to close performance gaps using credible, client-identified, and client-supported actions (Hale 1998). As a result, performance consultants will have reached their ultimate goal—improved performance in support of their client's business goals. Robb (1998, 253) believes that prior to implementing solutions, performance consultants should develop written agreements to implement the performance improvement interventions and projects identified by clients in the assessment phase (contracts). They should develop internal and external partnerships that are critical to a performance consultant's success (partnerships), and they should develop the performance improvement actions the client has agreed to take (performance improvement interventions). Finally, they should specify the expected outcomes and determine how success will be measured (results).

Silber (1992) maintains that performance consultants execute four responsibilities when implementing performance improvement interventions. First, they analyze performance problems, decide on appropriate solutions, and design specifications for the solutions. Second, they turn existing specifications for performance solution(s) into a program or intervention. Third, performance consultants implement a solution of their design. Fourth, they assess the solution to guarantee that it has solved the problem as well as provide cost and benefit data to the client to demonstrate the solution's return on investment.

Managing Performance Consulting Projects

Project management skills and techniques are invaluable to planning, organizing, and monitoring one's work or that of others. Performance consultants may be called upon to communicate benefits at various stages of a performance improvement intervention, facilitate the removal of barriers, or resolve issues affecting the performance change process or project team (Gilley and Maycunich 1998a).

Measuring and Reporting Results

Based on the impact measures agreed to in the assessment phase, performance consultants should (1) measure the results of actions taken; (2) broker for resources to measure results; or (3) manage a project to design, develop, and implement the measurement process (Robinson and Robinson 1996). Results reporting follows completion of the measurement process. Reporting results requires planning, tact, and tailoring the message to the audience in terms that are practical and easily understood.

Performance Technology Model

Although many acceptable approaches to performance consulting exist, most involve a performance improvement process or system that includes performance analysis, cause analysis, and intervention selection as shown in the generic model in Figure 11.2. Deterline and Rosenberg (1992) developed such an approach, which they refer to as the performance technology model.

FIGURE 11.2 Performance Technology Model

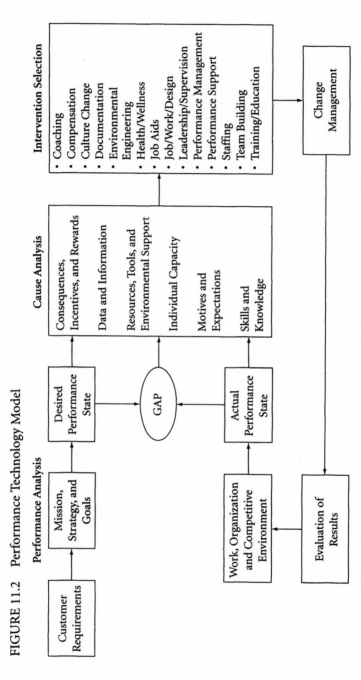

SOURCE: Reprinted, by permission from the publisher, from W. A. Deterline and M. J. Rosenberg, *Workplace Productivity: Performance Technology Success Stories* (Washington, D.C.: International Society for Performance Improvement, 1992).

Performance Analysis

Rosenberg (1996) describes performance analysis as a process of identifying the organization's performance requirements and comparing them to its objectives and capabilities. Harless (1986) previously described this as "front-end analysis," which identifies what must be done to correct a specific performance problem or to capitalize on opportunities for improvement.

Since the goal of performance analysis is to measure the gap between desired and actual performance (Rossett 1999b), performance consults develop competency profiles. To measure actual performance, performance consultants conduct a comprehensive assessment of employees' current capabilities, the efficiency of organizational structure, the appropriateness of organizational culture, and the organization's competitive position. The result of the analysis identifies the gap between desired and actual performance levels. The nature of the gap frames development of interventions designed to bring actual and desired performance levels closer together.

A variety of tools and techniques may be employed during a performance analysis, from reviews of organizational information, interviews, and focus groups to observations from subject matter experts, customers, suppliers, and performers. People's attitudes influence their perception of a problem's importance, the value of solving it, and the likelihood of succeeding with a particular solution. Rossett (1999b), therefore, suggests identifying the feelings of senior management in regard to performance problems and related solutions.

Cause Analysis

At this point the root causes of a past, present, or future performance gap are identified. Even after a performance analysis has been completed, however, it may be too soon to plan a solution because analysis may have identified only *symptoms* of the problem. According to Rosenberg (1996), a common mistake made during the performance improvement process is moving too hastily to adopt a solution or intervention (such as training). It is critical that the underlying cause(s) of a performance problem be identified. Each cause must be examined carefully to ascertain its contribution to a performance breakdown and impacts on performance.

Intervention Selection

Performance problems are often "multicausal"; hence, they may require a combination of interventions (Rummler and Brache 1995). Training, combined with changes in the work environment (structure) or motivation strategy (compensation system), is more likely to be successful. Rosenberg (1996) argues that the rate of success increases if management engages in the training and provides the workforce with post-training support.

Spitzer (1992) identified several intervention design principles for promoting successful performance improvement interventions. Performance improvement interventions should be based on a comprehensive understanding of the entire performance problem or situation. They should be carefully targeted and have a clear, visible sponsor. Interventions should be based on what is most important, possible, and needed within the organization. Intervention design should use a team approach in order to maximize opinions and ideas as well as obtain a cross section of the organization. Interventions should be cost-effective but comprehensive, given the resources available. Finally, interventions should be integrated into the organization's culture and operations in order to ensure their sustainability over time.

Types of Interventions

One of the best ways to consider interventions is to organize them by category. To this end, Rosenberg (1996) suggested four major categories of interventions:

1. *Human resource development* emphasizes improving individual employee performance through training, career development, individual feedback, incentives, and rewards.
2. *Organizational development* centers on improving the performance of groups or teams. It involves organizational design, team building, culture change, group feedback, incentives, and rewards.
3. *Human resource management* is concerned with coaching and managing individual and group performance, as well as recruiting and staffing. Intervention topics include supervision, leadership, succession planning, and personnel selection.
4. *Environmental engineering* focuses on providing tools and facilities for improving performance. Examples include ergonomics, job aids, electronic resources, systems design, job and organizational design, and facilities design.

Change Management

When organizational change isn't addressed adequately, implementation may fail. Resistance to change—particularly change that affects performance—can be a powerful obstacle. Performance improvement interventions often cause some kind of change that affects employees or the organization and requires much time and careful planning. Therefore, change management techniques are a critical aspect for successful implementation. As summarized by Rothwell (1996a, 9), "a good solution that's poorly implemented becomes a poor solution."

HRD professionals should monitor the intervention as it is being implemented by considering the following questions:

- How well does the intervention address the root cause(s) of human performance gaps?
- What measurable improvements can be shown?
- How much ownership have stakeholders vested in the intervention, and what steps can be taken to improve that ownership?
- How are changing conditions inside and outside the organization affecting the intervention? (Kissler 1991)

This step generates an intervention that is properly monitored and managed in a way consistent with desired results.

Evaluation

After applying or implementing the performance improvement solution, monitoring its effect on performance improvement and on the organization reveals its degree of success (Deterline and Rosenberg 1992). We examine this issue and provide several evaluation strategies and techniques in Chapter 17.

Conclusion

Improving the client's performance is the performance consultant's main goal. The performance consultant may be a client liaison, interviewer, analyst, project team member, or project manager whose responsibilities vary depending on the structure of the assignment or his or her level of performance, skill, and knowledge. Performance consultants utilize the logical steps of a performance consulting model and may be involved in delivering results in each phase of the performance improvement process in their quest to meet and exceed client needs.

PART IV

Organizational Change

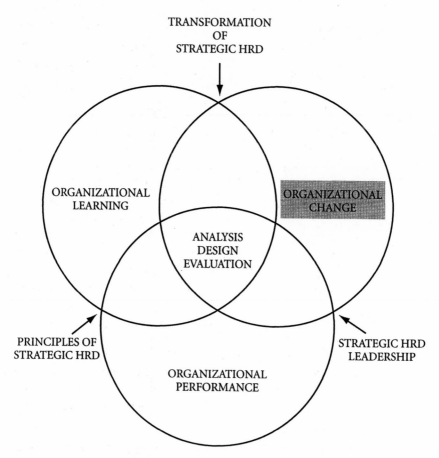

TRANSFORMATION
OF
STRATEGIC HRD

ORGANIZATIONAL
LEARNING

ORGANIZATIONAL
CHANGE

ANALYSIS
DESIGN
EVALUATION

PRINCIPLES OF
STRATEGIC HRD

STRATEGIC HRD
LEADERSHIP

ORGANIZATIONAL
PERFORMANCE

ORGANIZATIONAL LEARNING, PERFORMANCE, AND CHANGE

CHAPTER 12

Organizational Change

Organizations are in a constant state of change. Preskill and Torres (1999, 3) point out that "what has become crystal clear is that organizations will never again be stable and predictable. No longer do organizations offer one product or service for twenty more years with a homogeneous workforce that experiences little movement." Vaile (1996) has captured the spirit of these unprecedented organizational changes as "permanent white water." He asserts that organizational white water means that organizational life will be (a) full of surprises; (b) increasingly complex; (c) poorly organized and structured, and ambiguous; (d) quite costly; and (e) brimming with problems.

Several factors drive organizational change, including costs, market competition, market share, uncontrolled financial disasters, declining revenue and profits, and technology (Kissler 1991). Watkins and Marsick (1993, 4–5) maintain that several influences move organizations to adopt a continuous learning and change perspective. For example, changes in technology require learning new ways of thinking and working; the total quality movement requires employees to monitor their own work, reduce errors, and contribute suggestions for making the organization more competitive; and the customer service movement requires new learning to understand and satisfy customer needs and expectations. Additionally, they maintain that high-performing and self-directing work teams necessitate learning how to work effectively together to manage projects, influence people, and get the job done. Furthermore, they believe participatory management requires managers to share decisionmaking responsibility, empower employees, and assume more responsibility for jobs that are increasingly less clear and less narrowly defined. Gilley and Maycunich (2000) believe that competitive pressures require organizations to reduce unnecessary work processes and steps in production. They also contend that global turmoil and competition require organizations to adopt new human resources philosophies in order to enhance their competitive readiness and renewal capacity. Watkins and Marsick (1993, 5) conclude that "to survive in the turbulent environment created by these forces, organizations and their workforces must be flexible, farsighted, and able to learn continuously."

Technology is a major force affecting organizational change (Preskill and Torres 1999). Our increasing reliance on technology has revolutionized the world's production and consumption capacities and needs, as well as the way work is accomplished (Drucker 1997; Judy and D'Amico 1997; McLagan and Nel 1996; March 1995; Kissler 1991). This requires that people change how they make things, provide services, and communicate with one another.

Regardless of the efforts made by HRD professionals (performance consultants or organizational development change agents) to improve performance or bring about organizational change, some organizations fail to embrace change. Some of the most common reasons are the lack of management support for change, internal conflict for resources, recognition, and rewards, organizational overconfidence, lack of critical reflective skills (the ability to examine current and past performance), and lack of commitment to change (Ulrich 1998). Burke (1992) believes some organizations fail to change because of a lack of agreed-upon organizational mission and strategy and differing organizational values. Others fail to change due to a lack of payoff for change, lack of consequences for inadequate or poor performance, or lack of support for change by employees. Block (1981) cited several additional reasons such as a desire for confirmation, differing realities, lack of trust among employees, managers, and executives, and lack of change agent credibility. Each of these reasons contributes to the failure of organizations, employees, and leaders to embrace individual and organizational change. It is, however, the responsibility of HRD professionals to address each of these issues.

Conditions for Organizational Change

Several conditions must be present for organizational development interventions to bring about desired change (Nadler 1998). Management and all those involved must have highly visible commitment to change. Additionally, management must remain committed to change throughout all phases, from diagnosis through implementation and evaluation. Decisionmakers need to have advanced information so that they know what is to happen and why they are doing what they are doing (Dyer 1989, 7–8).

Effective change efforts are intertwined with multiple parts of the organization, directed by managers and assisted by a change agent (HRD professional), based on an effective diagnosis of the firm, and consistent with organizational conditions. Employees must clearly see the relationship between the change effort and the organization's mission, goals, and guiding principles. The change agent (HRD professional) must be competent and credible within the firm. Evaluation is essential and must consist of quantitative as well as qualitative data. Finally, organizations must be at an optimal point of readiness for change in order for it to occur. When these conditions are present within a firm, HRD professionals are more successful in implementing interventions that bring about or improve organizational effectiveness.

Nature of Change

"Change is a constant" is a common saying throughout organizations. Understanding change helps individuals and organizations prepare for and integrate change (Conner 1992, 79). One key aspect of the nature of change involves its type:

- *Micro changes* are small, manageable, and common transitions, such as a promotion or transfer.
- *Organizational changes* are large-scale transitions that affect interactions, reporting relationships, and responsibilities.
- *Macro changes* are massive transitions that alter one's life or change one's assumptions, values, or beliefs.

Micro change occurs when "I" change; organizational change is when "we" change; macro change involves "everyone." Even though the term *macro* sounds big, it actually has the least effect on an individual's daily behavior. Macro changes such as environmental pollution or increasing crime seem so far removed from us that they do not appear to be tangible. Only when change affects us personally do we take notice. The recent recession in Asia was an event with only macro implications—unless you conducted business there or worked for a company that did. Then it became a micro issue as well.

Process of Change

Change process fundamentals can be traced back to original research conducted by Lewin in 1951. Although other elaborate change models have been developed, the basic premises laid out by Lewin appear to be the most appropriate when initiating organizational change designed to improve effectiveness. He identified three steps in the change process: *unfreezing, moving,* and *refreezing.*

Unfreezing refers to conditioning organizations for change and establishing ownership within the firm. This effort creates momentum when decisionmakers, stakeholders, and influencers align to introduce change. Once organizations are ready for change, HRD professionals identify possible interventions to help the organization maximize its developmental opportunities. Lewin (1951) claims these actions change the organizational system from its current level of behavior and operations to its new, desired level. The moving phase, often referred to as transformation, occurs when organizations are in the process of redefining and reinventing themselves to achieve their goals and objectives. The final phase of the change process is refreezing, or establishing equilibrium within the organization. The HRD professional's primary focus during this time is to help the organization reestablish itself so that it can achieve higher-level performance.

Organizational Culture and Change

Kotter (1996) believes that *culture* refers to norms of behavior and shared values among a group of people. *Norms* are common or pervasive ways of acting that are found in a group and that persist because group members tend to behave in ways that teach these practices to new members, rewarding those who fit in and sanctioning those who do not. *Shared values* are important concerns and goals shared by most of the people in a group that tend to shape group behavior and that often persist over time, even when group membership changes.

Culture is shared, providing cohesiveness among people throughout an organization, and developed over time. An organization's existing culture is the product of beliefs, behaviors, and assumptions that have in the past contributed to success. Based on these characteristics, organizational culture can be defined as the *interrelationship of shared beliefs, behaviors, and assumptions that are acquired over time by members of an organization* (Conner 1992, 164).

Much has been learned in the past few years about culture change and HRD professionals' central role in its accomplishment (Ulrich 1997a, 169–170). Five steps reflect the essence of the HRD professional's role in successful culture change: (1) define and clarify the concept of culture change; (2) articulate why culture change is central to business success; (3) define a process for assessing the current culture, the desired future culture, and the gap between the two; (4) identify alternative approaches to creating culture change; and (5) build an action plan that integrates multiple approaches to culture change. To build an action plan for implementing culture change, Ulrich (1997a, 183) believes the following seven critical success factors should be considered.

Leading Change

Organizations need to identify a sponsor for the culture change effort. A sponsor is a leader who owns and champions the change, publicly commits to making it happen, gathers the resources necessary to sustain change, and invests in the personal time and attention needed to follow through.

Creating a Shared Need

Organizations need to align the rationale for culture change to business results and to articulate a clear reason for culture change efforts. Ulrich (1997a, 138) contends that employees need to understand the reason for change, why it is important, and how it will help them and/or the business in the short and long term.

Shaping a Vision

The desired outcomes of the culture change must be communicated. Employees need to see the outcomes of change in behavioral terms (what they will do differently as a result of the change). They must be enthusiastic about the results of accomplishing culture change and understand how customers and other stakeholders will benefit (Ulrich 1997a, 138).

Mobilizing Commitment

Organizations need to identify key stakeholders who must accept the desired culture. Stakeholders must recognize who else needs to be committed to the change to make it happen and how to build a coalition of support for the change (Ulrich 1997a, 138). They need to enlist the support of critical individuals in the organization and build a responsibility matrix to make culture change happen.

Changing Systems and Structures

Organizations need to realign and reengineer HRD practices to be consistent with the desired culture. Sponsors of the change need to understand how to link change to other HR and HRD systems (e.g., staffing, training, appraisal, compensations and rewards, structure, communication) and to recognize the systems' implications of the change (Ulrich 1998).

Monitoring Progress

Tracking change and the new culture that evolves requires sponsors to have a means of measuring success. They need to benchmark progress of the results of the change and the process of implementing the change.

Making Change Last

Organizations need to take specific actions, assign accountabilities and time frames, and integrate multidirectional activities (top-down, side-to-side, and bottom-up) to bring about lasting, long-term change. Ulrich (1998, 138) believes that this can be facilitated when sponsors of the change recognize the first steps in getting started, have short- and long-term plans to keep attention focused on the change, and have a plan for adapting the change over time. As HRD professionals help executives work through these success factors, they create an integrated culture-change action plan (Nadler 1998).

Several characteristics are crucial when examining the relationship between culture and change. First, culture is composed of three components: *beliefs, behaviors,* and *assumptions.* According to Conner (1992, 164–165),

> Beliefs are the set of integrated values and expectations that provide a framework for shaping what people hold to be true or false, relevant or irrelevant, good or bad about their environment. . . . Behaviors are observable actions that constitute the way people actually operate on a daily basis. Whereas beliefs reflect intentions that are often difficult to discern, behaviors can be verified in a more objective manner. . . . Assumptions are the unconscious rationale we use for continuing to apply certain beliefs or specific behaviors. When people develop belief and behavior patterns that are successful, they rely on those patterns when similar circumstances arise.

The prevailing *beliefs, behaviors,* and *assumptions* of an organization guide what are considered appropriate or inappropriate actions in which individuals and groups engage.

An organization's collective beliefs, behaviors, and assumptions affect daily business decisions, actions, and operations on two levels, overt and covert. The overt level represents observable, intentional, and direct influences on operations (e.g., goals, policies and procedures, and corporate mission statements). The covert level is characterized by obscure, unintentional, and indirect influences on operations (e.g., informal ground rules, unofficial guidelines, or "the way things are around here") (Conner 1992, 166). These latter influences are difficult to change because employees are often unaware of them.

On the overt level, an organization operates on beliefs and observable behaviors. At the covert level, the organization is influenced by employees' collective assumptions. These combine to influence oral and written communications, organizational structure, power and status, policies and procedures, compensation and reward systems, and the design and use of physical facilities.

If an organization's current culture and the change desired have little in common, the chances of successfully achieving that change are minimal. The odds of implementing the desired change grow as the similarity grows between the current culture and the beliefs, behaviors, and assumptions required by the new initiative. Rummler and Brache (1995) believe that whenever a discrepancy exists between current organizational culture and the objectives of change, the culture always wins. Effective management of organizational culture is an essential contributor to the success of a change initiative.

Because organizational culture is durable and resistant to major change, a great deal of time, energy, and resources must be used in its modification. HRD professionals encounter minimum resistance when a change initiative is consistent with organizational culture. When facing an organizational culture that may hinder desired change, Conner (1992, 178) believes an HRD professional should do one of three things: (1) modify the change to be more in line with existing beliefs, behaviors, and assumptions of the organization's culture; (2) modify the beliefs, behaviors, and assumptions of the current culture to be more supportive of the change; or (3) prepare for the change to fail.

Understanding Resilience

Although organizational effectiveness implies continuous change and development, individuals and organizations differ in their ability to adapt to or recover from change. The capacity of an organization and its members to absorb change without draining the firm or individual energies is referred to as resilience (Patterson 1997, 6). Resilience represents a personal energy account that people draw from to pay (time and effort) for change and their ability to adapt and adjust appropriately to it.

Organizations are challenged to strengthen their employees' adaptability to change, both personally and professionally. Connor (1992) believes that personal energy accounts become depleted in the face of continuous change unless the spiral of ongoing withdrawals is broken. He suggests two approaches to breaking the downward spiral and, thus, becoming more resilient. First, employees can increase their energy by developing adaptive skills. Second, they can decrease their energy expenditures by accepting the inevitability of change and adjusting accordingly.

Organizational leaders and HRD professionals are responsible for discovering ways to help employees strengthen the skills needed to adapt to change and thus remain resilient during change. They must create an environment that provides support for change and resiliency.

Resilient employees share several important characteristics. They are "positive, focused, flexible, organized, and proactive," according to Connor (1992, 238). They display a sense of security and self-assurance based on their view of life as complex yet filled with opportunity (positive). Resilient employees view disruptions as the natural result of a changing world and see major change as uncomfortable yet offering hidden opportunities. They believe that there are important lessons to be learned from challenge and see life as generally rewarding.

Resilient employees clearly focus on what they want to achieve. They maintain a strong vision that serves both as a source of purpose and as a guidance system to reestablish perspectives following significant disruption (Conner 1992, 239).

Conner (1992), Patterson (1997), and Nadler (1998) suggest that resilient employees demonstrate a special adaptability when responding to uncertainty (flexible). Resilient employees believe that change is a manageable process and have a high tolerance for ambiguity, needing only a short time to recover from adversity or disappointment. Resilient employees feel empowered during change, recognize their own strengths and weaknesses, and know when to accept internal or external limits. They challenge change and, when necessary, modify their own assumptions or frames of reference. Finally, they rely on nurturing relationships for support and display patience, understanding, and humor when dealing with change.

Connor (1992, 240) suggests that resilient employees develop structured approaches to managing ambiguity (organized). They identify the underlying themes embedded in confusing situations and consolidate what appear to be several unrelated change projects into a single effort with a central theme. They establish priorities and, when necessary, renegotiate during change. Resilient employees manage many simultaneous tasks and compartmentalize stress so that it does not carry over to other projects or parts of their lives. They recognize when to ask others for help and engage in major action only after careful planning.

Finally, Conner (1992, 240) believes that resilient employees engage change rather than defend against it (proactive). They realize when change is inevitable, necessary, or advantageous and use resources to creatively reframe a changing situation, improvise new approaches, or maneuver to gain an advantage. Resilient employees take risks despite potentially negative consequences; draw important lessons from change-related experiences that are then applied to similar situations; respond to disruption by investing energy in problem solving and teamwork; and influence others to resolve conflicts (Conner 1992, 240).

Myths and Realities Concerning Organizational Change

Myths and Assumptions About Change

According to Connor (1992, 7), organizations have an immeasurable impact on how employees view themselves in relation to change. From their experiences, most employees hold several unconscious assumptions about organizational change. Although firmly held, these assumptions are based mostly on fears and prejudice rather than fact. Some common myths include the following: it is impossible to understand why people accept or resist change; bureaucracies cannot really be changed; change will always be mismanaged; organizational efficiency and effectiveness inevitably decrease when changes are attempted; management is inherently insensitive to problems caused during the implementation of change; and what leaders say about change should never be confused with reality. Some believe that those who help implement positive changes are heroes, whereas those who resist are villains. Finally, there are those misguided individuals who believe that employees are prone to resist any change that is good for the business.

Patterson (1997, 7) has found that ten fatal myths permeate organizational change activities:

1. People act first in the best interest of the organization.
2. People want to understand the "what" and the "why" of organizational change.
3. People engage in change because of the merits of change.
4. People embrace change when they trust their leaders to do the right think.
5. People opt to be architects of the change affecting them.
6. Organizations are rationally functioning systems.
7. Organizations are wired to assimilate systemic change.
8. Organizations operate from a value-driven orientation.
9. Organizations can effect long-term systemic change with short-term leadership.
10. Organizations can achieve systemic change without creating conflict within the system.

HRD professionals are better prepared to help organizations and their employees adapt to change when they proactively address these myths and assumptions. Conversely, these can lead to disaster if not appropriately handled.

Realities of Change

Numerous harsh realities face organizations during times of change (Patterson 1997). *First,* most employees act in their own best interests, not in that of the organization. When people feel the winds of change blowing across an organization, the natural response is to say, "What's in it for me? How will I benefit? Why should I change?" (Block 1987). Two decades ago Hall and Loucks (1978) revealed that people respond predictably to organizational change. First, they want to know what the change is about. Second, they demand to know how organizational change will affect them personally as well as professionally. Third, people want to know how they can possibly fit change into their busy lives. People express concern about organizational interests only after they satisfactorily resolve their self-interests (which some never do).

It is natural for people to think first of themselves (Patterson 1997). Acting out of self-interest does not mean people are selfish or disloyal to the organization; such behavior simply reflects individuals' need to conserve their scarce energy. Thus, believing that employees will automatically rally around every change initiative within the organization is unrealistic. Employees spend their energy on change initiatives that offer a payback.

Implications for HRD Professionals.   Although the natural tendency of individuals is to act in their own self-interests, the logical tendency of those leading change initiatives is to sell change on the basis of how good it will be for the organization. Change agents erroneously assume that if they can rationally build a case for change based on the benefits to the organization, people will rationally embrace the change and everyone will win.

Second, according to Patterson (1997), most employees don't care to know the "what" and the "why" of organizational change—they simply want to know what's in it for them. Simply because the initiators of change have legitimate, compelling reasons for the need to change and do a competent job of presenting the case for change doesn't mean employees will enthusiastically embrace it. Instead, employees will often disregard meaningful, worthwhile organizational change simply because they fail to recognize its personal benefits.

Implications for HRD Professionals.   HRD professionals sometimes fail to recognize the distinctions between receiving and understanding communication. HRD professionals can convey information and employees can receive it without real understanding taking place. Genuine understanding does not occur until employees attach personal meaning to the message being communicated. HRD professionals must be aware of communications gaps in the system and trace the source of communication channel breakdowns.

Burden of proof poses yet another concern. Employees reason that as long as the system fails to communicate anticipated changes and accompanying expectations, they cannot be held responsible for fulfilling expectations. HRD professionals overcome the burden of proving organizational change has been effectively communicated by shifting significant responsibility for understanding back to those receiving the information.

Third, most employees engage in organizational change to avoid unnecessary difficulties or personal "pain" rather than to implement change based on its merits (Patterson 1997). Individuals need more than strong arguments for the merits of change; they need to weigh the pain of changing against the pain of clinging to the status quo. Patterson (1997) suggests that organizational leaders and HRD professionals pose a series of questions: What will our organizational life be like five years from now if we continue to do business as usual? How painful will it be to change to meet market demands? What will life be like if we accept the proposed changes? Will the short-term pain of changing be less than the long-term pain of holding on to how we currently do business? Honest responses to these questions help organizational leaders and HRD professionals determine whether a proposed change, even with the inevitable discomfort, will be worth the effort.

Implications for HRD Professionals.   HRD professionals must resist the natural tendency to "sell" proposed change using logical organizationally based benefits. Instead they should communicate the need for change by exposing the pain that will result from not changing (i.e., lost productivity, revenue, quality, profits, etc.). In essence, HRD professionals must help organizational leaders understand the urgency for change, which Tichy and Charan (1995) call "the burning platform theory of change." Employees must see that the platform is burning, whether or not the flames are visible. The burning platform is a metaphor for taking advantage of the opportunity to solve problems now and manage situations before they spin out of control.

Fourth, most employees view change with a great deal of skepticism and cynicism, even though they outwardly appear to be supportive (Patterson 1997). Lack of trust in decisionmakers and implementers underlies employee cynicism, eventually sabotaging change efforts. Often, seemingly trustworthy employees question the trustworthiness of those proposing the change. Mistrust leads "trustworthy" targets of change to resist the efforts of change agents (HRD professionals). Consequently, HRD professionals must prove their trustworthiness to those being asked to change.

Implications for HRD Professionals.   Attacks on trustworthiness can hurt deeply, and harsh reactions to mistrust are usually counterproductive. Furthermore, HRD professionals must examine their own conduct. Fisher and Brown (1988) encourage HRD professionals to think about whether they have possibly given others reasons to mistrust by asking the following questions about their behavior: Did I communicate clearly? Did I actually deceive or mislead others? Did my conduct in any way prevent successful change?

Along with strengthening interpersonal trust, HRD professionals must increase trust in the organization. Operationally, this means that they must build an environment that enables employees to challenge the actions, conduct, or intentions of organizational leaders without fear of retribution. One way is to create a forum that allows executives, managers, and other employees to discuss issues surrounding trust in a safe environment. By improving interpersonal and organizational trust, HRD professionals are more likely to be viewed as having good intentions by those whom they are asking to initiate change.

Finally, HRD professionals, through genuine, frequent, and even intentionally redundant communication must forecast any possibility of change and its linkage to organizational values and guiding principles. HRD professionals must assume responsibility for demonstrating that the proposed change is anchored to core organizational values and guiding principles and that the change rests on the burning platform.

Fifth, many people opt to be victims rather than architects of change (Patterson 1997; Nadler 1998). The literature on organizational behavior and development is replete with calls for employee involvement. Organizational leaders are advised to give employees considerable autonomy in constructing how proposed change initiatives will impact their personal and professional lives. Unfortunately, many employees have a tendency to avoid autonomy and embrace dependency.

As paradoxical as it may seem, people have a love-hate relationship with autonomy (Block 1987). On one hand, employees sincerely claim they want to be architects of change affecting them. On the other hand, they fall into the dependency trap of wanting someone to nurture or care for them, or someone to blame (Conner 1992).

Patterson (1997, 24) believes that "autonomy carries with it responsibility, which translates into being held accountable for one's own actions. Dependency carries with it a patriarchal contract, which translates into being protected by those above . . . as long as one does what he or she is told." It is natural, however, for employees to choose the safety of being dependent victims of change rather than to choose the ambiguity and risk inherent in being held accountable as architects shaping how change affects them (Conner 1992).

Implications for HRD Professionals.   Employees remain trapped in the victim state because they often think and act based on their worst fears. Consequently, they lose any sense of control over their lives. Employees encouraged to think and act based on their highest hopes for the future find new energy and creative possibilities (Patterson 1997). HRD professionals need to help employees clarify their choices. Further, they need to provide support, information, and resources to help employees successfully make the more painful choice to become architects of change that will provide opportunities for growth and development.

Executives and managers sometimes unintentionally contribute to employees' victim status by demonstrating parent-like behavior between themselves and employees. They take care of those they supervise in exchange for loyalty.

To create more resilient organizations, HRD professionals need to break the dependency spiral by creating a climate of trust. Open communications and honoring employees as valued members of the organization is a start. In a trusting climate, employees are encouraged to take the risks associated with being architects of change (Patterson 1997).

Sixth, most organizations operate irrationally (Patterson 1997). Patterson, Purkey, and Parker (1986) suggest that we develop a common understanding of rational and nonrational organizations. Formal rational systems function with a single set of uniform goals that provide stable, consistent direction to the organization over time. The formal organizational chart reflects who has power and who does not. In rational organizations, decisionmaking is a logical, problem-solving process leading to the "best solution" for the firm. The external environment doesn't interface with the organizational culture; thus, the organization makes its own strategic and tactical decisions.

In stark contrast, the nonrational organization is guided by multiple, competing sets of goals developed through negotiation, compromise, and synergy. Power and authority are distributed throughout the organization, and decisionmaking is a collaborative process designed to satisfy a number of constituencies. The external environment serves as a filter for the continuing development of the culture.

Implications for HRD Professionals.   HRD professionals are challenged to provide rational leadership in the midst of a seemingly nonrational environment. Patterson (1997) asserts that HRD professionals provide a measure of stability for their organizations by addressing goals, power relationships, decisionmaking, and the external environment as they pertain to fundamental change.

Seventh, most organizations are designed to protect the status quo. Many researchers (Katz and Kahn 1978; Watkins and Marsick 1993; Preskill and Torres 1999; Gilley and Maycunich 1998a; Ulrich and Lake 1990) have characterized organizations as organic, as living, growing systems in which various units contribute to overall vitality in complex ways, not in simple, linear ways. Thus, organizations constantly struggle to ward off threats to their very existence. Just like other living organisms, organizations are wired to survive by resisting change. O'Toole (1995) summarizes this condition by explaining that "individuals are what they believe, and groups are their cultures; hence, to require a group to change its shared beliefs is to threaten its very existence." Unfortunately, the natural tendency toward resistance typically does not allow firms to differentiate between necessary and unnecessary change. Consequently, the natural tendency to preserve the status quo in organizations can pose grave risks for organizations and their leaders.

Implications for HRD Professionals.   HRD professionals have an obligation to look at the big picture when planning for an organization's future. When evidence accumulates that systemic, organic change is requisite to the vitality of the organization's future, HRD professionals must initiate and sustain change against heavy odds. Therefore, HRD professionals need to create a sense of urgency and appeal to employees' self-interests by clearly explaining that their future well-being is at stake. If, indeed, the platform of the organization is on fire, it becomes an HRD professional's difficult assignment to help people see the flames, or at least smell the smoke (Patterson 1997, 33).

Eighth, Patterson (1997) believes that most organizations react to outside pressures such as the need for greater revenue, market share, or improved profitability rather than refer to their guiding principles and values when initiating change. As Sarason (1996) discovered, the more things change, the more they stay the same . . . or get worse. One reason is that many organizations move through their organizational lives in an event-driven fashion and are not anchored to a set of values and guiding principles that focus their energy, efforts, and direction. An event-driven approach means that change is characterized by a series of episodes, unconnected to each other, unconnected to a core set of principles, and occurring for a short time before being relegated to the proverbial last year's new-thing shelf (Patterson 1997, 33).

Most organizational members don't intend to be driven by events, but instead sincerely believe their actions are based on key organizational principles. In fact, most can point to a laminated mission statement somewhere in the office. Despite good intentions, organizations sap their energy by chasing a string of disconnected initiatives that end up on the junk heap of failed reform (Patterson 1997).

Implications for HRD Professionals.   HRD professionals are obligated to thoroughly understand the distinction between slogans and real change (Nadler 1998). Moving organizations beyond putting words on paper and declaring the assignment finished requires reflective time to visit and revisit the meaning outlined in mission statements and the concrete strategies for leading groups through this difficult process (Patterson 1993). Until a group achieves a common understanding and commitment to the principles underlying a change initiative, any support for change is built on a weak foundation. When organizational leaders leap quickly into a discussion of solutions or outcomes, HRD professionals must return the focus to core values and guiding principles. Acknowledging the importance of outcomes is important, yet organizational leaders must possess a clear understanding of and commitment to the reasons why they are doing what they are doing.

Ninth, most organizations unfortunately implement long-term change with short-term leadership (Patterson 1997). Outside consultants on short-term assignments are often brought into the organization to initiate long-term change, instead of using internal HRD professionals and qualified managers and employees who must live with the decisions made.

Systematic change takes a long time to design, plan, implement, and monitor before it becomes embedded into the culture of "how we do business around here" (Schein 1992). How long is long? Some experts (Fullan 1991; Burke 1992; Sarason 1996; Ulrich and Lake 1990) believe that systemic change can take from seven to ten years. This means an organization needs to persistently and passionately pursue a single initiative for almost a decade in order to increase the chances that the change will be integrated into the firm's fabric. Thus, long-term changes call for long-term leadership.

Implications for HRD Professionals. Having core organizational values drive the system is vital to achieving long-term success. Organizations that anchor themselves to core values and guiding principles can transcend the tenure of organizational leaders and managers. In fact, core values and guiding principles become the basis for selecting future leaders. The stability of the organization then rests on the extent to which values and principles shape the organization's future.

Collins and Porras (1994) maintain that the distinguishing factor separating truly outstanding organizations from their closest rivals is the concept of organizational values. Furthermore, they report that organizations maintain their stability across economic cycles and changes in executive leadership when they make long-term commitments to core values and guiding principles.

Tenth, most organizations are unrealistic about the amount of conflict that occurs as a result of change and naively expect change to be accepted wholeheartedly by employees (Patterson 1997). Many organizational leaders worry that acknowledging existing conflict may send signals to employees that things aren't under control. Thus, if things aren't going smoothly, someone will need to be held accountable for straightening them out. That someone usually is the leader.

Change creates conflict, which creates tension among employees. Excellent growth opportunities are often missed by putting an abrupt halt to resolving conflict or by pretending that it doesn't exist. Organizational leaders and employees can hide conflict temporarily, denying its existence for short periods of time. They can even blame the sponsor or change agent who initiated the change, but they cannot ignore it forever. Suppressing or denying conflict results in dysfunctional behavior organizationally and interpersonally, which harms everyone.

Implications for HRD Professionals. What can HRD professionals do to alter the natural tendency to avoid conflict? First, they need to accept the reality that conflict is inevitable but not the issue; conflict is the condition (Patterson 1997). The real issue is how organizational leaders and employees choose to handle conflict.

Second, HRD professionals need to understand employees' reactions and resistance to change. Connor (1992) described the phases people go through when they originally embrace a change perceived to be positive, only to resist it later. The five phases of positive resistance to change are (1) uninformed optimism; (2) informed pessimism; (3) hopeful realism; (4) informed optimism; and (5) completion.

During the first phase, sometimes referred as the "honeymoon," employees feel extremely positive about change, which produces naive enthusiasm based on insufficient data. The second phase occurs when employees begin to doubt the rightness of the change initiative. Some employees even withdraw from the change engagement, "checking out" because they have serious reservations or a low tolerance for pessimism. Although informed pessimism is inevitable, checking out is not.

Pessimism doesn't suddenly disappear; instead it lessens as employees move into "hopeful realism" (Connor 1992). This isn't a return to the "everything is wonderful" days of uninformed optimism; it simply means that employees begin to understand the positive possibilities of change.

As more and more concerns are resolved, employees become increasingly confident and move into the "informed optimism" stage, which is characterized by the acceptance of change as a positive growth and development opportunity or a positive career decision. Personal stability and wholeness, representing a state of equilibrium and tranquillity, characterize completion.

Third, HRD professionals need to create a safe environment for confronting conflict in a constructive way. By valuing the energy of dissent, they show people inside and outside the organization that honest conflict in a safe environment nourishes the seeds of rich solutions to organizational issues. When conflict surfaces, organizational leaders and managers need to move to the tension point, not away from it. Tension can be used creatively by capitalizing on the energy of dissent and leading people to reach solutions everyone can accept. The resistance resolution method developed by Gilley and Eggland (1992) offers one means by which to tap this energy (Chapter 11).

Roles in the Change Process

Five distinct roles are critical to the change process: sponsors, change agents, appliers, analysts, and advocates.

Sponsors

A sponsor is the "individual or group who has the power or influence to sanction, support, or legitimize change" (Connor 1992, 114). Sponsors consider the potential changes facing an organization and assess the barriers, dangers, and opportunities these transitions offer. They assess when change will occur, how it will be achieved, and in what form it will be presented. They are responsible for communicating new priorities to the organization, providing the resources needed to foster change, and providing the reinforcement needed to assure success. Sponsors are responsible for creating an environment that enables these changes to be made on time, at the appropriate level of quality, and within budget.

Connor (1992, 114–115) believes that a good sponsor must have the organizational power to legitimize change with appliers. He or she must create a level of discomfort with the status quo that makes change attractive. Good sponsors clearly envision what change must occur, thoroughly understand the organizational resources (time, money, people) necessary for successful implementation, and possess the ability and willingness to commit them. They have an in-depth understanding of the effect the change will have on the organization and the capacity to fully appreciate and empathize with the personal issues that major change raises. They understand thoroughly the size of the group to be affected by change and are able and willing to demonstrate the public support necessary to convey strong organizational commitment to change.

Good sponsors have the ability and willingness to meet privately with key individuals or groups to convey strong personal support for the change. They promptly reward those who facilitate acceptance of change and express displeasure with those who inhibit it. Sponsors ensure that monitoring procedures are established to track both the transition's progress and problems. Finally, good sponsors are willing to make sacrifices in order to bring about change, have the capacity to demonstrate consistent support for change, and reject any short-term action inconsistent with long-term change goals (Connor 1992, 114–115).

Change Agents

A change agent is the individual (typically an HRD professional) or group responsible for actually facilitating change (Chapter 13). Change agent success depends on the ability to identify and diagnose potential problems, develop appropriate change interventions, execute them effectively, and evaluate their impact on the organization. Such participation on the part of change agents is critical to the success of any change initiative.

Appliers

Appliers are the individuals or groups who actually implement change. Gilley (1998) uses the term applier because these people are the instruments of the change effort and play a crucial role in the short- and long-term success of a project. To enhance the likelihood of success, appliers comprehend the changes they are expected to implement and are appropriately involved in the process (Conner 1992). Their focus is a pragmatic attempt to improve performance or organizational efficiency. Their world is the daily pursuit of performance improvement while using limited resources. Their most frequently asked question is, "How will the change impact our daily lives?"

Appliers are decisionmakers who will have to live with change; hence it becomes a personal event for them. Their job is to implement and supervise change, and make it work. They understand the relationship between on-the-job success and accountability; therefore, they judge the impact of change on their employees, understanding that they will be blamed if the change fails and that others will be credited if it succeeds.

HRD professionals should make every attempt to reassure appliers that the proposed change has a solid base and will work. They should clearly define their commitment during design and implementation of the change in order to communicate an active involvement with and support of appliers. In addition, HRD professionals must clearly communicate what is in it for appliers and how it will help them improve employee performance.

Analysts

The analyst's role is simple: to screen change solutions and eliminate those that will not work. Analysts serve as gatekeepers by judging the quantifiable aspects of change solutions (Gilley 1998). They examine the technical specifications of a solution and determine whether it is a logical approach. In most decisionmaking situations, they do not have the authority to grant final approval but can advise sponsors not to move forward, and often do.

More than any other person involved in change initiatives, analysts examine the components of the change solution. According to Gilley (1998, 142), analysts "look at the pieces of the puzzle and see if they fit, which enables them to determine if the solution can be integrated into the organization's culture and blended with its values and leadership philosophy."

Unfortunately, some HRD professionals avoid or discount the role of analysts. The proper way to work effectively with analysts is to understand their importance and address their concerns with quantifiable information.

Advocates

In every change situation someone serves as an internal coach. These are advocates, who act as guides during the interaction between sponsors, HRD professionals, and clients. Advocates are the individuals or groups who want to achieve a change but lack the power and authority to bring it about (Conner 1992). They provide and interpret information about the problem, its potential causes, the types of sponsors involved, their expectations, and ways of proceeding (Gilley 1998).

Advocates can be found anywhere in the organization, including the HRD sector. Advocates can influence others to provide the leadership or support needed to foster change. Far too many change initiatives die an early death because they fail to gain support from the appropriate advocates. Advocates are concerned about the success of a change and want the change solution to succeed because it will improve the organization. According to Gilley (1998, 143), they ask one simple question: "How can we pull this off?" Their role becomes one of an ambassador serving the needs and wants of both HRD professionals and decisionmakers.

Advocates meet three criteria. They (1) have credibility with decisionmakers, (2) want the solution being presented, and (3) have credibility with HRD professionals (Miller and Heiman 1987). To facilitate change, HRD professionals need to identify credible advocates and work closely with them. They should follow advocates' advice unless it seriously violates their guiding principles, values, or ethics. Since advocates have already interacted with sponsors, appliers, change agents, and analysts involved in the change process, they understand their various operating styles and interests. Advocates are also aware of how each one of these individuals will benefit from implementation of a successful change solution, which is invaluable information for HRD professionals.

Barriers to Organizational Change

A number of barriers prevent organizations from implementing long-term, systemic change. Watkins and Marsick (1993) identified three such barriers: disconnected learning, learned helplessness, and tunnel vision.

Disconnected learning occurs when a training-for-training-sake approach prevails. The ghosts of learning efforts that never really took root because they were interrupted or were only partially implemented haunt many organizations. In such circumstances, little or no effort is made to transfer learning to the job or connect learning to business goals and objectives. Employees are on their own to implement learning, while managers and supervisors focus on other pressing issues. Disconnected learning occasionally interacts with the next barrier, learned helplessness, because people learn to ignore new initiatives that they think will disappear. They develop a habit of passivity that, over time, can lead to learned helplessness.

Employees learn helplessness when efforts at taking control meet with resistance or even punishment. Thus, *learned helplessness* hinders motivation and inhibits attentiveness to learning opportunities. In effect, employees are rewarded for not taking responsibility for their own actions. Watkins and Marsick (1993) contend that learned helplessness is also observed in teams when members allow their managers to passively direct them. Employees passively observe until the change initiative dissipates and, in so doing, guarantee organizational stagnation.

Employees who are aware of their own perspective but not the complexity of the entire situation experience *tunnel vision* (Watkins and Marsick 1993), which is the inability to see oneself and a situation from a systems point of view (and act accordingly). Tunnel vision causes employees to react blindly without fully considering the source of change or to become frozen into place due to the overwhelming complexity of change.

Change initiatives fail to bring about change for several reasons (Ulrich 1997a, 157). Change fails to occur when its initiatives are not tied to strategy or when change is seen as a fad or quick fix. Change fails when leaders are short-term focused, fail to lead, are afraid of the unknown, are unable to mobilize commitment to sustain change, or allow political realities to undermine change. Change also fails when expectations are not realistic, change designs are inflexible, and when HRD professionals neglect to generate measurable, tangible results. Consequently, HRD professionals are obligated to overcome these barriers before initiating change.

Models of Organizational Change

There are several models of organizational change that can be examined. We have selected four models that provide HRD professionals with differing perspectives of organizational change: (1) change process model, (2) building capacity for change model, (3) commitment to change model, and (4) leading change model.

The Change Process Model

For substantial change to occur, HRD professionals must adopt and implement the *change process model* (Gilley and Maycunich 2000). The change process model entails five activities: identifying assumptions, analyzing choices, making commitments, selecting appropriate actions, and engaging in critical reflective activities (Figure 12.1).

Identifying Assumptions.   Organizations first identify their assumptions about change prior to initiating the change process. Assumptions are beliefs about reality that are taken for granted, rules of thumb that guide one's actions, or a common set of beliefs and conventional wisdom (Brookfield 1992, 13).

According to Schwinn (1996), assumptions are an explicit set of conditions, principles, ethics, and expectations considered true regarding the basis for choosing actions and studying their consequences. In essence, assumptions are the anchors to which most decisions are tied. As a result, identifying one's assumptions about circumstances or events prior to engaging in change activities is critically important. Unless assumptions are identified and understood, individuals or or-

FIGURE 12.1 Change Process Model

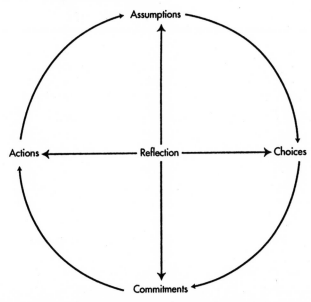

SOURCE: J. W. Gilley and A. Maycunich, *Beyond the Learning Organization: Creating a Culture of Continuous Growth and Development Through State-of-the-Art Human Resource Practices* (Cambridge, Mass.: Perseus Publishing, 2000).

ganizations will have difficulty promoting and accepting change, particularly when adopting a radical change such as organizational transformation.

Analyzing Choices.   Analyzing organizational choices reveals key elements of the decisionmaking process, allowing HRD professionals to understand the rationale behind the decisions made. The benefits of understanding organizational decisionmaking are invaluable. The process of analyzing choices involves examining *how* decisions are made, *who* participates in the decisionmaking process, *what* criteria are invoked, and *what* consequences follow. Engaging in this process places organizations in a better position to determine whether their decisions brought about desired change.

Making Commitments.   Commitment is crucial to bringing about real, lasting change. Absent sincere, dedicated commitment from all organizational members, change initiatives are destined to fail.

Selecting Appropriate Actions.   Implementing change requires organizations to take action. Appropriate actions may include allocating financial and human resources, restructuring the organization, identifying developmental strategies, and so forth, all of which enable individuals and organizations to make changes designed to bring about desired results.

Engaging in Critical Reflective Activities.   Critical reflection reveals the meaning of what was previously unknown or unrecognized and illuminates differences between prior and current expectations (Schwinn 1996). Individuals and organizations engage in critical reflective activities to understand their decisionmaking processes.

Critical reflection has been described as the "practice of analyzing one's own actions, decisions, or products by focusing on the processes involved" (Killion and Todnem 1991, 14). Individuals and organizations are able to develop a greater level of self-awareness of the nature and impact of their performance decisions, which provides additional opportunities for professional growth and development (Preskill 1996). Thus, critical reflection enhances awareness of why one acts as one does.

According to Saban, Killion, and Greene (1994), three types of critical reflection prevail: reflection *in* action, reflection *on* action, and reflection *for* action. *Reflection in action* occurs when individuals observe themselves from the outside, similar to an out of body experience. This exterior view provides individuals with a different perspective on their behaviors. *Reflection on action* focuses on the past. Individuals replay a situation in their minds, which they review, critique, and relive. As a result, they formulate opinions and judgments regarding their behavior. *Reflection for action* frames the future and allows organizations to utilize what they have learned from past experience. Preskill (1996) believes that this type of critical reflection allows organizations to better plan and sculpt change opportunities. Critical reflection, a quality improvement step in the change process, enables organizations to truly understand and embrace the change process.

The Building Capacity for Change Model

People change only when they have the capacity—ability and willingness—to do so (Connor 1992). *Ability* involves possessing the necessary skills and knowing how to use them. *Willingness* is motivation to apply essential skills to a particular situation. When one lacks either ability or willingness, it is unlikely that he or she will successfully adapt to change. Inadequate skills or knowledge causes deficiency in ability and should be addressed by training or informal mentoring. Unwilling behavior stems from a lack of motivation and should be addressed through performance management and coaching.

Successfully building change capacity relies on the following steps:

Step 1: Identify Key Success Factors for Building Capacity for Change. According to Ulrich (1997a), HRD professionals, acting as change agents, must turn knowledge about change into know-how for accomplishing change, and success factors for change into action plans for accomplishing change.

The first step is to have a clearly defined change model. A model identifies the key factors for a successful change and the essential questions that must be answered to put the model into action. Specific questions determine the extent to which key success factors exist within an organization. There are seven key success factors:

- Leading change: Having a sponsor of change who owns and leads the change initiative.
- Creating a shared need: Ensuring that individuals know why they should change and that the need for change is greater than the resistance to change.
- Shaping a vision: Articulating the desired outcome from the change.
- Mobilizing commitment: Identifying, involving, and pledging the key stakeholders who must be involved to accomplish the change.
- Changing systems and structures: Using HRD and management tools (staffing, development, appraisal, rewards, organization design, communication, systems, and so on) to ensure that the change is built into the organization's infrastructure.
- Monitoring progress: Defining benchmarks, milestones, and experiments with which to measure and demonstrate progress.
- Making change last: Ensuring that change happens through implementation plans, follow-through, and ongoing commitment (Ulrich 1997a).

Step 2: Profile the Extent to Which These Key Success Factors Are Being Managed. Resolving the paradox of change means transforming the seven key success factors from a theoretical exercise into a managerial process. Using the following questions, the seven factors' capacity for change in a given organization can be profiled. Ulrich (1997a, 73) believes that HRD professionals assigned to integrate change should answer these questions to ensure that the resources needed for making change happen will be available.

- To what extent does the change have a champion, sponsor, or other leader who will support the change? (Leading Change)
- To what extent do the people essential to the success of the change feel a need for change that exceeds the resistance to the change? (Creating a Need)

- To what extent do we know the desired outcomes for change? (Shaping a Vision)
- To what extent are key stakeholders committed to the change outcomes? (Mobilizing Commitment)
- To what extent have we institutionalized the change through systems and structures? (Changing Systems and Structures)
- To what extent are indicators in place to track our progress on the change effort? (Monitoring Progress)
- To what extent do we have an action plan for getting change to happen? (Making Change Last)

HRD professionals as change agents do not implement change, but they must be able to *get the change done*. By identifying and profiling key factors for change, they lead teams through the steps necessary for increasing change capacity.

The probabilities of implementing any change initiative improve dramatically when these seven success factors and their corresponding questions are assessed and discussed (Ulrich 1997a). HRD professionals leading the change should ask questions that reveal underlying assumptions.

Step 3: Identify the Improvement Activities for Each Success Factor. After conducting profiling activities, the organization identifies actions that will improve performance on those factors that received a low rating. The dialogue about the seven factors is generally more important than any "right" answer. The previous questions may be used to discuss action plans for each of the seven success factors.

As change agents, HRD professionals sometimes erroneously believe that they must "own" all the actions to make change happen. In reality, the primary job of change agents is to guide the change process. Therefore, it is critical that HRD professionals guide organizational leaders through discussions using the previous questions as a guide. Afterward, a comprehensive action plan for making change happen can be developed (Ulrich 1997a). Profiling transfers what is known about successful change into what can be done to make change successful.

Step 4: See the Seven Key Factors as an Iterative Process, Not an Event. In recent years many companies have initiated turnaround efforts. Through downsizing, rightsizing, outsourcing, and reengineering, these organizations have reduced costs and shed unprofitable businesses, while quality and reengineering efforts removed inefficient steps in work processes. Turnaround, however, is not transformation. Transformation results when customers and employees move from different images of a firm to similar issues (Ulrich 1997a, 14). Transformation changes the fundamental image of the business, as seen by customers and employees, and focuses on creating mind share more than market share. In other words, "real change" is not an event used to temporarily fix something but rather is a process used to re-design and enhance an organization, its operations, systems, and functions.

The Commitment to Change Model

According to Conner (1992), the commitment to change model has three specific stages: preparation, acceptance, and commitment. The horizontal axis of the commitment to change model reflects the length of time an employee has been exposed to change, whereas the vertical axis displays the degrees of support for change.

Preparation.   Introduction to change varies according to one's role in the change process (sponsor, change agent, applier, analyst, or advocate). Regardless of one's role, the preparation phase of the commitment model has two stages: contact and awareness.

Contact

Any activity by which sponsors, change agents, appliers, analysts, or advocates meet to exchange their perspectives regarding potential change is a contact. There are two possible outcomes of the contact stage: unawareness and awareness. Awareness, of course, advances the preparation process, whereas unawareness reduces the chances of adequate preparation for commitment.

Awareness

Organizations move into the awareness stage of the commitment process once they realize that modifications within the firm are underway. However, awareness does not necessarily mean that organizational leaders and employees have a complete understanding of the impact of change. For example, employees may know that a change is coming but may be uncertain about the specific effects the change may have. They may be unclear about the nature, depth, breadth, or basic rationale for the change.

Conner cites two possible outcomes of the awareness stage: confusion and understanding. Confusion reduces the probability of adequate preparation, whereas understanding advances the change process to the second phase—acceptance.

Acceptance.   The acceptance phase is a "mental period" of change where individuals struggle with the idea of altering their lives. It is characterized by two elements: understanding and positive perception.

Understanding

Understanding the nature and intent of change is the first step in acceptance. People who are aware of and comprehend a change can encourage and facilitate it.

When this has occurred, employees have crossed over the disposition threshold. The possible outcomes for the understanding stage are negative perception and positive perception. Employees who have a negative perception decrease their support for change and may exhibit behaviors that foster resistance. Employees with a positive perception of change will increase support for change, which enhances the likelihood of change acceptance.

Positive Perception

Once employees perceive a change as positive, they must decide whether they are going to support it. It should be pointed out that a positive perception of change and the actions required for making change happen are quite different efforts. Employees may not have the energy to implement change regardless of their perception of it. When employees perceive a change as positive, however, they are better prepared to move on to the commitment phase. How commitment will be manifested differs according to one's role as sponsor, change agent, or target. Sponsors use their organizational power and authority to legitimize change and ensure that it takes place. Change agents actively carry out the sponsor's decision, whereas targets support the change initiative willingly and are actively involved in implementing change. The two possible outcomes of the positive perception stage are either a decision not to support implementation or a formal decision to initiate the change.

Commitment. Commitment occurs when employees have decided to embrace change. The change initiative is now operational, and a second milestone has been reached—the "commitment threshold." The commitment phase consists of four subphases: installation, adoption, institutionalization, and internalization.

Installation

During installation the change is tested for the first time, which is sometimes referred to as the pilot-testing period. This period is the first opportunity for true, committed action to arise. In order to be successful, the change initiative requires consistency of purpose, an investment of resources, and the subordination of short-term objectives to long-range goals.

Problems and difficulties are inevitable during this period as change agents and targets attempt to modify and adjust the change initiative. During this period, some pessimism is common. As a result, HRD professionals must create a work environment that encourages open discussion of questions and concerns. Such actions facilitate and encourage problem-solving activities that build commitment. As problems and difficulties are resolved, a more realistic level of conviction toward the change develops, which allows commitment to advance to the adoption level. There are two possible outcomes for the installation stage: change is aborted or adopted.

Adoption

A considerable degree of commitment is required for organizations to reach the adoption stage. During this subphase, a change initiative is still being evaluated and cancellation is still an option. Conner (1992, 152–153) cites a number of reasons why change projects are aborted at this stage. First, logistic, economic, or political problems could surface after a significant testing period. Second, the need that sparked the initial commitment may no longer exist. Third, the overall strategic goals of the organization may have shifted and now do not include the change outcomes. Fourth, people in key sponsorship or agent positions may have left the organization or may not be as active in the project as they once were. At the conclusion of the adoption stage an organization can terminate the change initiative or institutionalize it as standard operating procedure.

Institutionalization

Employees no longer view the change as temporary once the change initiative has been institutionalized. They expect to employ the change as a matter of routine practice and begin to embrace it as a "way of daily life." Institutionalized change becomes a part of the organizational culture and is adopted as an important value or guiding principle. Once institutionalization occurs, the organizational system alters to accommodate the change, which can impact the compensation and rewards system, policies and procedures, managerial practices, work climate, and employer-employee relations. In short, once change is institutionalized the organization is never the same again. The expanding use and integration of technology is a prime example.

Internalization

When change reflects employees' personal interests, goals, or values, the ultimate level of commitment forms—internalization. Thus, employees "own" the change. They become deep-seated advocates and take personal responsibility for the change initiative's success. Internalization is stronger than any organizational mandate. Once reached it generates enthusiasm, high-energy involvement, and persistence on the part of employees.

Finally, Conner (1992, 155–160) identified six guidelines for obtaining employee and organizational commitment to change. First, people respond to change at different intellectual and emotional rates. Second, commitment is expensive; don't order it if the organization can't pay for it. Third, don't assume commitment will be generated without a plan of action. Fourth, keep in mind that building commitment is a developmental process. Fifth, either build commitment or prepare for the consequences. Sixth, slow down to increase the speed of change.

The Leading Change Model

Eight errors are common to organizational change efforts that result in predictable consequences: (1) allowing too much complacency, (2) failing to create a sufficiently powerful guiding coalition, (3) underestimating the power of vision, (4) undercommunicating the vision, (5) permitting obstacles to block the new vision, (6) failing to create short-term wins, (7) declaring victory too soon, and (8) neglecting to anchor changes firmly in the corporate culture (Kotter 1996, 16). These common errors can lead to several negative, often costly consequences: new strategies aren't implemented well, acquisitions don't achieve expected synergies, reengineering takes too long and costs too much, downsizing doesn't get costs under control, and quality programs don't deliver desired results. Kotter developed the leading change model to address these eight common errors.

Establishing a Sense of Urgency.   To bring about change, organizations should establish a sense of urgency to gain needed cooperation (Kotter 1996). When complacency is high, change usually goes nowhere because few organizational leaders are interested in working on transforming their organizations. Consequently, it is difficult to cultivate leaders with enough power, credibility, and influence to create and communicate a change vision. When complacency exists, it is equally difficult to energize employees to address problems within the firm. Without a sense of urgency, the momentum for change never materializes.

Gilley and Boughton (1996, 10–11) refer to this period as organizational equilibrium, which occurs when stress levels are low and productivity is adequate. However, they warn that this period is where "the organization gets too comfortable and fails to maintain its competitive spirit. If this period last too long, disaster can result. . . . Therefore, managers must be responsible for innovations and change during this period. They must recognize when apathy has taken root and take corrective action to eliminate it. Maintaining an attitude of continuous improvement is one of the best ways of combating apathy."

People will find a thousand ingenious ways to withhold cooperation from change that they sincerely think is unnecessary. Kotter (1996, 40) identified several sources of complacence, including absence of a major crisis, too many visible resources, low overall performance standards, and organizational structures that direct employees toward narrow functional goals. Others include internal measurement systems that focus on the wrong performance standards and lack of sufficient performance feedback. Some organizations exhibit kill-the-messenger culture, which adds to complacence. Still others include individual capacity for denial or too much overconfidence by upper management. Any of these excuses lead to apathy and indifference.

Kotter (1996, 44) identified nine ways to raise the urgency level. Although each may generate results, the first four are primarily perceived as negative attempts at raising the urgency level. First, organizations can create a crisis by allowing a financial loss, exposing managers to major weaknesses vis-à-vis competitors, or allowing errors to blow up instead of being corrected at the last minute. Second, they can eliminate obvious examples of excess (e.g., company-owned country club facilities, multiple company planes, gourmet executive dining rooms). Third, organizations can establish revenue, income, productivity, customer satisfaction, and cycle-time targets so high that they can't be reached by conducting business as usual. Fourth, organizations can stop measuring subunit performance based solely on narrow functional goals and insist that more people be held accountable for broader measures of business performance.

Five positive means exist to raise the urgency level (Kotter 1996, 44). First, organizations can make available more data about customer satisfaction and financial performance. This information typically demonstrates the organization's weaknesses vis-à-vis the competition. Second, organizations can insist that people interact regularly with unsatisfied customers, unhappy suppliers, and disgruntled shareholders. Third, organizations can use consultants and other means to provide more relevant data and honest discussion at management meetings. Fourth, they may promote honest discussions of their problems in company newspapers and senior management speeches and stop senior management "happy talk" about real, serious problems. Fifth, organizations can provide employees with information on future opportunities, on the wonderful rewards for capitalizing on those opportunities, and on the organization's current inability to pursue those opportunities.

Creating the Guiding Coalition.   The first step in putting together a guiding coalition that can direct a change effort is to find the right membership. Four key characteristics are essential to effective guiding coalitions:

1. *Position power:* Are enough key players on board so that those left out cannot easily block progress?
2. *Expertise:* Are the various points of view—in terms of discipline, work experience, and so forth—relevant to the task at hand adequately represented so that informed, intelligent decisions can be made?
3. *Credibility:* Does the group have enough people with good reputations in the firm so that its pronouncements will be taken seriously by other employees?
4. *Leadership:* Does the group include enough proven leaders to be able to drive the change process? (Kotter 1996, 57)

Organizations need both management and leadership skills on the guiding coalition; and they must work in cooperation with one another. Management skills enable leaders to organize and control the change process whereas leadership skills engender commitment to and drive change (Nadler 1998). Both are essential in bringing about long-term systemic change.

HRD professionals operate as change agents and guide the coalition to work together as a team. Although teamwork can be enhanced in many different ways, one component is crucial—trust. The presence of trust allows HRD professionals to foster teamwork; its absence hinders any efforts.

Developing a Vision and Strategy.   Organizations must create a vision to help direct the change effort and develop strategies for achieving that vision (Kotter 1996). *Vision* means a picture of the future with some implicit or explicit commentary on why people should strive to create that future.

In the change process, a good vision serves three important purposes. First, an effective vision clarifies the general direction for change. Second, vision motivates people to take action in the right direction and helps overcome employees' natural reluctance to change. Kotter (1996, 70) contends that a good vision "acknowledges that sacrifices will be necessary but makes clear that these sacrifices will yield particular benefits and personal satisfactions that are far superior to those available today—or tomorrow—without attempting to change." Third, a good vision coordinates the actions of different people by aligning individuals in a remarkably efficient way. Without a shared sense of direction, interdependent people may constantly conflict, whereas a shared vision clarifies the direction of change and helps employees agree on the importance and value of change.

An effective vision is *imaginable* in that it conveys a picture of what the future will look like. It is *desirable* because it appeals to the long-term interests of employees, customers, stockholders, and others who have a stake in the enterprise. An effective vision is *feasible,* enabling organizations to develop realistic, attainable goals. It is also *focused,* providing guidance in decisionmaking. Such a vision is *flexible,* allowing individual initiative and alternative responses in light of changing conditions. Finally an effective vision is *communicable* in that it is easy to communicate (Kotter 1996, 72).

Communicating the Change Vision.   Organizations must use every vehicle possible to communicate a new vision and strategies and rely on the guiding coalition to model the behavior expected of employees (Kotter 1996). Creating a communications plan achieves these goals.

An effective communications plan should be simple; all jargon and technical terms should be eliminated. It should paint a verbal picture worth a thousand words, while incorporating all possible media forums (memos, e-mail, and newsletters, formal and informal interactions). Such plans utilize repetition, which allows ideas to sink into the subconscious of all employees. An effective communication plan fosters two-way communication, which is always more powerful than one-way communication. Finally, an effective plan relies on leadership by example in that the behavior of managers is consistent with the message being communicated (Kotter 1996, 90).

Empowering Broad-Based Action.   Empowering broad-based action is designed to eliminate obstacles to change, modify systems or structures that undermine the change vision, and encourage risk taking and nontraditional ideas and actions. Kotter (1996, 115) identified five ways of empowering employees to effect change. Organizations can communicate a sensible vision to employees, make structures compatible with the vision, provide the training employees need to obtain the appropriate knowledge and skills to feel empowered, align information and personnel systems to the vision, and confront supervisors who undercut needed change and require their cooperation.

Generating Short-Term Wins.   Short-term improvements (wins) lay the foundation for sustainable long-term change and help transformation in at least six ways (Kotter 1996, 123). First, they provide evidence that sacrifices are worth the effort. Short-term improvements justify the short-term costs involved. Second, they reward change agents by providing positive public recognition. After a lot of hard work, positive reinforcement and recognition builds morale and motivation. Third, short-term improvements fine-tune vision and strategies by providing the guiding coalition with concrete data on the viability of their ideas. Fourth, they undermine cynics and self-serving resisters by demonstrating the benefits of change. Fifth, they keep organizational leaders involved and supportive by providing evidence that the transformation is on track. Sixth, short-term wins build momentum, thus turning neutrals into supporters, reluctant supporters into active helpers, and so forth.

Consolidating Gains and Producing More Change.   An organization should hire, promote, and develop people who can implement the change vision (Kotter 1996). Concurrently, HRD professionals operate as change agents to modify systems, structures, and policies that don't fit together or align with the transformation vision. In this way organizations consolidate gains and produce more change.

Anchoring New Approaches in the Culture.   Culture powerfully influences human behavior and can be difficult to change, and its near invisibility makes it hard to address directly (Kotter 1996, 150–151). Generally, shared values, which are less apparent but more deeply ingrained in culture, are more difficult to change than norms of behavior. Consequently, culture is powerful for three reasons: (1) individuals are selected and indoctrinated so well, (2) culture exerts itself through the actions of hundreds or thousands of people, and (3) all of this happens without much conscious intent and, thus, is difficult to challenge or even discuss. When a change initiative is not compatible with the relevant culture it will be subject to regression. Changes in work groups, a division, or an entire organization can unravel, even after years of effort, when new approaches haven't been anchored firmly in group norms and values—its culture.

HRD Professionals' Responsibilities When Implementing Change

An HRD professional's primary responsibility in implementing organizational change is to help organizations and employees to increase their resilience. That is, they assist the organization and its employees increase their capacity and ability to adapt to change. Patterson (1997) offers several suggestions. He believes that ample time must be invested in understanding the various group members' self-interests and in finding ways of satisfying their concerns while implementing change.

Another strategy involves helping members of the organization see the connections between change initiatives and the general direction in which the organization is headed. HRD professionals must create a sense of urgency for major change by "selling" the change initiative to critical decisionmakers, stakeholders, and influencers. Trust must be established with this group prior to engaging in sincere yet potentially redundant communications about the proposed change. Also, the linkage between change and the organization's guiding principles must be clear. Establishing trust is accomplished by allowing employees to challenge, without fear of reprisal, the conduct and intentions of those initiating change (Patterson 1997, 46).

HRD professionals must help employees understand that they do indeed have the choice between being a victim or an initiator of change (Nadler 1998). This effort includes helping employees approach change as an opportunity for advancement and improvement, rather than as a limiting activity. The urgency of proposed change will be underscored when employees realize that their future well-being is at risk if change is not achieved.

HRD professionals are responsible for helping organizational leaders understand and accept the reality that organizational conflict is inevitable, change will occur continuously, and creating a safe environment that promotes constructive handling of conflict is the most appropriate action. This type of environment should actively embrace conflict resolution and consensus building as an accepted operational practice. HRD professionals can help the organization develop long-term commitment to change by linking proposed changes to its guiding principles and core values. They need to help their organizations approach change rationally by continually clarifying the organization's goals in relation to its overall vision. HRD professionals should create and follow clearly articulated decisionmaking practices that align with the organization's values, and serve as a filter so that external forces do not cause major disruptions within the firm. Finally, the organization must learn to resist the natural tendency to deny the harsh realities of organizational change (Patterson 1997, 47). Instead, HRD professionals should help organizations acknowledge these realities and apply strategies that help the organization become more adaptive to change.

Conclusion

One of the most important professional practice domains of strategic HRD is organizational change. It requires HRD professionals to shift their attention to the dynamics of the organization, assume new and exciting roles, examine the myths of change, identify and develop resilient employees, understand the relationship between organizational culture and change, and embrace change models that can be used to positively impact the organization.

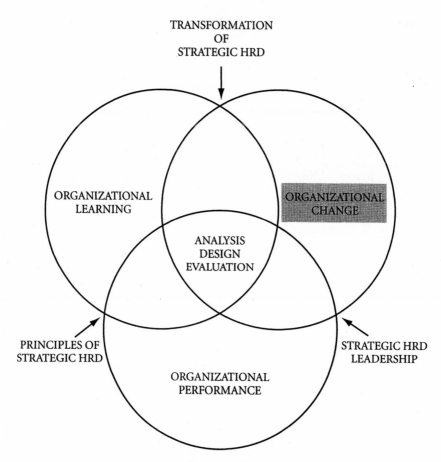

TRANSFORMATION
OF
STRATEGIC HRD

ORGANIZATIONAL
LEARNING

ORGANIZATIONAL
CHANGE

ANALYSIS
DESIGN
EVALUATION

PRINCIPLES OF
STRATEGIC HRD

STRATEGIC HRD
LEADERSHIP

ORGANIZATIONAL
PERFORMANCE

ORGANIZATIONAL LEARNING, PERFORMANCE, AND CHANGE

CHAPTER 13

Organizational Development Change Agents

Engaging in organizational development (OD) activities requires HRD professionals to select strategies that narrow or close performance gaps by addressing their underlying cause(s) (Rothwell 1996a, 201–221). To do this effectively, OD change agents create enthusiasm among others about planning and implementing OD strategies on an organizational scale. They involve and empower others in the process of selecting OD strategies organization-wide and those linked to work and individual development and change. Finally, they excite others about planning and implementing human performance enhancement strategies specific to work methods or processes. Finally, they need to be able to involve and empower others in the process of selecting OD strategies.

Burke (1992, 177–178) believes that an OD change agent's effectiveness depends on his or her ability to tolerate ambiguity. Obviously every organization is different, and what works in one may not work in another. Thus, every change intervention must fit the unique circumstances within an organization. Burke (1992) also believes that a change agent's effectiveness depends upon his or her ability to influence others, discover and mobilize human energy (both within oneself and within the client organization), maintain a sense of humor and perspective, have self-confidence, and be interpersonally competent. Finally, a sense of mission about his or her work as an OD practitioner offers change agents meaning.

Although most of these abilities can be learned, many HRD professionals have difficulty making the transition from trainer to organizational development change agent because they are not prepared for the complexity, ambiguity, and uncertainty common in the world of consulting (Robinson and Robinson 1996). To make the transition, HRD professionals must be able to understand and apply the objectives of organizational development consulting, adopt its roles and responsibilities, develop and exhibit specialized OD consulting competencies and skills, and implement the organizational development process.

Edgar Schein (1992) contrasts the process consultant role with the purchase and doctor-patient models. The purchase model represents the most prevalent form of consultation, in which the client purchases expert services and information. An example is a client's employment of a consultant to conduct market research. The doctor-patient model occurs when clients describe to consultants the symptoms of what is wrong with the organization ("Turnover is too high," "We're losing market share with respect to product X," "Our management information system is a mess") and then expect consultants to prescribe a remedy for the problem.

Schein contrasts these two models with the process consultant, one who helps the client's organization diagnose its own strengths and weaknesses more effectively, view organizational problems more clearly, and with the consultant's help, propose a remedy. Schein asserts, "It is a key assumption of change that the client must share in the process of diagnosing what may be wrong (or learn to see the problem for himself), and must be actively involved in the process of generating a remedy because only the client ultimately knows what is possible and what will work in his culture and situation" (1987, 30). Thus the primary though not exclusive function of OD consultants is to help clients learn how to help themselves more effectively.

Values of Organizational Development Change Agents

Change agents subscribe to a set of values that constitute four primary beliefs of applied behavioral scientists. First, change agents believe that the needs and aspirations of human beings are the reason for an organized change process. Second, work and life become more meaningful if employees are allowed to participate in decisions affecting their organization. Third, employing action research techniques improves organizational effectiveness. Fourth, they believe in the democratization of organizations through power equalization processes (French and Bell 1995). McLean (1982) argues that the ability to develop an approach that is internally consistent—that is, based on theories validated in the consultant's personal experience as well as congruent with his or her values, skills, abilities, and personality—may be the single most important ingredient to a change agent's success.

Roles and Skills of Organizational Development Change Agents

In order to function as an organizational development change agent, HRD professionals must assume additional roles and subroles. Three roles and nine subroles offer HRD professionals opportunities to enhance their organizational impact and influence (Figure 13.1). The roles include organizational expert, employee champion, and performance consultant.

FIGURE 13.1   Pyramid of HRD Roles, Subroles, and Competencies

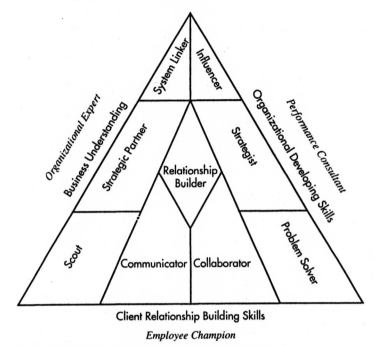

Client Relationship Building Skills

Employee Champion

SOURCE: J. W. Gilley and A. Maycunich, *Beyond the Learning Organization: Creating a Culture of Continuous Growth and Development Through State-of-the-Art Human Resource Practices* (Cambridge, Mass.: Perseus Books, 2000).

Organizational Expert

Gilley and Maycunich (2000) believe that HRD professionals improve their organizational impact and influence by demonstrating business understanding, political awareness, and organizational consciousness. HRD professionals also enhance their effectiveness through proficiency in the subroles of scout, strategic partner, and system linker (Figure 13.1).

Business Understanding.   Knowledge of business fundamentals, systems theory, organizational culture, and politics reveals understanding of organizational philosophy that guides business action. An awareness of how organizations work is essential for OD change agents and enables them to think like their clients. This understanding requires knowledge of how things get done and how decisions are made inside an organization. OD change agents possessing business understanding are better able to facilitate change without disrupting the organization's operations.

HRD professionals add value to the organization by understanding business operations, thus enabling human resource personnel to adapt their practices and activities to changing business conditions (Ulrich 1997a). Although HRD professionals may be experts in learning, performance, and change initiatives, these skills are of little value to the organization unless they are able to adapt their practices to business conditions and circumstances. Consequently, HRD professionals need to gain experiences in functional areas such as marketing, finance, operations, or sales to generate pertinent, practical solutions for their clients HRD.

As a member of the organizational family responsible for its improvement, HRD professionals promote business initiatives that help the organization improve its competitive readiness, performance capacity, and renewal capabilities. They design and implement change initiatives that enhance employee productivity and performance, which leads to overall organizational improvement.

HRD professionals also demonstrate business understanding through their knowledge of stakeholder needs and expectations. This knowledge enables HRD professionals to adapt their practices, procedures, products, innovations, and services to better serve their clients.

Political Awareness

Regardless of its size and complexity, an organization has a political structure, work environment, and culture that influence its decisions and behavior and that ensure stability and continuity. However, these components are often a major reason why organizations experience difficulties. When employees and managers are unable to convince organizational leaders of organization dysfunction, objective third-party change agents are needed and become the formal representatives of change.

Organizational Consciousness

OD change agents' understanding of organizational operations enables them to promote organizational change. This knowledge aids them in identifying organizational needs, selecting solutions, implementing interventions, and evaluating the results of change. Knowing where to go for information, insight, recommendations, and coaching helps OD change agents avoid the pitfalls common in organizational life. Another benefit of organizational awareness is a better understanding of the organization's political structure and decisionmaking procedures. These are critical in gaining the support needed to implement meaningful change.

Subroles of Organizational Expert.   Understanding client needs and expectations, being aware of the financial and business issues facing the organization, and creating long-term solutions to difficult problems provide excellent opportunities to improve the organization's strength and viability. Business understanding, political awareness, and organizational consciousness facilitate an HRD professional's ability to improve the firm's performance. Three subroles exhibit business understanding: *scout, strategic partner,* and *systems linker* (Figure 13.1) (Gilley and Maycunich 1998a).

When change agents operate as visionaries within the organization, they are performing as scouts. Scouts guide the organization through uncharted territory in the quest for change. In short, change agents lead the organization into areas it has not gone before. In the scout role, OD change agents generate innovative solutions to complex problems, set priorities, synthesize client input, translate these into action plans, and direct the organization toward achieving its business goals.

As strategic partners, OD change agents possess a thorough understanding of business fundamentals, core processes, operations, and procedures. Consequently, they comprehend the critical factors affecting organizational competitiveness and have the ability to communicate the benefits that change strategies and innovations provide the firm.

System linkers help divisions, departments, units, and functions work in harmony to achieve desired business results. They align these separate entities around a common set of guiding principles that define the organization's direction and provide its purpose and focus. Thus, organizational members pull in the same to direction to achieve a collective set of business results. By communicating the value and importance of teamwork, HRD professionals are then able to establish connections between departments. As a result, affected parts of the organization work together in harmony.

Employee Champion

OD change agents are in a unique position to serve as employee champions because they help employees identify legitimate work demands and thus help workers set priorities (Ulrich 1997a). They also help employees balance work demands through the proper allocation of resources. As employee champions, OD change agents identify creative ways of leveraging resources so that employees do not feel overwhelmed by what is expected of them.

Ulrich (1997a, 135) identified ten questions that help OD change agents determine whether employees and organizations are responding appropriately to demand situations:

1. Do employees control key decisionmaking processes that determine how work is done?
2. Do employees have a vision and direction that commits them to working hard?
3. Are employees given challenging work assignments that provide opportunities to learn new skills?

4. Do employees work in teams to accomplish goals?
5. Does the work environment provide opportunities for celebration, fun, excitement, and openness?
6. Are employees compensated and rewarded for work accomplishments?
7. Do employees enjoy open, candid, and frequent information sharing with management?
8. Are employees treated with dignity? Are differences openly shared and respected?
9. Do employees have access to and use of technology that makes their work easier?
10. Do employees have the skills necessary to do their work well?

Responses to these questions enable an organization to determine the adequacy of employee control, commitment to the organization, the type of challenging work provided to employees, the degree to which collaboration and teamwork are employed, the adequacy of organizational culture, the quality of the compensation and reward system used, the quality and quantity of organizational communications, the concern for due process, the adequacy of technology, and employee competence (Ulrich 1997a, 136).

When serving as employee champions, OD change agents devote a majority of their time helping their organization positively answer each of the above ten questions. Doing so enables them to increase their influence within the organization, which positively impacts its business results.

As effective employee champions, OD change agents develop client relationship-building skills such as interpersonal and conflict resolution skills. Thus, OD change agents build mutual acceptance and positive regard, develop a sense of trust, promote rapport, and enhance their credibility with clients. Over time, clients will be more willing to accept change recommendations.

Client Relationship-Building Competency.   Effective OD change agents develop mutual acceptance and positive regard with their clients, which requires mastery of interpersonal and conflict resolution skills. These skills help clients develop a sense of trust when implementing change for the first time, promote rapport, and enhance credibility. Trusting clients are more willing to trust OD change agents' recommendations.

According to Burke (1992), OD change agents support and nurture others, particularly during periods of conflict and stress. He emphasizes that this skill is critical just before and during change initiatives and that it builds rapport with clients.

Interpersonal Skills

At the heart of the change agent/client relationship are interpersonal skills. When OD change agents serve as employee champions, they demonstrate respect for the personal boundaries and values of their clients through interpersonal skills such as active listening and questioning. Interpersonal skills structure the communication process between change agents and their clients, enabling agents to develop the acceptance and positive regard of their clients. Burke (1992) cites that the ability to listen well and empathize is especially important during interviews, in conflict situations, and when client stress is high. Finally, through the use of interpersonal skills, change agents create a working relationship and an environment where clients feel safe and secure. Consequently, clients are more willing to try out new and unfamiliar behaviors, technologies, and so forth.

Conflict Resolution Skills

Conflicting goals, ideas, policies, and practices make it almost impossible to implement meaningful change. Mastery of conflict resolution skills by OD change agents allows them to guide executives, managers, and employees through the change process in a way that minimizes resistance. Conflict resolution skills enable OD change agents to understand why resistance occurs, how to respond accordingly, maintain an objective viewpoint, and demonstrate fairness. Such insight is advantageous in overcoming resistance to change. Finally, the ability to confront difficult issues is essential for change agents because much of their work consists of exposing issues that organization members are reluctant to face (Burke 1992).

Subroles of Employee Champion. To serve as employee champions, OD change agents need to assume three subroles that develop client relationship-building skills (Gilley and Maycunich 1998a). They are *relationship builder, collaborator,* and *communicator.*

One of the best ways of improving client relationships involves helping them learn new skills and competencies. Learning enhances client self-esteem, which in turn improves the OD change agent–client relationship. OD change agents enhance client relationships by encouraging development of critical thinking skills, which improve clients' professional practices, approaches to accomplishing work, and performance. Several activities help OD change agents become competent relationship builders. These include turning assertions into questions, giving clients options, making meetings and reports meaningful, helping clients implement solutions and interventions, being accessible, and always, always adding value.

As collaborators, OD change agents establish credibility and gain employee confidence to implement change. Collaborators tailor communications to their audience, listen and ask appropriate questions, present ideas clearly and concisely through well-organized written and interpersonal communications, engage in informal communications that build support, and identify commonalties among their various client groups to determine shared interests.

Important skills such as active listening, using silence, demonstrating understanding, establishing rapport, communicating empathy, clarifying statements, and appropriately employing summarization techniques enable change agents to serve as communicators. In this subrole, OD change agents increase clients' understanding of change, identify the need for change, and enumerate the importance and benefits of change. As communicators, OD change agents continually engage in interactions that enhance their organizational influence by building positive and effective client relationships, thus enabling OD change agents to better serve their organizations. Thus, the role of employee champion has a profoundly positive impact on an organization's performance capacity and competitive readiness.

Performance Consultant

The role of performance consultant effectively enhances an HRD professional's organizational influence and impacts organizational results. Many human resource professionals are unable to make the transition to performance consultant because they are not prepared for the complexity, ambiguity, or uncertainty common in consulting. According to Robinson and Robinson (1996), to make the transition HR professionals must develop and apply specialized consulting competencies and skills, apply the role of performance consulting to improve organizational effectiveness, and appreciate and understand the performance consulting process.

Organizational Development Skills.   To avoid the pitfalls common in organizational life, OD change agents must be operationally intelligent. Fundamental to this outcome is organizational awareness—an insight that helps change agents better understand its political structure, decisionmaking, and procedures. Each of these is essential in rallying support needed to implement meaningful change.

When operating as performance consultants, OD change agents rely on a set of guiding principles to direct their behavior and anchor them during difficult times. Consequently, change agents acquire problem-solving, conceptual, research, and analytical skills in order to become effective in managing and implementing organizational change (Hale 1998). They respond to unforeseen contingencies, provide appropriate solutions to complex and sensitive issues, and conduct a wide variety of activities designed to modify established policies and procedures (French and Bell 1995).

Rothwell (1996a, 206) believes that performance consultants should be able to identify possible OD strategies, apply them at the individual worker level, and decide when training or other learning activities are most appropriate to close performance gaps. All of these situations require organizational development skills that include conceptual, technical, integrative, and analytical skills.

Conceptual Skills

Performance consultants operating as change agents help clients analyze performance problems, implement change initiatives, and evaluate their thinking about the organizational system. According to Burke (1992), performance consultants develop conceptual skills to achieve these outcomes. He believes that it is necessary for them to think and express certain relationships, such as the cause-and-effect and if-then linkages, that exist within the systemic context of the client organization. These skills allow performance consultants to create a framework to guide their behavior—one that they continuously use to test solutions and recommendations. Such a framework should also be used when conducting organizational analysis, implementing change interventions, and evaluating outcomes.

Technical Skills

Performance consultants analyze data gathered during diagnosis, examine solutions, and evaluate the organizational impact of change interventions. These technical skills are used to analyze and evaluate change interventions, and develop new initiatives to meet the specific client need. A commonly forgotten technical skill is the ability to respond to unforeseen contingencies.

Analytical Skills

It is a performance consultant's responsibility to know how to generate information, analyze it, distinguish among problems, symptoms, and causes, identify solutions to problems, and recommend appropriate solutions. Such experience is gained by dealing with difficult situations throughout an organization and requires advanced analytical skills.

Objectivity

Hale (1998) reports that effective performance consultants possess the ability to remain impartial regardless of their personal values and biases, and in spite of an organization's culture, traditions, and vested interests. This ability is referred to as objectivity, which is often difficult for performance consultants to master because of their perspectives. However, it is almost impossible to effectively address most organizational issues without a high degree of this skill. In fact, remaining objective enables performance consultants to function as the social conscience of the organization and is, perhaps, the greatest single benefit of this OD change agent role.

Intuition

Performance consultants should have the ability to quickly recognize one's own feelings and intuition, according to Burke (1992). He argues that this is important in order to distinguish one's own perceptions from those of the client and to use these feelings and intuitions as interventions when appropriate and timely.

Integrative Skills

Integrative skills link ideas, concepts, and strategies resulting in dynamic, innovative approaches to problem solving. Integrative skills require consultants to identify the components of a problem, define their interrelationships, and then fashion interventions that improve performance.

Specialized Knowledge

Robinson and Robinson (1996) contend that performance consultants must possess a unique set of skills and specialized knowledge in order to be useful to an organization. They believe that far too many performance consultants lack the depth of understanding needed to be successful. Today, the term consultant has been used to describe those individuals who design and deliver training programs and workshops rather than those who maintain a unique set of skills and/or specialized knowledge in performance management and organizational development. This is having a profoundly negative impact on the credibility of HRD and on OD performance consultants in particular.

Subroles of Performance Consultants. As performance consultants, OD change agents engage in three subroles capable of responding to unforeseen contingencies, providing appropriate solutions to complex, sensitive issues, and conducting a wide range of activities designed to modify or enhance results. These subroles include *influencer, strategist,* and *problem solver* (Gilley and Maycunich 1998a).

As influencers, performance consultants are directive in their efforts to influence client thinking, initiate change, or provide specific recommendations that address difficult performance problems. OD change agents, however, guard against their own personal biases and overpowering opinions, remaining receptive to others' views, ideas, and recommendations in order to be successful in the influencer subrole. Simultaneously, they encourage organizational members to take risks to achieve their goals and objectives.

Performance consultants as strategists are responsible for assessing organizational needs using quantifiable and qualifiable methodologies, developing and executing business initiatives, and evaluating the effectiveness of performance improvement interventions and other change initiatives. Additionally, strategists incorporate the ideas of others into directive action plans.

When performance consultants take an active role in the decisionmaking and change management process, they are serving as problem solvers. In this subrole, performance consultants spend a majority of their time helping clients make decisions that are beneficial to achieving desired results. Problem solvers strive to make certain that the perceived problem is indeed the one critical to the organization.

Finally, performance consultants are experts in applying the consulting process, which serves as a guide in establishing client relationships, identifying organizational performance problems and developmental needs, revealing client resistance to change, conducting diagnoses, providing clients with feedback, selecting and implementing appropriate change interventions, and evaluating results (Chapter 14). These steps represent the phases of the OD consulting process. When applied, this process ensures that root causes of problems have been identified and appropriate solutions have been selected and implemented resulting in suitable outcomes.

Organizational Development Change Agents

The role of organizational development change agent is the level at which HRD professionals wield the greatest influence to impact an organization's operations and outcomes (Figure 13.1) (Gilley and Maycunich 2000; Ulrich 1997a; and Burke 1992). This role requires knowledge of HRD practices, partnering and negotiating skills, business understanding, client relationship building, and organizational development skills. In essence, this role is a microcosm as well as an aggregate of all roles previously discussed. Organizational development change agents have the greatest ability to institute true organizational change. When HRD professionals act as change agents, they establish high levels of credibility within the organization and influence with key decisionmakers, line managers, and employees.

Robinson and Robinson (1996) assert that the roles of performance consultant and change agent are very similar. The primary difference is that performance consultants' interventions are directed at improving individual and organizational performance, enhancing performance management, and increasing productivity and quality. On the other hand, organizational development change agents' interventions include those that directly impact the organizational system, such as an examination of organizational culture, work climate, mission, strategy, structure, policies, procedures, managerial practices, and leadership.

Responsibilities of Organizational Development Change Agents

OD change agents accept a variety of responsibilities. Each is designed to maximize the effectiveness of change initiatives and achieve change goals (e.g., improve communications, enhance client relationships, improve organizational performance capacity, enhance the organization's culture, or improve work environments).

Providing Information

OD change agents are responsible for interpreting and imparting information in order to communicate what changes are needed. When OD change agents provide information, they are fulfilling the traditional role of consulting. As such, their primary responsibility is to provide information needed by individuals, groups, and the organization to define problems and make decisions.

OD change agents gather, analyze, and synthesize information the client needs to make a decision. In short, change agents serve as researchers. This activity requires a high level of competence in designing and developing questionnaires, conducting structured interviews, and facilitating focus groups activities. This often-overlooked activity supports the problem-solving and decisionmaking process and is, perhaps, one of the most critical activities of a change agent.

Advocating Solutions

Advocating solutions requires OD change agents to influence the organization to choose particular actions or solutions that improve performance, efficiency, and quality. Meeting this responsibility requires change agents to be very directive, proactive, and persuasive in performance-related issues. It could be said that change agents are "selling" organizational leaders during this activity.

As information experts, change agents help the organization establish a vision of its future. Consequently, it is important that the change agent function as a futurist, providing multiple options, ideas, and possibilities. The value of this activity is in the several alternatives generated for the firm.

Providing Objective Observations

As an objective observer, change agents use reflective questioning to help clients clarify a given situation. Furthermore, change agents observe the effects that performance standards have on quality and performance, the effectiveness of performance appraisals and reviews, the impacts of job design and redesign activities, and the impact and results of other organizational change interventions. This nondirective activity enables change agents to guide clients in overcoming barriers that prevent change.

Sometimes change agents are asked to observe training programs in order to develop follow-up strategies and training aids and to identify opportunities for applying the skills taught. They advise managers on how to facilitate learning transfer, improve the application of new skills, and assess performance feedback.

Solving Problems

As problem solvers, change agents' primary responsibility is making certain that the perceived problem is indeed the one that needs solving. Change agents spend the majority of their time accurately defining the problem rather than providing solutions to problems that may not exist. A useful consulting approach involves working with the problem as "defined" by the client in such a way that more useful definitions emerge (Turner 1983).

Change agents take an active role in the problem-solving process. Their objectivity helps them evaluate existing problems and explain possible solutions. In addition, change agents use a synergistic approach, collaborating with clients in the perceptual, cognitive, and action-taking processes involved in solving organizational problems (Lippitt and Lippitt 1986).

Implementing Change

In addition to helping the organization plan for change, change agents are often asked to implement change. Their involvement in this activity is a matter of considerable debate. Some OD change agents believe managers should be primarily responsible for implementing change, while others believe change agents should be responsible. The transference of this responsibility to change agents stems from managers' lack of specialized skills and knowledge.

A poorly implemented change initiative wastes time and money and further complicates an already difficult situation. Change agents must, therefore, be familiar with the organization and have an appropriate level of authority to effectively implement change. In addition, change agents must understand the potential outcomes and impacts of their recommendations. Managers should, however, participate in implementing solutions while serving as linkages between important client groups. Without these key connections, implementation (change) will not occur, regardless of the change agent's efforts.

Rothwell (1996a, 217–221) maintains that OD change agents must have the ability to implement, or coordinate implementation of, OD strategies, integrating them with organizational strategic plans, organizational culture and structure, work processes, and worker input.

Improving Organizational Effectiveness

The ultimate responsibility of an OD change agent is to improve organizational effectiveness. Gilley and Coffern (1994, 184) define organizational effectiveness as "an organization's ability to adapt strategies and behaviors to future environmental change by maximizing contribution of the organization's human resources." Organizational effectiveness implies that management is dedicated to developing and maintaining the most important systems and linkages to improve performance and quality (Fallon and Brinkerhoff 1996).

Improving organizational effectiveness requires change agents to assist decisionmakers in selecting the best solutions to their problems. Solutions include the approaches, plans, strategies, processes, and programs most appropriate for the organization. Recommendations and solutions can be tailored to the organization's immediate and future problems. At the same time, change agents help organizational members overcome the obstacles that prevent change.

Successful change agents demonstrate their ability to assess organizational dynamics by identifying and managing such things as the political environment, communication breakdowns, hidden agendas, stakeholder conflict, client resistance, and departmental competitiveness. Managing these barriers fosters organizational change. In essence, change agents demonstrate their organizational savvy in order to be successful.

Identifying Alternatives and Resources

Most OD change agents are responsible for identifying alternatives and resources and helping clients assess consequences. Although change agents set up relative criteria for assessing alternatives, develop cause-and-effect relationships for each alternative, and establish a proper set of strategies, they are not directly involved in decisionmaking.

Identifying alternatives and resources is often overlooked as one of the least formal of all responsibilities. Some HRD programs receive as many as fifty requests each month. In many cases, information is conveyed through telephone conversations with the interested parties, whereas at other times requests result in extensive projects.

Facilitating Learning

OD change agents are responsible for helping organizations acquire new skills, knowledge, insights, awareness, and attitudes needed to implement change (Burke 1992). These could include problem-solving skills, giving and receiving performance feedback, listening skills, leadership development, goal setting, resolving conflicts, and diagnosing group interactions. Further, Burke (1992) has found that client development of these skills and knowledge enables them to rely less on change agents as they apply what they have learned.

On occasion, OD change agents facilitate learning activities to improve performance and create organizational change. In some situations, change agents are simply asked to recommend which learning processes are best to use. At other times, they are asked to provide training activities to help their clients obtain needed knowledge and skills. Change agents rely on their understanding of the teaching/learning process, appropriate use of instructional methods, application of experiential learning activities, and presentation, listening, and facilitation skills.

Finally, Burke (1992) believes that change agents must have the ability to *teach* or create learning opportunities. This ability should not be reserved for classroom activities but should be utilized on the job, during meetings, and within the mainstream of the overall change effort.

Negotiating Solutions

Negotiating solutions requires change agents to use a synergistic participatory approach and to collaborate with clients in perceptual, cognitive, and action-taking processes to solve problems. This approach requires change agents to become active participants in the problem-solving process. By blending directive and objective approaches, clients are encouraged to define existing problems and test alternatives for an effective resolution. To execute this responsibility correctly, change agents use a partnership approach as they focus their attention on identifying problems and evaluating, selecting, and carrying out alternatives.

Encouraging Consensus and Commitment

Any change useful to an organization will rely on the members of the organization working together. Change agents build consensus and commitment among organizational decisionmakers and members in bringing about lasting and needed change. Each member is encouraged to consider the good of the overall firm before considering personal and professional goals. For this to occur, change agents must provide sound and convincing recommendations and present them persuasively.

As consensus and commitment builders, change agents monitor their clients' readiness and commitment to change by considering the following questions:

- How willing are members of the organization to implement change?
- Is upper-level management willing to learn and utilize new management methods and practices?
- What types of information do members of the organization readily accept or resist?
- What are members' attitudes toward change?
- What are executives' attitudes toward change?

- To what extent will individual members of the organization regard their contribution to overall organizational effectiveness as a legitimate and desirable objective? (Turner 1983)

Evaluating the level of enthusiasm for a particular recommendation is another way to gauge readiness for change. By identifying the level of enthusiasm, change agents instantaneously measure resistance or support for a given solution. Once identified, change agents are able to withdraw or encourage recommendations prior to implementation.

Building consensus and commitment requires change agents to establish a collaborative working relationship with each client. From the beginning, an effective relationship becomes a collaborative search for acceptable answers to the client's real needs and concerns (Turner 1983). Ideally, this will be a mutually beneficial relationship, where trust and a readiness for change are developed quickly during the OD consulting process.

Improving Performance and Change

Performance improvement and change are critical responsibilities of OD change agents. Change agents help clients develop diagnostic skills to address specific performance problems, and focus on *how* things are done rather than on *what tasks* are performed. This responsibility requires change agents to examine organizational structure, job design, work flow, performance appraisal and review, employee attitudes, performance management procedures, performance standards, and quality improvement processes. During this examination, change agents develop a high level of interpersonal and group skills to improve performance and impact organizational change. The primary goal of this activity is for employees to become more effective and improve their performance.

Planning, Managing, and Evaluating Organizational Development Projects

Every performance improvement, organizational development, or change initiative is a project that must be planned, managed, and evaluated (Gilley and Maycunich 1998a). Project management involves planning objectives and activities for successful results, organizing people to get things done, directing and controlling people to keep them focused on achieving desired results, and measuring progress to provide useful feedback. Therefore, every OD change agent functions as a project manager. It comes as no surprise that change agents must become competent at managing projects in order to bring about long-term, systemic change. As project managers, OD change agents achieve specific objectives using proven tools and techniques such as critical paths (charts), scheduling technologies (Gantt charts), goal and risk analysis, stakeholder analysis, controlling techniques, and project diagrams.

Furthermore, project management is a method and set of techniques based on the accepted management principles of planning, organizing, influencing, and controlling. Each principle is used in combination to reach a desired end result, on time, within budget, and according to established specifications. Project management is also a way of thinking that keeps desired results in focus. Consequently, personnel are organized and their efforts are directed toward achievement of desired results. Finally, project management requires evaluation of project objectives against measurable criteria.

Planning

Planning involves identifying clear, specific goals and objectives to be attained on time, within budget, and at a desired level of quality. Work activities to be carried out by members of the project team must be specified, including individual tasks and expected outcomes. Specific dates, time, and individuals responsible for producing the desired results must also be identified.

In order to control the outcomes of a project, OD change agents develop comprehensive plans—no plan means no control. Alternatives should be assessed and more than one way of accomplishing the desired result should be identified. Identifying alternatives is an effective means by which to guard against unforeseen changes, which can alter the outcome of the project. For example, change agents must be able to adjust to unexpected contingencies such as having funds drastically reduced or eliminated, which can dramatically affect the quality and timeliness of project outcomes. To alleviate the impact of unanticipated difficulties and ensure successful project completion, controls must be built in (Gilley and Maycunich 1998a).

Organizing

When change agents create a structure useful in executing project plans, they engage in the process of organizing. Organizing is a set of activities, responsibilities, and authoritative relationships used in implementing the project plan. According to Gilley and Coffern (1994), organizing includes determining who is responsible for what activities, objectives, and results; who reports to whom; what activities are carried out where in the organization; and who is authorized to make critical project decisions.

To carry out work plans, change agents assemble necessary material and financial resources. Additionally, span of control most appropriate for the project must be identified. Too many or too few activities or people can inhibit achievement of desired results.

Change agents are the principal project managers; hence they are ultimately responsible for achieving project objectives. Change agents are, therefore, accountable for identifying work divisions based on the tasks and activities to be achieved, balancing the authority and responsibility necessary to complete the project, and delegating work to other project team members.

Influencing

Influencing a project requires change agents to communicate, motivate, coach, supervise, and provide performance feedback to project team members. Influencing is not a singular event but an ongoing activity. Formal and informal communication may be required which can include memos, directives, meetings, reports, e-mail, and telephone and informal conversations with project team members as needed.

As a project managers, change agents are likened to orchestra conductors, who, at all times, know where they are in the plan and direct each team member in order to produce a quality performance. One of their chief responsibilities is to build synergy around project outcomes, encouraging participation and ownership during the process.

Controlling

Controlling is the process of observing, monitoring, and directing human and material resources throughout a project and of identifying and assembling resources into a workable structure. Actual results must be compared to plan results, and their discrepancies isolated. Based on the feedback obtained, change agents make decisions necessary to narrow the gap between expectations and performance.

Change agents must possess knowledge of performance measurement as well as a clear, specific understanding of their client's expectations in order to minimize discrepancies between actual and desired performance. To avoid unnecessary problems, change agents establish reporting relationships at specific points throughout the project, which serve as an early warning of discrepancies that may threaten project outcomes. These controls allow time to redesign and/or adjust the project and its activities in order to produce deliverables on time, within budget, and at quality specifications. These quality and quantity checks and balances determine project success. Checks and balances guarantee continuous improvement of change agents, project team members, and others involved in planning and controlling the project.

Project management includes systematic measurement of actual progress compared to expectations in order to identify deviations. Decisionmaking activities used in correcting and redirecting the project keep it on track.

According to Gilley and Maycunich (1998a, 312),

> Project management differs from regular management in several ways. First, project management is a comprehensive approach to planning and directing complex activities. Planning is the cornerstone of success of project management, while it is not as critical to regular management. Project management emphasizes results—getting the job done on time, within budget, and with specific controls to gauge progress and provide feedback. Regular management incorporates planning, organizing, directing, and controlling as part of the process of managing people, work flows, and achieving results. Project management uses systems analysis and measurement to make certain that expected results are achieved.

Conclusion

The role of OD change agent is one of the most important that strategic HRD professionals can perform. It is a role that enables them to influence organizational leaders regarding the structure and systems of the firm as well as the business and work processes used to produce products and deliver services that satisfy clients needs and exceptions. Furthermore, the OD change agent role enables HRD professionals to positively impact the organization's strategic direction, mission, strategy, and practices to improve its competitive readiness and effectiveness.

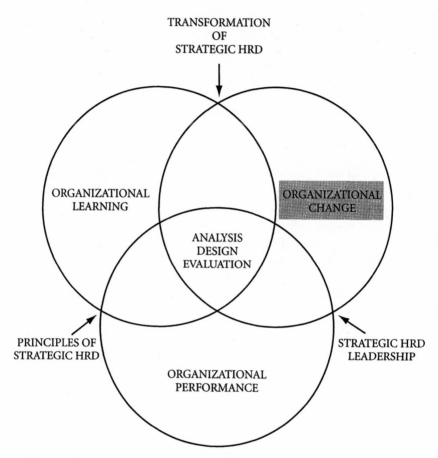

TRANSFORMATION
OF
STRATEGIC HRD

ORGANIZATIONAL
LEARNING

ORGANIZATIONAL
CHANGE

ANALYSIS
DESIGN
EVALUATION

PRINCIPLES OF
STRATEGIC HRD

STRATEGIC HRD
LEADERSHIP

ORGANIZATIONAL
PERFORMANCE

ORGANIZATIONAL LEARNING, PERFORMANCE, AND CHANGE

CHAPTER 14

Organizational Development Consulting

Organizational development consulting aims at improving organizational performance capacity, growth, and competitiveness. It is a long-term process requiring all members of the organization to get involved. OD consulting incorporates action research and the scientific method as ways to develop the organization's problem-solving capabilities. According to Gilley and Eggland (1989), OD consulting is not a "fix it" strategy but rather a continuous way of managing organizational change that, over time, becomes a way of organizational life. Therefore, it is useful to think of OD consulting as planned, data-based approaches to change, involving setting goals, planning action, monitoring feedback, and evaluating results. OD consulting also involves a systems approach that closely links human resources to technology, business processes, and change.

Burke (1992) further defines organizational development consulting as a planned process of change in an organization's culture through the utilization of behavioral science technologies, research, and theory. According to his definition organizational development leads to fundamental change in the way things are done, modifying the essence of organizational culture.

Burke (1992, 9) believes that OD consulting efforts (1) respond to an actual and perceived need for change on the part of the client, (2) involve the client in the planning and implementation of change, and (3) lead to change in the organization's culture. Therefore, organizational development consulting is a process of fundamental change in an organization's culture. Fundamental change implies "that some significant aspect of the organization's culture will never be the same" (Burke 1992, 9).

Many HRD professionals conduct sessions and processes that rely on OD technology. According to French and Bell (1995), such technologies include interviewing both individuals and groups, observing the situation, analyzing and organizing the data collected (diagnosis), reporting back to those from whom the data were obtained on the collective sense of the organizational problems (feedback), analyzing what the data mean, planning the steps to be taken as a consequence (discussion), and taking appropriate steps (action). Burke (1992), however, does not think that simply using OD techniques results in providing OD consulting.

Ackoff (1981) contends that for an organization to develop, change must occur. However, this does not mean that *any* change will be acceptable; development and change are not the same. Change may not result in growth. Further, he argues that "growth can take place with or without development (and vice versa) because development is an increase in capacity and potential, not an increase in attainment. . . . It has less to do with how much one has than with how much one can do with whatever one has" (34–35).

OD consulting, therefore, is a process of bringing to the surface those implicit behavioral patterns that help and hinder development (Burke 1992). In other words, OD consulting enhances employee conscious awareness so they can reinforce behaviors that help them develop and change. Furthermore, OD change agents are responsible for helping clients help themselves.

Burke (1992, 12) maintains that OD change agents are concerned with change that more fully integrates individual needs with organizational goals and improves an organization's effectiveness through better utilization of resources, especially human resources. He suggests involving organization members more in the decisions that directly affect them and their working conditions.

Burke (1992) asked an interesting question: If an organization's culture does not need any change, is OD consulting appropriate? OD consulting is not appropriate unless some fundamental change is desired. How does an HRD professional (change agent) know when fundamental change is needed? Perhaps the best way of determining the appropriateness of OD consulting is to examine the solution pattern of a problem. To do so, HRD professionals measure the impact that previous solutions have had on an organizational problem. If solutions consistently fail to solve the problem, it is necessary to identify the "root cause," not just treat the overt symptoms. This is when OD consulting becomes useful (Rothwell 1996a). When the real causes of organizational problems are uncovered, solutions can be devised to eliminate them.

OD consulting encompasses many interventions, including organizational design, team building, cultural change, leadership, strategy development, management systems, and a variety of other techniques intended to transform firms (Kissler 1991). OD practitioners constantly seek opportunities to improve the human part of a system and, thus, focus on humanistic rather than behaviorist strategies. The field draws its theory from psychology and organizational behavior.

Beer and Eisenstat (1996) consider organizational development from several perspectives, each with its own implications for HRD. The first, *OD as general management*, focuses on the organization's operation and general management. Of specific concern is organizational culture, particularly how to manage or change it. Organizational culture can enhance performance by espousing a supportive environment or hinder performance by inhibiting risk taking, change, or growth. HRD professionals must understand the culture of an organization in order to implement interventions likely to succeed. Leadership, another aspect, can be an effective vehicle for change, including change in performance. Effective HRD professionals employ leaders to set a vision, model behaviors, and challenge others.

The second perspective proposed by Beer and Eisenstat is that of *OD as creating adaptive organizations*, which is the organizational redesign component. Innovative, responsive, and flexible organizational structures enhance worker performance; in turn, worker performance helps create adaptive organizations. Firms that are more flexible and adaptive are more likely to respond to HRD-related initiatives. Inflexible or rigid organizations, in contrast, make it difficult for new performance improvement strategies to succeed, especially if they involve changes in work patterns, introduction of new tools or methodologies, or realignment of jobs.

The third perspective, *OD as human resource management*, is an effort to "develop high-commitment work systems that will attract, motivate, and retain superior employees" (Beer and Eisenstat 1996, 353). Compensation, benefits, and labor relations are examples. HRD is challenged to use these human resource functions appropriately in an integrated approach to improving performance.

OD as implementing change, a fourth perspective, embodies much of the research on change and how to make it happen, incorporating change theory and processes. Lasting positive change in the workforce, its productivity, and its competence is the goal of any performance improvement system. Change-oriented strategies have been instrumental in enabling the HRD field to expand from individual to organizational results.

Organizational Development Consulting: A Total System Approach

Organizational development consulting relies on learning as a means of bringing about change; however, the focus is on improving the organization's performance system rather than on individual employees. OD partnerships primarily benefit the organization itself, with employees as secondary benefactors.

When implementing change, it is crucial for HRD professionals to consider the scope and intensity of their efforts. French and Bell (1995) likened organizations to icebergs. Formal parts of the organization represent that part of the iceberg seen above the water. Informal parts lie beneath the water's surface—unseen, unknown, unnamed, yet clearly organizational elements. They believe that the formal organization consists of publicly observable, structural components that include span of control, hierarchical levels, and the organization's mission, goals, policies, procedures, and practices. On the other hand, informal organizational components are not observable and consist of personal perceptions of the organization, including its informal power structure, patterns of intergroup and intragroup relationships, prevalence of trust, openness, and risk-taking behaviors, and relationships between managers and employees.

HRD professionals consider both the formal and informal organization when implementing change. Tichy (1989) believed that the scope and intensity of organizational problems manifest themselves in the informal parts of the firm. He concluded that the depth of intended change referred to how far management would be willing to go into the organizational iceberg to solve a problem. Furthermore, real change occurs only when the informal organization and all of its behaviors and practices are radically altered. Consequently, changes that occur in the formal organization rarely penetrate deeply enough to have a positive impact on the organization's effectiveness or performance capacity. He further added that the greater the depth of the intervention, the greater the risk of failure and the higher the cost of change. Consequently, HRD professionals must be able to condition the organization and establish ownership for change prior to implementing interventions.

The target for change is the organization (i.e., total system), not necessarily individual members, according to Burke and Schmidt (1971). They believe that individual change is typically a consequence of system change because individual behavior is modified by the new conforming pattern. Therefore, organizational development is a total system approach to change (Burke 1992).

Gilley and Eggland (1989, 76) present a differing perspective:

> OD consulting fails to account for the fact that all organizations are made up of a myriad of individuals. Regardless of the intervention employed and changes made by the organization, people are responsible for implementing change. Organizations are made up of people who accept a common set of organizational goals and objectives by which others outside the organization benefit. In return, each employee receives financial compensation as well as other intrinsic rewards. Organizations do not run themselves; individuals release their personal power and control to organizational leaders in order that the organization can be run more efficiently. Without this compliance, organizations could not maintain control or operate efficiently. Consequently, the macro perspective of organizational development consulting must take into consideration that changes cannot occur, nor can performance improve, without each member of the organization improving respective skills, competencies, knowledge, and attitudes.

Most HRD professionals agree that OD consulting is an approach to a total system. They also believe that an organization is a socio-technical system in that every organization has a technology, whether it is producing something tangible or rendering a service. Although technology is a subsystem of the total organization, it represents an integral part of the culture (Burke 1992). Every organization also comprises people who interact to accomplish performance activities in order to generate performance outputs; thus, the human dimension constitutes the social subsystem. Regardless, OD consulting is most effective when the total organizational system is examined to determine the root cause of a problem and solutions are presented and applied to bring about long-term systemic change.

Goals and Objectives of OD Consulting

The primary goals of OD consulting are to improve organizational effectiveness and performance capacity, enhance organizational renewal, and increase employee performance and productivity. To accomplish these goals, organizations must improve their efficiency, enhance their health, increase collaboration, and develop an appropriate human resource philosophy.

Improving organizational efficiency requires firms to identify a better way of producing products and services, improve communication, and advance the performance management and learning systems. It also requires organizations to redesign their compensation and rewards system, improve job design, and may require a new organizational structure. Such changes require OD change agents to completely examine an organization's operation in search of incremental improvements as well as improved practices and procedures.

Organizations desirous of improving employee morale, creativity, and work climate concentrate on organizational health. Organizational health reflects the relationship between employees and the firm. Relationship quality improves by effectively integrating individual and organizational goals, increasing their problem-solving capacities, and creating organizational environments that encourage individual and organizational growth. Each of these goals can be achieved through OD consulting.

Neilsen (1984) sees the primary objective of OD consulting as initiating a collaborative form of organization possessing four characteristics. First, organizations have structures and policies that facilitate understanding of and commitment to organizational goals. Second, they have reward systems that emphasize group performance while still recognizing individual contributions. Third, collaborative organizations have a measurement system that is used as a yardstick of performance improvement and productivity rather than as rigid performance criteria that become an end in themselves. Finally, they have participatory human resource procedures that examine individual career aspirations based on the organization's long-term needs, as well as the present and future competencies the individual brings to the organization.

When organizational leaders believe that employees are valuable resources and are committed to the welfare of the firm, the collaborative form of organization evolves most naturally. Unfortunately, many firms adhere to a "revolving door" philosophy of human resources based on supply-side economics, in which the supply of qualified personnel exceeds the organization's demands. The revolving door philosophy fosters the attitude that employees exist for the purpose of the organization and that the organization has control over their career advancement, professional growth, and work assignments. As Burke (1992, 183) has observed,

> It is painfully obvious that most organizations treat their most valued resources—employees—as if they were expendable. If OD helps correct these imbalances, it is long overdue, but what about the organization? If it doesn't survive, there will be no jobs, no imbalances to correct. Of the two words represented by OD, practitioners heretofore have spent more time on development than on organization. They are equally important, however; if either is out of balance, the OD change agent's goal is to redress the imbalance.

Additionally, a generally accepted belief is that certain individuals are perceived to be more valuable than others. Although this cultural bias exists, it should be understood that the modern organization would grind to a stop if certain employees (such as its secretarial and support staff) decided to collectively strike. Consequently, many organizations have recognized that the revolving door philosophy is not the most efficient approach to the management and development of human resources or to the improvement of organizational effectiveness. Gilley and Maycunich (2000) report that a by-product of OD consulting is that organizations change their overall philosophy of human resources and adopt the belief that *employees are their greatest assets* and should be treated accordingly.

Beckhard (1969) identified several characteristics of an effective organization that serve as goals for OD consulting. First, the organization, its significant subparts, and individuals manage their work against goals and plans for achievement of these goals. Second, form follows function; that is, the program, task, or project determines how human resources are organized. Third, decisions are made by and near the sources of information, regardless of where those sources are located on the organizational chart. Fourth, the reward system is such that managers and supervisors are rewarded or punished comparably for short-term profit or production, performance, growth, and development of subordinates, and creating a viable working group. Fifth, lateral and vertical communication is relatively undistorted. People are generally open and confronting, sharing all relevant facts, including feelings. Sixth, there is a minimum of inappropriate win-lose activities between individuals and groups. Constant effort is made at all levels to treat conflict and conflict situations as problems, subject to problem-solving methods.

Seventh, high conflict (clash of ideas) exists about tasks and projects, and relatively little energy is spent in clashing over interpersonal difficulties because they generally have been worked through. Eighth, the organization and its parts see themselves as interacting with each other and with a larger environment—the firm is an open system. Ninth, there is a shared view, and management strategy to support it, of trying to help each person or unit in the organization to maintain integrity and uniqueness in an interdependent environment. Tenth, the organization and its members operate in an action-research way. General practice is to build in feedback mechanisms so that individuals and groups can learn from their own experience.

French and Bell (1995) believe that OD consulting is not separate or single events but rather a series of events interacting over an extended period of time. The intent of OD consulting is not to make decisions for management but to identify the root causes of complex problems and to help clarify their choices. OD consulting helps organizations generate valid data useful in improving the organizational culture and performance management system. OD consulting helps organizational leaders make strategic choices based on a diagnosis of the current state and helps them clarify desired outcomes.

Characteristics of OD Consulting

There are several characteristics of OD consulting. First, OD consulting is supported by top management and is focused on the total organizational system. Second, it uses action research, experiential learning, and behavioral science techniques to identify, diagnose, and evaluate performance problems and organizational issues. Third, OD consulting uses planned activities directed by third-party change agents. Fourth, it views organizations from a systems approach. Fifth, OD consulting involves ongoing and relatively long-term processes. Sixth, it increases organizational performance capacity and effectiveness. Seventh, OD consulting emphasizes the importance of goal setting and action planning through strategic planning. Eighth, it is group- and team-oriented (Gilley and Eggland 1989).

Purposes of OD Consulting

According to Burke (1992), one of the largest and most heated debates among OD change agents and academics is whether OD consulting is a contingent or normative process. The contingent group argues that OD change agents should allow clients to determine the direction of change, and then OD change agents help clients achieve this end. By contrast, a significantly smaller group, the normative, argues that although the OD process should be facilitative, OD change agents have a responsibility to recommend specific directions for change.

The normative approach addresses values more than any other aspect of the organization's culture in that changes in certain operational norms would require a value shift that had already been determined (Burke 1992, 196–197). The shift is generally toward a more humanistic treatment of all employees. In fact, the direction of change would be toward an organizational culture where growth and development of organization members is just as important as making a profit or meeting the budget. It would be a culture where equal opportunity and fairness for people in the organization are commonplace; it is the rule rather than the exception. Burke (1992) contends that such a culture would encourage managers to exercise their authority more participatively than unilaterally and arbitrarily; and authority is associated more with knowledge and competence than role or status.

A normative approach to OD would create an organizational culture in which cooperative behavior is rewarded more frequently than competitive behavior, and organization members are kept informed or at least have access to information, especially concerning matters that directly affect their jobs or them personally. Burke (1992) believes change can help develop an organizational culture in which members feel a sense of ownership of the organization's mission and objectives, and conflict is dealt with openly and systematically, rather than ignored, avoided, or handled in a typical win-lose fashion. A normative approach creates an organizational culture where rewards are based on a system of both equality-fairness and equity-merit. Finally, it creates an environment in which organization members are given as much autonomy and freedom to do their respective jobs as possible, to ensure both a high degree of individual motivation and accomplishment of organizational objectives.

According to Neilsen (1984, 22), "organizational development consulting is most likely to succeed . . . with organizations whose members are mature, psychologically healthy adults, who are committed to the organization's welfare and who have important resources to offer, and whose leaders are willing to risk experimentation to enhance individual and organizational health." Others believe that the ultimate value of OD consulting is that it allows organization members to become mature, psychologically healthy, and committed to the organization (Burke 1992). Still others believe that OD consulting encourages the development of personal skills and competencies that the organization can utilize in its effort to remain competitive and productive (Gilley and Eggland 1989). Thus, the principal value of OD consulting is its development of people as well as organizations.

Burke (1992, 183) concluded that if OD change agents hold humanistic values they will act accordingly as change agents, believing that organizations should serve humans, not the reverse. Thus, he maintains that OD change agents are supportive of interventions that help employees (1) be more involved in decisions that directly affect them, (2) be assertive regarding their needs, if not their rights, (3) plan their careers, (4) become more a part of the work group, (5) obtain more interesting jobs or to enrich the ones they have, (6) have opportunities for additional training, education, and personal development, (7) be more involved with their superiors in establishing the objectives and quotas they are expected to reach, and in general, (8) receive respect and fair treatment.

Over the years, several researchers and authors (Lippitt and Lippitt 1986; Turner 1983; Burke 1992; Ulrich 1997a) have identified a number of critical purposes of OD consulting. They remain as important today as when they were first introduced. They are separated into three categories: traditional, client oriented, and organizationally oriented.

Traditional Purposes of OD Consulting

The traditional purposes of OD consulting, and those most often requested by employees, managers, and executives, include providing information and solving problems, conducting effective diagnosis and making recommendations, and implementing change.

Providing Information and Solving Problems.   The most common reason for conducting OD consulting activities is to obtain information and solve problems. Organizations expect the OD consulting process to solve difficult performance, managerial, and/or organizational problems. Though problems vary from organization to organization and from department to department, OD consulting is used to make certain that the identified problem is indeed the one that needs to be solved. Organizations that can identify the root causes of their problems do not need to conduct OD consulting activities. Therefore, the majority of OD consulting projects focus on helping clients define the correct problem, and then work with the problem in such a way that more useful definitions emerge (Turner 1983).

Conducting Effective Diagnosis and Providing Recommendations.   The second purpose of OD consulting is to conduct an effective diagnosis and provide recommendations for the organization, which includes identifying problems, data gathering, data analysis, and making recommendations (French and Bell 1995). The focus of these activities includes examining the economic conditions facing the organization, analyzing the political and technological status of its industry, determining the appropriateness of the organizational structure, measuring managerial abilities and attitudes, or auditing the organizational culture.

One of the difficulties facing change agents responsible for OD consulting projects is that much of the information being gathered is confidential. Many managers are reluctant to share data, fearful that they might be blamed for poor performance or falling productivity. Consequently, the diagnosis and recommendation process can sometimes strain the change agent/client relationship. Nevertheless, it is critical that managers and executives become involved in the process, which ensures they understand their roles and responsibilities. Such participation allows them to develop critical diagnostic skills that may be needed during future analysis.

OD change agents must present a consistent, logical action plan designed to solve the problem(s) facing the organization. Such a plan includes suggestions on how clients should implement a solution(s).

Implementing Change.   OD consulting is often used to implement change, which is a matter of considerable debate among change agents and managers. Some believe that implementing change is the primary responsibility of managers or executives who are familiar with the organization and have the authority to make things happen (Kissler 1991). Conversely, implementing change often requires specialized skills or knowledge not present among many managers and executives. Implementing change also requires an understanding of change's impact on an organization, which can only be gained through firsthand experience acquired by change agents through their numerous consultative engagements. The most compelling reason for using OD change agents is that a poorly implemented change intervention has a devastating impact on the organization in terms of expense, demoralized employees, and reduced productivity. Change agent expertise avoids these problems.

Managers and executives should, however, participate in change implementation because they serve as linkages between important client groups (Ulrich and Lake 1990). Absent these key linkages change will not occur nor will people be willing to do things differently, regardless of potential positive outcomes. Another reason for manager and employee involvement is that they must "live with" the change initiative and make it work.

Client-Oriented Purposes of OD Consulting

OD consulting is used to meet the needs and expectations of clients, which requires OD change agents to build consensus and commitment and facilitate client learning.

Building Consensus and Commitment.   Effective organization consulting builds consensus and commitment to change, which is critical because positive organizational change requires organization members to work together. Employees, managers, and executives are responsible for considering the overall good of the organization prior to considering their own personal and professional agendas and goals. To build consensus and commitment, change agents provide sound, convincing recommendations and present them persuasively. Moreover, they convince participants of the steps required to bring about lasting change, which requires identification of essential decisionmakers and involving them in the change process.

Managers' and executives' enthusiasm for a particular recommendation also gauges readiness for change. This provides an instantaneous measure of cooperation, interest, resistance, reluctance, or resentment by which OD change agents can decide whether to encourage a specific recommendation.

Building positive working relationships with clients, which can happen during the entry and contracting phases of the OD consulting process, provides yet another way of developing consensus and commitment (Block 1981). Positive relationships can also be heightened when gathering information or during the implementation phase. A successful relationship becomes a collaborative search for acceptable answers to the client's real needs and concerns. Ideally, this will be a mutually beneficial relationship.

Facilitating Client Learning.   OD consulting encourages client learning. To achieve this purpose, change agents help clients develop the knowledge and skills needed to adjust to future conditions and address potential problems (Hale 1998). Soliciting client participation in the consulting process is one of the best ways of facilitating client learning. Participation enables clients to gain valuable experience, develop a different organizational perspective, and build problem identification, diagnostic, and implementation skills. Their participation also helps them develop an understanding of the importance of consensus and commitment to bringing about change. Furthermore, the organization begins to develop a learning culture that fosters additional change, which is essential to enhancing an organization's renewal capacity.

Organizationally Oriented Purposes of OD Consulting

These higher-level consulting objectives are designed to improve organizational effectiveness, enhance organizational renewal and performance capacity, improve organizational capability, overcome employee depression, and increase employee productivity and performance.

Improving Organizational Effectiveness.   OD consulting as a strategy to improve organizational effectiveness helps organizations adapt future strategies and behavior to environmental change and optimize the contribution of their human resources. Organizational effectiveness implies senior management's dedication to developing and maintaining the most important systems and linkages needed for improving productivity, efficiency, and profitability. OD consultants develop tailor-made recommendations and solutions to the organization's immediate and future problems and enable decisionmakers to select the most appropriate change interventions.

To enhance organizational effectiveness, OD consulting gathers, diagnoses, and evaluates data about an organization to provide recommendations for change. Additionally, it identifies the steps needed when implementing change and develops linkages within the organization. Finally, OD consulting fosters employee involvement in bringing about change.

Enhancing Organizational Renewal and Performance Capacity.   OD consulting is like nature in that

> every spring the earth re-awakens after the long winter; rebirth, rejuvenation, renewal—call it what you like, the cycle completes itself. Nature's ability to re-build after a long dormancy or catastrophe is astounding. New plant life and young animals are testimony to the ultimate regeneration—a promise fulfilled by tomorrow. Furthermore, each year exhibits growth as those creatures able to survive the test of time are typically larger or stronger than the year before. (Gilley and Maycunich 2000, 25)

OD consulting provides organizations and their employees with creative, safe outlets through which to provide innovative and creative solutions to complex problems. OD consulting enables organizations to identify and incorporate new ideas, processes, or procedures that help them rebuild their market share and create successful business strategies.

OD consulting brings about change within an organization. Change occurs as a result of gaining new insight, awareness, and understanding through critical reflection. The outcome of change is the reconfiguration of organizational structure, culture, work climate, mission, and strategy. Once an organization changes, whether slightly or significantly, a new organizational self-image emerges that filters current realities through an understanding of the present state. That is, change brings about new meaning that alters an organization to the point that it can never return to it original state. Consequently, new meaning leads organizations to desire to change the way they interact on a daily basis. This permanent change propels the organization to a higher plane in which continually evolving employees nourish organizational renewal.

OD consulting fuels *continuous growth and development.* As organizations grow and develop, they constantly renew, improving their reservoir of performance capabilities, which enhances organizational renewal and performance capacity. As an organization improves its overall renewal and performance capacity, it enjoys enhanced competitive readiness, allowing it to avoid the plateau periods of maturity as well as the slippery slopes of decline.

Improving Organizational Capability.   According to Ulrich and Lake (1990, 40), "organizational capability is a business's ability to establish internal structures and processes that influence its members to create organization-specific competencies and, thus, enable the business to adapt to changing customer and strategic needs." They contend that organizational capability includes people management and the means through which organizations implement policies and procedures to develop and sustain employee commitment.

Organizational capability depends greatly on teamwork and the ability of an organization to capitalize on synergy to produce results. Ulrich and Lake have captured the essence of OD consulting: building ongoing success by establishing the structures (foundations) and processes (human resource practices) needed to facilitate required competencies that ensure organizational competitiveness.

Successful organizations avoid the natural tendency to view enhanced organizational capability as merely increased employee productivity, which, although impressive, is not sufficient to ensure long-term business viability. Enhancing organizational capability is the result of the aggregate growth, development, reflection, and renewal abilities of employees. Healthy organizational members are far more qualified to lead the organization to long-term success. As employees maximize their knowledge, skills, and abilities, these are transferred to and improve the organization, which is the fundamental purpose of OD consulting.

Overcoming Employee Depression.   Employee depression is a psychological condition brought about by apathy and the underutilization and alienation of employees, who feel they are not perceived to be vital, contributing members of the firm (Ulrich 1997a). Other psychological dimensions of employee depression include feeling overwhelmed, lost, or fatigued as a result of excessive work demands or productivity requirements. In any case, employees feel unappreciated.

Ulrich (1997a) suggests that OD consulting is useful in overcoming employee depression by addressing excessive demands on employees and their feelings of inadequacy. Organizations need to be encouraged to strike a balance between the two. He believes that one solution is to adopt a philosophical approach to employee enhancement—that of the developmental organization (see Chapter 6). This approach enables employees to exert control over their careers, reestablish commitment to the organization, and participate in challenging work. It also helps them engage in collaborative, team-oriented activities, share in a culture that fosters personal improvement, and receive the performance feedback and support necessary to motivate continuous growth and development.

Increasing Employee Productivity and Performance. OD consulting provides an organization the opportunity to support employee excellence by virtue of their participation in change initiatives and growth and development activities (Rothwell 1996a). In return, employees are able to reach their performance peak because the organization provides a supportive, collaborative, nurturing, healthy environment.

When OD consulting is used for this purpose, change agents are asked to identify critical competencies required to produce exceptional results (performance outcomes), performance standards for outputs, and design improvement activities that enrich performance (Rummler and Brache 1995). Furthermore, OD consulting gives change agents the opportunity to develop and implement a systematic, well-organized performance management process useful in improving employee productivity, quality, performance, and overall development. Such systems improve manager-employee relations by encouraging supervisors to develop positive alliances with employees through timely feedback and coaching activities.

Outcomes of OD Consulting

The optimal outcomes of OD consulting are improved organizational effectiveness and performance capacity. According to Gilley and Eggland (1989, 89), there are, however, several other important outcomes. First, OD consulting provides opportunities for employees to function as human beings, with a complex set of needs and values, rather than as resources in the productivity process. Second, it provides opportunities for each organization member and the organization itself to develop to their fullest potential. Third, OD consulting increases an organization's effectiveness by helping it achieve its strategic business goals and objectives. Fourth, it helps create an environment in which employees find exciting and challenging work. Fifth, OD consulting provides opportunities for employees and managers to influence the way in which they relate to work, the organization, and the work environment.

Phases of OD Consulting

Strategic HRD leaders are first and foremost change agents. As such, it is important that HRD leaders understand the stages of the organizational development process, their purpose, and the role of change agents during each stage. Table 14.1 outlines the roles of organizational change agents at each stage.

To bring about organizational improvement and change, OD change agents embrace a comprehensive approach that they use over and over. This approach guides them throughout the organizational development process. Although the number of steps in the OD process varies from one theoretical framework to another, there is general agreement that it consists of ten phases.

TABLE 14.1   Stages of the Organizational Development Process

OD Process	Purpose	Role of Change Agent
1. Entry	First information sharing	To provide information on background, expertise, and experience of client team
2. Establishing Client Relationships	Build synergistic collaborative client relationships	To provide professional background and expertise of change agents
3. Contracting	Sufficient elaboration of needs, interest, fees, services, working conditions, arrangements; and to establish the specific goals and strategies to be used	To specify actual services, fees to be charged, time frame, and actual work conditions, and to agree mutually with the client team on the goals and strategies to be used
4. Identifying Problems	To obtain an unfiltered, undistorted, and objective view of the organization's problems and processes	To clearly identify the performance problem or organizational issue
5. Diagnosing Problems	To obtain, organize, analyze interpret, and evaluate data	To collect data concerning organizational problems and processes, and to provide feedback
6. Identifying Root Causes	To identify root causes of problems	Analyze possible causes of performance and organizational problems, and isolate the most obvious
7. Providing Feedback	To provide timely feedback to client regarding the status of the change initiative responsibilities	To maintain a clear understanding of the nature and scope of the change initiative and of one's perspective
8. Planning Change	To design a change initiative that will achieve the project goal(s)	To design and develop a change initiative
9. Implementing Interventions	To implement an intervention	To work with the client team to implement a change intervention
10. Evaluating Results	To determine the effectiveness of intervention strategies, energy, and resources used, as well as the change agent-client system relationship	To gather data on specified targets and report findings to the client

Phase 1: Entry

Contact between the change agent and client initiates in the entry phase. This contact may occur in one of two ways. First, the client may call a change agent for an exploratory discussion about the possibility of an OD effort. Second, the change agent may suggest to the client that such an OD effort might be worthwhile. For an internal change agent, either mode could occur. Since a majority of internal change agents feel some commitment to their organizations, or because it is a part of their job descriptions to contact managers (clients) in the organization, the latter approach is most common. Internal change agents may have experienced success with a change initiative in another department or division of the organization and may wish to apply the process elsewhere within the firm. Initiating contacts with clients therefore comes naturally for internal change agents, where there is certainly more opportunity for informal contacts to occur—at committee meetings, informal meetings, and so forth—when questions can be asked and suggestions explored (Burke 1992).

Phase 2: Establishing Client Relationships

After the initial contact, the change agent and the client begin the process of exploring with one another the possibilities of a working relationship. The client usually assesses whether the change agent's previous experience applies to the present situation, whether the change agent is competent and can be trusted, and most importantly, whether he or she can relate well with the change agent.

The most critical element in implementing change initiatives involves establishing the change agent/client relationship, which is critical for fostering trust and cooperation between change agents and clients. The relationship should promote an environment of open and honest communication that improves understanding and reduces resistance. Also, a positive client relationship reduces the incidence of hidden agendas so commonly found during organizational change.

While developing client relationships, the change agent assesses (1) the probability of relating well with the client, (2) the client's motivation and values, (3) the client's readiness for change, (4) the extent of resources for supporting a change effort, and (5) potential leverage points for change—whether the client has the power to make decisions that will lead to change or whether higher authority must be sought (Gilley and Maycunich 1998a). During this phase, control is the most important issue to be resolved as the balance of power between clients and change agents is established. Additionally, a clear understanding of the rules of engagement—who will make what decisions, how they are to be made, and how the change agent's knowledge and skills are to be used—must be determined. Researchers maintain that consulting power can be shared in one of three ways (Gilley 1998; Burke 1992; Lippitt and Lippitt 1986). First, power to make decisions can reside with the change agents. Second, it can reside with clients. Third, it can be mutually shared, where clients and change agents have mutual responsibility for diagnosing needs, generating and selecting remedies, and implementing and evaluating solutions. Except for the client's ultimate veto, neither clients nor change agents have greater power.

Phase 3: Contracting

Assuming that the mutual explorations of the change agent and client in the entry and relationship phases are satisfactory, the next phase in the process is negotiating a contract, which is likely to be brief. The contract is essentially a statement of agreement that succinctly clarifies what the change agent and clients agree to do respectively (French and Bell 1995). The contract may be nothing more than a verbal agreement, with a handshake, perhaps, or it may be a formal document. Most often, the contract is informal, typically involving an exchange of letters between the two parties (Burke 1992).

Prior to engaging in a comprehensive, time-consuming, and very costly OD consulting activity, change agents must discover exactly how serious their clients are. In order to do so, four steps are necessary. First, change agents discuss the parameters of the OD consulting process, revealing the scope and depth of analysis in detail. Second, they discuss the respective roles all parties will play during the OD consulting process, including the client's responsibility to work closely with change agents and to be prompt and responsive when asked for access to employees, files, and other pertinent information. Third, change agents discuss the procedures to be used during the OD consulting process, including gathering and analyzing data, conducting informal discussions with clients, presenting findings to decisionmakers, and determining action sequences for the remaining steps in the process. Fourth, OD change agents ask permission of their clients to move forward and to establish time lines for completion of the change initiative (Gilley and Maycunich 1998a). Once these four issues have been properly addressed and clients have granted permission to proceed, the process of gathering data can begin.

Burke (1992) suggests that, in good practice, OD consultants renew or renegotiate the contract periodically. He believes that the timing of the renewal or renegotiations is not as important as seeing that this phase is periodically repeated. It is also a good practice to have the agreement in writing in order to avoid misunderstandings.

Phase 4: Identifying Problems

The principal responsibility of OD change agents is identifying the performance, managerial, cultural, or system problem(s) affecting organizational productivity, performance, quality, or competitiveness. These problems are often viewed as the difference between "what is" and "what should be." Consequently, most organizations use the OD consulting process to narrow the gap between these two conditions.

A cardinal rule of OD is that change agents begin as facilitators, focusing on what the client considers to be the problem, not necessarily what the change agent deems important (Ulrich 1998). Later, the change agent can recommend or advocate specific changes. Many OD consulting projects fail when change agents identify the wrong problem, in contrast to selecting the wrong solution to solve the right problem. Obviously, identifying the correct problem facing the organization is of critical importance. Furthermore, successful change initiatives begin with a rigorous diagnosis of the current organizational state to determine how the organization is presently functioning. Such information helps change agents correctly determine whether the identified problem actually exists.

Phase 5: Diagnosing Problems

Diagnosing problems involves obtaining, organizing, analyzing, interpreting, and evaluating data. Burke (1992, 75) asserts that

> diagnosis has usually begun even at the entry phase—if the change agent is alert. How the client reacts to the possibility of change at the outset may tell a great deal not only about the client as an individual but also about the part of the organization's culture that he or she represents. Initially, therefore, information gathering is accomplished through the change agent's observations, intuitions, and feelings. Later, more systematic methods are used, such as structured interviews, questionnaires, and summaries of such organizational documents as performance records and task force reports.

Once data are collected, change agents interpret, categorize, analyze, and summarize in order to make certain that all information is accounted for. Next, they organize the information so that the client can easily understand it, analyze it, and take appropriate action.

Burke (1992) adds that change agents gather data directly or indirectly through interviews, questionnaires, focus groups, records, reports, or observations. In order to develop an effective diagnosis, change agents must make certain that all divisions, departments, and units are represented, which helps them to guarantee they have selected an appropriate diagnostic approach.

Phase 6: Identifying Root Causes

All too often, change agents jump to conclusions and make recommendations before they have uncovered the "real" cause of a problem. If the problem's cause and effect relationship has not been established, most likely it will not be resolved (Rothwell 1996a). It is essential to identify the root cause of a problem prior to wasting material, financial, and human resources. Hence, change agents must examine all possible causes of the problem prior to suggesting solutions.

Phase 7: Providing Feedback to Clients

Once organizational problems have been identified, organizational development change agents present their preliminary findings to their clients, which gives clients an opportunity to examine the data and offer their reactions and opinions. Providing feedback gives change agents the opportunity to determine client readiness for change. In addition, change agents can make certain that their strategy is appropriate for the organization prior to implementing a costly and time-consuming intervention that may not help the firm achieve desired results.

French and Bell (1995) report that the success of the feedback phase greatly improves when change agents effectively summarize and analyze the data. The feedback phase consists of holding meetings with the client—usually the decision-maker—alone and then the remainder of the project team. Feedback sessions should encourage discussion and debate, and a small group that does not involve multiple levels of management is best for such purposes (Robinson and Robinson 1996).

A feedback session generally has three steps (Burke 1992, 76). First, the change agent provides a summary of the data collected and some preliminary analysis. Second, general discussion ensues, in which questions of clarification are raised and answered. Third, some time is devoted to interpretation, allowing changes in the change agent's analysis and interpretation. This approach enables change agents to work collaboratively with clients to arrive at a final diagnosis that accurately describes the current state of the organization.

Phase 8: Planning Change:
Identify, Evaluate, and Select Solutions

Following completion of the feedback phase, OD change agents identify the most appropriate change intervention by identifying the sources of organizational problems and matching appropriate solutions to them (Kissler 1991). Thus, change agents must be familiar with the variety of intervention strategies available and be able to group them in a meaningful fashion.

According to Burke (1992), the planning phase sometimes becomes the second half of the feedback session because a good diagnosis determines the solution to be used. If this is the case, he believes that the only required planning may be the implementation steps (i.e., what to do). However, the more complex the organization, the more complex the diagnosis. Thus, the planning phase becomes a separate event, following the feedback sessions.

One purpose of the planning phase is to identify solutions that correlate to the problems identified in the diagnosis. Another purpose is to decide on the next steps to be taken. The OD change agent again works collaboratively with the client team during this phase, primarily by helping them identify and explore alternative solutions. Moreover, the client decides which solution is to be adopted, not the change agent. Once several appropriate solutions have been identified, change agents, in cooperation with their clients, evaluate and select the most feasible one.

Phase 9: Implementing Interventions

The action taken by an organization to bring about meaningful change is generally referred to as an intervention. The possibilities are numerous, and the selected intervention(s) should be a direct reflection of and response to the diagnosis.

An intervention's success depends on several factors, such as executives' and senior managers' support, type of organizational resistance, employees' and managers' readiness for change, amount and type of employee involvement in the OD process, and payoff and rewards associated with change (French and Bell 1995).

Organizational development change agents monitor the progress of an intervention once it has been implemented and determine whether adjustments are required. Failure to communicate may result in missed opportunities to bring about meaningful change; hence effective communication between change agents and clients is essential.

One of the biggest barriers to implementing meaningful change is employees' beliefs and feelings regarding change (Patterson 1997). Since change affects the way employees interact and the way they accomplish work and threatens employee stability, change agents must identify and manage such concerns carefully. They should look for signs of employee resistance and respond accordingly.

Phase 10: Evaluating Results

Because change agents cannot be totally objective, someone else should be asked to conduct an evaluation of the OD consulting activity. Evaluation may range from informal client testimonials that reflect their perception of outcomes to systematic research activities employing controls and multiple data analyses. Burke (1992, 78) asserts that "a more objective and systematic evaluation is obviously better, at least for determining cause and effect." However, such evaluations are very difficult to conduct. The problem is control due to the near impossibility of developing a proper control group for comparison during an OD consulting engagement. Furthermore, the client is usually more interested in implementing solutions to problems than objectively determining whether results were attributable to the OD intervention (Burke 1992). Guba and Lincoln (1988) suggest that the most important outcome of an evaluation is the stakeholders' perception of the change and its respective organizational impacts, which they refer to as fourth generation evaluation.

Organizational Development Frameworks

A model or framework anchors an OD change agent's approach to organizational development consulting. Following are three models of OD consulting and development that provide differing perspectives and approaches.

Burke-Litwin Model

Burke and Litwin (1992, 532) present a model of organizational performance and change (Figure 14.1). According to Burke (1992), the model is consistent with accepted thinking about organizations from general systems theory. The external environment box represents input, and the individual and organizational performance box represents output. Feedback loops go in both directions. The remaining boxes of the model represent the throughput aspect of general systems theory. Arrows in both directions convey the open-systems principle that change in one factor will eventually impact the others. If the model could be diagrammed so that the arrows were circular, reality could be represented more accurately in this causal model.

Burke and Litwin (1992) deliberately positioned the model to highlight the relative weight of influence various elements have on each other. Kissler (1991) suggests that organizational change is driven more by environmental impact than by any other source. According to Burke (1992), the relative positioning of the remaining variables also indicates that strategy, leadership, and culture more directly affect organizational change than structure, management practices, and systems (e.g., policies and procedures). The individual elements of the model include the following:

- *External environment:* External political, financial, and marketplace forces.
- *Mission and strategy:* A collective understanding of the overall purpose and direction of the organization by its people.
- *Leadership:* Executive behavior and values that energize others to act.
- *Culture:* Collective beliefs, visible and sometimes hidden rules and practices that have been shaped by the organization's history and past momentum.
- *Structure:* The placement of people into positions that allows for an optimal alignment of authority and responsibility needed to achieve the organization's strategic objectives.

FIGURE 14.1   The Burke-Litwin Model of Organizational Performance and Change

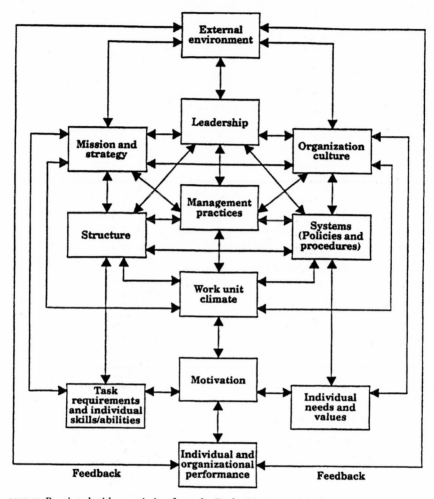

SOURCE: Reprinted with permission from the Burke-Litwin Model of Individual and Organizational Performance. Copyright ©1992, W. Warner Burke Associates, Inc.

- *Management practices:* The management activity that draws upon technical, financial, and human assets to carry out the organization's strategy.
- *Systems:* The procedures, written guidelines, and other mechanisms that constitute predetermined answers to guide people in decisionmaking. The budgeting process, reward system, and human resource flow processes are examples.

- *Climate:* The collective current impressions, expectations, and feelings of the members of local work units. These influence relationships in multiple directions throughout the organization.
- *Task requirements and individual skill/abilities:* The skills and knowledge required to be successful in a specific assignment, which can be considered a job-person match.
- *Individual needs and values:* The internal psychological factors that provide attraction to and assign value to specific outcomes. These can be tangible or intangible.
- *Motivation:* The force that propels humans toward desired objectives. This energy comes from such basic motives as achievement, power, affection, discovery, security, and freedom.
- *Individual and organizational performance:* Organizational outcomes such as productivity, profit, service level, and the satisfaction of both internal and external stakeholders. (Burke 1992)

Burke and Litwin (1992) separate organizational change into two categories. The distinctions are as follows:

- *Transformational Factors:* External environment, leadership, mission and strategy, organization culture, and individual and organizational performance
- *Transactional Factors:* Management practices, structure, systems (policies and procedures), task requirements and individual skills/abilities, work unit climate, motivation, individual needs and values, and individual and organizational performance.

Areas where altercation is likely caused by interaction with external forces and that requires overt behavioral change by employees are referred to as transformational. Shifts in the external environment require modification in transformational factors. When these elements change, they dramatically affect the way the organization functions and require dramatic behavioral shifts on the part of employees. Over time, a "new organization" forms.

Transactional refers to alterations that occur primarily through relatively short-term reciprocity among employees and groups (Burke 1992). Change in these elements affects the way employees interact as well as their attitudes, sense of direction, commitment, and motivation. These reactions are personal and individualized behaviors rather than ones driven by individualized values and guiding principles influenced by organizational culture.

Burke and Litwin (1992) believe that organizational performance and change can be affected by both transactional and transformational change. The former is short-term and immediate, whereas the latter is long-term and systematic. Both are acceptable approaches, and it is the responsibility of OD change agents to help organizations determine which approach is the most acceptable.

Change Management Organization Model

According to Kissler (1991, 258), the fundamental issue facing leaders and managers is

> how best to capture the essence of their organizations when considering how to position them for coming change. This suggests that, whereas the description and alignment of primary segments is important, it is even more important to understand how to anticipate the potential impact of change and assess the organization's readiness to deal with it.

The change management organization model has three distinct levels within it (Figure 14.2). At its broadest level are four primary organizational dimensions. Beneath each dimension are several influence systems: leadership, structure, process, and workforce.

- *Leadership.* The primary ingredients are the people and systems propelling the organization into the future.
- *Structure.* As the organization sets its overall course, it must examine its internal strengths and weaknesses as well as its external opportunities and threats. Once this is done, the strategy should lead to the formation of roles and relationships among organizational units and individuals.
- *Process.* How work is planned, performed, measured, and controlled. This dimension draws upon the technical and financial resources of the organization.
- *Workforce.* The characteristics of the organization's people. (Kissler 1991, 258–260)

A second level of detail, called *influence systems,* lies beneath these dimensions. Organizations comprise several of these influence systems, which affect whether and to what extent change can be implemented and sustained (Kissler 1991, 269). Table 14.2 shows twenty-two of these second-level elements.

Although each of the influence systems relates primarily to one organizational dimension, they are not exclusive. Their purpose is to target specific changes and systematically coordinate the impacts of each of the influencing systems. Because of their highly interactive and interdependent nature, change to any one will result in change in other influencers. Kissler (1991, 261–264) provided a definition for each of the influence systems as follows:

FIGURE 14.2   Change Management Organization Model

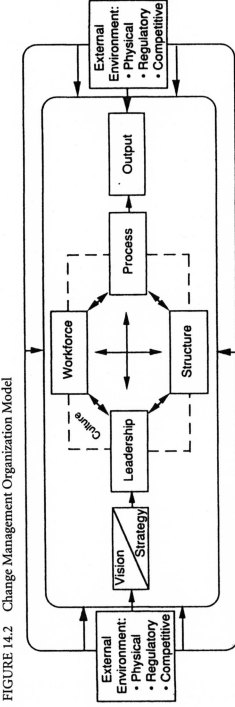

SOURCE: Reprinted, by permission from the publisher, from G. D. Kissler, *The Change Riders: Managing the Power of Change* (Cambridge, Mass.: Perseus Books, 1991).

TABLE 14.2   Organizational Influence Systems

Leadership	Structure	Process	Workforce
Vision	Role	Planning	Values
Image	Relationship	Operations	Skills
Power	Form	Control	Knowledge
Innovation		Communication	Motivation
Style		Automation	Commitment
Risking		Education	
Allocation			
Rewards			

Leadership Influence Systems.

- *Vision* is what the organization imagines or wants to achieve in the future.
- *Image* represents the perception that individuals or groups have of the organization.
- *Power* is the ability or capacity to influence the behaviors of others.
- *Innovation* is the process of bringing new problem-solving or value-adding ideas into use.
- *Style* is the pattern of behaviors throughout the organization, often reflective of its management or leadership.
- *Risking* is the tendency to take chances when the conditions are uncertain.

Structure Influence Systems.
- *Role* is the "expected-perceived-enacted behavior patterns attributed to a particular job or position."
- *Relationship* shapes the interaction among organizational units and their members. They are the interpersonal components of a job.
- *Form* is the configuration or shape of an organization (i.e., structure and strategies).

Process Influence Systems.

- *Planning* determines what factors are required to achieve goals before an activity takes place.
- *Operations* are the primary prescribed processes conducted by any organization.
- *Control* includes the mechanisms by which deviations from plans and standards are prevented, detected, and corrected, and assumes adherence

to plans and standards to achieve objectives. Controls exist at all levels (strategic, operational, or production) and apply to all organizational units (corporate, division, department, project, or work team).

- *Communication* is the exchange of data, information, or meaning.
- *Education* is the development of abilities into specific, required, or desired skills, knowledge, or attitudes.
- *Allocation* is the distribution of resources within an organization.
- *Rewards* and the systems that provide them offer positive reinforcement to shape the work behavior of individuals.

Workforce Influence Systems.

- *Values* are the principles, enduring beliefs, and customs held dear by individuals and groups in an organization.
- *Skills* are abilities that contribute to performance.
- *Knowledge* includes employees' familiarity with facts, conditions, or principles (pertaining to the conduct of certain processes or work tasks is termed *skill* for our purposes).
- *Motivation* is a state of mind that causes one to behave in certain ways.
- *Commitment* is the desire to persist.

The change management organization model calls attention to some familiar variables such as workforce, leadership, strategy, structure, and output. Moreover, it highlights the vision needed to set the stage for managing various types of organization transformation. Vision is a key element that underscores an issue that continues to be debated: whether such activity is needed and, if attempted, can actually yield benefits to an organization (Kissler 1991, 264–265). The model demonstrates a close relationship between formation of a future state and development of a supporting strategy. Furthermore, Kissler (1991) uses a "close in" framework beginning with a vision and ending with actual output, thus separating the organization and external variables.

Kissler (1991, 265) summarizes by saying, "It becomes clear that managing the impact of change demands that leaders and managers begin with a rigorous examination of their organizations in terms of their major dimensions, underlying systems, and techniques that could be used to effect change."

Organizational Effectiveness Framework

Gilley and Maycunich (1998a) designed an open system model to help isolate breakdowns in organizational performance, quality, and effectiveness. The organizational effectiveness framework (OEF) is based on a relationship design similar to the human body in that it has independent but interdependent components (i.e., circulatory, digestive, skeletal, nervous system, and so forth) essential to maintaining good health and life. Similarly, the OEF consists of both an organizational system and a performance management system (see Figure 14.3).

The organizational system consists of interdependent components on which the organization is dependent in order to remain viable. These seven interdependent functions include leadership, structure, work climate, organizational culture, mission and strategy, managerial practice, and policies and procedures. As illustrated in Figure 14.3, each of these seven components is dependent on the others, as represented by the arrows. Nevertheless, each component is an independent component of the organization, not unlike that of vital organs within the human body.

Within the OEF, the performance management system is comprised of eight interdependent components. Once again, both an interdependent and independent relationship exists among these eight components. They include human and material resources, compensation and reward system, learning system, work design, career planning, recruiting and selection, performance coaching, and performance appraisal process.

The arrows in both directions convey an open system principle; changes in one factor will eventually impact the others (Burke 1992). Connection points exist between the organizational system and performance management system, demonstrating the linkage between the two.

According to Gilley and Maycunich (1998a, 69–70), applying an organizational effectiveness strategy is important to OD change agents for seven reasons. First, this framework enables an approach to organizational change from both micro and macro perspectives. When approaching change from a micro perspective, change agents rely on the performance management system to enhance individual and organizational performance. Macro-level changes require the focus of attention on the organizational system since it is commonly shared across departmental lines and divisions. Second, change agents analyze the relationships between various components within the organizational and performance management systems to determine potential breakdowns or areas of weakness. Third, change agents examine any or all of the fifteen functions to determine whether one, a few, or all are contributing to a breakdown in performance or output. Fourth, OD change agents can better develop change initiatives by focusing on the most appropriate components and their interdependencies. Fifth, the OEF can identify appropriate layers that consist of groupings both within each respective system and across system lines. Sixth, change agents use the framework to examine the organizational system and performance management system separately allowing for completely different interventions. Seventh, OD change agents can focus their of consulting activities, depending upon whether they are examining the organi-

FIGURE 14.3   Organizational Effectiveness Framework

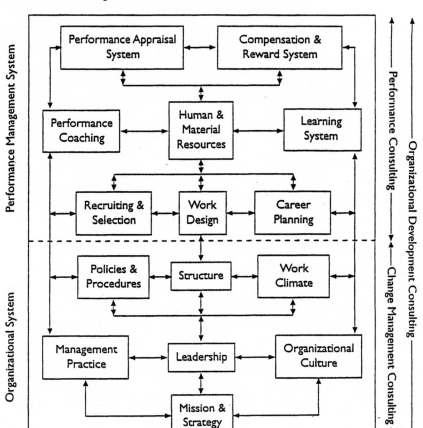

SOURCE: J. W. Gilley and A. Maycunich, *Strategically Integrated HRD: Partnering to Maximize Organizational Performance* (Cambridge, Mass.: Perseus Books, 1998a).

zational system, performance management system, or a combination, using change management consulting, performance consulting, and organizational development consulting, respectively.

Gilley and Maycunich (1998a) maintain that the OEF can improve performance capacity, continuous development, efficiency, and organizational effectiveness. One need only step back and examine the issues, relationships, and logical characteristics of each of the fifteen components of the organization effectiveness framework in order to employ it. OD change agents should think of the OEF as a trouble-shooting guide useful in identifying areas of inquiry or concern surrounding a problem or difficult issue. For example, to isolate problems or breakdowns, electronic technicians use electronic diagrams (schematics), automobile mechanics rely on diagnostic tools, and building contractors refer to blueprints. Similarly, OD change agents use the OEF to isolate problems or identify areas that require attention in order to craft a solution for which an intervention can be constructed.

Gilley and Maycunich (1998a, 84) state that applying the organizational effectiveness framework involves the following seven steps:

1. Identify the *most logical components* that should be taken into account in determining the extent of a performance problem or organizational breakdown. (Identify only those components that have a "direct" impact on the problem. Recommendations and interventions may require addressing additional components).
2. Define each component and identify its importance within one's organization.
3. Identify the relative strengths and weaknesses of each component.
4. Examine the relationship among components.
5. Determine any negative impacts that components have on each other.
6. Isolate areas of concern or breakdowns.
7. Identify recommendations and/or interventions that should be used to neutralize negative impacts.

For example, improving organizational performance requires HRD professionals to examine:

- the adequacy of human and material resources;
- the hiring and selection practices used to match employees with jobs (recruiting and selection);
- the ability of managers and supervisors to provide formal feedback and to design corrective action and developmental plans (performance appraisal process);
- the impact of financial and intrinsic rewards on employee motivation (compensation and reward system);
- the manager's ability to train, mentor, and provide constructive performance feedback (performance coaching);
- the managerial practices of the organization (management practice); and
- organizational practices (policies and procedures).

Once an HRD professional has examined each of these components, he or she can determine their importance and relative strength or weakness within the organization as well as their relationship and impact on one another. Next, he or she can isolate areas of concern or breakdown. Finally, an HRD professional can identify recommendations or solutions in order to neutralize negative impact. When used this way, the organizational effectiveness framework is an excellent tool in analyzing complex organizational and performance problems.

Gilley, Boughton, and Maycunich (1999) suggest using the organizational effectiveness framework during organizational, managerial, performance, and needs analysis activities to identify gaps between current and desired expectations (see Chapter 15). They believe that OD change agents can use the framework to conduct brainstorming activities to identify factors that contribute to performance problems or organizational breakdowns. Additionally, the framework can be used to assign areas of inquiry during the problem identification phase of a performance consulting project. When used to isolate potential problems, define relationships between and among various components, or identify intervention possibilities, the applications are endless.

Conclusion

Beer (1983) defined organizational development consulting as a systemwide process of data collection, diagnosis, action planning, intervention, and evaluation aimed at (1) enhancing congruence between organizational structure, processes, strategy, people, and culture; (2) developing new and creative organizational solutions; and (3) developing the organization's self-renewing capacity. OD consulting occurs only when organization members work collaboratively with change agents (OD consultants) using behavioral science theory, research, and technology. In short, OD consulting focuses upon improving overall organizational effectiveness by developing innovative approaches to problem solving and by establishing a "survivalist attitude" in a continuously evolving environment of technological advancement and cultural change. Consequently, organizational development consulting can be viewed as both a philosophy and a collection of methods for organizational improvement. Both are characterized by an emphasis on collaborative participation in data collection, diagnosis, planning, intervention, and evaluation in order to improve the entire firm.

PART V

Essential Practices in Organizational Learning, Performance, and Change

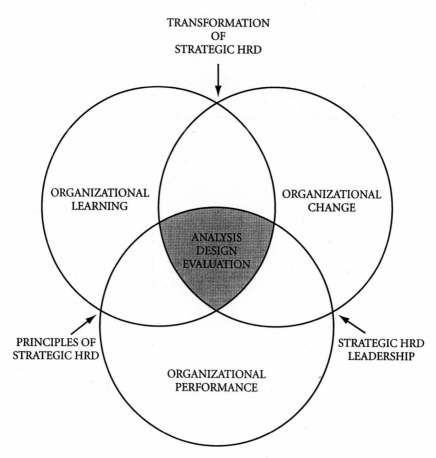

TRANSFORMATION
OF
STRATEGIC HRD

ORGANIZATIONAL
LEARNING

ORGANIZATIONAL
CHANGE

ANALYSIS
DESIGN
EVALUATION

PRINCIPLES OF
STRATEGIC HRD

STRATEGIC HRD
LEADERSHIP

ORGANIZATIONAL
PERFORMANCE

ORGANIZATIONAL LEARNING, PERFORMANCE, AND CHANGE

CHAPTER 15

Analysis in Organizational Learning, Performance, and Change

Identifying organization, performance, and learning needs provides HRD professionals the opportunity to improve organizational effectiveness while building strategic business partnerships, management development partnerships, and organizational development partnerships. Identifying needs allows HRD professionals to improve their credibility and enhance the image of the HRD program, its interventions, and consulting services.

Brinkerhoff (1998) reports that effective analysis reflects a continuous, value-based, nonjudgmental activity that is closely aligned to stakeholder expectations. Analysis should be integrated and linked with organizational strategy and, thus, not used to justify HRD professionals' actions and behaviors. He further warns HRD professionals to avoid the following dangers that could bias the analysis process: (1) using data to support or justify predetermined outcomes; (2) viewing data as evidence of a need that requires an action; and (3) interpreting data incorrectly.

Sleezer (1992) suggests three possible results of analysis: information gathering, priorities setting, and management involvement and support. Holton (1995a) adds that analysis should include solutions and recommendations for closing the gap between "what is" and "what should be." In other words, HRD professionals not only identify needs but also isolate causes and suggest solutions. Holton (1995a) suggests that HRD professionals need to be proactive leaders in performance and organizational enhancement, not simply analysts. Thus, they should interpret data for the purpose of determining solutions and obtaining support from management to implement performance improvement interventions and change initiatives.

Goals for Analysis

The analysis process should be based on clear and understandable goals—ones that are specific, measurable, attainable, realistic, and tied to a timetable (SMART). Rossett (1999a) identified six goals for analysis. HRD professionals should identify (1) managers' and employees' perceptions of reality; (2) information about optimal performance (what would the organization be doing if it were functioning splendidly and employees' performance was done at optimal levels?); (3) information about actual performance, which determines what employees are doing now and what incentives, tools, and participation programs influence their performance; (4) information regarding how decisionmakers, organizational leaders, managers, and centers of influence (critical employees) feel about the relationship between optimal and actual performance; (5) information about solutions that enhance performance or improve organizational effectiveness, which allows HRD professionals to avoid the "power and mystery of analysis" by focusing on positive outcomes; and (6) information regarding the cause of performance problems, the most common of which are employees' lack of skill or knowledge, environmental dysfunction, lack of or improper incentives, and unmotivated workers.

Obstacles to Analysis

Although analysis is an important component of HRD practice there are several obstacles that prevent its execution.

Lack of Support for Analysis

Many organizations view analysis as a waste of time, energy, and effort. Consequently, there is often very little support for conducting analyses within the organization. Gaining support for analysis is critical as it conditions the firm to the use of such activities prior to implementing costly interventions. According to Rossett (1999b, 108), three strategies can be used to increase support for analysis. First, HRD professionals can conduct effective analyses, document what has been done, and how it has contributed to the bottom line. Second, HRD professionals can make the case for analyses by demonstrating their importance (for example, a physician doesn't prescribe treatment without cautious diagnosis). Third, HRD professionals can avoid using terms such as analysis, needs assessment, or front-end analysis if management does not respond well to these (using instead terms such as planning, study, or research).

Identifying internal sponsors or advocates for such activities is a means of garnering support for organizational performance analysis. Internal sponsors must possess credibility within the firm and have opportunities to encourage and promote analysis within the firm. To be successful, sponsors need an appropriate network and access to important contacts within the firm, as well as the ability to articulate ideas in a persuasive manner.

Additionally, HRD professionals need to participate in high-profile assessment activities. These are typically of great importance to senior managers and executives because they impact a large number of employees. As a result, analysis has the potential of enhancing the image and credibility of HRD professionals within the firm.

Analysis Paralysis

Common in many organizations is a situation known as analysis paralysis. Typically, this resistance to analysis occurs when executives, managers, and employees fear that incompetence will be revealed, for which they will be held accountable. Analysis paralysis prevents well-intended, well-meaning examination of critical performance problems and organizational deficiencies, which leads to unacceptable customer service, poor quality, and negative business results. Another type of analysis paralysis occurs when organizations become concerned that analysis may become an end unto itself. This attitude toward analysis stands in the way of identifying solutions to serious problems.

When HRD professionals do not possess credibility, analysis paralysis is a common result. To overcome this obstacle, HRD professionals must be able to clearly articulate the goals for analysis, identify the questions that will reveal the most appropriate information, assess the cost of material and human resources necessary for analysis, and resolve potential areas of disagreement. In other words, HRD professionals must know what they are doing in order to conduct an effective and efficient analysis.

HRD professionals can increase their credibility within the organization by clearly demonstrating the benefits of analysis activities. When they provide valuable information for making critical organizational decisions, HRD professionals make a strong case for the continued use of analysis within the firm.

Lack of Value of Analysis

Little analysis is conducted by vendor-driven HRD programs since their focus is on the number of training courses provided and participants served. In some situations, needs analysis is conducted for the purpose of identifying skill and knowledge deficiencies—and used as a justification for more training activity.

When organizations fail to embrace the analysis process, Rossett (1999a) asserts that the only viable solution is to advocate the use of analysis as a problem-solving activity. The analysis process then becomes a strategic weapon used to improve organizational effectiveness. In this way, HRD programs can make the transition from activities-driven practices to results-driven practices. The outcomes generated through this process will evidence the value of incorporating analysis into the organization's everyday activities, and analysis will become a routine activity within a firm (Gilley and Maycunich 1998a).

A Strategic Approach to Analysis

Rothwell (1996a, 103–104, 139–140) reports that several competencies are required of analysts in HRD. As analysts, HRD professionals should be able to examine the needs and expectations of customers, suppliers, distributors, and stakeholders; formulate, assess, and convert organizational plans to HRD efforts; link performance improvement efforts to organizational mission and strategy; identify organizational strengths and weaknesses; examine work flow within and between departments; detect bottlenecks in work processes; assess present competency levels of workers; and assess workforce supply in light of workforce needs, taking inventory of the organization's present human capability.

HRD professionals engage in the analysis process as a means of uncovering the diverse needs of the organization. According to Gilley and Coffern (1994), HRD professionals should consider using these five strategic questions to effectively conduct the analysis process:

1. Does a performance problem or an organizational problem exist within the firm?
2. Does the problem exist because of a learning, performance, management capability, or organizational effectiveness gap?
3. Should an analysis be conducted at the individual, performance, or organizational level?
4. What data gathering methods should HRD professionals use to isolate and investigate problems?
5. Once a problem has been isolated, how should HRD professionals ensure the successful implementation of performance improvement interventions or change initiatives?

Answering these questions increases HRD professionals' understanding of the problem and the type of analysis that is appropriate.

Question 1: Does a performance problem or an organizational problem exist within the firm?

The analysis process begins by identifying the expectations (i.e., revenue, production, quality, service, return on investment) of executives and managers and comparing them to actual performance. Such expectations are the *desired state, condi-*

tions, or circumstances preferred by management, which represent targets for all operational units, divisions, and departments. Existing productivity and performance represent the *current state*. Problems occur when there is a gap between the current and desired states. In other words, a problem is a difference between "what is" and "what should be."

Rothwell and Sredl (1992) describe analysis as being either deficiency oriented or opportunity oriented. Most analysis activities are deficiency oriented, designed to identify and address existing deficiencies or gaps in performance. By definition, a deficiency approach is focused on the present. Opportunity-oriented analysis is future oriented, identifying performance gaps likely to occur in the future and proactively implementing solutions to prevent them. Holton (1995, 7) indicates that today's fast-changing organizations should incorporate future-oriented analysis.

Revans (1994) classified analysis activities into four types, varying along two dimensions. One dimension defines the type of problem, known or unknown, while the other dimension expresses the conditions under which the problem occurs, also divided into known and unknown. According to Holton, (1995, 7), a four-cell matrix describes the following four types of analysis:

- Corrective analyses are those that analyze existing problems in existing circumstances to identify performance problems.
- Adaptive analysis occurs in organizations that find themselves performing under new conditions but facing the same job demands as in the past.
- Developmental analyses are designed to improve an organization's ability to deal with additional problems in the existing environment and conditions.
- Strategic analysis requires anticipation of unknown problems or deficiencies that are likely to occur in the future under changing, but unknown, conditions. (See Appendix E)

Holton (1995, 7) contends that "traditional learning assessment and performance analysis methodologies are strong tools for corrective analysis, limited tools for adaptive and developmental analysis, and weak tools for strategic analysis."

Question 2: Does the problem exist because of a learning, performance, management capability, or organizational effectiveness gap?

Four types of deficiencies commonly exist within organizations. Each contributes to organizational inefficiency and ineffectiveness if not properly addressed. These are learning, performance, management capability, and organizational effectiveness gaps.

Learning Gaps.   When HRD professionals engage in analysis to identify learning needs, they identify the skills, knowledge, and attitudes required of employees to perform their jobs. These serve as the foundation for designing and developing performance improvement interventions needed to overcome a plethora of skill and knowledge deficiencies. When employees adopt these proficiencies, they should be able to increase productivity and achieve better outcomes.

A learning need results from a deficiency of knowledge, skill, or attitude and is thus a specialized need. Rothwell and Cookson (1997, 127–128) classify learning needs into five categories:

- *Unfelt needs* are deficiencies unknown to the learner.
- *Felt needs* are deficiencies that learners recognize in themselves or that other stakeholders recognize in learners.
- *Expressed needs* are ones learners identify and know why they are needed.
- *Normative needs* constitute a deficiency or gap between a "desirable" standard and one that really exists.
- *Comparative needs* are differences between two or more similar individuals, groups, or teams.

Performance Gaps.   Identifying performance deficiencies requires HRD professionals to engage in a variety of activities to ascertain the impact of the organizational and performance management systems on performance outcomes. Performance gaps are deficiencies in the way the organization manages performance, designs jobs, or reinforces and rewards performance. HRD professionals must go beyond such rudimentary analyses to uncover true causes of performance shortfalls. Performance gaps can be examined through performance and causal analysis activities (Chapters 9 and 11).

HRD professionals need to distinguish between those practices that are being performed adequately and those that are being performed below standard. According to Elliott (1998), this can be done by reviewing existing data; observing exemplary performance and comparing it to average performance; and interviewing performers, managers, and technical experts. He suggests that HRD professionals should look for best practices that are not being performed safely, fast enough, or at all (1998, 72–73). Additionally, HRD professionals should look for best practices in which steps are performed out of order or in which steps can be eliminated. They should determine whether the deficient performance of practices occurs at a particular time or place. After identifying deficient practices, they can generate cause hypotheses for why the practices are not being performed adequately.

Management Capability Gaps.   The quality of managers is one of the biggest problems facing organizations. Gilley and Boughton (1996) report that managers should provide guidance and direction for employees and serve as liaisons between executives and employees, interpreting the organization's vision and ensuring that goals and expectations are met. Consequently, HRD professionals need to identify deficiencies in the way employees are managed and motivated within the organization, which refers to management capability gaps.

Gilley and Boughton (1996, 15) believe that far too many organizations allow managers to act indifferently toward their employees, to maintain superior attitudes, or to consider employees as vessels to be used and abused. Managers are allowed to possess poor listening and feedback skills and are not disciplined when they are unable to build positive, productive relationships with employees.

When organizations retain managers who are unable to delegate responsibility, develop their personnel, conduct performance appraisals, or establish priorities, they are fostering *managerial malpractice*. Allowing managerial malpractice to flourish in organizations leads to diminished business results. Fortunately, HRD professionals are frequently asked to determine ways of improving managers' proficiencies and skills. The analysis process is often used to expose managerial gaps within the firm. Closing the gap between desired results and actual performance sometimes involves performance coaching.

As a result of the analysis process, HRD professionals cultivate management development partnerships that improve overall performance within the organization. Another appropriate intervention includes designing and implementing competency-based selection tools to recruit and select individuals with the aptitude to become efficient managers capable of securing results through people.

Organizational Effectiveness Gaps.   Organizational effectiveness gaps are a result of the way the organization is conceived, designed, and managed. Kaufman, Rojas, and Mayer (1992) believe that the entire organizational system must be examined in order to identify organizational gaps. Consequently, analyses focused on uncovering organizational effectiveness deficiencies are complex and aimed at the macro level.

To improve their effectiveness, organizations often solicit the help of HRD professionals to reinvent themselves. Organizational gaps need to be identified and corresponding interventions designed, which include organizational development and change initiatives. Organizational analysis activities are extremely complex and time-consuming and require the greatest amount of skill among HRD professionals.

Question 3: Should an analysis be conducted at the individual, performance, or organizational level?

One of the most important questions on the minds of executives and managers gets to the heart of the analysis process: Where is the "pain?" The answer to this question provides direction and focus for HRD professionals as they engage in analysis projects throughout the firm. Locating the "pain" determines which type of analysis is most appropriate and when it should be used. Three types of analysis are common in organizations:

- Individual analysis (learning analysis);
- Performance analysis (performance analysis);
- Organizational analysis (organizational analysis and impact mapping)

Each is examined in greater detail later in this chapter (see models of analysis).

Question 4: What data gathering methods should HRD professionals use to isolate and investigate problems?

As part of the analysis process, HRD professionals must gather data that either supports or rejects their hypotheses. Doing so allows them to compile the evidence needed to make thoughtful, reasonable recommendations that address the organization's problems. A number of methods are available to uncover evidence from the various constituencies within the organization. The seven most useful to HRD professionals are (1) is/should analysis, (2) focus groups, (3) critical analysis, (4) interviews, (5) observations, (6) questionnaires, and (7) root-cause analysis.

Each method solicits the thoughts and ideas of executives, managers, and employees regarding organizational, performance, and learning needs. Some are more appropriate than others, and it is HRD professionals' responsibility to ascertain under what conditions and circumstances various methods will be used. Usually, employing several sources is preferable to just one; HRD professionals are more confident of the data collected, particularly when differing methodologies produce identical results.

Is/Should Analysis. The is/should method of data collection is most useful when users are not familiar with a particular process or performance occurring within the organization. The easiest way to use this method is by developing an is/should chart, which is a simple list of issues related to a specific problem, reporting the current state in the left column and the desired state in the right column. This method organizes information in order to compare what is happening as opposed to what should be happening. Discovering the current state and identifying standards representative of the desired state requires HRD professionals to solicit opinions of leaders, managers, and employees. Therefore, other related methods (focus groups, critical incidents) must be used.

The "is" side of the chart should be free of bias—constructed from actual observations, interviews, focus groups, or other research. The "should" side of the chart may reflect only a particular group's or individual's perspective of what the desired state is, which is often established by predetermined industrial or performance standards common in an industry.

The is/should analysis method is particularly useful at the beginning of the analysis process. The primary strengths of the is/should method are that it can be used by groups or individuals; it asks the user to be solution oriented during problem identification; and it is simple and easy to use and understand.

Two weaknesses, however, are associated with this method: (1) it does not, by design, force the user to prioritize processes or problems; and (2) it does not lend itself to comparison of multiple problems or processes.

The is/should method can be use separately by different individuals to compare perceptions of the current and desired states. In this way, the method can validate a common issue or confirm opposing viewpoints. Furthermore, this method enhances discussion, which may lead to agreement about performance standards for the desired state. The method itself does not inherently offer reliability or validity.

Focus Groups.   Focus groups are small discussion groups consisting of ten to twelve employees led by a facilitator. The purpose is to focus on a topic or idea and to take an in-depth look at the group's opinions regarding the topic. Focus groups offer valuable insights as to cause and often lead to recommendations for interventions. Ideally, a focus group should comprise no more than ten people, who represent a cross-section of the organization, and meet for no longer than one and one-half hours at a time. If possible, focus groups should be conducted on the organization's time, as participants will be more receptive if they are paid. In selecting participants, a random sample is recommended; placing peer groups together increases the probability of honesty, comfort, and disclosure.

To gain information from as many sources as possible, several focus groups should be used. Although a total representation of opinions is very difficult to achieve, the more diverse the groups, the more accurate overall analysis will be.

Focus groups can be a time-consuming and thus costly activity. The only other method providing this level of insight is the use of personal interviews, which are even more time-consuming and costly. Other feedback mechanisms such as questionnaires and observation answer the "what" but not the "why" questions that focus groups do.

Focus groups help HRD professionals explain the "what" and the "why" behind employees' opinions, ideas, and perspectives. They provide an interpersonal method for eliciting information through a collaborative process. Focus groups are useful for gathering information necessary in developing questionnaires for quantitative study. Finally, they provide easy, fairly reliable access to ideas and attitudes.

However, the focus group method also has several weaknesses. First, it relies on qualitative, not quantitative, information, which prevents HRD professionals from determining how widespread attitudes or opinions might be throughout the firm. Second, focus groups often lack statistically significant representation of the organization, regardless of how groups are assembled. Third, focus groups are very expensive because they require a great deal of time and effort to conduct and lead to losses in productivity due to the participation of group members. Fourth, some group participants may harbor fears of disclosing and providing honest responses regardless of the facilitator's skill level. Fifth, more persuasive participants may sway the group's opinions. Sixth, focus groups require a great deal of work, typically requiring 120 to 150 hours of typing, writing, editing, and analyzing the data collected.

Preplanning requires HRD professionals to identify a facilitator to conduct the focus group and to randomly select participants. HRD professionals must determine the focus group's purpose in order to isolate the problem that the focus group is intended to address. Focus groups require HRD professionals to create a general outline of the topic to be explored, project time commitment, and establish an agenda that includes participant roles, purposes, and processes for procedures. Finally, HRD professionals need to create the climate—arrange for a private room where the general outline will be introduced, the purpose explained, and participants told what will be done with the information gathered.

HRD professionals should be neutral during meetings. They must have the ability to ask questions that address specific needs, concerns, and opinions of participants. They may choose to educate group members on the particular topic prior to gathering individual or group responses and should ask participants to brainstorm solutions to specific situations and make corresponding recommendations for change. Critical incident analysis or individual interviews may be conducted in advance to provide information to be examined during the meeting.

During focus group meetings, participants are allocated roles (e.g., facilitator, recorder, or participant). Introducing each participant and reviewing the agenda (which includes participant roles and focus group purpose) begins the meeting. Process rules are then introduced, as well as the anticipated amount of time for meetings. Next, the focus group is facilitated through controlled dialogue and conflict while moving beyond the general to the specific. At the close of the meeting, HRD professionals review the gathered information and determine whether the group's purposes have been met, explaining the next steps and how the information will be used and thanking participants for their time and contributions. Finally, a follow-up report summarizes outcomes, and participants are sent a copy of the report along with a thank-you note expressing appreciation for the member's time, energy, and effort.

Critical Incident Analysis.   In order to make the transition from general organizational and performance problems to specific details, HRD professionals use critical incident analysis. A critical incident analysis (sometimes referred to as a significant incident report) records an example of extreme behavior or performance. Critical incident analysis examines specific events by detailing successful and unsuccessful performance and can be used to determine optimal and actual performance. To qualify as a critical incident, the event must involve performance that actually took place on the job, have a clear purpose and identifiable consequences, and have firsthand witnesses of the performance situation. Critical incident analysis can serve as a needs analysis in itself, but it is more significant when used as a part of another method such as an interview or focus group.

When HRD professionals want to identify details of a problem and its contributing factors, critical incident analysis is extremely useful and is beneficial in determining individuals' feelings and perceptions of a situation. The critical incident method is valuable when investigating the effectiveness of on-the-job performance and examining organizational effectiveness. The critical incident technique should not be used to study every job but seems most appropriate for analyzing jobs that are somewhat ambiguous, flexible, or where there are an undefined number of ways to achieve the same outcome. According to Gilley and Maycunich (1998a, 206), the critical incident method addresses the following questions:

1. What was done that led to effective job performance and/or organizational effectiveness?
2. What was done that detracted from effective job performance/organizational effectiveness or led to ineffective job performance/organizational effectiveness?
3. What, if done differently, would have been more effective?
4. What attitudes, values, abilities, knowledge, or skills (present or absent) seem to have led to success or failure?

When using the critical incident technique, HRD professionals ask a series of questions that allow individuals to feel comfortable enough to answer openly and honestly. Simultaneously, HRD professionals lead participants through a series of thoughts that ultimately lead to recommendations. Seven questions help HRD professionals move from general problem solving to specific details of performance analysis:

1. What occurred recently on the job that caused job dissatisfaction? (Direct the individual's attention)
2. What part of the job caused the most problems? (Focus on specific events)
3. How did this incident make you feel about your job? (Surface underlying feelings or perceptions)

4. What do you see as the cause of this problem? (Identify causes)
5. What could have been done to prevent this from occurring? (Pinpoint solutions)
6. What should be done to avoid a repeat of this incident? (Seek recommendations)
7. What did you discover that you can support? (Conclude with confirmation) (Gilley and Maycunich 1998a, 206)

The critical incident technique is an excellent tool to capture essential behaviors of jobs and tasks that allow a high degree of individuality. However, when this technique is used to capture elements of a very simple, highly repetitive, and procedurally limited job, results are somewhat disappointing.

Individual Interviews.   One-on-one interviews with employees, managers, and executives are another useful technique for gathering information. This method allows employees to share ideas, clarify misconceptions, and express their points of view. It is most appropriate when examining confidential problems or issues that people may feel uncomfortable discussing in a group. For example, managers and supervisors usually prefer to voice their opinions about the organization in a more private setting.

Interviews have several strengths. First, they reveal more than just verbal information, since they provide HRD professionals an opportunity to observe body language, gestures, and nonverbal behaviors. Such information may be more telling than an individual's verbalized ideas and opinions. Second, interviews are flexible. However, they should be developed around a well-designed structure or framework to maintain continuity from one individual to the next. Third, interviews are an excellent technique when soliciting opinions from subject matter experts who have a great deal to say about a particular organizational or performance problem. Fourth, interviews provide excellent opportunities for HRD professionals to build rapport and relationships with members of the organization, which can enhance HRD's image.

The principal weakness of interviews involves their unpredictability; interviewees may simply vent frustration, anger, or overall resentment of the organization. Obviously, HRD professionals cannot always control the information gathered or the meeting outcomes. Under such circumstances, interviewers should remain neutral, expressing no opinions as to whether the interviewee is correct in his/her ideas or beliefs. Finally, conducting interviews is an extremely difficult technique to master. The challenge to HRD professionals is to develop the skills necessary to solicit information while maintaining and building rapport with clients.

Gilley and Maycunich (1998a, 207–208) provide the following steps for conducting effective interviews:

1. Preparation for the interview.
   A. Identify the interview's purpose.
   B. Review the tasks of the interview.
   C. Develop the interview agenda.
   D. Schedule date(s).
2. Opening the interview.
   A. Make the participant feel comfortable.
   B. Explain your role as interviewer.
   C. Explain participant's role as interviewee.
   D. Discuss the interview's purpose and how information will be used.
3. Conducting the interview.
   A. Ask questions and record answers.
   B. Listen responsively to the interviewee's answers.
   C. Take notes on the interviewee's responses.
4. Conclude the interview.
   A. Give the interviewee an opportunity to ask questions.
   B. Discuss additional information.
   C. Thank the interviewee for his/her time, effort, and opinions.

Observation. Gathering data by watching one or more persons performing a series of tasks or exhibiting skills employs a technique known as observation. Observation is used when detailed information is necessary and when acquired skills need to be measured for accuracy and effectiveness. Observation can also be used to measure qualitative characteristics, but only when job activities are observable. To guarantee quality and accuracy, the observer and the person under observation should never interact during the activity. Familiarity with the task of a job being observed is essential in order to determine if performance meets existing standards.

When attempting to establish best practices, where subject matter experts or exemplary performers are observed, observation is an excellent technique. Additionally, HRD professionals can elect to use observation to determine gaps between actual and desired performance (rather than using is/should charts previously discussed).

Observations can be structured or unstructured. When the observation is guided through the use of checklists to determine whether the performance has been completed correctly, it is a structured observation. This activity isolates which tasks are performed correctly and which ones involve errors. Checklists contain a list of tasks along with explanations as to how each is to be performed.

Unstructured observations do not follow a predetermined checklist. HRD professionals simply record what they observe (including the steps the observee used in completing the task) along with detailed descriptions (such as general information about the performer and performance). It is critical that information be captured in exactly the form in which it is observed since it is an undocumented, unsubstantiated method of gathering data.

Observation is perhaps most useful when deciding or setting standards for job tasks. HRD professionals identify the person being watched and his/her corresponding job function, describing the procedures being studied in sufficient detail to allow persons with no knowledge of the activity to follow resulting instructions. Additionally, they outline the order in which subtasks are completed, listing any forms used to carry out the task, identifying decision points, and constructing decision trees showing any alternatives resulting from those decisions. HRD professionals determine the circumstances under which the task takes place and choose the best time for observation. Finally, they prepare a checklist, if one is to be used, and compare performance with existing standards.

Questionnaires. The thoughts, feelings, beliefs, experiences, and attitudes of employees, managers, and executives can be gathered through questionnaires. These are a concise, preplanned set of questions designed to yield specific information on a particular topic. Because they are designed to gather preliminary data, questionnaires should be used only after all other sources of information have been thoroughly researched, including the use of other analysis methodologies.

Questionnaires provide an effective means of obtaining information from a large group, as they can be used to sample large populations in diverse locations. As a result, they are very cost effective. Questionnaires are relatively time efficient, typically requiring less than twenty minutes to complete. They are also perceived as confidential, which is crucial when respondents desire anonymity.

Questionnaires are one of the most difficult analysis methodologies to design because they are very difficult to write in a clear, concise, neutral manner. Moreover, questionnaires are not particularly useful in determining intensity of feelings, even though Likert Scales (ranking scales) are often used. Another disadvantage of questionnaires is that questions are open to interpretation, potentially skewing outcomes and findings. Finally, questionnaires do not lend themselves to flexibility; therefore, HRD professionals must know exactly what they are looking for prior to designing the instrument.

Obtaining acceptable response rates is the major weakness of questionnaires. Improving response rates requires choosing the sample population carefully, keeping the questionnaire as brief as possible, and limiting the number of open-ended questions. The survey should ensure anonymity and provide an easy return method (a return envelope or instructions to return questionnaire to an easily accessible location).

According to Gilley and Coffern (1994, 38–39), an effective questionnaire has the following characteristics:

1. Deals with a specific topic—one that individuals in the sample recognize as important enough to allow for the time needed to complete the questionnaire. The significance should be clearly stated in the accompanying letter or on the questionnaire.
2. Is attractive in appearance—neatly and logically arranged and clearly printed.
3. Contains clear, complete directions and definitions of necessary terms.
4. Is objective—containing no leading questions that signal the desired response.
5. Is logical and flows from general to specific.
6. Is easy to tabulate and interpret.
7. Includes a cover letter explaining the questionnaire's purpose and response deadline.

When constructing a questionnaire, HRD professionals keep in mind several rules. First, they define or qualify terms that may be easily misunderstood or misinterpreted. Second, they eliminate descriptive adjectives and adverbs that contain no agreed-upon meaning, such as frequently, occasionally, or rarely. Third, HRD professionals avoid using double negatives, which may be confusing to the respondent. Fourth, they underline words to be emphasized. Fifth, they give an example or point of reference when asking for a ranking or rating. Sixth, HRD professionals avoid unwarranted assumptions and phrase questions so that they are appropriate for all respondents. Seventh, they design questions that give complete possibilities for comprehensive responses and provide for a systematic qualification of responses.

Writing an effective cover letter is perhaps the key to obtaining a high response. Cover letters communicate to respondents the purpose of the survey and persuasively request their cooperation. Confidentiality should be stressed as well as how the information will be used. It is important to identify high-ranking sponsors such as organizational executives or managers. Additionally, respondents should be guaranteed a copy of the study's results, which allows them to compare their own perspectives with that of others. This heightens their curiosity, interest, and participation. Cover letters request the immediate return of the questionnaire with a clearly stated completion date and express appreciation for respondents' time and cooperation.

Root-Cause Analysis.   When managers and executives do not fully understand the causes of problems, root-cause analysis is in order. Root-cause analysis is an excellent tool for identifying "hidden causes" of performance problems and organizational breakdowns. Failure to identify the root cause can result in wasted financial, material, and human resources. Moreover, root-cause analysis establishes a framework by which to identify the real cause of organizational and performance deficiencies.

Root-cause analysis uses brainstorming techniques to reveal all possible causes. This helps to eliminate preconceived or predetermined ideas about the problem. Thus, root-cause analysis is a bias-free technique, which helps organizations make significant improvements in their performance and efficiency.

Gilley and Maycunich (1998a, 212) identify several steps of root-cause analysis. They are as follows:

- Identify and agree on the definition(s) of the problem(s). For example, survey results and individual interviews indicate that employees feel there are no opportunities for promotion.
- Identify possible causes of the problem. Utilize brainstorming and cause/effect diagrams to surface ideas. Write down all ideas; later the group will discuss and eliminate as appropriate.
- Verify causes with data. Use existing data or, if needed, identify additional data necessary to help decide which are actual causes of the problem. If more information is needed, identify what it is and who will obtain it.
- Check your conclusions about causes. Do people with knowledge of the issue/processes agree with the conclusions? Do the conclusions make sense? Is additional information needed to support the results?

Following these simple steps, HRD professionals guide members of the organization through a process of determining the real reasons that problems exist within the firm. However, stand-alone root-cause analysis can be very unreliable; therefore, other analysis techniques should be used to support results.

Question 5: Once a problem has been isolated, how should HRD professionals ensure the successful implementation of performance improvement interventions or change initiatives?

HRD professionals often struggle with how to best proceed in the analysis phase of their practice. One way of determining the most appropriate way to proceed involves considering three critical principles of change: congruence, predisposition, and succession (Bowers and Franklin 1977).

- The *principle of congruence* implies that the analysis process must be selected, designed, and adjusted to fit the structure and function of the organization. Such requirements infer that the analysis must be tailored to better suit the organization.

- The *principle of predisposition* suggests that change is more likely to succeed at certain points within the organization. By identifying these *penetration* or *leverage points,* analysis is more likely to be successfully adopted and integrated into the organization, allowing the rest of the firm to benefit.
- The *principle of succession* means that change does not occur in a direct fashion, but rather indirectly. That is, some change will occur only after barriers and obstacles are removed from the organizational culture.

These three principles of change guide HRD professionals in drafting strategic approaches to organizational, management, and performance analysis. HRD professionals should incorporate all three principles simultaneously. An appropriate approach includes removing obstacles and barriers that prevent implementation of organizational performance analysis, identifying the penetration points where organizational performance analysis is most likely to succeed, and designing, developing, and implementing organizational performance analysis that fits the organization.

Certainly, most analysis activities are important; however, some are more so than others. Therefore, analysis activities must be prioritized. It is critical that HRD professionals understand the difference between analysis actions that produce limited results (e.g., learning needs) as opposed to those that enhance the organization's overall effectiveness (e.g., organizational analysis).

Models of Analysis

Selecting analysis models must be balanced by consideration of those deemed most urgent. Assessing urgency can be difficult as it is human nature to respond to individuals who create the most noise, have the loudest voices, and/or are in a position within the organization to command immediate attention (i.e., senior management). Limited human and material resources force HRD professionals to identify those analysis models that will have the greatest impact on organizational effectiveness, efficiency, and quality. These become an HRD professional's highest priority.

Needs Analysis

According to Watkins and Kaufman (1996) and Rothwell and Kazanas (1998), *needs analysis* is the process of determining the seriousness and importance of learning, performance, and organizational needs. In other words, needs assessment reveals what gaps exist, whereas needs analysis determines their importance, severity, and why they exist.

According to Foshay, Silber, and Westgaard (1986, 27), a needs analysis plan addresses seven key questions:

- What results are desired from the needs analysis? (Objectives)
- Whose needs will be assessed? (Target audience)
- What methods will be used to select a representative group of people from the target audience for participation in the needs analysis? (Sampling procedures)
- How will information be gathered? (Data collection methods)
- What instruments should be used during needs analysis, and how should they be used? What approvals or protocols are necessary for conducting needs analysis, and how will the instructional designer interact with members of the organization? (Specifications for instruments and protocols)
- How will the information collected during needs analysis be analyzed? (Methods of data analysis)
- How will needs be identified from the results of data collection and analysis? (Descriptions of how decisions will be made based on the data)

These vary in importance depending on project constraints and stakeholder expectations (Phillips and Holton 1995).

HRD professionals will find it helpful to use the following ten-step method to guide their needs analysis actions (Rothwell and Cookson 1997, 138-140):

1. Clarify the problem or need: distinguish learning needs from management needs. Rothwell and Cookson (1997) provide the following questions as a guide:
   - Who or what is the focal point for needs analysis?
   - What is known about the problem or need?
   - What is happening and what should be happening?
   - When did the problem or need first become apparent?
   - How has it changed over time, if at all?
   - How did the problem or need first become apparent?
   - Who is affected by the problem?
   - Where is the problem or need most keenly felt?
   - Why is the problem or need important?
   - Who are the stakeholders interested in solving the problem or meeting the need?
   - What accounts for their interest at this time?
   - How much is the problem or need costing the organization?
   - What benefits will result from solving the problem or meeting the need?

These questions guide HRD professionals' efforts as they determine the problems that can be solved by instruction and those that need management action.

2. Collect background information: discover as much as possible about the organization, its stakeholders, the problem, the need, and other issues relevant to the needs assessment effort.

3. Refine the problem or need: focus the needs analysis effort by examining problems that affect current performance instead of conducting a comprehensive needs analysis.

4. Formulate questions: decide exactly what questions need to be addressed by the needs analysis.

5. Construct the study design: clarify ways to control variables and clarify how outcomes will later be evaluated.

6. Specify how information about problems or needs will be collected: determine which data collection methods will be used, how, and in what combinations.

7. Specify how information about problems or needs will be analyzed: choose analytical methods.

8. Implement the needs analysis project: collect information about the problems or needs using the methods identified previously.

9. Evaluate the results, draw conclusions, and note issues for future interventions: analyze the results of data collection efforts, drawing conclusions and interpretations.

10. Present results to key stakeholders and establish an action plan for solving problems and meeting needs: establish agreement for subsequent steps to be taken, if warranted.

Contingency-Based Needs Analysis Model

Rothwell and Cookson (1997, 140) disagree that needs assessment must be conducted in a systematic, linear manner. They contend that HRD professionals can conduct needs analysis through a "collaborative approach, in which they would work on a team, committee, or task force with representatives of key stakeholder groups such as managers and targeted program participants." Their primary responsibility is to brief committee members on the process and assume a leadership role. Committee members are, however, actively and personally involved in each step.

Rothwell and Cookson maintain that HRD professionals should only facilitate the needs analysis process when key stakeholders are actively involved in the process. This is a nondirective approach in which HRD professionals consult with key stakeholders and assemble a project team that collectively possesses the abilities necessary to conduct the needs analysis. HRD professionals outline the problem or need and the steps of the needs analysis process itself. Team members are then given the responsibility to conduct the needs analysis (all ten steps). A leader is selected to oversee the process while the HRD professional serves as an expert resource on needs analysis. Finally, team members plan and execute the needs analysis project.

Performance Analysis Model

Performance analysis, sometimes called *front-end analysis*, distinguishes performance deficiencies from learning and organizational needs. It focuses on identifying the causes of performance breakdowns and the impact of the work environment, motivational factors, and managerial impact on employee productivity and performance. Performance analysis is critically important because organizations cannot afford to waste scarce resources on interventions that fail to solve performance problems. Rothwell (1996a) argues that HRD professionals lack the time to focus on learning activities when deficiencies do not stem from individual knowledge, skills or attitudes. Instead, they should use their performance consulting skills to guide the organization in management actions addressing the work environment or motivational factors.

Performance analysis diagnoses reveal the causes of a performance problem by examining why differences exist among performers, whether performance is acceptable or unacceptable, or below standard (Rothwell and Cookson 1997). It also helps determine whether jobs are designed correctly (performance alignment model, Chapter 11), the relationship between jobs (managing the white spaces model, Chapter 11), factors affecting performance (human performance system, Chapter 9), causal relationships (performance technology model, Chapter 9), and the impact of performance alignment, compensation, and developmental philosophy (performance alignment model, Chapter 11). In Chapter 11, we examined a performance consulting model (Robinson and Robinson 1996) that can be used to conduct performance audits and frame the performance consulting process.

Mager and Pipe (1984) described the most famous performance analysis model, in which they identified a series of questions useful when conducting performance analysis. This model answers questions about a performance problem, guiding decisions on appropriate solutions.(See Appendix F.)

First, *describe a performance discrepancy.* A performance discrepancy is the difference between actual and desired results. Determine the difference between what is being done and what is expected. Any discrepancy is cause for concern since accepted variations are rarely the basis for taking corrective actions. Discrepancies may surface as differences between actual and desired production outputs or in quality measures, revenue measures, or customer service measures. HRD professionals should also provide reliable evidence of the discrepancy.

Second, *determine the importance of the discrepancy.* What happens if we do nothing? Is it worth improving? If it is not important, then no further action is warranted, and managers, employees, and HRD professionals should turn their attention to more important discrepancies.

Third, *determine the cause of the discrepancy.* Does it result from a skill or knowledge deficiency by an individual (or group), or does it result from another deficiency? Could performers do the job if their lives depended on doing it correctly? Are present skills at least adequate? If it is caused by a skill or knowledge deficiency, HRD professionals should ask additional questions:

- *Were they able to perform successfully in the past?* If not, the problem may be solved by arranging formal (structured, planned) training. If the answer is yes, the discrepancy does not result from lack of knowledge or skill, and HRD professionals should continue diagnosing the problem.
- *Are employees used to performing often or are the needed skills or knowledge used frequently?* If the answer is no, the problem may be solved by arranging practice. If yes, the discrepancy is not caused by lack of practice. Therefore, HRD professionals need to determine exactly how employees learn how they are doing and whether they are getting regular feedback about their job performance. If workers are not receiving appropriate feedback, HRD professionals should arrange for it.

Once these questions have been addressed, additional questions may surface and should be asked about performance discrepancies that appear to result from a skill or knowledge deficiency:

- *Is there a simpler way to address the skill or knowledge deficiency?* Alternatives to consider may include changing the job (job redesign), arranging on-the-job training (OJT), or writing clearer job descriptions that contain specific performance standards, output requirements, and activities.
- *Does the performer have the potential to perform?* If the answer is no, action should be taken with the performer, such as termination or transfer to a job for which he or she is better qualified.

If the performance discrepancy is not caused by a skill or knowledge deficiency, the following four related questions are warranted:

1. *Is the desired performance being punished in some way?* Are employees somehow punished for performing correctly? If not, another cause should be considered; if so, the deficiency can usually be eliminated by removing the punishment.

2. *Is nonperformance rewarded or is there some pressure not to perform?* In other words, is there some reward for incorrect performance, does doing it wrong draw attention, or are employees somehow benefiting by not performing properly? If the answer is yes, arranging positive consequences can rectify the deficiency. In other words, "employees should be given appropriate incentives or rewards for performing as they are expected or desired to perform" (Rothwell 1996a, 41).

3. *Does doing the job correctly really matter?* Is there an unfavorable outcome for not doing well, and do performers understand what consequences result from their actions? If not, the problem may be corrected by articulating consequences or improving the feedback that performers receive regarding their performance results.

4. *Are there obstacles to performing?* An obstacle is anything that prevents people from performing their job adequately. If the answer to this question is yes, the obstacle needs to be removed. If the answer is no, the performance discrepancy may result from a different cause, such as lack of motivation or the inability to adhere to organizational policies and procedures. The following questions provide additional insight as to whether obstacles exist in the workplace: Do employees know *what* is expected? Do they know *when* it is expected? Are there too many competing demands? Are resources available to do the job?

Two final steps involve (1) *selecting the best solution(s)* and (2) *implementing the solution(s)*. By using these questions, HRD professionals can analyze nearly any performance problem facing their organization and identify one or more strategies to address performance problems (adapted from Mager and Pipe 1984).

Organizational Analysis

The most comprehensive and complex type of analysis attempts to identify the deficiencies between current and desired organizational results, which Gilley and Maycunich (1998a) refer to as organizational analysis. Kaufman, Rojas, and Mayer (1992) refer to organizational analysis as a macro-analysis due to its complexity and disruptive nature—one that all members of the organization are aware of, participate in, and are affected by.

Organizational analysis offers HRD professionals an excellent opportunity for creating and developing organizational development partnerships responsible for uncovering the root causes of organizational deficiencies. To do so, HRD professionals need to understand the nature of business and the organization. Additionally, they must focus the organizational analysis process at the correct level within the firm. Organizational analysis consists of eight discrete steps designed to identify why there is a discrepancy in organizational results (Figure 15.1).

FIGURE 15.1 Organizational Analysis

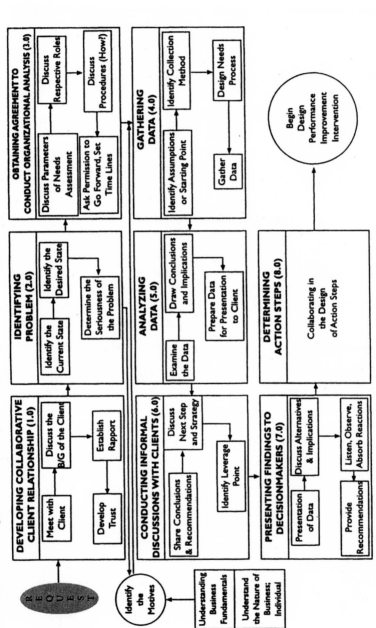

SOURCE: Reprinted, by permission from the publisher, from J. W. Gilley and A. Maycunich, *Strategically Integrated HRD: Partnering to Maximize Organizational Performance* (Cambridge, Mass.: Perseus Books, 1998a).

Developing Collaborative Client Relationships.   The first step in the organizational analysis process is developing positive working relationships with clients. Doing so initiates client partnerships, which is essential during the analysis process. HRD professionals engage in four activities to accomplish this, including meeting with the client, discussing the client's background, establishing rapport, and developing trust. At first glance these seem to be very straightforward, commonsense efforts; however, they are far more difficult to master than originally thought.

Identifying the Problem.   During organizational analysis, the is/should process is put into action, the most important part of which is determining the seriousness of the problem. Additionally, critical incident analysis and structured interviewing are other effective methods used in determining the size of the discrepancy and its intensity. Organizational analysis addresses discrepancies that directly impact business outcomes or results, whereas needs analysis typically focuses on identifying skill and knowledge deficiencies.

Demonstrating an Understanding of the Organization

HRD professionals must demonstrate their organizational understanding before being allowed to participate in organizational analysis projects. In some organizations, this includes working alongside assembly workers, riding in disposal trucks hauling trash, or participating in job exchange programs. In any case, invaluable insight is gained about the organization's operations and personnel functions. Additionally, HRD professionals need to be able to communicate effectively and efficiently with executives and stakeholders about problems important to them.

Gilley and Maycunich (1998a) contend that lack of credibility within organizations is the Achilles' heel of most HRD professionals. If HRD is to achieve the status equal to that of other operational divisions within the organization this problem must be remedied. Consequently, HRD professionals need to develop an understanding of operations, the decisionmaking process, and the relationships between and among jobs within the organization. Failure to actively improve one's organizational knowledge, and thus one's credibility, may produce catastrophic effects.

Identifying the Motives

Identifying the motives of organizational leaders and decisionmakers (clients) for organizational analysis must be completed prior to moving forward. Identifying the motives of individuals sponsoring the analysis helps to eliminate problems and difficulties later in the process. Furthermore, HRD professionals must guard against simply reacting to the requests of clients by considering whether the request will help the organization achieve its strategic business goals and objectives; this helps to isolate the motives of individual sponsors. In this way, the integrity of the process, the HRD program, and its professionals remains protected.

Obtaining Agreement to Conduct Organizational Analysis.   Unfortunately, far too many clients simply want to confirm that a problem exists rather than take the steps to eliminate it. Furthermore, closing the gap between current and desired results may be extremely painful, often requiring unpleasant decisions and actions. Consequently, clients may be reluctant to move forward. Thus, it is important to request permission from clients prior to moving forward. Although many HRD professionals assume that being asked to conduct an organizational analyses is permission enough to move forward, Gilley and Maycunich (1998a) believe that it is important to obtain permission because some clients are not fully aware of the consequences when they make analysis requests. Moreover, HRD professionals need to determine whether clients are really dedicated to solving problems or whether they are only interested in confirming that they exist.

Gathering Data.   During the data-gathering process, HRD professionals need to think strategically about how to gather data in an efficient and cost-effective manner. This includes designing a process that is objective and that guards against using favored analysis methods, which may not be appropriate. Biases should be addressed in the first part of the data gathering process, which is the identification of assumptions and starting points. Certain assumptions serve to focus analysis and offer direction as to how information is to be gathered.

Three additional steps remain during this part of the analysis process. First, HRD professionals must design a data-gathering framework, which includes defining the critical question to be addressed. This is sometimes referred to as the problem statement. Second, the design process incorporates relevant information and/or literature, which provide insight into the situation. Third, the procedures by which questions will be investigated require discussion, including the identification of samples and data collection methods. To ensure that the proper mix is selected, the relevance and appropriateness of each methodology should be discussed. Once the appropriate methodology is identified, the final step of this process is engaging in the collection of data.

Analyzing Data.   HRD professionals are concerned with examining the data gathered in step four and interpreting it for the purposes of drawing conclusions and identifying implications during this phase of the organizational analysis process. This seemingly straightforward process can be quite rigorous, as data is seldom obtained in an absolute, clean, and understandable form. If an adequate job has been done of gathering information and selecting analysis methodologies, analyzing data becomes a much simpler procedure. HRD professionals can prepare the data for presentation to clients once an interpretation has been completed.

Conducting Informal Discussions with Clients.   Gilley and Maycunich (1998a) suggest that it is never a good idea to present findings, conclusions, implications, or recommendations to clients in a formal setting because HRD professionals run the risk of catching clients off guard or sharing information that is perceived to be confidential. They contend that embarrassing interactions such as this can forever destroy an HRD professional's credibility with clients. Therefore, they suggest that informal meetings be arranged where such information can be shared. Of course, the information shared should be held in strictest confidence. Information that is perceived to be controversial or politically damaging can be eliminated from the final report and presentation. Additionally, informal meetings allow clients the opportunity to provide reactions before the findings and recommendations become official. They are also an excellent opportunity to integrate the insights, perceptions, and suggestions of clients regarding how data and/or recommendations should be presented.

Another purpose of informal meetings is to afford clients an opportunity to discuss strategies and identify potential leverage points with HRD professionals.

Presenting Findings to Decisionmakers.   Next, the findings, conclusions, implications, and recommendations are presented formally to the decisionmaking team responsible for implementing solutions. During this meeting, appropriate alternatives and implications can be discussed. At this point, HRD professionals should listen, observe, and absorb clients' reactions to the data collected, making certain that they have been heard during the final presentation. That is, clients must clearly hear and understand HRD professionals' recommendations. Review and reiteration of suggestions during a summary activity support a powerful conclusion.

Determining Action Steps.   Once findings, conclusions, implications, and recommendations have been thoroughly examined and discussed, attention must be turned collectively to formulating action steps. Action steps include the identification of performance improvement interventions, change management strategies, and change initiatives designed to help the organization achieve its business goals. Additionally, these interventions, strategies, and initiatives help the organization improve its performance capacity. Regardless of the solution selected, HRD professionals must help their clients design, develop, implement, transfer, and eventually evaluate each solution.

Impact Mapping

According to Brinkerhoff and Gill (1994, 73–74), impact mapping can be used to tie together the performance objectives, job results, business objectives and goals, and strategic goals of the organization. Although impact mapping was not originally designed to be an analysis framework, it is an excellent tool for conducting organizational analysis activities that link learning, performance, and change efforts to the organization's business goals. It consists of nine interdependent steps. First, HRD professionals should *specify business results* from each business function (department or unit). These should represent the final outputs generated by a business function. Second, they should *determine the relative order of goals and objectives* by creating a functional hierarchy such that the progression from unit and department goals to company-wide goals is clear to all. Brinkerhoff and Gill (1994, 73) contend that achieving less important goals creates a foundation for achieving the next goal while creating a stronger organization in the process.

Third, HRD professionals should *design input-output models for each job* by identifying and clarifying the specific and critical resources that are needed to achieve the desired outcomes of the job. Fourth, they should *link key inputs and results to a business operations sequence*, which requires that the functional dependencies among jobs be described. Fifth, HRD professionals should *clarify how several jobs result in a business outcome* by demonstrating how each job's output contributes to the aggregate of the organization's business results.

Sixth, HRD professionals should *identify each employee's performance objectives* by identifying the knowledge, skills, and attitudes required for each job. Seventh, they should *produce a draft map* by putting together the pieces of information from the tasks described above. Eighth, they should *review the draft map with stakeholders* from all levels of the organization. Ninth, they should *repeat steps seven and eight if necessary. (See Appendix G for sample)*

Conclusion

Identifying organizational and performance needs is a complex and difficult process requiring HRD professionals to think strategically about their clients' requests, develop support for the analysis process, and overcome analysis paralysis within the organization. Five critical questions must be answered as they prepare to participate in this credibility-enhancing activity. Finally, HRD professionals prepare themselves to conduct organizational, management, performance and learning analysis when appropriate. It is fundamentally important that HRD professionals develop the skills and abilities to expertly, efficiently perform each of these types of analyses, as well as determine when each is appropriate.

Holton (1995, 10–11) identified several recommendations that may help HRD professionals become excellent analysts. They include learning all the methodologies, becoming skilled at qualitative methods, adopting strategic assessment techniques, using multiple methods to collect data, assessing on multiple levels (preferably three levels: organizational, process, and performer), and thinking performance analysis, not just learning needs assessment.

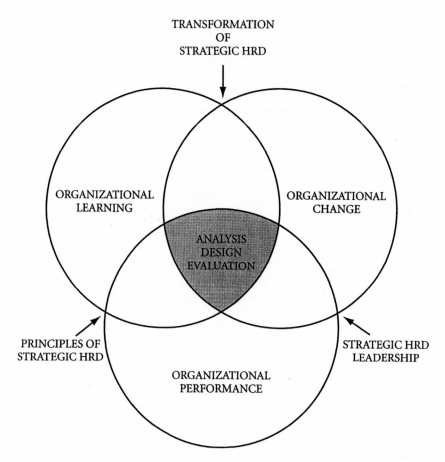

TRANSFORMATION
OF
STRATEGIC HRD

ORGANIZATIONAL
LEARNING

ORGANIZATIONAL
CHANGE

ANALYSIS
DESIGN
EVALUATION

PRINCIPLES OF
STRATEGIC HRD

STRATEGIC HRD
LEADERSHIP

ORGANIZATIONAL
PERFORMANCE

ORGANIZATIONAL LEARNING, PERFORMANCE, AND CHANGE

Designing Learning and Performance Improvement Interventions and Change Initiatives

The design process incorporates a systematic approach to identifying and solving performance problems, suggest Rothwell and Kazanas (1998, 3), including learning and nonlearning interventions and initiatives. Nonlearning activities include developing job aids, conducting strategic planning activities, building and implementing performance management systems, redesigning the organizational structure, redesigning motivational systems, redesigning jobs, creating competency-based employee selection methods, reengineering feedback systems, and identifying, implementing, and managing change management projects. All of these interventions and initiatives incorporate use of the design process.

Design Principles and the Role of the Designer

Spitzer (1992, 116–122) identified several critical design principles useful in linking problems and their respective solutions. Design principles guide HRD professionals, allowing them to increase their probability of success. These principles should be used to direct the design of all interventions and initiatives regardless of their intent. Interventions and initiatives should be based on a comprehensive understanding of the situation, including the organizational context and the causes of a performance problem. They should be carefully targeted in order to have the greatest impact within the organization.

An intervention or initiative requires a sponsor who has something to gain as a result of its success. Interventions/initiatives should be designed with a team approach to inspire employee involvement, appropriate representations, and support throughout the organization. Intervention/initiative design should be sensitive to cost and based on comprehensive, prioritized employee needs and expectations. Effective designers investigate cost-effective solution alternatives. Well-planned interventions/initiatives emphasize long-term effectiveness, are sustainable over time, and have a lasting effect on the organization. They should be designed with development and implementation in mind and with an iterative approach utilizing formative evaluation techniques to continuously improve their outcomes.

The role of the designer is often the most misunderstood of the fundamental roles in HRD. It is easily overlooked when compared with more visible roles such as performance consultant or organizational development change agent. In many organizations, the same individual who facilitates learning interventions does intervention and initiative design; therefore, it is viewed by many as a part of organizational learning. The designer role drives the design, development, and evaluation of learning and performance interventions and change initiatives used to improve organizational performance, effectiveness, and profitability.

Brinkerhoff (1998, 161–162) offers the following questions to guide HRD professionals in designing learning and performance improvement interventions and change initiatives:

- Have correct and sufficient performance improvement methods, tools, and other support aids been identified?
- How likely is it that the organization will provide the necessary methods, tools, and other support aids?
- To what extent do senior and mid-level managers agree to and support the targeted performance improvement objectives?
- To what extent do performers themselves agree with the targeted performance improvement objectives?
- How likely is it that the support of key persons (as identified in tertiary analysis) will be provided as needed?
- How politically and economically feasible is the performance improvement plan?
- Is the performance improvement plan the most cost-effective alternative for achieving the needed performance improvement and business impact?
- Is there sufficient senior and mid-level management support to enhance learning acquisition?

Simonsen (1997, 233) identified several questions for determining design:

- Who are your customers (target population)?

- If your target population is varied, such as both professional and production employees, will one intervention/initiative work for all or will variations be required?
- Will a pilot program or group be useful? If so, how will group members be chosen?
- Will budget constraints, staff availability, or time constraints create a need to roll out in phases, or will you plan for full-scale implementation?
- How will you link and build on existing resources and systems?
- What kind of accountability will there be?
- How will participants be rewarded or acknowledged for changing their behavior and accepting the challenge of managing their careers strategically?
- How will you measure success?
- What baseline data is needed now for comparison after implementation?
- Who will pay for participation?
- Will employee participation be on their time, company time, or some combination of both?
- Who will be involved in the further design?

Intervention Design Models

HRD professionals can choose from several design models to create learning and performance improvement interventions and change initiatives. We examine four: Learning Acquisition and Transfer Model; ADDIE Model; Critical Events Model; and the Instructional Systems Design Model developed by the International Board of Standards for Training, Performance, and Instruction (IBSTPI).

Learning Acquisition and Transfer Model

According to Gilley, Boughton, and Maycunich (1999, 133), the learning acquisition and transfer process begins by identifying employees' current performance baselines. This is achieved by comparing their performance with standards to isolate performance gaps. These become an employee's "performance benchmark," revealing areas requiring performance improvement.

Next, managers and employees isolate competency areas critical to the successful execution of organizational initiatives and determine employees' areas of strength and weakness. These become the focus of employee learning acquisition plans. Thus, employees acquire and transfer learning that helps them to overcome performance gaps or to capitalize on strengths. Once performance baselines and areas of focus (strengths or weaknesses) have been identified, employees should answer the following questions:

- What do I need to learn or do differently to improve my performance?
- What resources (human and material) are needed to achieve my performance objectives?
- When will I complete my learning acquisition plan?
- How will I apply what I have learned on the job?
- How will I know when I have successfully achieved my performance objectives?
- What criteria or means will I use to validate measurement indicators?
- How will I celebrate my new learning, increased skills, or improved attitudes?
- What rewards and recognition are appropriate?

The answers to these questions guide employees in the successful design of learning acquisition and transfer plans. Let's consider each in greater detail.

First, employees must identify what they intend to learn, which helps them translate identified performance needs into performance objectives. According to Gilley and Maycunich (1998a, 251), "a well-written performance objective should be clear and understandable, identify what the employee will learn, describe the observable behavior that will demonstrate that learning occurred, identify the acceptable level of performance for the learned behavior, describe the conditions under which performance will be measured, and be stated in such a way that the degree to which it is accomplished can be estimated or measured."

Second, employees need to identify resources they will use to achieve their performance objectives. These include human resources such as peers and superiors as well as material resources including books, journal articles, handouts, newspapers, suggested readings, videotapes, cassette tapes, and the like.

Third, employees determine the date by which each performance objective will be completed. This provides employees with planning parameters that force appropriate time management techniques. Fourth, employees identify how they will implement learning on the job. Strategizing the precise application forces review and understanding of current job processes and planning of implementation methodologies.

Fifth, employees need to identify learning measurement to ensure that they have achieved their performance objectives. Measuring performance improvement requires employees to clearly identify indicators of accomplishment—the criteria and means of validating success. Gilley, Boughton, and Maycunich (1999) point out that this process involves gathering performance improvement data, comparing this data with performance standards, contrasting performance improvement data with performance baselines, and determining the amount and degree of improvement. They provide the following questions as a way of helping HRD professionals, managers, and employees identify indicators of accomplishment (1999, 264):

- How will employees know when they have successfully achieved their performance objectives?
- Who will employees rely on to determine that they have successfully completed their performance objectives?
- What evidence will employees use to judge that they have successfully completed their performance objectives?
- How will employees measure what has been learned or what they are able to do differently?
- How will employees measure the performance produced by their new knowledge, skills, or behavior?

Sixth, as a way of illustrating growth and development, employees gather performance data and compare it to performance standards and their baselines. This reveals the amount and degree of employee improvement and whether individual performance objectives have been achieved.

Finally, employees should be rewarded and recognized for continuous development, and their successes celebrated as further encouragement. One of the principal outcomes of learning acquisition and transfer plans is that organizations create an environment where development is perceived as an important ingredient to organizational success.

ADDIE Model

One of the most common design models is ADDIE. According to Carnevale, Gainer, and Villet (1990, 30), the ADDIE model consists of five stages: Analysis of learning needs, Design of learning programs, Development of learning materials, Implementation (delivery), and Evaluation (Figure 16.1).

Analysis Phase. During the analysis phase of the ADDIE model, HRD professionals "distinguish instructional needs from non-instructional needs, thus distinguishing performance gaps that would be appropriately addressed through instruction from gaps more appropriately addressed through management action" (Rothwell and Cookson 1997, 196). HRD professionals examine the organizational environment, potential participants, and occupational demands and expectations that will impact the application of learning. Once learning needs are identified, they are examined in greater depth through need analysis (see Chapter 15).

The analysis of needs allows HRD professionals to determine the performance required after instruction has occurred. Additionally, performance requirements focus instructional requirements.

FIGURE 16.1   The ADDIE Model

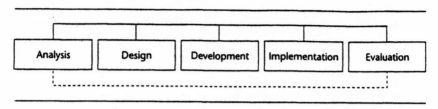

Design Phase.   During the design phase, HRD professionals determine how to meet a learning need or solve a performance problem. One of the important elements of the design phase is the identification of course content, which becomes a critical input in the learning process. As a result, learning activities, materials specifications, and instructional strategies can be identified.

Performance objectives are also identified during this phase. They define the desired outcomes of the intervention, selection of strategies and methods of instruction and facilitation, criteria for development, and criteria for evaluation.

Development Phase.   During the development phase, HRD professionals translate instructional design information and content into instructional materials to be implemented. Important outputs of the development phase include lesson plans, instructional strategies and media, and learner materials. During this phase, the testing and validation of media, material, and instruction should be accomplished.

Implementation Phase.   Implementation is commonly thought to be an HRD professional's primary responsibility. Managers should assume a lion's share of this responsibility because they are ultimately responsible for employee growth and development. Indeed, managers are held accountable for their employees' performance and productivity; therefore, they should also be responsible for their employees acquiring the skills, knowledge, and attitudes to perform their jobs.

HRD professionals facilitate implementation of learning and performance improvement interventions by training managers as instructors and facilitators. They also design and develop interventions since the design process is highly technical and time consuming.

Evaluation Phase.   Rothwell and Cookson (1997) contend that evaluation is a thread running throughout all phases of the ADDIE model. Therefore, evaluation should not be viewed as a linear, summative process in which each phase follows the previous phase in order, ending in evaluation. Rather, evaluation is cyclical and linked to every phase to ensure accountability and quality (see Chapter 17).

Nadler's Critical Events Model

Nadler and Nadler (1994) developed a nine-step design model, which they refer to as the Critical Events Model. (Appendix H.)

Identify Organizational Needs.   Nadler and Nadler's (1994) model begins by identifying organizational needs. Three important questions help HRD professionals determine whether intervention design is appropriate: (1) Do performance problems exist? (2) Can the causes of performance problems be distinguished from their symptoms? (3) Are the causes of performance problems traceable to deficiencies of knowledge, skill, or attitude, or deficiencies of management, or a combination of the two?

Answers to these questions indicate when "symptoms are indistinguishable from causes or when problems stem from management rather than performer deficiencies" (Rothwell and Cookson 1997, 29). Performance problems traceable to these deficiencies should be solved by management action, whereas those linked to deficiencies of performer knowledge and skill should be solved by planned learning experiences. Conversely, learning interventions designed and delivered to address problems caused by management deficiencies only compound the performance shortfall and waste scarce resources. Thus, HRD professionals' first responsibility is to determine the types of deficiencies that exist and then identify their origin and respond accordingly.

Specify Job Performance.   Nadler and Nadler (1994) suggest that HRD professionals should undertake at least one form of job analysis to obtain information about job-related performance. They identify three forms of job analysis: task analysis based on observation, simulation, and interview.

Identify Learner Needs.   Identifying learner needs reveals who will participate in the program; where they are located; their experience, education, and training; their job requirements and responsibilities; their cultural and language proficiencies; their levels of motivation to learn; and their physical and mental characteristics (Nadler and Wiggs 1986). HRD professionals compare actual to desired levels of learner knowledge, skills, and attitudes in order to distinguish deficiencies that are important and critical from those that are not (Nadler and Nadler 1994).

Determine Objectives.   Deficiencies frame the type of objectives needed. Nadler and Nadler (1994) identified three types: (1) general *program objectives* clarify the purpose to be served by designing and delivering a planned learning experience; (2) general *instructional objectives* guide the program planning process by focusing on the results to be achieved; (3) *learner objectives* clarify (a) tasks to be achieved that are stated as observable actions, (b) conditions in which learners are to demonstrate successful performance, and (c) standards to indicate how acceptable performance will be assessed in terms of quantity, quality, cost, or time.

Build the Curriculum.   According to Rothwell and Cookson (1997, 32),

> planned learning can be sequenced in several different ways, such as in psychological order, job-related (procedural) order, logical order, or problem-oriented or issue-oriented order. If learning is organized in *psychological order,* the content is sequenced to facilitate learning from past to present, simple to complex, known to unknown, concrete to abstract, practical to theoretical, or present to future. Learning organized in *job-related order* presents the content to learners in the same way in which work tasks or decisions are performed on the job. *Logical order* sequences content in building blocks, perhaps based on limited assumptions about what learners already know. If instruction is organized in a *problem-oriented* or *issue-oriented order,* the content is usually described inductively, that is, beginning with a practical problem so that learners can discover the problem's solution.

Select Instructional Strategies.   Having identified what is to be learned, HRD professionals then decide which learning process is most appropriate and select instructional methods and materials useful in achieving objectives. Selecting these methods and materials requires consideration of the following: learning or performance objectives; content, instructors, and targeted learners; facilities and equipment; time available for instruction and practice; and costs of learning interventions in terms of opportunity costs (lost productivity for participants) and actual cost.

Obtain Instructional Resources.   Once HRD professionals have developed the learning plan, sequenced content, and chosen methods and materials, they are ready to obtain the resources necessary to deliver planned learning experiences.

Conduct Training.   The next step of the Critical Events Model is conducting training. Although a rather straightforward activity, learning plans remain flexible to be responsive to contingencies. Achieving skills, knowledge, and attitudes required to overcome learning and performance deficiencies should be the primary purpose of the learning event.

Conduct Evaluation.   Typically, the final step in a design model is conducting an evaluation. However, Nadler and Nadler (1994) believe that evaluation is a continuous, iterative process that is used to improve each step of the design process (see Appendix H). Thus, evaluation is formative as a feedback mechanism for HRD professionals.

Instructional Systems Design Model (IBSTPI)

Foshay, Silber, and Westgaard (1986) identified a comprehensive design model applicable for learning and performance improvement interventions as well as change initiatives. Their instructional design model has become the basis by which instructional design standards have been developed. It is perhaps the most complete design framework in the field of HRD, and it consists of ten phases.

Conducting a Needs Assessment. The first step in the Instructional Systems Design (ISD) model is conducting a needs assessment. According to Rothwell and Kazanas (1998, 54), the "purpose of needs assessment is to uncover, more precisely than performance analysis does, what the performance problem is, who it affects, how it affects them, and what results are to be achieved by learning and performance improvement interventions." Needs assessment is crucial because the entire ISD model depends on its results (Rothwell and Sredl 1992). However, Rossett (1990) stresses that several obstacles must be overcome to effectively perform needs assessment. First, many senior managers perceive that HRD professionals are self-interested parties in the needs assessment process who stand to benefit from the results (Bengtson 1994). Second, needs assessment sometimes requires too much time, especially in an era of dynamic change (Lewis and Bjorkquist 1992). Third, some managers believe that HRD professionals lack in-depth technical knowledge of specific jobs, which hinders their ability to adequately perform needs assessment (Bengtson 1994).

Assessing Relevant Characteristics of Adult Learners. In assessing characteristics of adult learners, Rothwell and Cookson (1997, 116–117) identified five that are important to the design of interventions and initiatives:

- Physical characteristics—the physical, mental, learning, or emotional states of employees.
- Backgrounds—the education, skills, knowledge, and experiences of employees.
- Work habits—the way employees go about doing their jobs.
- Attitudes—the beliefs, feelings, and perceptions of employees.
- Interests—the way employees prefer to spend their time, sometimes referred to as their passions or strengths.

Analyzing the Characteristics of a Work Setting. Rothwell and Kazanas (1998, 103) report that HRD professionals need to "assess the appropriateness of the setting for what is to be accomplished, and make appropriate changes to provide a better fit between themselves and the setting." This refers to the work setting, which is the place were work occurs and interactions between employees happen. It is where work conditions, reporting relationships, culture, structure, mission, strategy, policy and procedures, and leadership interact for the purpose of achieving an organization's goals and objectives.

Dubois and Rothwell (1996) and Watkins and Marsick (1993) emphasize the importance of the setting in which people apply what they learn. They argue that ignoring the environment when applying new knowledge is a recipe for failure. In order for HRD professionals, acting as change agents, and managers to have the ability to use or change the environment they must possess *environmental competence* (Steele 1973, 8). According to Rothwell and Kazanas (1998, 102), this is the "ability to be aware of one's environment and its impact."

When HRD professionals ignore the environment in which learning will be designed, delivered, and subsequently applied, they experience resistance from managers and employees. This is because learning may be inappropriate or poorly matched with everyday work conditions and specialized technology.

Performing Job, Task, and Content Analysis. The "process of gathering detailed information about the work that people do in organizations is called *work analysis* . . . and encompasses three different kinds of investigation—*job analysis, task analysis,* and *content analysis,*" state Rothwell and Kazanas (1998, 116). In combination, these are the most technical activities HRD professionals perform during the design process. Because work analysis is expensive and time consuming, a performance analysis should be conducted first. In this way, performance problems are identified that can be further examined through needs analysis activities. Once isolated and deemed serious, learning and performance improvement interventions can be designed to address them.

Rothwell and Kazanas (1998, 116) point out the "work analysis takes up where needs assessment leaves off" because it is the basis for developing performance objectives as well as the foundations for the design process. They also remind us that work analysis is the last of the analysis activities carried out before performance objectives are written and instructional materials are developed.

Job Analysis

Denis (1992) defines *job analysis* as a systematic examination of what people do, how they do it, and what results are achieved. Job analysis is simply a collection of related activities, duties, or responsibilities used in achieving specific outputs and business results. It is a prerequisite for more detailed task or content analysis. When job descriptions are nonexistent, outdated, inconsistent with information desired by decisionmakers, or inadequate for guiding more detailed task analysis, job analysis should be conducted. Clifford (1994) suggests that job analysis helps formulate accurate job descriptions.

Rothwell and Kazanas (1998, 118–119) report that job analysis identifies what people do, which provides information for selecting, appraising, compensating, developing, growing, and disciplining employees. Werther and Davis (1996, 117) maintain that job analysis helps evaluate how environmental challenges affect individual jobs and eliminates unneeded job requirements that can cause discrimination in employment. Additionally, job analysis reveals job elements that help or hinder quality of work life, plans for future human resource requirements, and matches job applicants with job openings. Job analysis also helps to determine learning needs for new and experienced employees, to create plans to develop employee potential, and to set realistic performance standards. Finally, job analysis aids employee placement in jobs that use their skills effectively and compensate them fairly.

Job analysis reveals the activities employees should be held accountable for doing or achieving and how employee work activities contribute to achieving organizational objectives. It also uncovers barriers to performance, enabling these to be addressed by management.

When conducting a job analysis, Rothwell and Kazanas (1998, 120–124) believe that HRD professionals should engage in the following steps:

1. Identify the jobs to be analyzed.
2. Clarify results desired from the analysis.
3. Prepare a plan that answers these questions:
   - Who will conduct the job analysis?
   - What is the purpose of the analysis?
   - How will results be used?
   - What sources or methods will be used to collect and analyze job information?
4. Implement the job analysis plan.
5. Analyze and use results of the job analysis.

Task Analysis

Rothwell and Kazanas (1998, 125) define *task analysis* as an "intensive examination of how people perform work activities," determining exactly what workers do, how, and why. They continue by identifying several purposes of task analysis: (1) to determine components of competent performance; (2) to identify activities that may be simplified or otherwise improved; (3) to isolate precisely what a worker must know, do, or feel to learn a specific work activity; (4) to clarify conditions (equipment and other resources) needed for competent performance; and

(5) to establish minimum expectations (standards) for how job incumbents should perform each task appearing in their job descriptions (125). Task analysis is not limited to any single method or technique.

Content Analysis

Content analysis is defined as "the process of breaking large bodies of subject matter or tasks into smaller and instructionally useful units" (Gibbons 1977, 2). Rothwell and Kazanas (1998, 133) state that "content analysis . . . differs from job or task analysis because it stems from an examination of information or knowledge requirements rather than from sequences or procedures in conducting work activities or achieving work results." It is intended to identify and isolate single idea or skill units for instruction and provide guidance to sequence topics in instruction (133).

As reported by Rothwell and Kazanas (1998, 134), content analysis is important because it is a "process of identifying the essential information that learners should translate into work-related knowledge, skills, and attitudes through planned instructional experiences." HRD professionals are responsible for organizing and translating information discovered during content analysis into meaningful learning exercises.

HRD professionals should apply the following steps to perform a content analysis, according to Swanson and Gradous (1986):

1. Identify the subject or topic.
2. Investigate what experienced performers know about the topic.
3. Investigate how people perform the mental (covert) activity by
   - Asking them.
   - Observing the results of work activity.
   - Using other methods.
4. Conduct a literature search on the topic.
5. Synthesize results using any one of several methods to develop a model of the subject.
6. Describe the subject or content.

Writing Performance Objectives. Regardless of its type and length, every intervention/initiative has a set of desired outcomes that indicate what the learner should be able to know or do as a result of the program. These outcomes are known as performance objectives. Rothwell and Kazanas (1998, 151) contend that performance objectives "guide remaining steps in the design process by describing precisely what the participant should know, do, or feel on completion of a planned learning experience."

Performance objectives are statements focused on what should result from instruction. They provide a standard by which HRD professionals and managers guide and direct learners, and they serve as the goals for learners, helping them monitor their own progress. Performance objectives should guide the process of selecting instructional methods and media and provide criteria for the evaluation of learning.

Writing performance objectives is challenging, as so many commonly used words and phrases are open to misinterpretation. Objectives such as "to understand," "to appreciate," and "to believe" are difficult if not impossible to measure. Gilley and Eggland (1989) assert that the best way to communicate objectives like these is to describe the learner's desired behavior using action words and terms that are specific enough to preclude individual misinterpretations. They believe that well-written performance objectives describe or imply the behavior that should be observed and verified as a result of learning. In order for this to happen, performance objectives should contain three components: (1) identification of the desired performance or learning, (2) the conditions or circumstances under which the task must be performed or the learning duplicated, and (3) the minimal level of performance or knowledge (standard) required.

Performance objectives are useful because they describe precisely what learners are expected to know, do, or feel upon program completion (Rothwell and Cookson (1997, 157). They establish evaluation criteria to measure and distinguish adequate from inadequate participant performance and focus individuals on desired program results so they can organize their own efforts and activities. Moreover, performance objectives reduce participant anxiety and frustration by clarifying desired program outcomes.

Performance objectives permit instructors to identify participants who lack necessary prerequisite abilities and help participants determine how well they have achieved mastery of the subject. They ensure consistency and agreement between what is learned and what is evaluated, help instructors appropriately sequence planned learning activities, and supply evidence of systematic planning to support participant learning. Finally, performance objectives provide a basis for instructor accountability and responsibility while helping program planners during the design stage (Rothwell and Cookson 1997, 157).

Developing Performance Measurement. Immediately following the preparation of performance objectives, HRD professionals should create *performance measurements,* which are ways of monitoring learner achievement. These include observations on the job, simulations, paper-and-pencil tests, and interviews.

Performance measurements guide the preparation of interventions and initiatives. Rothwell and Kazanas (1998) believe performance measurement provides a basis for learner accountability, ensuring learner progress toward predetermined performance goals that can be monitored during and after instruction. Brown (1995) and Brinkerhoff and Gill (1994) report that performance measurements allow linkage of learner achievements to organizational strategic plans.

Rothwell and Kazanas (1998, 173) believe that HRD professionals should be able to answer two basic questions before they prepare instructional materials: (1) What should be measured? (2) How should it be measured? Determining the purpose of measurement and focusing on appropriate methods of measuring instruction will answer the first question. Next, they should be able to design and develop appropriate instruments to achieve the intended purpose.

Sequencing Performance Objectives. Effective instruction should be sequenced so that learners will be systematically introduced to work activities in ways appropriate to the performance objectives as well as the situations or conditions in which they must learn. Sequencing performance objectives provides a logical framework for an intervention or initiative. In this way, participants are given a clear understanding of the focus, direction, and importance of learning and change. Sequencing performance objectives helps the facilitator manage various learning activities to meet the needs of learners and satisfy program demands.

Some methods of sequencing instruction are simply more appropriate than others, depending on the performance objectives, learners, and the learning environment. Rothwell and Kazanas (1998) identified nine approaches to sequencing performance objectives:

- Chronological sequencing: Content is arranged by time sequence with the presentation of later events preceded by discussion of earlier ones.
- Topical sequencing: Learners are immediately immersed in the middle of a topical problem or issue.
- Whole-to-part sequencing: Learners are first presented with a complete model or a description of the full complexities of a physical object or work duty. Instruction is then organized around parts of the whole.
- Part-to-whole sequencing: Learners are introduced to each part of a larger object, abstraction, or work duty.
- Known-to-unknown sequencing: Learners are introduced to what they already know and are gradually led into what they do not know.
- Unknown-to-known sequencing: Learners are *deliberately* disoriented at the outset of instruction.
- Step-by-step sequencing: Learners are gradually introduced to a task or work duty.
- Part-to-part-to-part sequencing: Learners are treated to a relatively shallow introduction to a topic, move on to another topic that is also treated superficially, move on to yet another topic that is treated superficially, eventually returning to the original topic for more in-depth exposure, and so on.

- General-to-specific sequencing: Learners are introduced to the "big picture," then led through discussion of specific topics.

Specifying Instructional Strategies. An *instructional strategy,* in the simplest sense, involves *what will be taught* and *how it will be taught.* Rothwell and Kazanas (1998, 210) state that an instructional strategy consists of "decisions that result in a plan, method, or series of activities aimed at obtaining a specific goal." Therefore, it is a plan for systematically exposing learners to experiences that will help them acquire knowledge, skills, or new attitudes. They contend that an instructional strategy should be based on work analysis (job, task, and content analysis) and linked to the performance objectives established to achieve desired results.

Dick and Carey (1990, 175–176) suggest that once an instructional strategy has been devised, HRD professionals develop instructional materials, establish a set of criteria to evaluate and revise existing materials, and create a framework guiding facilitation, interactive group exercises, and transfer of learning activities. Foshay, Silber, and Westgaard (1986, 65) report that an instructional strategy should determine (1) the methods, materials, devices, settings, and people needed to transmit the instructional message, (2) the media to be used, (3) the physical location in which learners will receive instruction, and (4) the methods of integrating these elements.

Additionally, HRD professionals need to consider how various instructional events and lessons should be structured, sequenced, and timed. The following questions can help during this process:

- How much time is required to accomplish performance objectives?
- How much time is required for instructional presentations, application, practice, and review, respectively?
- How many performance objectives can be covered in each instructional period?
- How many aspects of a topic can be grouped for practice? (Gilley and Eggland 1989, 225)

Quite simply, an instructional strategy allows HRD professionals to conceptualize the instructional process, enabling them to match instructional methods with performance objectives. HRD professionals can select from several different instructional methods to convey their message to learners:

- Lectures: one-way communication of a series of facts or information about a particular subject
- Buzz groups: a large group discussion allowing questions and feedback

- Role play: learners create situations and assume the role of one or more individuals
- Case studies: presentation, either written or verbal, of an incident that did or could have happened
- Games: simulations made competitive
- Demonstrations: a show-and-tell technique used to illustrate a point or feature
- Nominal group techniques: problem-solving group techniques designed to encourage participation
- Brainstorming: technique used to elicit as many ideas and responses as possible regarding a problem
- Question-and-answer sessions: learners obtain needed and vital information through inquiry
- Simulations: a dramatic representation of reality combining case studies and role playing (Gilley and Eggland 1989, 225)

Designing Instructional Materials.   The steps in the ISD process culminate in instructional materials that assist learners in achieving desired performance objectives. According to Rothwell and Kazanas (1998, 234), HRD professionals should take several steps to select, modify, or design instructional materials: (1) prepare a working outline, (2) conduct research, (3) examine existing instructional materials, (4) arrange or modify existing materials, (5) prepare tailor-made instructional materials, and (6) select or prepare learning activities.

Evaluating Instruction.   Successful interventions and initiatives meet specific performance objectives and measure the effectiveness of facilitators (managers) and the competencies of HRD professionals. Evaluation determines the impact of learning on individuals and whether changes in behavior have occurred. Finally, evaluation measures the overall impact of learning on the organization and its employees in order to determine its benefits.

The primary reason for evaluation is to assess whether the intervention or initiative accomplished its assigned objectives. As Gilley and Eggland (1989, 229) ask, "Did the intervention or initiative help participants develop adequate knowledge, skills, and attitudes used to improve their performance or to implement appropriate organizational changes?" They believe that another reason for evaluating interventions involves isolating their strengths and weaknesses. Each intervention/initiative should be evaluated to determine the effectiveness of the design, the designer's competence, the quality of implementation, the effective use of project controls, the cost-to-benefit ratio, and the impact on organizational effectiveness.

Conclusion

Designing learning and performance improvement interventions and change initiatives is an important activity. Well-designed interventions and initiatives follow proven models that address specific individual and organizational needs, frame achievable objectives, specify job performance, utilize appropriate instructional methods, measure performance, and effectively evaluate their results.

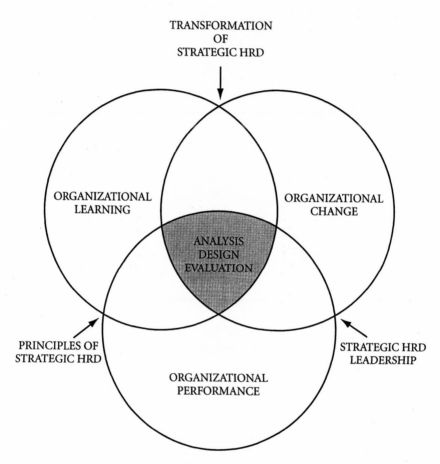

TRANSFORMATION
OF
STRATEGIC HRD

ORGANIZATIONAL
LEARNING

ORGANIZATIONAL
CHANGE

ANALYSIS
DESIGN
EVALUATION

PRINCIPLES OF
STRATEGIC HRD

STRATEGIC HRD
LEADERSHIP

ORGANIZATIONAL
PERFORMANCE

ORGANIZATIONAL LEARNING, PERFORMANCE, AND CHANGE

CHAPTER 17

Evaluation in Organizational Learning, Performance, and Change

*E*valuation is the process of estimating value of a planned learning experience, report Rothwell and Cookson (1997). They maintain that evaluation involves two steps: (1) comparing results and objectives, and (2) appraising or judging the value of the differences assessed. In many respects, evaluation is similar to analysis in that both compare *what is* and *what should be*, and interpret the results of that comparison. They describe five program issues worthy of evaluation:

1. *Quality*–the value or utility of an intervention or initiative.
2. *Suitability*–the needs and expectations of sponsors and participants regarding an intervention or initiative.
3. *Effectiveness*–the impact or results of an intervention or initiative.
4. *Efficiency*–the cost/benefit of an intervention or initiative.
5. *Importance*–the long-term influence on an organization as a result of an intervention or initiative.

It is important to distinguish between evaluation and measurement. Laird (1985, 242) believes "*measurement* refers to the act of collecting information relative to the dimensions, quantity, or capacity of something, while evaluation involves making judgments about ideas, works, solutions, methods, or materials related to the intervention." The purpose of the judgment is to determine something's value or worth. Geis and Smith (1992, 132) assert that evaluation is a systematic process relying on many special skills, such as collecting information, interpreting data, drawing conclusions, and communicating outcomes.

Purpose of Evaluation

Stufflebeam (1975, 19) reports that "evaluation is the process of delineating, obtaining, and applying descriptive and judgmental information . . . concerning some object's merit; as revealed by its goals, structure, process, and product; and for some useful purpose such as decisionmaking or accountability." He cites two major purposes of evaluation. The first involves *decisionmaking* to produce information for improvement and to guide choosing among possible modifications. Evaluation of this kind is referred to as *formative* (or *proactive*) (Rothwell and Cookson 1997), which is developmental. It should be used as the basis for constructively modifying the intervention or initiative, not simply to keep it alive or, alternatively, complete the process (Gilley and Eggland 1989).

The second purpose of evaluation is *accountability,* or justification of the program's value to employers, sponsors, and decisionmakers. This is *summative* (or *retroactive*) evaluation (Rothwell and Cookson 1997), and it involves gathering information after program completion to describe and defend its achievements. Bowers and Franklin (1977) report that summative evaluation assesses overall outcomes of an intervention or initiative and supports a decision to continue or terminate the process. Evaluators seek descriptive and judgmental information from everyone involved with the intervention or initiative as well as from those who influence or who might be influenced by the same.

Organizations "measure so that they can monitor, control, and improve system performance at the organization, business process, and job/performer levels," according to Rummler and Brache (1995, 135). They argue that without measures, managers have no basis for specifically communicating performance expectations to employees or knowing what is going on in their organizations (137). Without measures, managers cannot isolate performance gaps, provide feedback that compares performance to a standard, identify performance that should be rewarded, or effectively make and support decisions regarding resources, plans, policies, schedules, or structure. Furthermore, Rummler and Brache (1995, 137) assert that without measures, employees at all levels have no basis for "knowing specifically what is expected of them, monitoring their own performance and generating their own feedback, generating their own rewards and understanding what performance is required for rewards from others, or identifying performance improvement areas."

Guba and Lincoln (1988) ask several important questions pertaining to the purpose of evaluation: What decisions need to be made? Who has to make them? When will the decisions be made? What criteria will the decisions be based on? The answers to these questions reveal whether an evaluation is formative or summative.

Stufflebeam (1975) does not conceptualize the process of evaluation as a fixed sequence of steps. For both formative and summative evaluation, the basic scheme involves obtaining information for four classes of variables—goals, design, process, and product—each of which corresponds to a different aspect of the intervention or initiative (Rothwell and Cookson 1997).

Brinkerhoff and Gill (1994) report that the benefits of evaluation include identifying opportunities for training, determining client deficits in needed knowledge, skills, and attitudes, and enhancing the learning process. Additional benefits are managing critical value-adding events, identifying training problems and their potential solutions, and assessing the business impact of training. Other important benefits include providing accountability for the use of resources and monitoring changes in attitudes and perceptions related to training.

Brinkerhoff (1999) identifies several important but less common purposes of evaluation, which include fulfilling one's HRD responsibility to the organization, improving the quality of the performance management system, and improving project management execution. Moreover, he believes that evaluation includes providing feedback on individual and organizational learning, performance improvement, and organizational development and change; educating organizational leaders to the values and benefits of HRD; and demonstrating HRD capacity and capability. Finally, evaluation should improve intervention design and development, guide HRD practice, and improve its effectiveness.

When to Evaluate

Evaluation can be conducted at various points during the HRD process. Typically, evaluation is viewed as a linear process in which evaluation is the last phase (i.e., Analyze–Design–Develop–Implement–*Evaluate*). In many circumstances evaluation serves as a feedback process to revise and improve HRD. This formative evaluation is linked to a final summative evaluation that determines the impact or outcomes of the intervention or initiative. In essence, Analyze–Design–Develop describes formative evaluation, whereas Revise–Implement is summative.

Nadler and Nadler (1994) and Geis and Smith (1992) maintain that evaluation can and should occur during and after each phase of the HRD process (i.e., Analyze–Evaluate–Revise, Design–Evaluate–Revise, Develop–Evaluate–Revise, and Implement–Evaluate–Revise). For example, front-end analysis (needs, performance, organizational) should be evaluated. During the design stage, one evaluates alternative media, instructional strategies, performance objectives, different sequences, and so on. During the implementation phase HRD professionals evaluate the facilitation skills of managers during learning sessions and whether or not performance objectives are achieved.

Rummler and Brache (1995) assert that evaluation (measurement) should occur at the conclusion of each output phase of performance (job/performer, business process, organization). To accomplish this, organizations measure the quality of finished products or services to make certain they meet or exceed customers' expectations and are competitive in the marketplace. Next, business processes should be measured to guarantee that internal process outputs are delivered on time and at an acceptable level of quality. Finally, employees' individual performance outputs need to be compared to performance standards to determine whether they meet or exceed standards.

When evaluations are conducted at the business process and job/performer levels, HRD professionals utilize a *performance management system* to gather appropriate data, execute the evaluation, and provide appropriate feedback to employees. They rely on the overall *quality control system* to conduct organization-level performance evaluation and work cooperatively with senior managers in its execution and feedback of findings.

What to Evaluate

The principal objective of learning and performance improvement interventions and change initiatives is to improve individual and organizational performance as well as organizational capabilities, which results in increased organizational efficiency. An evaluation of the organization's behavioral environment is required prior to designing an intervention or initiative. After an intervention or initiative has been implemented and participants' have had significant time to internalize new knowledge, apply new skills, or incorporate change, another behavioral environment analysis should be conducted. The results should be compared and conclusions drawn regarding the impact of the interventions and initiative on the environment. Finally, behavior of employees who participated in the intervention or initiative should be compared to that of nonparticipating employees to obtain an accurate measure of program results.

As reported by Kirkpatrick (1995), evaluation should measure the effectiveness of the intervention or initiative, facilitation of instruction, learning that occurs, change in behavior on the job, performance improvement, productivity, and the impact on the organization. Although these are common elements evaluated in HRD, Geis and Smith (1992) suggest that there are other important elements that should be evaluated, including people, products, processes, purposes, facilities, resource rates, costs/benefits, and outcomes.

Evaluating interventions or initiatives allows HRD professionals to determine whether desired performance objectives have been achieved. Evaluation reveals whether an intervention or initiative makes a difference, what activities were worthwhile, whether on-the-job behavior has changed, and whether changes in specific knowledge, skills, and attitudes have been sufficient to alter behavior. Finally, evaluation determines whether an intervention or initiative *can* achieve such behavioral changes.

Evaluation determines the appropriateness of the design in terms of its practicality, theoretical soundness, and responsiveness. Brinkerhoff (1987) refers to this as the second stage of evaluation. Brinkerhoff (1998) believes evaluation should determine whether an intervention or initiative has been implemented in accordance with its design. Special attention is given to unplanned departures from the design and whether they were necessary. If such was the case, the intervention or initiative should be redesigned to account for such changes.

Learning facilitators, managers, and sometimes HRD professionals should be assessed on their ability to hold the learners' interest, to assist and relate to the learner, to summarize clearly, and to identify clear performance objectives. They should also be evaluated with respect to their ability to communicate ideas, facts, and emotions, to organize the teaming environment, and to establish a comfortable and supportive learning environment. Finally, they should be evaluated to determine whether they selected appropriate methods of instruction, selected appropriate learning activities, and knew the material being presented (Donaldson and Scannell 1986).

Gilley and Maycunich (1998a) assert that organizational performance and change efforts require evaluation. Assessing organizational performance considers consulting practices and processes, performance outcomes, transfer of learning strategies, competence of HRD professionals as performance consultants, and effectiveness of performance management systems. Evaluating organizational change involves reviewing value-added interventions and services, change management activities, organizational development strategies, components of the organizational system, and competence of HRD professionals as change agents. Finally, they contend that evaluation should measure the impact and results of HRD as well as its strategy, partnerships, and outcomes.

Building a Measurement System

As stated by Rummler and Brache (1995, 137),

> merely establishing measures is not enough; if we are going to manage the organization as a system, we must have sound measures that ensure we are monitoring the right things. A total measurement system [is] not a collection of unrelated—and potentially counterproductive—measures but a performance management process that converts the data provided by the measurement system into intelligent action.

Rummler and Brache (1995, 137–138) provide some guidelines to measure performance (outputs) at the organization, business process, and job/performer levels. Regardless of the level, they recommend the following measurement development sequence:

- Identify the most significant outputs of the organization, process, or job.
- Identify the "critical dimensions" of performance for each of these outputs (i.e., *quality*: accuracy, reliability, appearance; *productivity*: quantity, rate, and timeliness; *cost*: labor, materials, and overhead).
- Develop the measures for each critical dimension.
- Develop goals, or standards, for each measure.

Several authors and researchers maintain that organizational effectiveness comes about only when the organization, process, and job/performer levels are all headed in the same direction (Gibson, Ivancevich, and Donnelly 1997; Fallon and Brinkerhoff 1996; Rummler and Brache 1995; Swanson 1994). According to Rummler and Brache (1995, 139), however, the key to achieving this result is to develop a "measurement network that ties the three levels together into a system." They contend that the outcomes of such a measurement system make it possible to monitor performance at all levels and eliminate failure before it negatively impacts outputs. Additionally, all performers see and measure their impact on critical organization outputs.

Rummler and Brache (1995, 139) suggest that the process of building the measurement system has two stages: (1) establishing the output linkage from organization output to process output to job/performer output, and (2) overlaying relevant measures on these outputs following the "sound measures" sequence described above.

Using Evaluation to Avoid Critical Errors

Brinkerhoff (1998, 151–152) identified five critical errors in performance improvement interventions. Once these errors are identified and understood, HRD professionals can establish evaluation strategies to prevent their reoccurrence.

1. *Error of direction:* focusing the performance improvement intervention in the wrong direction; attempting to resolve performance deficits that are not worthwhile to the organization.
2. *Error of analysis:* identifying the wrong causes for performance deficits, or failing to connect the right performance objectives to the business goal.
3. *Error of design:* failing to construct the right performance improvement tools, incentives, aids, and techniques.
4. *Error of implementation:* failing to implement the performance improvement plan so that the right performance improvement techniques are made available.
5. *Error of impact:* failing to improve performance or to achieve the business goal.

Five-Phase Evaluation Framework

Brinkerhoff (1998, 153) developed a five-phase framework that parallels the five fundamental errors of evaluation discussed above.

1. Analyze goals to determine the merits of the performance improvement intervention effort.
2. Audit the performance analysis process used in determining the performance factors and roles that must be improved in order to achieve the business goal.
3. Evaluate the design of performance improvement interventions.
4. Analyze the implementation of the performance improvement intervention, including the following:
   - Examine the adequacies of steering controls used to guide and direct the project.
   - Assess the usage of implementation techniques.
   - Provide the accountability and documentation of project activities and results.
5. Determine the impact/results of the performance improvement intervention (153).

This framework evaluates performance improvement interventions and monitors change initiative assessment. It also audits the accuracy of an HRD professional's work.

Roles in Evaluation

Preskill and Torres (1999, 186) believe that evaluators should be collaborators, facilitators, interpreters, mediators, coaches, and educators of learning and change processes. They are involved initially in establishing an evaluation framework, but in some cases they periodically intervene thereafter to keep employees actively involved in the inquiry process. They are responsible for facilitating dialogue and reflection by asking questions and identifying and clarifying organization members' values, beliefs, assumptions, and knowledge as they engage in each phase of the inquiry.

Effective evaluators encourage employees to be heard and hold them accountable for any behaviors that discourage growth and development during the evaluative inquiry process. Preskill and Torres (1999, 186) contend that evaluators are "responsible for maintaining a climate that supports a spirit of inquiry, reciprocity, and community." Finally, evaluators work collaboratively with stakeholders, decisionmakers, and program participants to determine the strengths and weaknesses of various interventions and initiatives and to maintain a climate that supports the continuous learning of all employees.

Stufflebeam (1975) reports that the role of evaluator entails three principal functions:

- *delineating*, which involves holding as many face-to-face meetings between the evaluator and decisionmakers as necessary to identify needed evaluative information;
- *obtaining*, which includes physically gathering and processing the information; and
- *applying*, which is using the information obtained from evaluation to make decisions and establish accountability (jointly shared between program planners and stakeholders).

Rothwell (1996a, 297–298) identified several abilities of evaluators. Evaluators are able to

- integrate evaluation processes with organizational strategy evaluation;
- integrate evaluation processes with corporate culture, structure, and politics;
- integrate evaluation processes with work processes and work methods;
- give each worker a say in evaluation processes and in feeding results back into future human performance enhancement strategies.

The Evaluation Process

As stated by Brinkerhoff (1998, 149), evaluation is a process of asking key questions, then collecting and using data to answer them. He maintains that some questions represent internal concerns, such as whether a needs analysis procedure has uncovered valid needs, or whether a team of performers can efficiently use a draft job aid. Other questions represent external stakeholder concerns, such as whether the intervention has achieved performance objectives, or whether a business goal has been affected.

Smith and Geis (1992, 151–158) and Brinkerhoff (1998, 168–171) combine to identify an eight-step approach to planning an evaluation inquiry.

Design Step 1: Identify All Clients and Stakeholders and Clarify Their Needs

The first step in the evaluation process is to clearly identify the needs and expectations of decisionmakers (clients), and managers and employees (stakeholders)

(Smith and Geis 1992). Clients of performance improvement interventions and change initiatives authorize and guide the project, whereas managers and employees, who are the recipients of performance improvement and change efforts, are stakeholders (Brinkerhoff 1998).

Interviewing the decisionmaker that sponsors the evaluation is usually the best way of determining needs and expectations. Next, stakeholders should be interviewed. If possible, HRD professionals should obtain the criteria by which needs and expectations will be measured, clients' and stakeholders' biases on what kinds of data are credible, the names of other stakeholders to be consulted, and constraints on project planning (Smith and Geis 1992).

Design Step 2: Identify the Performance Improvement Initiative to Be Evaluated

Brinkerhoff (1998) believes that HRD professionals need to have a clear understanding of the organization's performance improvement and change goals and strategy. They need to describe the initiative fully by addressing the following questions:

- What are the goals and objectives of the performance improvement project?
- How is it supposed to influence business needs?
- Who is involved? How, and when?

Design Step 3: Identify and Clarify the Purposes for the Evaluation

Evaluation purposes are used to guide the evaluation process. They determine how well interventions and initiatives work, what makes them work or prevents them from being successful, and whether they produce desired results. HRD professionals must identify and clarify the purpose of the evaluation and measure the outcomes of interventions and initiatives against them.

Design Step 4: Determine the Critical Research Questions That the Evaluation Must Address

The next step involves restating clients' and stakeholders' concerns in terms that direct the evaluation design. Smith and Geis (1992, 152) report that restated questions should indicate (1) the type of *data* to be collected, (2) the types of *people* who will provide the data (or who will be measured), and usually (3) the *standard* or benchmark for evaluating the program's success. Furthermore, research questions should identify what data will be valid for the decision and credible to decisionmakers.

Brinkerhoff (1998, 170) identified several potential research questions for a typical evaluation:

- What gains in performance have been achieved for various employee groups (for example, tellers, customer service representatives, and loan officers)?
- What job aids have been most effective?
- What problems have employees encountered in improving their performance?
- How have employees reacted to the new incentives?
- What revisions are needed to job aids to make them more useful?
- What are the critical supervisory behaviors needed to support performance improvement?
- How much have revenue and profits improved?

Design Step 5: Develop an Evaluation Design

The next step involves expanding research questions into a design outline (Smith and Geis 1992). The design outline specifies the information needed and the steps to be followed in completing the evaluation. This includes identifying specific measurement techniques, standards that will be used to evaluate performance, and who is responsible for steps of the evaluation. Next, HRD professionals outline the remaining steps in the evaluation process, which includes steps 6, 7, and 8.

Design Step 6: Analyze Resources and Constraints

Before completing the evaluation design, HRD professionals analyze what is realistic for the situation. They review the design outline to determine what resources are necessary for completion. These may include time, staff, access to data, authority to conduct the evaluation, and an acceptable budget. Constraints on the evaluation plan may include lack of resources or development of contingency plans.

Design Step 7: Determine the Best Data Collection Methods

The data collection plan must be consistent with the evaluation questions previously identified. Data collection methods abound, and their applicability varies with the purposes for the evaluation, information needs, and expectations of clients and stakeholders. Additionally, HRD professionals identify how the various sets of data will be summarized, what statistics will be computed, and what numbers will be compared in order to answer each of the evaluation research questions.

Design Step 8: Plan Reporting and Communications Actions

Client and stakeholder needs and expectations drive evaluation. Therefore, HRD professionals need to plan their delivery of evaluation results to people who need them. According to Brinkerhoff (1998, 171), HRD professionals should not "simply prepare an evaluation report, then give it to everyone who may have an interest. Rather they should plan to provide concise and targeted evaluative summaries that are specifically focused on the needs and expectations of the clients and stakeholders." In addition to formal written reports, presentations, workshops, and discussions of findings are appropriate. Brinkerhoff (1998, 171) concludes that the "more interactive the format the better, as clients and stakeholders typically need and want assistance in interpreting evaluation findings and applying solutions to performance problems."

Outcomes of Evaluation

Preskill and Torres (1999) identified several outcomes associated with effective evaluations. Outcomes for *individuals and team members* help them understand how their actions affect others in the organization, ask more questions than give solutions/answers, and develop a greater sense of personal accountability and responsibility for the organization's outcomes. Moreover, effective evaluations help individuals and team members become more self-directed learners and take more and higher risks. They become more consultative and coachable and are more likely to ask for help. As a result, individuals and team members become more effective listeners, develop creative solutions (willingness to do something different), and share the work that needs to be done.

Preskill and Torres (1999) report that the outcomes of effective evaluation for *organizations* include the opportunity to develop new products and services, deploy changes more quickly, increase productivity, improve morale, enhance organizational work climate, and reduce turnover. They also cite that organizations experience less sabotage, fewer errors, improved financial performance, increased efficiency, less work redundancy, and more effective service to customers.

Effective evaluations establish buy-in and commitment within the organization, according to Brinkerhoff (1998). He contends that effective evaluations demonstrate the value-added nature of HRD, encourage active involvement of stakeholders in achieving results, and provide opportunities to gather eclectic perspectives and viewpoints from multiple stakeholders, which can establish a continuous, consistent feedback process.

Models of Evaluation

Models come in different formats, philosophical approaches, levels of evaluation, and matrices of measurement techniques. This section offers brief descriptions of six models—selected because they have influenced practice significantly or represent new approaches that have stimulated interest among professional evaluators.

Kirkpatrick's Four Levels of Evaluation Model

Kirkpatrick (1996) identified different levels of evaluation, each for a different purpose. This is the most commonly used model within the field of HRD because of its usefulness in determining the focus and importance of interventions and initiatives. The levels are reaction, learning, behavior, and impact. Robinson and Robinson (1989) reported that the majority of HRD functions conduct only reaction and learning evaluations, with only 40 percent of functions conducting impact evaluations. Of this 40 percent, only 20 percent of them do so more than 20 percent of the time. Consequently, impact evaluations are rarely used to measure the effectiveness of HRD efforts.

Level 1: Reaction Evaluation.   It is sometimes useful to obtain the opinions, feelings, and perspectives of participants regarding an intervention or initiative for the purpose of improving it (Kirkpatrick 1996). Reaction evaluations indicate whether participants enjoyed the intervention and how much they liked the facilitator and the method of instruction used. Reaction evaluations are the easiest to develop and administer, which is one reason they are the most widely used by HRD departments. Although they are important and serve a useful purpose, they do not determine whether learning occurred or behavior changed or improved as a result of the intervention or initiative. Moreover, this approach does not reveal whether the organization benefited as a result of employee participation.

Level 2: Learning Evaluation.   The second level of evaluation is known as learning evaluation. This type determines whether performance or change objectives were achieved and what participants learned. It measures which principles, facts, skills, and attitudes were obtained from the intervention. A learning evaluation is much more difficult to develop and administer, as it requires HRD professionals to develop evaluation questions that are directly linked to the performance or change objectives. HRD professionals should administer a test before and after an intervention to determine whether learning has occurred and at what level.

Level 3: Behavior Evaluation.   A behavior evaluation identifies any behavioral change that occurred as a result of the learning and change process. Rothwell and

Kazanas (1998) believe that behavior evaluations measure on-the-job performance changes that occurred as a result of learning. They contend that an HRD professional's primary responsibility at this level is to gather evidence of on-the-job change and to assess how accurately employees transferred learning from the classroom to the job.

Behavioral evaluations should be conducted several months after learning or change occurs to allow participants time to internalize the knowledge, skills, procedures, practices, or attitudes obtained during an intervention or initiative. To obtain an accurate measurement of behavioral change, HRD professionals identify a *behavior baseline* for each participant prior to the intervention or initiative. Three to six months later, behavior must be measured and compared to the original baseline to determine whether a change has occurred. The primary difference between learning and behavior evaluation is that the latter is a measurement of the outward manifestation of learning.

The following questions can be used when conducting a behavior evaluation:

- What are the desired outcomes in behavioral terms?
- How will HRD professionals, managers, executives, and employees know when on-the-job performance has improved?
- What is a reasonable time period for skills and knowledge transfer to occur?
- How does the work environment affect skill and knowledge transfer?
- How do motivational factors affect skill and knowledge transfer?

Answers to each of these questions help HRD professionals determine the appropriateness of a behavior evaluation.

Level 4: Impact Evaluation.   The fourth level is known as impact evaluation, which addresses the following question, "How has the organization been affected by the results of learning and performance improvement interventions or change initiatives?" Gilley and Eggland (1989, 234) argue that "they are the most difficult to develop and administer because so many variables must be controlled in order to obtain evidence that the organization improved as a result of an intervention or initiative." To isolate and control such variables, HRD practitioners employ exacting research methodologies and conduct statistical analyses to determine their effects.

When conducting an impact evaluation, HRD professionals identify discrete, specific behaviors to be measured. However, it is important to determine the way impact is to be measured before designing an impact evaluation. One way to determine organizational impact is to interview clients (decisionmakers) and stakeholders (employees and managers) to ascertain their perspectives. Another is to examine "before" and "after" results and assess whether an intervention or initiative produced the change. Still another approach is to interview customers to gather their opinions and perspectives of organizational effectiveness before and after the intervention or initiative.

Context-Input-Process-Product (CIPP) Model

Stufflebeam (1983) developed the context-input-process-product (CIPP) model, which was designed for educational planners and administrators. Its purpose is to provide feedback loops throughout the definition-design-implementation cycle of intervention development. Smith and Geis (1992, 161) report that the CIPP model presents the evaluator with four sets of issues:

- context issues (performance objectives versus stakeholders' needs; environmental variables that affect program design and implementation),
- input issues (intervention design strategy; adequacy of available resources; appropriate policies),
- process issues (intervention implementation, especially what happened versus what was intended), and
- product issues (attainment of performance objectives; outputs generated; unintended consequences).

According to Smith and Geis (1992), the CIPP model can be applied to organizations in four ways. First, the CIPP evaluation can be used to conduct a needs analysis. Second, it is used as an input evaluation of alternatives for addressing the needs identified when used as a needs analysis. Third, the evaluation can monitor the design and implementation of interventions and initiatives. Fourth, the CIPP evaluation helps HRD professionals examine the outcomes of an intervention or initiative in terms of its impact on the organization and its outcomes.

Cost-Benefit Model

According to Kearsley (1986), the cost-benefit analysis model addresses the concerns of decisionmakers for justifying the investment in interventions and initiatives. It is also an excellent framework for comparing alternatives for future investment. He believes that the cost-benefit method takes one of four forms. First, it lists the cost factors to consider in comparing alternatives (alternative method). Second HRD professionals can divide cost by some outcome measure (ratio method). Third, HRD professionals can express benefits and costs in the same units (return on investment method). Fourth, they can calculate the relationship between the program and performance (consulting method).

Smith and Geis (1992) state that "cost-benefit models lend themselves to decision making and often lead to a better understanding of the entire performance system." Brinkerhoff (1987, 188–189) reports that six basic steps are involved in conducting a cost-benefit analysis:

1. Identify decisionmakers and their values. Indicate which people are to be included in the analysis and how different values are to be weighted relative to one another.
2. Identify alternatives and clearly understand the decision choices. When the alternative to program A is program B, use benefit-cost ratios that compare the two programs directly rather than ratios that compare each program to the null alternative of no program.
3. Identify costs, including all direct and indirect expenses as well as opportunity costs.
4. Identify benefits that individuals, groups, or organizational elements will enjoy as a result of the program.
5. If possible, translate the potential worth to beneficiaries and the possible costs in terms of some comparable data, such as dollars saved, absences reduced, productivity gained, and so on.
6. Aggregate and interpret valued effects. The various valued effects of a program can be combined in a calculation of net benefits or a cost-benefit ratio.

Return-On-Investment (ROI) Analysis

The return-on-investment (ROI) method provides HRD professionals with the expected return (benefits) on investment (costs) expressed as a percentage or in actual dollars. As a percentage, HRD professionals identify the benefits of an intervention or initiation in financial units and divide them by their actual cost. The higher the percentage the greater the benefit to the organization in financial terms. Another way of calculating ROI involves identifying the performance improvement or change value resulting from an intervention or initiative in financial terms and subtracting their respective costs (Swanson 1999, 815). The higher the number, the greater the benefit. Of course, both methods can reveal a negative ROI.

The investment (cost) portion of the formula represents capital expenditures such as HRD professionals' salaries, facilities or equipment, opportunity cost (loss productivity for participants), development or production costs, and so on. ROI may be calculated prior to an intervention or initiative to estimate its potential cost effectiveness or afterward to measure achieved results. ROI calculations are most useful and powerful when the intervention or initiative benefits can be clearly documented and substantiated. Also, the nature of the intervention or initiative can impact whether it is appropriate to calculate a return on investment.

According to Swanson and Gardous (1988), two other methods for evaluating investments can be used: the payback period method and the future value method. The payback method divides total investment by annual savings to arrive at a time period (years and months) when the intervention or initiative will be expected to "pay back" the original investment. The future value method is appropriate when determining long-term effects of more than one decision. Since today's investments have various returns, future value analysis indicates the future benefits of various investments and illustrates the option with the highest return. As a result, HRD professionals help organizational decisionmakers decide how best to allocate resources. ROI, however, poses a difficult method to operationalize as most benefits derived from interventions and initiatives cannot be quantified. ROI does prove valuable when discussing the qualitative benefits (skills, intellectual capital, specialized expertise and knowledge, industry knowledge, human capital) that will be of the most importance to the organization in the future.

Formative Evaluation

Rothwell and Kazanas (1998, 268–273) introduced a seven-step model for conducting formative evaluations. The model is most useful when evaluating instruction, but it can also be used to improve performance improvement and change interventions.

Step 1: Determine Purpose, Objectives, and Participants.   The first step of formative evaluation is determining its purpose, objectives, and participants. When assessing purpose, Rothwell and Kazanas (1998) suggest answering the following questions: Why is this evaluation being conducted? Who will be reviewing the findings? How has learning affected performance and productivity? What impact did the intervention or initiative have on the organization?

When these questions have been addressed, they clarify the desired results of the formative evaluation. For each purpose identified, HRD professionals establish measurable objectives for the evaluation, which enable them to compare results against planned intentions. Additionally, HRD professionals consider who wants the evaluation and why, as well as what information they need from it. This information frames the importance of the evaluation and its priority.

Finally, HRD professionals identify who will participate in the formative evaluation and make certain that they are a representative population. This activity ensures that the purposes and objectives of the evaluation are accomplished.

Step 2: Assess Information Needs.   HRD professionals need to assess the information needs of clients and stakeholders to understand what information is desired as a result of the formative evaluation. Rothwell and Kazanas (1998, 269) believe that clients and stakeholders provide important clues regarding information needs:

- *HRD professionals* will usually be interested in how they can revise interventions or initiatives to make them more effective for participants.
- *Key decisionmakers* will usually be interested in how well the intervention or initiative meets previously identified organizational needs, solves employee performance problems, or enhances organizational effectiveness.
- *The managers* of participants will usually be interested in familiarizing themselves with the content so they can hold learners accountable for applying what they learned on the job.
- *Participants* may be interested in how to apply what they learn.

Step 3: Consider Proper Protocol.   HRD professionals are wise to regard and observe proper protocol. Rothwell and Kazanas (1998, 269) point out a number of considerations for proper protocol during a formative evaluation:

- How much do the targeted audiences expect to be consulted about a formative evaluation *before, during,* and *after* it is conducted?
- What permissions are necessary to carry out the study?
- Whose permissions are necessary?
- What formal or informal steps are needed to secure the necessary permissions to conduct a formative evaluation, select subjects, correct data, and report results?

Five key factors affect protocol: (1) the decisionmakers' experience with formative evaluation and its purposes, (2) labels, or terms that confuse leaders as to the intent of a formative evaluation, (3) timing of the formative evaluation, (4) participation and permissions needed to conduct a formative evaluation, and (5) method of evaluation most appropriate and acceptable within the organization.

Step 4: Describe the Population to Be Studied and Select Subjects.   HRD professionals are responsible for describing the population for study and selecting participants. This fairly straightforward activity must be completed with care to ensure that an appropriate representation is selected for the organization. Failure to do so may produce statistical errors or introduce bias—both of which may jeopardize the evaluation.

Step 5. Identify Other Variables of Importance.   HRD professionals are challenged to identify other variables of importance to a formative evaluation. Rothwell and Kazanas (1998, 271) provide several questions useful in identifying these variables:

1. What settings should be used for the formative evaluation?
2. What specific program issues are particularly worth pre-testing before widespread delivery of instruction?
3. How much should the formative evaluation focus solely on instructional issues, and how much (if at all) should it focus on other important but noninstructional issues such as equipment or staff needs, required financial resources, facilities needs, and noninstructional needs of participants?
4. What *positive* but post-instructional outcomes of the planned learning experience can be anticipated? What *negative* post-instructional outcomes can be anticipated?
5. What estimates should be made about expected costs of the instructional program?
6. How accurate are the prerequisites previously identified?

Step 6: Formulate a Study Design.   Sixth, HRD professionals formulate an evaluation design that addresses how the formative evaluation will be conducted. An evaluation design is a planning document used when carrying out the evaluation. Rothwell and Kazanas (1998, 272) suggest that HRD professionals make certain to (1) define key terms; (2) clarify the purpose and objectives of the evaluation; (3) provide a logical structure or series of procedures for assessing instructional materials and methods; (4) identify the evaluation's methodologies, such as surveys, trial runs or rehearsals, and interviews; (5) identify populations to be studied and means by which representative subjects will be selected; and (6) summarize key standards by which the instructional materials and methods will be judged.

Step 7: Formulate a Management Plan to Guide the Study.   A management plan is a comprehensive schedule of procedures, events, or tasks to be completed in order to implement the evaluation design. Included in a management plan are milestones, due dates, descriptions of tangible products resulting from the evaluation, data collection analysis, contingency plans, and communication and report plans.

Evaluative Inquiry Model

Preskill and Torres (1999, xix) challenge the belief that a rationalist approach to evaluation inquiry can be achieved—in which everyone thinks rationally on behalf of the organization, everyone will arrive at the same conclusion, and all implementation follows discovery of the one best strategy. They ask,

> How can evaluative inquiry contribute to the development, maintenance, and growth of organizations in a dynamic, unstable, unpredictable environment? What we propose . . . is that evaluative inquiry can not only be a means of accumulating information for decision making and action (operational intelligence) but that it also be equally concerned with questioning and debating the *value* of what we do in organizations. (Preskill and Torres 1999, xix)

They further assert that learning from evaluative inquiry is a "social construction occurring through the involvement of multiple constituencies, each representing different perspectives. It is socially situated and is mediated through participants' previous knowledge and experiences" (1999, xix).

Preskill and Torres (1999, xx) see evaluative inquiry as a kind of "public philosophy in which organization members engage in dialogue with clients and other stakeholders about the meaning of what they do and how they do it." Such dialogue forces participants to focus on the historical, political, and sociological aspects of the objects of inquiry (Schwandt 1995). Accordingly, Preskill and Torres (1999, xx) believe that evaluative inquiry for organizational learning and change encompasses a focus on program and organizational processes as well as outcomes, shared individual, team, and organizational learning, and education and training of organizational practitioners in inquiry skills. They further contend that evaluative inquiry encompasses modeling the behaviors of collaboration, cooperation, and participation, establishing linkages between learning and performance, and searching for ways to create greater understanding of the variables that affect organizational success and failure. Finally, they maintain that evaluative inquiry uses a diversity of perspectives to develop understanding about organizational issues.

Torres, Preskill, and Piontek (1997) argue that evaluation efforts fail to significantly impact organizations because traditional evaluation practice is inadequate for helping organizations meet the complex challenges of a global economy and the emergence of the knowledge era. Therefore, the goals for the Evaluative Inquiry Model are to "describe the role of evaluative inquiry in learning organizations, provide a framework for conducting evaluative inquiry within an organizational learning context, and stimulate reflection and conversation among evaluators, researchers, organizational members, and consultants about their own practice" (Preskill and Torres 1999, xxi). Their model offers HRD professionals a way of integrating evaluative inquiry into organizational work processes. As a result, organizational members are better able to adapt to ever-changing conditions. The model consists of six phases:

Phase 1: Learning in Organizations. As discussed in Chapter 5, learning in organizations consists of three focus areas: individual, team, and organizational. Each of these elements is critical in the Evaluative Inquiry Model (Figure 17.1).

Phase 2: Evaluative Inquiry Learning Processes. One of the unique characteristics of the Evaluative Inquiry Model is the focus on the learning process. Preskill and Torres (1999) believe that the learning process consists of four major elements: reflection, dialogue, asking questions, and identifying and clarifying values, beliefs, assumptions, and knowledge.

Reflection

Reflection allows individuals and groups to review their ideas, understandings, and experiences through introspective thought. Individually, reflection allows us to interpret our own behavior holistically, both in terms of how our behavior is impacted by others and in terms of how others are affected by our actions. Team members, similarly, explore and better understand each other's perceptions, experiences, values, beliefs, assumptions, and knowledge through reflection. In addition, they begin to understand how and why things happen the way they do within the organization.

According to Mezirow (1991), there are three types or foci of reflection: content, process, and premise. *Content* reflection focuses on the description of the subject or problem. *Process* reflection involves analyzing the methods and strategies used to resolve the problem. *Premise* reflection considers why the problem is an issue in the first place. Thorough reflection, which promotes the greatest learning, often involves work teams engaging in each type of reflection at some point.

Individual or team reflection can occur before, during, or after completion of an activity. Reflection prior to an action involves deciding how lessons learned from past reflective experiences will be employed in this activity. During an activity, reflection occurs as participants observe and assess their thought processes and actions. Reflection upon completion allows individuals or team members to review what occurred, assessing the results of actions that led to success and suggesting improvements for those that fell short (Saban, Killion, and Green 1994).

Unfortunately, barriers to reflection abound in the workplace. According to Shaw and Perkins (1991), common barriers include performance pressure, competency traps, and absence of learning forums or structures. Performance pres-

FIGURE 17.1   Evaluative Inquiry Model

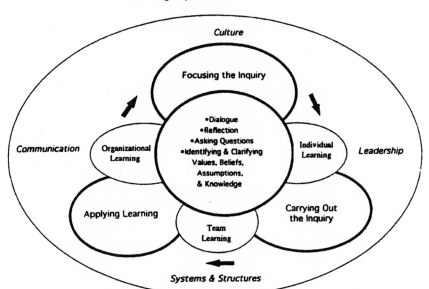

SOURCE: Reprinted, by permission from the publisher, from H. Preskill and R. T. Torres, *Evaluative Inquiry for Learning in Organizations* (Thousand Oaks, CA: Sage Publications, 1999).

sure affects most of us on the job—where we are evaluated based on productivity, efficiency, profitability, and so forth. Organizational pressures such as competition, shareholder demands, and tight labor markets contribute to short-term focus and lack of time for reflection. We fall into competency traps when workers are perceived to be performing skillfully; hence, no reason to change exists. Finally, learning structures are absent when organizational culture or leadership fails to encourage or reward learning.

Often barriers to learning reflection, whether individual, team, or organizational, can be minimized or overcome, if reflection's benefits are conveyed to and understood by learners, teams, managers, and the firm.

Preskill and Torres (1999, 55) report that reflection enables team members to think more deeply and holistically about an issue, leading to greater insights and learning. It also helps connect the rational decisionmaking process to a more affective and experiential learning process. Furthermore, reflection challenges individuals to be honest about the relationship between what they say and what they do, and creates opportunities to seriously consider the implications of any past or future action. Finally, refection acts as a safeguard against making impulsive decisions.

Questioning

How do individuals or teams know what is expected of them, clarify ambiguous statements or goals, and gather necessary information? By asking. The act of questioning may indicate curiosity, interest, desire to proceed, appropriate caution, skepticism, or pursuit of excellence. Asking questions is a fundamental characteristic of learning organizations. Historically, managers and their organizations have not encouraged questioning. Those asking questions are often perceived as troublemakers, challengers of authority, or whiners. Enlightened organizations, on the other hand, view questions as opportunities "to acquire information, insight, clarity, or direction that would resolve problems more efficiently and effectively, . . . [promoting] learning at deeper levels" (Preskill and Torres 1999, 60).

Questioning helps identify issues of key importance to the organization, acknowledges employees' prior knowledge, and uncovers a broad range of issues upon which to focus discussion. Questioning also helps develop a culture of curiosity, which stimulates continuous learning and results in deeper levels of understanding and knowledge. Finally, questioning challenges organization members' current knowledge and understanding (Preskill and Torres 1999, 61). Failure to ask questions may lead to improper planning, unsupported assumptions, unsatisfied stakeholders, hasty actions, or unsubstantiated leaps from problem to solution.

Dialogue

The American Heritage Dictionary defines dialogue as an exchange of ideas or opinions. Preskill and Torres (1999, 53) call dialogue "a sustained collective inquiry into everyday experience and what we take for granted," implying a spirit of understanding. They maintain that

> through dialogue, individuals seek to inquire, understand complex issues, and uncover assumptions. In other words, dialogue is what facilitates the evaluative inquiry learning processes of reflection, asking questions, and identifying and clarifying values, beliefs, assumptions, and knowledge. Through dialogue, individuals make connections with each other and communicate personal and social understandings that guide subsequent behaviors.

Through dialogue, individuals and groups share attitudes, reflections, and experiences regarding the organization, thus facilitating understanding (learning) of the firm's goals, objectives, culture, policies, and procedures. Dialogue enables group members to "suspend judgment in order to create new understandings" (Preskill and Torres 1999, 53).

Dialogue brings to the surface multiple points of view that need to be addressed and negotiated. It also helps make individual and hidden agendas visible so they can be addressed. Dialogue allows team members to develop shared meanings that are important for further inquiry activities, which contributes to building a sense of community and connection. Additionally, dialogue illuminates the organization's culture, policies, and procedures and increases the likelihood that learning at the team level will lead to learning throughout the organization. Finally, dialogue enables difficult topics to surface and be addressed, which facilitates individual, team, and organizational learning (Preskill and Torres 1999, 57).

Identifying and Clarifying Values, Beliefs, Assumptions, and Knowledge

Preskill and Torres (1999, 66) report that organizational learning requires individuals and teams to continually identify and clarify their values, beliefs, assumptions, and knowledge—a process involving constant questioning, testing, and validating. "Without examining what underlies our thinking, we are prone to continue operating in old ways, limiting the potential for learning and change." The following questions can help individuals identify and understand their values, beliefs, assumptions, and knowledge regarding specific issues they face within organizations:

- What are my roles/responsibilities with respect to this issue?
- How did I become involved in these roles/responsibilities?
- What experiences have I had with respect to this issue? Were they positive, negative, or neutral?
- What experiences in other settings have I had with respect to this issue? Were they positive, negative, or neutral?
- Have I had an experience with this issue where my expectations were not met? If so, why were they not met?
- How do I think this situation can be improved?
- Based on my answers to these questions, what underlying assumptions and values does my perspective on this issue reflect?
- In what ways might my values influence my position on this issue? (Preskill and Torres 1999, 67)

When individuals and teams engage in activities that enhance their understanding of self, team, and organization, a climate of learning grows. Additionally, identifying and clarifying values, beliefs, assumptions, and knowledge facilitates a common understanding of key terms and phrases so that language is less likely to be a barrier to effective communication and learning. It also helps bring to the surface motivations, opinions, and attitudes, which lead to greater understanding among team members. Furthermore, it helps individual team members accept change, modify their thinking and behaviors, and mediate potential conflicts among team members more quickly and effectively. Finally identifying and clarifying values, beliefs, assumptions, and knowledge helps confirm that prior experiences and attitudes affect individuals' behavior in the work environment (Preskill and Torres 1999, 67).

Phase 3: Focusing the Evaluative Inquiry.   When organizations experience low employee morale, high turnover, poor employee performance and productivity, or poor employee-employer relations, they must make some difficult decisions to overcome these discouraging conditions. According to Preskill and Torres (1999, 72), "the approach organization members use to address these issues is what differentiates organizations that learn from their experiences from those that do not." In their model, they describe how a team focuses an inquiry through dialogue, reflection, asking questions, and identifying and clarifying values, beliefs, assumptions, and knowledge in order to define the evaluative issues, identify key stakeholders, and determine a set of evaluative questions that will guide the inquiry (72).

Preskill and Torres (1999, 91) believe that focusing the inquiry enables team members to view a specific problem or issue within the larger context of the organization and clarifies the relationships among program goals, designs, and intended outcomes. Focusing the inquiry also helps competing expectations of the program to be explored and understood and highlights potential barriers or obstacles to further evaluative inquiry processes. Moreover, it helps clarify intended users and uses of evaluative inquiry outcomes and identify potential misuses of evaluative inquiry processes. In addition, focusing the inquiry increases the likelihood that meaningful, useable data will be obtained in carrying out the inquiry phase and identifies questions that may provide insights into other issues that would benefit from additional inquiry. Finally, it helps ensure that the most significant questions will be addressed in the evaluative inquiry process.

Phase 4: Carrying Out the Inquiry.   As with most evaluation frameworks, the Evaluative Inquiry Model includes a section that deals with designing the evaluative inquiry process, identifying methods and procedures for data collection, analyzing data, providing communication and writing reports, and implementing inquiry activities. Preskill and Torres (1999, 98) believe that

> The work of evaluative inquiry in this phase most closely resembles traditional evaluation or action research efforts—with the crucial enhancement being that the four learning processes of dialogue, reflection, asking questions, and identifying and clarifying values, beliefs, assumptions, and knowledge are inextricably intertwined throughout the design, data collection, analysis and interpretation, and communicating and reporting activities. The key task at this time is to clearly link the information needs of the stakeholders to the evaluative questions and the kinds of data that will best answer those questions.

Implementing the inquiry provides trustworthy, credible information upon which to base actions within the organization. It gives fuller consideration to the mutual impact of contextual/political issues and data collection activities, resulting in a more sensitive, relevant, and productive inquiry design. Carrying out the inquiry helps answer specific questions and reduces uncertainties about particular programs, policies, and procedures within the organization. Moreover, it provides a means for interpreting findings in terms of crucial, mediating aspects of the organization's internal and external context; and it also provides a vehicle for deeper understanding of issues within the organization and further nourishes individual, team, and organizational learning. Finally, carrying out the inquiry provides specific information (recommendations) on which to take action (Preskill and Torres 1999, 125).

Phase 5: Applying Learning.   Preskill and Torres (1999, 131–132) suggest that

> applying learning takes place when organizations believe they have enough information to inform changes that will address the original object of the evaluative inquiry. This usually occurs when the findings and recommendations of an evaluative inquiry are available. . . . The *applying learning* phase consists of three distinct activities: (1) identifying and selecting among action alternatives, (2) developing an action plan, and (3) implementing the action plan and monitoring its progress.

There are several benefits of applying learning. First, applying learning provides for judicious, carefully reasoned selection among action alternatives. Second, it provides a means for understanding the implications of various potential actions. Third, it provides a means for developing realistic, contextually sensitive action plans. Fourth, applying learning allows for the exploration of potential barriers or obstacles to implementing the inquiry's recommendations. Fifth, it ensures that those potentially affected by the actions are involved in planning for implementation. Sixth, applying learning ensures that the findings from inquiry are being used to support individual, team, and organizational learning. Seventh, it reinforces an organization's focus on continuous improvement and learning throughout implementation (Preskill and Torres 1999, 150).

Phase 6: Building the Infrastructure for Evaluative Inquiry.   Preskill and Torres (1999, 154) report that the four most important components of building an organization's infrastructure are culture, leadership, systems and structures, and communication. Each of these components has been addressed throughout this book and our treatment of them does not vary greatly from that expressed in the Evaluative Inquiry Model. Therefore, we will not examine them further.

Conclusion

Evaluation can be simply defined as systematic reflection. Reflection requires all parties to pause occasionally and assess how things are going, determine whether expected results are being achieved, notice unanticipated outcomes, or figure out why results are not as expected. It is important to acknowledge and nurture successful efforts and equally important to modify strategies that do not work.

Evaluation is systematic in that organizations and HRD professionals plan for it and commit resources to implementing evaluation actions. Using a systematic approach to evaluation ensures that "pauses" are planned to collect data, ask questions, think critically, and consider the course of subsequent performance improvement project plans and actions.

Appendices

<pre>
                    FUTURE/STRATEGIC
                         FOCUS
                           │
   Management of   │   Management of
   Strategic Human   │   Transformation
   Resources   │   and Change
                           │
PROCESSES ────────────────┼──────────────── PEOPLE
                           │
   Management of   │   Management of
   Firm Infrastructure   │   Employee
                           │   Contribution
                           │

                 DAY-TO-DAY/OPERATIONAL
                         FOCUS
</pre>

APPENDIX A   HRD Roles in an Organization

SOURCE: Ulrich, D. (1997). *Human resource champions.* Boston, MA: Harvard Business School Press.

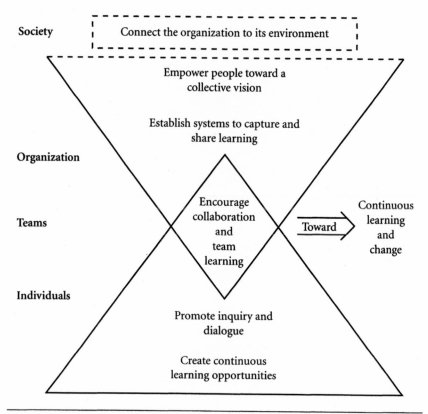

APPENDIX B   Learning Organization Action Imperatives

SOURCE: Watkins, K. E. & Marsick, V. J. (1993). *Sculpting the learning organization: Lessons in the art and science of systematic change.* San Francisco: Jossey-Bass.

APPENDIX C   Comparing Traditional, Learning, and Developmental Organizations

Characteristics	Traditional Organization	Learning Organization	Developmental Organization
Orientation	Training	Learning	Development
Capacity for Organizational Renewal	Low	Moderate	High
Importance of Human Resources	Not Critical	Critical	Essential
Assumption of Growth and Development	Training will Enhance Organization	Building Capability to Create through Learning	Continuous Development is Key to Competitiveness. Profitability, and Renewal
Expectation of Growth and Development	Improved SKA's	Continuous Learning	Organizational Renewal and Competitive Readiness
Types of Developmental Activities	Accidental Learning Conversational Learning Incidental Learning Anticipatory Learning	Deutero Learning Action Learning	Developmental Learning
Focus of Developmental Activities	Knowledge Acquisition	Application and Reflection	Change and Continuous Growth and Development
Outcomes of Developmental Activities	Comprehension	Mastery and Self-Awareness	New Meaning, Renewal, and Performance Capacity

(continues)

APPENDIX C (*continued*)

Organizational Priorities	Market Share, Profits, Productivity, Margin	Learning is Key to Improving Business Results	Achieving Business Goals and Objectives through Employee Growth & Development
Type of Leadership	Autocratic	Transactional Tranformational	Developmental
Structure and Work Climate	Departmental, Formal Hierarchical, Little or No Employee Participation	Team/Project-Oriented Encourage and Reward Individual and Group Learning	Organizational System Approach
Leader Role	Status Quo.	Synergist	Holistic Thinker and Developmental Champion
Manager Role	Status Quo.	Learning Partner	Performance Coach
Employee Role	Status Quo.	Self-Directed Learner	Developmental Enhancer
HR Professional Role	Status Quo.	Employee Champion	Performance Consultant and OD Change Agent
Actions Required to Move the Organization Forward	None	Focus on Learning	Focus on Development

SOURCE: J. W. Gilley and A. Maycanich, *Beyond the Learning Organization: Creating a Culture of Continuous Growth and Development Through State of the Human Resource Practices* (Cambridge, MASS: Perseus Books, 2000).

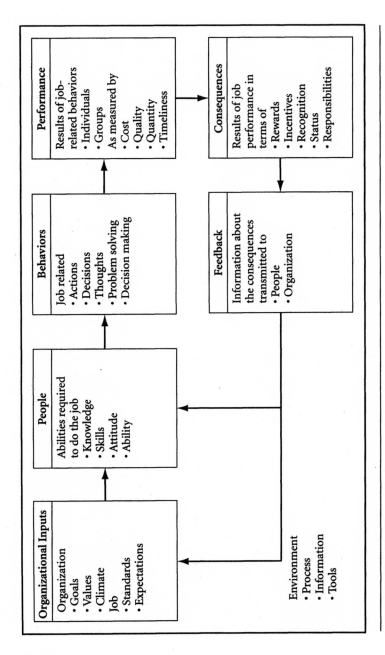

APPENDIX D   The Human Performance System

SOURCE: Fuller, J., & Farrington, J. (1999). *From training to performance improvement: Navigating the transition.* San Francisco: Jossey-Bass.

Problem

		Known	Unknown
Condition	Known	Corrective	Developmental
	Unknown	Adaptive	Strategic

APPENDIX E   Four Types of Needs Assessments

SOURCE: Phillips, J., & Holton, E., III (Eds.). (1995). *In Action: Needs Assessment.* Alexandria, VA: American Society for Training and Development.

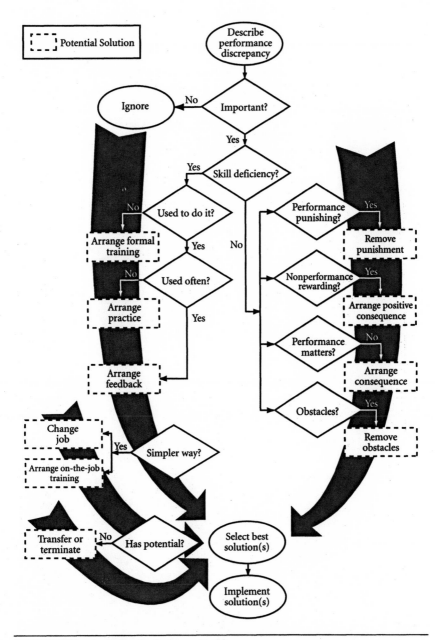

APPENDIX F   Analyzing Performance Problems

SOURCE: Excerpted from: R. Mager and P. Pipe, *Analyzing Performance Problems*, 2d ed. (Belmont, Calif.: Lake Publishing Company, 1984).

450

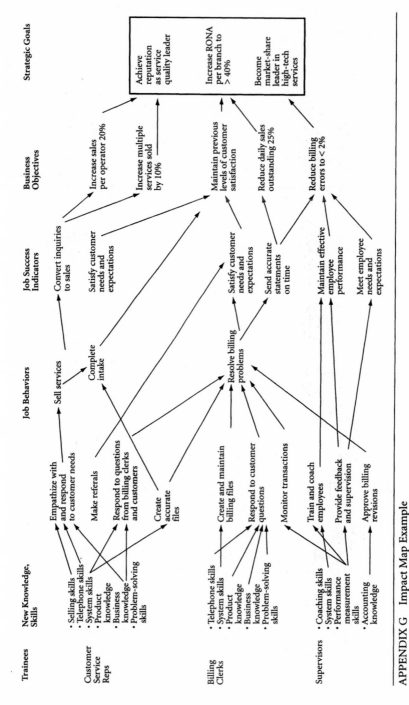

APPENDIX G   Impact Map Example

SOURCE: Reprinted by permission from the publisher, from Bunkerhoff, R. and Gill, (1994). The Learning Alliance. San Francisco: Jossey-Bass.

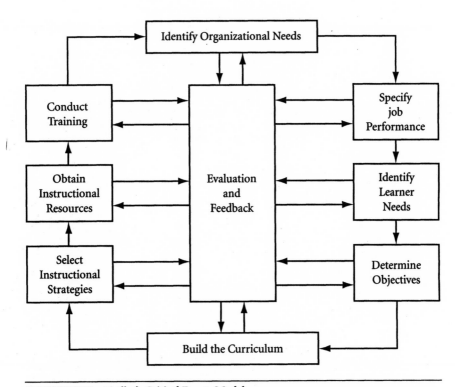

APPENDIX H   Nadler's Critical Events Model

SOURCE: From *Designing Training Programs: The Critical Events Model*, p. 15, by Leonard Nadler and Zeace Nadler. Copyright © 1994 by Gulf Publishing Company, Houston, Texas. Used with permission. All rights reserved.

References

Ackoff, R. L. (1981). *Creating the Corporate Future.* New York: Wiley.

Anderson, R. W. (1997). The Future of Human Resources: Forging Ahead or Falling Behind? In D. Ulrich, M. R. Losey, and G. Lake, eds., *Tomorrow's HR Management: 48 Thought Leaders Call for Change,* pp. 146–154. New York: Wiley & Sons.

Argyris, C. (1970). *Management and Organizational Development.* New York: McGraw-Hill.

Argyris, C., and D. Schon. (1996). *Organizational Learning II: A Theory of Action Perspective.* Reading, MA: Addison-Wesley.

Aronson, E. (1995). *The Social Animal,* 7th ed. New York: Freeman.

Barich, H., and P. Kotler. (1991). A Framework for Image Management. *Sloan Management Review* 4, 94–104.

Bates, R. A. (1999). Measuring Performance Improvement. In R. J. Torraco, ed., *Performance Improvement Theory and Practice,* pp. 47–67, San Francisco: Berrett-Koehler.

Beckhard, R. (1969). *Organization Development: Strategies and Models.* Reading, MA: Addison-Wesley.

Beer, M. (1983). What Is Organizational Development? In L. S. Baird, C. E. Schneiner, and D. Laird, eds., *Training and Development Sourcebook.* Amherst, MA: HRD Press.

Beer, M. (1997). The Transformation of the Human Resource Function: Resolving the Tension Between a Traditional Administrative and a New Strategic Role. In D. Ulrich, M. R. Losey, and G. Lake, eds., *Tomorrow's HR Management: 48 Thought Leaders Call for Change,* pp. 84–95. New York: Wiley & Sons.

Beer, M., and R. A. Eisenstat. (1996). Developing an Organization Capable of Implementing Strategy and Learning, *Human Relations,* 49 (5): 62–67.

Beer, M., R. A. Eisenstat, and R. Biggadike. (1996). Developing an Organization Capable of Strategy Implementation and Reformulation: A Preliminary Test. In B. Moingeon and A. Edmondson, eds., *Organizational Learning for Competitive Advantage.* London: Sage Publications.

Bellman, G. (1983). Untraining the Trainer: Steps Toward Consulting. *Training and Development Journal* 7 (1): 70–73.

Bellman, G. (1998). Partnership Phase: Forming Partnerships. In D. G. Robinson and J. C. Robinson, eds., *Moving from Training to Performance: A Practical Guide,* pp. 39–53. San Francisco: Berrett-Koehler.

Bengtson, B. (1994). *An Analysis of CEO Perceptions Concerning Trainer Roles in Selected Central Pennsylvania Manufacturing Firms.* Unpublished doctoral dissertation. Pennsylvania State University.

Berke, G. B. (1990). *How to Conduct a Performance Appraisal.* Alexandria, VA: ASTD Press.

Block, P. (1981). *Flawless Consulting: A Guide to Getting Your Expertise Used.* San Diego: Pfeiffer.

Block, P. (1987). *The Empowered Manager: Positive Political Skills at Work.* San Francisco: Jossey-Bass.

Bolton, R. (1986). *People Skills: How to Assert Yourself, Listen to Others, and Resolve Conflicts.* New York: Simon and Schuster.

Boud, D., R. Keogh, and D. Walker. (1985). *Reflection: Turning Experience into Learning.* London: Kogan Page.

Bowers, D. G., and J. L. Franklin. (1977). *Survey-Guided Development: Data-Based Organizational Change.* San Diego: University Associates.

Boyett, J. H., and J. T. Boyett. (1995). *Beyond Workplace 2000: Essential Strategies for the New American Corporation.* New York: Dutton.

Brassard, M. (1996). *The Memory Logger Plus+.* Methuen, MA: GOAL/QPC.

Brinkerhoff, R. O. (1987). *Achieving Results from Training.* San Francisco: Jossey-Bass.

Brinkerhoff, R. O. (1997). Clarifying and Directing Impact Evaluation. In S. M. Brown and C. J. Seidner, eds., *Evaluating Corporate Training Models and Issues,* pp. 141–166. Boston: Klumer Academic.

Brinkerhoff, R. O. (1998). Measurement Phase: Evaluating Effectiveness of Performance Improvement Projects. In D. G. Robinson and J. C. Robinson, eds., *Moving from Training to Performance: A Practical Guide,* pp. 147–174. San Francisco: Berrett-Koehler.

Brinkerhoff, R. O. (1999). Personal interview.

Brinkerhoff, R. O., and S. J. Gill. (1994). *The Learning Alliance.* San Francisco: Jossey-Bass.

Broad, M., and J. Newstrom. (1992). *Transfer of Training. Action-Packed Strategies to Ensure High Payoff from Training Investment.* Reading, MA: Addison Wesley.

Brockett, R. G., and R. Hiemstra. (1991). *Self-Direction in Adult Learning: Perspectives on Theory, Research, and Practice.* London and New York: Routledge.

Brookfield, S. D. (1987). *Developing Critical Thinkers: Challenging Adults to Explore Ways of Thinking and Acting.* San Francisco: Jossey-Bass.

Brookfield, S. D. (1992). Uncovering Assumptions: The Key to Reflective Practice. *Adult Learning* 16 (1): 13–18.

Brookfield, S. D. (1994). Adult Learning. In T. Husen and T. N. Postlethwaite, eds., *The International Encyclopedia of Educators,* 2nd ed., vol. 1, pp. 163–168. New York: Pergamon Press.

Brookfield, S. D. (1995). *Becoming a Critically Reflective Teacher.* San Francisco: Jossey-Bass.

Brown, K. (1995). Strategic Performance Measurements. *CPA Journals* 65 (10): 65.

Buckingham, M, and C. Coffman. (1999). *First, Break All the Rules: What the World's Greatest Managers Do Differently.* New York: Simon & Schuster.

Burke, W. W. (1992). *Organizational Development: A Process of Learning and Changing.* Reading, MA: Addison-Wesley.

Burke, W. W. (1997). What Human Resource Practitioners Need to Know for the Twenty-First Century. In D. Ulrich, M. R. Losey, and G. Lake, eds., *Tomorrow's HR Management: 48 Thought Leaders Call for Change,* pp. 96–11. New York: Wiley & Sons.

Burke, W. W., and G. H. Litwin. (1992). A Causal Model of Organizational Performance and Change. *Journal of Management* 18 (3): 532–545.

Burke, W. W., and W. H. Schmidt. (1971). In Primary Target for Change: The Manager or the Organization? In H. A. Hornstein, B. B. Bunker, W. W. Burke, M. Gindes, and R. J. Lewicki, eds., *Social Intervention: A Behavioral Science Approach*, pp. 373–385. New York: Free Press.

Caffarella, R. S. (1993). Self-Directed Learning. In S. B. Merriam, ed., *An Update on Adult Learning Theory. New Directions for Adult and Continuing Education*, no. 57. San Francisco: Jossey-Bass.

Cameron, K. (1980). Critical Questions in Assessing Organizational Effectiveness. *Organizational Dynamics* 9 (2): 66–80.

Carnevale, A., L. Gainer, and G. Villet. (1990). *Training in America: The Organization and Strategic Role of Training*. San Francisco: Jossey-Bass.

Cascio, W. F. (1995). *Managing Human Resources: Productivity, Quality of Work Life, Profits*. New York: McGraw-Hill.

Chadwick, R. P. (1982). *Teaching and Learning*. Old Tappens, NJ: Fleming Revelle.

Chalofsky, N. (1992). A Unifying Definition for the Human Resource Development Profession. *Human Resource Development Quarterly* 3 (2): 175–182.

Chalofsky, N. (1996). A New Paradigm for Learning in Organizations. *Human Resource Development Quarterly* 7 (3): 287–293.

Chalofsky, N., and C. Lincoln. (1983). *Up the HRD Ladder: A Guide for Professional Growth*. Cambridge, MA: Perseus Books.

Chalofsky, N., and C. Lincoln. (1989). What Is HRD? In D. Gradous, ed., *Systems Theory Applied to Human Resource Development*, pp. 12–19. Alexandria, VA: American Society for Training and Development.

Clark, R. E., and E. Estes. (1996). Cognitive Task Analysis. *International Journal of Educational Research* 25 (3): 403–417.

Clifford, J. (1994). Job Analysis: Why Do It, and How Should It Be Done? *Public Personnel Management* 23 (2): 321–340.

Clifton, D. O., and P. Nelson. (1992). *Soar with Your Strengths*. New York: Delacorte.

Collins, C., and J. L. Porras. (1994). *Built to Last: Successful Habits of Visionary Companies*. New York: Harper Business.

Conner, D. (1992). *Managing at the Speed of Change*. New York: Villard Books.

Craig, R., ed. (1976). *Training and Development Handbook*, 2nd ed. New York: McGraw-Hill.

Davis, L. N. (1984). *Planning, Conducting, and Evaluating Workshops*. San Diego: University Associates.

Dean, P. (1999). Designing Better Organizations with Human Performance Technology and Organization Development. In H. D. Stolovitch and E. J. Keeps, eds., *Handbook of Human Performance Technology: Improving Individual and Organizational Performance Worldwide*, pp. 321–334. San Francisco: Jossey-Bass.

Dean, R. L., and J. W. Gilley. (1986). A Production Model for Experiential Learning. *Performance and Instruction Journal* 25 (3): 26–28.

Denis, J. (1992). A Basic Course on Job Analysis. *Training and Development Journal* 46 (7): 67–70.

Denison, P. R. (1990). *Corporate Culture and Organizational Effectiveness.* New York: Wiley.

Dervarics, C. (1994). What's a Good Needs Assessment? *Technical and Skills Training* 5 (4): 22–26.

Deterline, W. A., and M. J. Rosenberg, eds. (1992). *Workplace Productivity: Performance Technology Success Stories.* Washington, DC: ISPI.

Dewey, J. (1938). *How We Think.* New York: Heath.

Dick, W., and L. Carey. (1990). *The Systematic Design of Instruction,* 3rd ed. New York: HarperCollins.

Donaldson, L., and E. E. Scannell. (1986). *Human Resource Development: The New Trainer's Guide.* Reading, MA: Addison-Wesley.

Dormant, D. (1992). Implementing Human Performance Technology in Organizations. In H. D. Stolovitch and E. J. Keeps, eds., *Handbook of Human Performance Technology: A Comprehensive Guide for Analyzing and Solving Performance Problems in Organizations,* pp. 167–187. San Francisco: Jossey-Bass.

Drucker, P. E. (1997). The Future That Has Already Happened. *Harvard Business Review* 75 (5): 19–23.

Dubois, D., and W. Rothwell. (1996). *Developing the High-Performance Workplace.* Organizational Assessment Package: Administrator's Handbook and Data Collection Instrument. Amherst, MA.: Human Resource Development Press.

Dyer, W. G. (1989). Team Building: A Microcosm of the Past, Present, and Future of OD. *Academy of Management OD Newsletter* 4, 7–8.

Ehrlich, C. J. (1997). Human Resource Management: A Changing Script for a Changing World. In D. Ulrich, M. R. Losey, and G. Lake, eds., *Tomorrow's HR Management: 48 Thought Leaders Call for Change,* 163–170. New York: Wiley & Sons.

Eichinger, R., and D. Ulrich. (1995). *Human Resource Challenges.* New York: Human Resource Planning Society.

Eisenstat, P. A. (1996). What Corporate Human Resources Bring to the Picnic: Four Models for Functional Management. *Organizational Dynamic* 3, 232–251.

Elliott, P. (1998). Assessment Phase: Building Models and Defining Gaps. In D. G. Robinson and J. C. Robinson, eds., *Moving from Training to Performance: A Practical Guide,* pp. 63–77. San Francisco: Berrett-Koehler.

Evans, P. (1995). *Business Strategy and Human Resource Management: A Four-Stage Framework.* Working paper, INSEAD, Fountainbleau.

Fallon, T., and R. O. Brinkerhoff. (1996). *Framework for Organizational Effectiveness.* Paper presented at the American Society for Training and Development International Conference.

Fisher, R., and S. Brown. (1988). *Getting Together: Building a Partnership That Gets to Yes.* Boston: Houghton Mifflin.

Flannery, T. P., D. A. Hofrichter, and P. E. Platten. (1996). *People Performance and Pay: Dynamic Compensation for Changing Organizations.* New York: Free Press.

Foshay, W., K. Silber, and O. Westgaard. (1986). *Instructional Design Competencies: The Standards.* Iowa City: International Board of Standards for Training, Performance, and Instruction.

Fournies, F. F. (1988). *Why Employees Don't Do What They're Supposed to Do and What to Do About It.* New York: Liberty Hall Press.

French, W. L., and C. H. Bell Jr. (1995). *Organizational Development: Behavioral Science Interventions for Organizational Improvement.* Englewood Cliffs, NJ: Prentice-Hall.

Fullan, M. (1991). *The New Meaning of Educational Change.* New York: Teachers College Press.

Fullan, M., and M. N. Watson. (1991). Beyond School-University Partnerships. In M. Fullan and Hargreaves, eds., *Teacher Development and Educational Change.* London, United Kingdom: Falmer Press.

Fuller, J. L. (1997). *Managing Performance Improvement Projects.* San Francisco: Jossey-Bass.

Fuller, J. L., and J. Farrington. (1999). *From Training to Performance Improvement: Navigating the Transition.* San Francisco: Jossey-Bass.

Galbraith, M. W., ed. (1991). *Facilitating Adult Learning: A Transactional Process.* Malabar, FL: Krieger.

Galpin, T. J. (1996). *The Human Side of Change: A Practical Guide to Organization Redesign.* San Francisco: Jossey-Bass.

Geis, G. L., and M. E. Smith. (1992). The Function of Evaluation. In H. D. Stolovitch and E. J. Keeps, eds., *Handbook of Human Performance Technology: A Comprehensive Guide for Analyzing and Solving Performance Problems in Organizations,* pp. 130–150. San Francisco: Jossey-Bass.

Gerber, M. E. (1995). *The E Myth Revisited.* New York: HarperCollins.

Gibbons, A. A. (1977). *Review of Content and Task Analysis Methodology.* San Diego: Courseware.

Gibbons, M. A. (1990). A Working Model of the Learning How to Learn Process. In R. Smith et al., eds., *Learning How to Learn Across the Life Span.* San Francisco: Jossey-Bass.

Gibson, J. L., J. M. Ivancevich, and J. H. Donnelly. (1997). *Organizations: Behavior, Structure, Process,* 9th ed. New York: McGraw-Hill.

Gilbert, T. F. (1978). *Human Competence: Engineering Worthy Performance.* New York: McGraw-Hill.

Gilbert, T. F. (1982a). A Question of Performance. Part 1, The PROBE Model. *Training and Development Journal* 36 (9): 20–30.

Gilbert, T. F. (1982b). A Question of Performance. Part 2, Applying the PROBE Model. *Training and Development Journal* 36 (10): 85–89.

Gilbert, T. F. (1996). *Human Competence: Engineering Worthy Performance* (Tribute edition). Washington, DC: ISPI.

Gilley, J. W. (1989). Career Development: The Linkage Between Training and Development. *Performance Improvement Quarterly* 2 (1): 6–10.

Gilley, J. W. (1992). *Strategic Planning for Human Resource Development*. Alexandria, VA: ASTD Press.

Gilley, J. W. (1998). *Improving HRD Practice*. Malabar, FL: Krieger.

Gilley, J. W., and N. W. Boughton. (1996). *Stop Managing, Start Coaching: How Performances Coaching Can Enhance Commitment and Improve Productivity*. New York: McGraw-Hill.

Gilley, J. W., N. W. Boughton, and A. Maycunich. (1999). *The Performance Challenge: Developing Management Systems to Make Employees Your Organization's Greatest Asset*. Cambridge, MA: Perseus Books.

Gilley, J. W., and A. J. Coffern. (1994). *Internal Consulting for HRD Professionals: Tools, Techniques, and Strategies for Improving Organizational Performance*. New York: McGraw-Hill.

Gilley, J. W., and S. A. Eggland. (1989). *Principles of Human Resource Development*. Cambridge, MA: Perseus Books.

Gilley, J. W., and S. A. Eggland. (1992). *Marketing HRD Programs Within Organizations: Improving the Visibility, Credibility, and Image of Programs*. San Francisco: Jossey-Bass.

Gilley, J. W., and A. Maycunich. (1998a). *Strategically Integrated HRD: Partnering to Maximize Organizational Performance*. Cambridge, MA: Perseus Books.

Gilley, J. W., and A. Maycunich. (1998b). The Role of the Integrated Human Resources Department in Strategic Planning. *Quality Observer* 7 (8): 22–25.

Gilley, J. W., and A. Maycunich. (2000). *Beyond the Learning Organization: Creating a Culture of Continuous Growth and Development Through State-of-the-Art Human Resource Practices*. Cambridge, MA: Perseus Books.

Greenberg, J. (1994). *Organizational Behavior: The State of the Science*. Hillsdale, NJ: Erlbaum.

Gregory, J. M. ([1884] 1978). *The Seven Laws of Teaching*. Reprint, Grand Rapids, MI: Baker Book House.

Guba, E. G., and Y. S. Lincoln. (1988). *Effective Evaluation: Improving the Usefulness of Evaluation Results Through Responsive and Naturalistic Approaches*. San Francisco: Jossey-Bass.

Hale, J. (1987). *Training: Preparing for the 21st Century*. Unpublished paper.

Hale, J. (1998). *The Performance Consultant's Fieldbook: Tools and Techniques for Improving Organizations and People*. San Francisco: Jossey-Bass and Pfeiffer.

Hall, D. T., and P. H. Mirvis. (1995). Career as Lifelong Learning. In A. Howard, ed., *The Changing Nature of Work*. San Francisco: Jossey-Bass.

Hall, G., and S. Loucks. (1978). *Innovation Configurations. Analyzing the Adaptations and Innovations*. Report no. 3049. Austin: University of Texas at Austin, Research and Development Center in Teacher Education.

Hamil, G., and C. K. Prahalad. (1994). *Competing for the Future*. Boston: Harvard Business School Press.

Hardy, R. E., and R. Schwartz. (1996). *The Self-Defeating Organizations: How Smart Companies Can Stop Outsmarting Themselves*. Cambridge, MA: Perseus Books.

Harless, J. H. (1974). *An Ounce of Analysis (Is Worth a Pound of Objectives)*. Newman, GA: Harless Performance Guild.

Harless, J. H. (1986). Guiding Performance with Job Aids. In M. E. Smith, ed., *Introduction to Performance Technology*, pp. 106–124. Washington, DC: National Society for Performance and Instruction.

Heiman, M., and J. Slomianko. (1990). *Learning to Learn on the Job*. Alexandria, VA: ASTD Press.

Heron, J. (1989). *The Facilitator's Handbook*. London: Kogan Page.

Hesselbein, F., M. Goldsmith, and R. Beckhard, eds. (1995). *The Leaders of the Future*. San Francisco: Jossey-Bass.

Hiemstra, R. (1991). Toward Building More Effective Learning Environments. In R. Hiemstra, ed., *Creating Environments for Effective Adult Learning. New Directions for Adult and Continuing Education*, no. 50. San Francisco: Jossey-Bass.

Hiemstra, R., and B. Sisco. (1990). *Individualizing Instruction: Making Learning Personal, Empowering, and Successful*. San Francisco: Jossey-Bass.

Holton III, E. F. (1995a). A Snapshot of Needs Assessment. In J. Phillips, and E. F. Holton III, eds., *In Action: Needs Assessment*. Alexandria, VA.: American Society for Training and Development.

Holton III, E. F. (1995b). In Search of an Integrative Model for HRD Evaluation. In *Proceedings of the 1995 Academy of Human Resource Development Annual Conference*. Austin, TX: Academy of Human Resource Development.

Hutchison, C. S. (1990). A Performance Technology Process Model. *Performance and Instruction* 29 (3): 1, 5.

Jackson, L., and D. Maelssac. (1994). Introducing a New Approach to Experiential Learning. In L. Jackson and R. S. Caffarella, eds., *New Directions for Adult and Continuing Education*, no. 55, 17–27. San Francisco: Jossey-Bass.

Jacobs, R. (1987). *Human Performance Technology: A Systems-Based Field for the Training and Development Profession*. Columbus: ERIC Clearinghouse on Adult, Career, and Vocational Education, National Center for Research in Vocational Education, Ohio State University.

Jacobs, R., and M. J. Jones. (1995). *Structured On-the-Job Training*. San Francisco: Berrett-Koehler.

Jarvis, R. (1992). *Paradoxes of Learning*. San Francisco: Jossey-Bass.

Jewell, S. F., and D. O. Jewell. (1992). Organization Design. In H. D. Stolovitch and E. J. Keeps, eds., *Handbook of Human Performance Technology: A Comprehensive Guide for Analyzing and Solving Performance Problems in Organizations*, pp. 211–232. San Francisco: Jossey-Bass.

Judy, R. W., and C. D'Amico. (1997). *Workforce 2020: Work and Workers in the 21st Century*. Indianapolis: Hudson Institute.

Katz, D., and R. Kahn. (1978). *The Social Psychology of Organizations*, 2nd ed. New York: Wiley.

Kaufman, R., A. M. Rojas, and H. Mayer. (1992). *Needs Assessment: A User's Guide.* Englewood Cliffs, NJ: Educational Technology Publications.

Kearsley, G. (1986). Analyzing the Costs and Benefits of Training. *Performance and Instruction* 25 (1): 30–32; (3): 23–25; (4): 13–16; (5): 8–10; (6): 8–9.

Killion, J. P., and G. Todnem. (1991). A Process for Personal Theory Building. *Educational Leadership* 48 (6): 14–16.

Kirkpatrick, D. (1995). *Evaluating Training Programs.* San Francisco: Berrett-Koehler.

Kissler, G. D. (1991). *The Change Riders: Managing the Power of Change.* Cambridge, MA: Perseus Books.

Kline, P., and B. Saunders. (1998). *Ten Steps to a Learning Organization.* Arlington, VA: Great Ocean Publishers.

Knicely, H. V. (1997). The Future of Human Resources: Superhuman Resource Leadership in the Twenty-First Century. In D. Ulrich, M. R. Losey, and G. Lake, eds., *Tomorrow's HR Management: 48 Thought Leaders Call for Change,* pp. 111–118. New York: Wiley & Sons.

Knowles, M. S. (1975). *Self-Directed Learning.* New York: Association Press.

Knowles, M. S. (1980). *The Modern Practice of Adult Education: From Pedagogy to Andragogy,* 2nd ed. New York: Cambridge Books.

Knowles, M. S., E. F. Holton III, and R. A. Swanson. (1998). *The Adult Learner,* 5th ed. Houston: Gulf Publishing.

Kolb, D. (1984). *Experiential Learning: Experience as the Source of Learning and Development.* Englewood Cliffs, NJ: Prentice Hall.

Kotter, J. P., and J. L. Heskett. (1992). *Corporate Culture and Performance.* New York: Free Press.

Kotter, J. R. (1996). *Leading Change.* Boston: Harvard Business School Press.

Labovitz, G., and V. Ronansky. (1997). *The Power of Alignment: How Great Companies Stay Centered and Accomplish Extraordinary Things.* New York: Wiley & Sons.

Laird, D. (1985). *Approaches to Training and Development,* 2nd ed. Reading, MA.: Addison Wesley Longman.

Larson, C. E., and F. M. La Fasto. (1989). *Teamwork: What Must Go Right/What Can Go Wrong.* Newbury Park, CA: Sage Publications.

Lawler III, E. E. (1995). Strategic Human Resources Management: An Idea Whose Time Has Come. In B. Downie and M. L. Coates, eds., *Managing Human Resources in the 1990s and Beyond: Is the Workplace Being Transformed?* pp. 46–70. Kingston: IPC Press.

Lawler III, E. E. (1996). *From the Ground Up.* San Francisco: Jossey-Bass.

Le Boeuf, M. (1985). *Getting Results: The Secret to Motivating Yourself and Others.* New York: Berkeley Books.

Levy, A. (1986). Second-Order Planned Change: Definition and Conceptualization. *Organizational Dynamics* 15 (l): 5–20.

Lewin, K. (1951). *Field Theory in Social Science.* New York: Harper.

Lewis, T., and D. Bjorkquist. (1992). Needs Assessment: A Critical Reappraisal. *Performance Improvement Quarterly* 5 (4): 33–54.

Lippitt, G., and R. Lippitt. (1986). *The Consulting Process in Action*, 2nd ed. San Diego: University Associates.

Mager, R., and P. Pipe. (1984). *Analyzing Performance Problems*, 2nd ed. Belmont, CA: Lake Publishing.

March, J. G. (1995). The Future, Disposable Organizations, and the Rigidities of Imagination. *Organization* 2 (3-4): 427–440.

Marquardt, M. J. (1996). *Building the Learning Organization*. New York: McGraw-Hill.

Marquardt, M. J. (1999). *Action Learning in Action: Transforming Problems and People for World-Class Organizational Learning*. Palo Alto: Davies-Black Publishing.

Marquardt, M., and A. Reynolds. (1994). *The Global Learning Organization*. Burr Ridge, IL: Irwin.

Marsick, V. J., and K. E. Watkins. (1990). *Informal and Incidental Learning in the Workplace*. London: Routledge.

Marsick, V. J., M. Volpe, and K. E. Watkins. (1999). Theory and Practice of Informal Learning in the Knowledge Era. In V. J. Marsick and M. Volpe, eds., *Informal Learning on the Job*, pp. 80–95. San Francisco: Berrett-Koehler.

Maxwell, J. C. (1998) *The 21 Irrefutable Laws of Leadership: Follow Them and People Will Follow You*. Nashville, TN: Thomas Nelson Publishers.

McGill, I., and L. Beaty. (1995). *Action Learning: A Practitioner's Guide*, 2nd ed. London: Logan Page.

McLagan, P. (1989). Models for HRD Practice. *Training and Development Journal* 43 (9): 49–59.

McLagan, R., and C. Nel. (1995). *The Age of Participation*. San Francisco: Berrett-Koehler.

McLagan, R., and C. Nel. (1996). The Shift to Participation. *Perspectives on Business and Global Change* 10 (1): 47–59.

McLean, A. J. (1982). *OD in Transition: Evidence of an Evoluting Profession*. New York: Wiley.

Merriam, S. B., and R. G. Brockett. (1997). *The Profession and Practice of Adult Education: An Introduction*. San Francisco: Jossey-Bass.

Merriam, S. B., and R. S. Caffarella. (1991). *Learning in Adulthood*. San Francisco: Jossey-Bass.

Meyer, E. C., and K. R. Allen. (1994). *Entrepreneurship and Small Business Management*. Mission Hills, CA: Glencoe/McGraw-Hill.

Mezirow, J. (1981). A Critical Theory of Adult Learning and Education. *Adult Education Quarterly* 32 (1): 3–24.

Mezirow, J. (1991). *Transformative Dimensions of Adult Learning*. San Francisco: Jossey-Bass.

Mezirow, J. (1997). Transformative Learning: Theory to Practice. In P. Cranton, ed., *Transformative Learning in Action: Insights from Practice. New Directions in Adult and Continuing Education*, no. 79, pp. 5–12. San Francisco: Berrett-Koehler.

Michael, D. N. (1973). *On Learning to Plan—And Planning to Learn: The Social Psychology of Changing Toward Future-Responsive Social Learning*. San Francisco: Jossey-Bass.

Miller, R. B., and S. E. Heiman. (1987). *Conceptual Selling.* Reno, NV: Miller Heilman.

Mills, G. E., R. W. Pace, and B. D. Peterson. (1988). *Analysis in Human Resource Training and Organization Development.* Cambridge, MA: Perseus Books.

Mink, O. G., P. W. Esterhuysen, B. P. Mink, and K. Q. Owen. (1993). *Change at Work: A Comprehensive Management Process for Transforming Organizations.* San Francisco: Jossey-Bass.

Mohrman, S. A., and E. E. Lawler III. (1997). Transforming the Human Resource Function. In D. Ulrich, M. R. Losey, and G. Lake, eds., *Tomorrow's HR Management: 48 Thought Leaders Call for Change,* pp. 241–249. New York: Wiley & Sons.

Mohrman, S. A., E. E. Lawler III, and G. McMahan. (1996). *New Directions for the Human Resources Organizations: An Organization Design Approach.* Los Angeles: Center for Effective Organizations.

Morris, L. (1995). Development Strategies for the Knowledge Era. In S. Chawla and J. Renesch, eds., *Learning Organizations: Developing Cultures for Tomorrow's Workplace,* pp. 323–336. Portland, OR: Productivity Press.

Nadler, D. A. (1998). *Champions of Change: How CEOs and Their Companies Are Mastering the Skills of Radical Change.* San Francisco: Jossey-Bass.

Nadler, L. (1970). *Developing Human Resources: Concepts and Models.* San Francisco: Jossey-Bass.

Nadler, L. (1983). *Human Resource Development: The Perspective of Business and Industry.* Columbus, OH: ERIC Clearinghouse on Adult, Career, and Vocational Education.

Nadler, L. (1990). *Developing Human Resources: Concepts and Models,* 3rd ed. San Francisco: Jossey-Bass.

Nadler, L., and Z. Nadler. (1994). *Designing Training Programs: The Critical Events Model.* Houston: Gulf.

Nadler, L., and G. Wiggs. (1986). *Managing Human Resource Development: A Practical Guide.* San Francisco: Jossey-Bass.

Neilsen, E. H. (1984). *Becoming an OD Practitioner.* Englewood Cliffs, NJ: Prentice-Hall.

Nilson, C. (1999). *The Performance Consulting Toolbook: Tools for Trainers in a Performance Consulting Role.* New York: McGraw-Hill.

O'Toole, J. (1995). *Leading Change.* San Francisco: Jossey-Bass.

Patterson, J. (1993). *Leadership for Tomorrow's Schools.* Alexandria, VA.: Association for Supervision and Curriculum Development.

Patterson, J. (1997). *Coming Clean About Organizational Change.* Arlington, VA: American Association of School Administrators.

Patterson, J., S. Purkey, and J. Parker. (1986). *Productive School Systems for a Non-rational World.* Alexandria, VA: Association for Supervision and Curriculum Development.

Pedler, M., ed. (1991). *Action Learning in Practice,* 2nd ed. Aldershot, England: Gower.

Peterson, D. B., and M. D. Hicks. (1995). *Development First: Strategies for Self-Development.* Minneapolis: Personnel Decisions International.

Peterson, D. B., and M. D. Hicks. (1996). *Leader as Coach: Strategies for Coaching and Developing Others.* Minneapolis: Personnel Decisions International.

Pfeffer, J. (1994). *Competitive Advantage Through People.* Boston: Harvard Business School Press.

Phillips, J., and E. F. Holton III, eds. (1995). *In Action: Needs Assessment.* Alexandria, VA: American Society for Training and Development.

Preskill, H. (1996). The Use of Critical Incidents to Foster Reflection and Learning in HRD. *Human Resource Development Quarterly* 7 (4): 335–347.

Preskill, H., and R. T. Torres. (1999). *Evaluative Inquiry for Learning in Organizations.* Thousand Oaks, CA: Sage Publications.

Pucel, D. J., and J. C. Cerrito, and R. Noe. (1989). Integrating Selections, Training, and Performance Evaluation. *Performance Improvement Quarterly* 2 (4): 21–29.

Randolph, A., and B. Posner. (1992). *Getting the Job Done: Effective Project Planning and Management.* Englewood Cliffs, NJ: Prentice-Hall.

Raudsepp, E. (1987). In R. L. Kuhn, ed., *Handbook for Creative Managers,* pp. 173–182. New York: McGraw-Hill.

Redding, J. (1994). *Strategic Readiness: The Making of the Learning Organization.* San Francisco: Jossey-Bass.

Regalbuto, G. (1992). Targeting the Bottom Line. *Training and Development Journal* 46 (4): 29–38.

Revans, R. (1994). Keynote presentation at the 1994 Academy of Human Resource Development annual meeting.

Robb, J. (1998). The Job of a Performance Consultant. In D. G. Robinson and J. C. Robinson, eds., *Moving from Training to Performance: A Practical Guide,* pp. 229–255. San Francisco: Berrett-Koehler.

Robinson, D. G., and J. C. Robinson. (1989). *Training for Impact: How to Link Training to Business Needs and Measure the Results.* San Francisco: Jossey-Bass.

Robinson, D. G., and J. C. Robinson. (1996). *Performance Consulting: Moving Beyond Training.* San Francisco: Berrett-Koehler.

Robinson, D. G., and J. C. Robinson. (1999). *Moving from Training to Performance: A Practical Guide.* San Francisco: Berrett-Koehler.

Rogers, C. R. (1969). *Freedom to Learn.* Columbus, OH: Merrill.

Rolls, J. (1995). The Transformational Leader: The Wellspring of the Learning Organization. In S. Chawla and J. Renesch, eds., *Learning Organizations: Developing Cultures for Tomorrow's Workplace,* pp. 101–110. Portland, OR: Productivity Press.

Rosenberg, M. J. (1982). Our Instructional Media Toots. *Performance and Improvement* 21 (3): 16–21.

Rosenberg, M. J. (1990). Performance Technology: Working the System. *Training* 27 (2): 43–48.

Rosenberg, M. J. (1996). Human Performance Technology: Foundation for Human Performance Improvement. In W. Rothwell, ed., *The ASTD Models for Human Performance Improvement: Roles, Competencies, and Outputs.* Alexandria, VA.: American Society for Training and Development.

Rosenberg, M. J., W. C. Coscarelli, and D. S. Hutchison. (1999). The Origins and Evolution of the Field. In H. D. Stolovitch and E. J. Keeps, eds., *Handbook of Human Performance Technology: Improving Individual and Organizational Performance Worldwide*, pp. 25–26. San Francisco: Jossey-Bass

Rossett, A. (1990). Overcoming Obstacles to Needs Assessment. *Training* 27 (3): 36–41.

Rossett, A. (1992). Analysis of Human Performance Problems. In H. D. Stolovitch and E. J. Keeps, eds., *Handbook of Human Performance Technology: A Comprehensive Guide for Analyzing and Solving Performance Problems in Organizations*, pp. 97–113. San Francisco: Jossey-Bass.

Rossett, A. (1999a). Analysis for Human Performance Technology. In H. D. Stolovitch and E. J. Keeps, eds., *Handbook of Human Performance Technology: Improving Individual and Organizational Performance Worldwide*, pp. 139–162. San Francisco: Jossey-Bass.

Rossett, A. (1999b). *First Things Fast: A Handbook for Performance Analysis*. San Francisco: Pfeiffer.

Rothwell, W. (1996a). *Beyond Training and Development: State-of-the-Art Strategies for Enhancing Human Performance*. New York: AMACOM.

Rothwell, W. (1996b). *The ASTD Models for Human Performance Improvement: Roles, Competencies, and Outputs*. Alexandria, VA.: American Society for Training and Development.

Rothwell, W., and R. Cookson. (1997). *Beyond Instruction: Comprehensive Program Planning for Business and Education*. San Francisco: Jossey-Bass.

Rothwell, W. J., and H. C. Kazanas. (1998). *Mastering the Instructional Design Process: A Systematic Approach*. San Francisco: Jossey-Bass.

Rothwell, W. J., and H. Sredl. (1992). *The American Society for Training and Development Reference Guide to Professional Human Resource Development Roles and Competencies*, 2nd ed. Amherst, MA: Human Resource Development Press.

Rothwell, W. J., R. K. Prescott, and M. W. Taylor. (1998). *Strategic Human Resource Leaders: How to Prepare Your Organization for the Six Key Trends Shaping the Future*. San Francisco: Davies-Black Publishing.

Rousseau, D. M., and K. A. Wade-Benzoni. (1995). Changing Individual-Organization Attachments: A Two-Way Street. In A. Howard, ed., *The Changing Nature of Work*. San Francisco: Jossey-Bass.

Rummler, G. (1998). The Three Levels of Alignment. In D. G. Robinson and J. C. Robinson, eds., *Moving from Training to Performance: A Practical Guide*, pp. 13–35. San Francisco: Berrett-Koehler.

Rummler, G. A., and A. P. Brache. (1992). Transforming Organizations Through Human Performance Technology. In H. D. Stolovitch and E. J. Keeps, eds., *Handbook of Human Performance Technology: A Comprehensive Guide for Analyzing and Solving Performance Problems in Organizations*, pp. 32–49. San Francisco: Jossey-Bass.

Rummler, G. A., and A. P. Brache. (1995). *Improving Performance: How to Manage the White Spaces on the Organizational Chart*. San Francisco: Jossey-Bass.

Saban, J. M., J. P. Killion, and C. G. Green. (1994). The Centric Reflection Model: A Kaleidoscope for Staff Developers. *Journal of Staff Development* 18 (3): 16–20.

Sarason, S. (1996). *Revisiting the Culture of the School and the Problem of Change*. New York: Teachers College Press.

Savage, C. (1990). *Fifth-Generation Management: Integrating Enterprises Through Human Networking*. Digital Press.

Schein, E. H. (1992). *Organizational Culture and Leadership*. San Francisco: Jossey-Bass.

Schein, E. H. (1996). The Cultures of Management: The Key to Organizational Learning. *Sloan Management Review* 38 (1): 9–20.

Schneider, B., and A. Konz. (1989). Strategic Job Analysis. *Human Resource Management* 28 (2): 51–63.

Schon, D. A. (1983). *The Reflective Practitioner*. New York: Basic Books.

Schon, D. A. (1987). *Educating the Reflective Practitioner*. San Francisco: Jossey-Bass.

Schrock, S. A., and G. L. Geis. (1999). Evaluation. In H. D. Stolovitch and E. J. Keeps, eds., *Handbook of Human Performance Technology: Improving Individual and Organizational Performance Worldwide*, pp. 185–209. San Francisco: Jossey-Bass.

Schuster, J. R., and P. K. Zingheim. (1992). *The New Pay: Linking Employee and Organizational Performance*. New York: Lexington Books.

Schwandt, D. R. (1995). Learning as an Organization: A Journey into Chaos. In S. Chawla and J. Renesch, eds., *Learning Organizations: Developing Cultures for Tomorrow's Workplace*, pp. 365–380. Portland, OR: Productivity Press.

Schwinn, D. (1996). *The Interactive Project Learning Model*. Concept paper. Transformation, Inc.

Senge, P. M. (1990). *The Fifth Discipline: The Art and Practice of the Learning Organization*. New York: Doubleday.

Shaw, R. B., and D. N. T. Perkins. (1991). Teaching Organizations to Learn. *Organization Development Journal* 9 (4): 1–12.

Shea, G. P. (1994). Mentoring: Helping Employees Reach Their Full Potential. In *AAIA Management Briefing*. New York: American Management Association.

Shipka, B. (1995). The Seventh Story: Extending Learning Organizations Far Beyond the Business. In S. Chawla and J. Renesch, eds., *Learning Organizations: Developing Cultures for Tomorrow's Workplace*, pp. 143–152. Portland, OR: Productivity Press.

Silber, K. (1992). Intervening at Different Levels in Organizations. In H. D. Stolovitch and E. J. Keeps, eds., *Handbook of Human Performance Technology: A Comprehensive Guide for Analyzing and Solving Performance Problems in Organizations*, pp. 50–65. San Francisco: Jossey-Bass.

Simerly, R. O. (1987). *Strategic Planning and Leadership in Continuing Education*. San Francisco: Jossey-Bass.

Simonsen, P. (1997). *Promoting a Developmental Culture in Your Organization: Using Career Development as a Change Agent.* Palo Alto: Davies-Black Publishing.

Sleezer, C. M. (1992). Needs Assessment: Perspectives from the Literature. *Performance Improvement Quarterly* 5 (2): 34–46.

Smart, B. D. (1983). *Selection Interviewing: A Management Psychologist's Recommended Approach.* New York: Wiley.

Smith, K. K. (1982). Philosophical Problems in Thinking About Organizational Change. In P. S. Goodman and Associates, eds., *Change in Organizations,* pp. 316–374. San Francisco: Jossey-Bass.

Smith, M. E., and G. L. Geis. (1992). Planning an Evaluation Study. In H. D. Stolovitck and E. J. Keeps, eds., *Handbook of Human Performance Technology: A Comprehensive Guide for Analyzing and Solving Performance Problems in Organizations,* pp. 151–166. San Francisco: Jossey-Bass.

Smith, R. (1988). *Human Resource Development: An Overview.* Washington, DC: Office of Educational Research and Improvement.

Spitzer, D. R. (1999). The Design and Development of High-Impact Interventions. In H. D. Stolovitch and E. J. Keeps, eds., *Handbook of Human Performance Technology: Improving Individual and Organizational Performance Worldwide,* pp. 163–184. San Francisco: Jossey-Bass.

Steele, E. (1973). *Physical Settings and Organization Development.* Reading, MA: Addison Wesley.

Steinburg, C. (1991). Partnerships with the Line. *Training and Development* 10, 28–35.

Stewart, T. A. (1997). *Intellectual Capital.* New York: Doubleday/Currency.

Stolovitch, H. D., and E. J. Keeps, eds. (1992). *Handbook of Human Performance Technology: A Comprehensive Guide for Analyzing and Solving Performance Problems in Organizations.* San Francisco: Jossey-Bass.

Stolovitch, H. D., E. J. Keeps, and D. Rodrigue. (1995). Skill Sets for the Human Performance Technologist. *Performance Improvement Quarterly* 8 (2): 40–67.

Stufflebeam, D. L. (1971). The Relevance of the CIPP Evaluation Model for Educational Accountability. *Journal of Research and Development in Education* 5 (2): 19–25.

Stufflebeam, D. L. (1975). Toward a Science of Education Evaluation. *Educational Technology* 7 (14): 329–344.

Stufflebeam, D. L. (1983). The CIPP Model for Program Evaluation. In G. F. Maddaus, M. Scriven, and D. L. Stufflebeam, eds., *Evaluation Models: Viewpoints on Educational and Human Services Evaluation.* Newall, MA: Kluwer-Nijhoff.

Swanson, R. A. (1987). *Human Resource Development Definition.* St. Paul, MN: Training and Development Research Center.

Swanson, R. A. (1994). *Analysis for Improving Performance. Tools for Diagnosing Organization and Documenting Workplace Expertise.* San Francisco: Berrett-Koehler.

Swanson, R. A. (1995). Human Resource Development: Performance Is the Key. *Human Resource Development Quarterly* 6 (2): 207–213.

Swanson, R. A. (1999). The Foundations of Performance Improvement and Implications for Practice. In R. J. Torraco, ed. *Performance Improvement Theory and Practice*, pp. 1–25. San Francisco: Berrett-Koehler.

Swanson, R. A., and D. Gradous. (1986). *Performance at Work: A Systematic Program for Analyzing Work Behavior.* New York: Wiley.

Swanson, R. A., and D. Gradous. (1988). *Forecasting Financial Benefits of Human Resource Development.* San Francisco: Jossey-Bass.

Tarraco, R. J., and R. A. Swanson. (1995). The Strategic Roles of Human Resource Development. *Human Resource Planning* 18 (4): 10–21.

Thiagarajan, A. J. (1980). *Experimental Learning Packages.* Englewood Cliffs, NJ: Educational Technology Publications.

This, L. E., and G. L. Lippitt. (1983). Learning Theories and Training. In L. S. Baird, C. E. Schneier, and D. Laird, eds., *Training and Development Sourcebook.* Amherst, MA: HRD Press.

Thompson, L. W. (1995). The Renaissance of Learning in Business. In S. Chawla and J. Renesch, eds., *Learning Organizations: Developing Cultures for Tomorrow's Workplace*, pp. 85–99. Portland, OR: Productivity Press.

Tichy, N. M. (1989). GE's Crotonvule: A Staging Ground for Corporate Revolution. *Academy of Management Executive* 102.

Tichy, N. M., and R. Charan. (1995). The CEO as Coach. *Harvard Business Review* (March-April): 69–78.

Torres, R. T. (1991). Improving the Quality of Internal Evaluation: The Evaluator as Consultant-Mediator. *Evaluation and Program Planning* 14 (3): 189–198.

Torres, R. T., H. Preskill, and M. E. Piontek. (1996). *Evaluation Strategies for Communicating and Reporting: Enhancing Learning in Organizations.* Thousand Oaks, CA: Sage Publications.

Torres, R. T., H. Preskill, and M. E. Piontek. (1997). Communicating and Reporting: Concerns of Internal and External Evaluators. *Evaluation Practice* 18 (2): 105–128.

Tosti, D. T. (1986). Feedback Systems. In M. E. Smith, ed., *Introduction to Performance Technology.* Washington, DC: National Society for Performance and Instruction.

Tough, A. (1979). *The Adult's Learning Projects*, 2nd ed. Toronto: Ontario Institute for Studies in Education.

Turner, A. N. (1983). Consulting Is More Than Giving Advice. *Harvard Business Review* 61 (5): 120–129.

Ulrich, D. (1997a). *Human Resource Champions.* Boston: Harvard Business School Press.

Ulrich, D. (1997b). Judge Me by My Future Than by My Past. In D. Ulrich, M. R. Losey, and G. Lake, eds., *Tomorrow's HR Management: 48 Thought Leaders Call for Change*, pp. 139–145. New York: Wiley & Sons.

Ulrich, D. (1998). A New Mandate for Human Resources. *Harvard Business Review* 76 (1): 124–134.

Ulrich, D., and D. Lake. (1990). *Organizational Capability: Competing from the Inside Out.* New York: John Wiley & Sons.

Vaile, P. (1996). *Learning as a Way of Being.* San Francisco: Jossey-Bass.

Watkins, K. (1989). Business and Industry. In S. Merriam and P. Cunningham, eds., *Handbook of Adult and Continuing Education.* San Francisco: Jossey-Bass.

Watkins, K. E., and V. J. Marsick. (1993). *Sculpting the Learning Organization: Lessons in the Art and Science of Systematic Change.* San Francisco: Jossey-Bass.

Watkins, R., and R. Kaufman. (1996). An Update on Relating Needs Assessment and Needs Analysis. *Performance Improvement* 35 (10): 10–13.

Weiss, J. W., and R. K. Wysocki. (1992). *Five-Phase Project Management: A Practical Planning and Implementation Guide.* Cambridge, MA: Perseus Books.

Werther, W. B., and K. Davis. (1996). *Human Resources and Personnel Management.* New York: McGraw-Hill.

Williams, V. L., and J. E. Sunderland. (1998). Maximize the Power of Your Reward and Recognition Strategies. *Journal of Compensation and Benefits* 2 (14): 11–17.

Wilson, L. (1987). *Changing the Game: The New Way to Sell.* New York: Fireside.

Zemke, R., and S. Zemke. (1995). Adult Learning: What Do We Know for Sure? *Training* 32 (6): 31–40.

Index

Printed in the United States
76771LV00004BB/4